Lecture Notes in Computer Science 7623

Commenced Publication in 1973
Founding and Former Series Editors:
Gerhard Goos, Juris Hartmanis, and Jan van Leeuwen

Marco Winckler   Peter Forbrig
Regina Bernhaupt (Eds.)

Human-Centered Software Engineering

4th International Conference, HCSE 2012
Toulouse, France, October 29-31, 2012
Proceedings

 Springer

Volume Editors

Marco Winckler
Regina Bernhaupt
ICS-IRIT Université Paul Sabatier
118 route de Narbonne, 31062 Toulouse Cedex 9, France
E-mail: {winckler, regina.bernhaupt}@irit.fr

Peter Forbrig
Universität Rostock
Fachbereich Informatik, Lehrstuhl Softwaretechnik
18055 Rostock, Germany
E-mail: peter.forbrig@uni-rostock.de

ISSN 0302-9743   e-ISSN 1611-3349
ISBN 978-3-642-34346-9   e-ISBN 978-3-642-34347-6
DOI 10.1007/978-3-642-34347-6
Springer Heidelberg Dordrecht London New York

Library of Congress Control Number: 2012949461

CR Subject Classification (1998): D.2, H.5.2, H.5, I.2, H.3-4, C.2

LNCS Sublibrary: SL 2 – Programming and Software Engineering

Typesetting: Camera-ready by author, data conversion by Scientific Publishing Services, Chennai, India

Printed on acid-free paper

Springer is part of Springer Science+Business Media (www.springer.com)

Preface

The International Conference on Human-Centered Software Engineering (HCSE) is a single-track working conference which aims at bringing together researchers and practitioners interested in strengthening the scientific foundations of user interface design, examining the relationship between software engineering and human–computer interaction and on how to strengthen user-centered design as an essential part of the software engineering process.

HCSE 2012 was the fourth edition of a series of conferences promoted by the IFIP Working Group 13.2 on WG 13.2 Methodologies for User-Centered Systems Design. Traditionally, this conference is organized in conjunction with other conferences in the field of human-computer interaction. The first edition (HCSE 2007) was organized in Salamanca, Spain, in conjunction with the conference Engineering Interactive Systems (EIS). The second edition (HCSE 2008) was held in Pisa, Italy, with the, conference Task Models and Diagrams (TAMODIA). The third edition (HCSE 2010) was organized in Reykjavik, Iceland, in conjunction with NordiCHI. For the first time, HCSE was organized as a standalone conference this year. The 2012 edition of HCSE was held in Toulouse, France, October 29–31 2012, at the Institute of Research of Informatics (IRIT), on the campus of the Paul Sabatier University (Toulouse III).

HCSE 2012 welcomed 12 full research papers (acceptance rate of 22%) and 14 short papers (acceptance rate of 33%) that are presented hereafter. This year, we improved the reviewing process by moving to two rounds of reviews. All contributions were first screened by the members of the international committee and received a set of suggestions for improving the submissions and a recommendation of likely accept/reject. Authors of contributions that received a recommendation of likely accept were then asked to send a rebuttal and a revised version of their contributions. Then, in a second round of reviews, a meta-reviewer screened the original version of the paper, the revised version, and the authors' rebuttal. The final decision took into account the way authors addressed the reviewers' comments, which included the edited paper and the argument in the rebuttal. This two-round review process requested extra work both from the authors and the reviewing committee and we are very thankful for all the efforts made. This procedure aimed to support scientific argumentation and guidance toward excellence in research and we believe that it fulfilled these goals. Our sincere gratitude goes to the members of our Program Committee, who devoted countless hours to ensure the high quality of the HCSE Conference.

We would like to thank Neville A. Stanton and Emilia Mendes, our keynotes, who accepted to give an inspiring speech at HCSE and for providing us with a written record that is also presented in these proceedings. In addition, sincere thanks must be extended to the local organizers, Veronique Debats and Sabine Lartigue, whose logistic support was essential to make this conference possible.

Finally, our thanks go to all the authors who did the scientific work and especially to the presenters who took on the additional task of discussing the results with their peers at HCSE 2012 in Toulouse.

Marco Winckler
Peter Forbrig
Regina Bernhaupt

Organization

HCSE 2012 Technical Committee

Organizers

Marco Winckler	ICS-IRIT, Université Paul Sabatier, France
Peter Forbrig	University of Rostock, Germany
Regina Bernhaupt	ICS-IRIT, Université Paul Sabatier, France

Program Committee

Ahmed Seffah	Université de Technologie Troyes, France
Alistair Sutcliffe	University of Manchester, UK
Andy Dearden	Sheffield Hallam University, UK
Anirudha N. Joshi	Indian Institute of Technology, India
Anke Dittmar	University of Rostock, Germany
Bertrand David	Ecole Centrale de Lyon, France
David Benyon	School of Computing Napier University, UK
Effie Law	ETH Zürich, Switzerland and University of Leicester, UK
Emilia Mendes	Zayed University, Dubai
Fabio Paternò	Istituto di Scienza e Tecnologie dell'Informazione "A. Faedo" (ISTI), Italy
Francisco Montero	University of Castilla - La Mancha, Spain
Frank Maurer	University of Calgary, Canada
Gerrit Meixner	German Research Center for Artificial Intelligence (DFKI), Germany
Gerrit Van Der Veer	Open University Netherlands (OUN), The Netherlands
Gustavo Rossi	Universidad National de La Plata (UNLP), Argentina
Hallvard Trætteberg	Norwegian University of Science and Technology, Norway
Janet Wesson	Nelson Mandela Metropolitan University (NMMU), South Africa
Jean Vanderdonckt	Université catholique de Louvain (UcL), Belgium
John Carroll	Virginia Tech, USA
José Campos	University of Minho, Portugal
Marcelo Pimenta	Federal University of Rio Grande do Sul (UFRGS), Brazil
Maria Dolores Lozano Perez	University of Castilla - La Mancha, Spain
Marta Kristín Lárusdóttir	Reykjavik University, Iceland

Matthias Rauterberg	Technische universiteit Eindhoven (TU/e), The Netherlands
Morten Borup Harning	Dialogical, Denmark
Natalia Juristo Juzgado	Universidad Politécnica de Madrid, Spain
Oscar Pastor	Universidad Politécnica de Valencia, Spain
Pedro Campos	Universidade da Madeira, Portugal
Philippe Palanque	Paul Sabatier University (Toulouse III), France
Simone Barbosa	PUC-Rio, Brazil
Stefan Sauer	University of Paderborn, Germany
Xavier Ferré	Universidad Politécnica de Madrid, Spain

Local Organizing Committee

Sabine Lartigue	IRIT-UPS, Toulouse, France
Veronique Debats	IRIT-UPS, Toulouse, France

Sponsors

The conference chairs and conference organizers would like to thank our sponsors:

Institute of Research in Informatics of Toulouse (IRIT)
interaction-design.org
University Paul Sabatier (Toulouse III)
Société de l'Electricité, de l'Electronique et des Technologies de l'Information et de la Communication (SEE)

Scientific Sponsors

IFIP WG 13.2 Methodologies for User-Centered Design

Table of Contents

Short Papers

Human Factors Engineering as the Methodological Babel Fish: Translating User Needs into Software Design

Neville A. Stanton

Faculty of Engineering and the Environment
University of Southampton
Highfield, Southampton, SO17 1BJ, UK
n.stanton@soton.ac.uk

Abstract. The aim of this paper is to show, by way of two case studies, the value of including Human Factors in interaction and interface design specification. It is argued that Human Factors offers and unique and useful perspective and contributes positively to design. Human Factors sits between subject matter experts and software engineers, translating user requirements though the applications of theory, models and methods. This results in software design requirements that have been intelligently interpreted and presented in a graphical manner. The two case studies demonstrate the differences between the interfaces with and without Human Factors input. Both cases show quantitative and qualitative benefits of including Human Factors in design. Performance improvements between 20-70 percent were demonstrated, which is typical of Human Factors design interventions.

Keywords: Human Factors Methods, Requirements Specification, Case Study.

1 Introduction to Human Factors Methods

The purpose of this paper is to show the benefit of Human Factors (HF) methods in system specification and design. Human Factors has a broad remit, covering all manner of analysis from human interaction with devices, to design of tools and machines, to team working, and general aspects of work and organisational design. The Human-Centred Design of Systems is also covered by the International Standard ISO13407. This emphasises the need to focus on the potential users of systems at all stages in the design and development process in order to ensure that requirements have been adequately defined and that functions are allocated between user and technology appropriately [23]. Much has been made about the timeliness of Human Factors input into projects, arguing that the appropriateness of the analysis will depend upon a number of factors [21][23][24], including which stage of design the project is at, how much time and resources are available, the skills of the analyst, access to the end-user population, and what kind of data are required [25]. Stanton and Young (1999) [25] showed that many of the methods they reviewed were flexible

M. Winckler, P. Forbrig, and R. Bernhaupt (Eds.): HCSE 2012, LNCS 7623, pp. 1–17, 2012.
© IFIP International Federation for Information Processing 2012

with regard to the design stage they could be applied to. Indeed many of the methods could be applied to very early stages of design, such as to concept models and mock-ups. Many methods may be used in a predictive as well as an evaluative manner. This flexibility of application to the various design stages bodes well for Human Factors methods. Other factors that the analyst needs to be aware of when choosing methods are: the accuracy of the methods (particularly where a predictive element is involved), the criteria to be evaluated (such as time, errors, communications, movement, usability, and so on), the acceptability and appropriateness of the methods (to the people being analysed, the domain context, resources available, and so on), and the cost-benefit of the method(s) and the product(s). Methods form a major part of the Human Factors discipline. For example, the International Encyclopaedia of Human Factors and Ergonomics [13] has an entire section devoted to methods and techniques. Many of the other sections of the encyclopaedia also reference to, if not provide actual examples of, Human Factors methods. In short, the importance of Human Factors methods cannot be overstated. These methods offer the ergonomist a structured approach to the analysis and evaluation of design problems. The Human Factors approach may be described using the scientist-practitioner model [23]. As a scientist, the Human Factors researcher is:

- extending the work of others;
- testing theories of human-machine performance;
- developing hypotheses;
- questioning everything;
- using rigorous data collection and analysis techniques;
- ensuring repeatability of results;
- disseminating the finding of studies.

As a practitioner, the Human Factors engineer is:

- addressing real-world problems;
- seeking the best compromise under difficult circumstances;
- looking to offer the most cost-effective solution;
- developing demonstrators and prototype solutions;
- analysing and evaluating the effects of change;
- developing benchmarks for best practice;
- communicating findings to interested parties.

According to Stanton et al (2005) [23] Human Factors will work somewhere between the poles of scientist and practitioner, varying the emphasis of their approach depending upon the problems that they face. Human Factors and Ergonomics methods are useful in the scientist-practitioner model, because of the structure, and potential for repeatability, that they the offer. There is an implicit guarantee in the use of methods that, provided they are used properly, they will produce certain types of useful products. It has been suggested that Human Factors and Ergonomics methods are a route to making the discipline accessible to all [10][26]. Despite the rigor offered by methods however, there is still plenty of scope for the role of experience. Annett and Stanton (2000) [3] summarised the most frequently asked questions raised by users of Human Factors methods as follows:

- How deep should the analysis be?
- Which methods of data collection should be used?
- How should the analysis be presented?
- Where is the use of the method appropriate?
- How much time/effort does each method require?
- How much, and what type, of expertise is needed to use the method(s)?
- What tools are there to support the use of the method(s)?
- How reliable and valid is/are the method(s)?

Annett (2002) [1] questions the relative merits for construct and criterion-referenced validity in the development of Human Factors theory. He distinguishes between construct validity (how acceptable the underlying theory is), predictive validity (the usefulness and efficiency of the approach in predicting the behaviour of an existing or future system), and reliability (the repeatability of the results). Investigating the matter further, Annett identifies a dichotomy of Human Factors methods: analytical methods and evaluative methods. Annett argues that analytical methods (i.e., those methods that help the analyst gain an understanding of the mechanisms underlying the interaction between human and machines) require construct validity, whereas evaluative methods (i.e., those methods that estimate parameters of selected interactions between human and machines) require predictive validity. This distinction is made in Table 1.

Table 1. Annett's dichotomy of Human Factors methods (adapted from Annett, 2002 [1])

	Analytic	**Evaluative**
Primary purpose	Understand a system	Measure a parameter
Examples	Task analysis, training needs analysis, etc.	Measures of workload, usability, comfort, fatigue, etc.
Construct validity	Based on an acceptable model of the system and how it performs	Is consistent with theory and other measures of parameter
Predictive validity	Provides answers to questions, e.g., structure of tasks	Predicts performance
Reliability	Data collection conforms to an underlying model	Results from independent samples agree

This presents an interesting question for Human Factors, are the methods really mutually exclusive? Some methods appear to have dual roles (i.e., both analytical and evaluative, such as Task Analysis For Error Identification), which implies that they must satisfy both criteria. However, it is plausible, as Baber (2005) [4] argues in terms of evaluation, that the approach taken will influence which of the purposes one might wish to emphasise. The implication is that the way in which one approaches a problem, e.g., along the scientist-practitioner continuum, could well have a bearing on how one employs a method. At first glance (particularly from a 'scientist' perspective) such a 'pragmatic' approach appears highly dubious: if we are selecting methods piecemeal in order to satisfy contextual requirements, how can be certain that we are producing useful, valid, reliable etc. output? While it may be possible for a method to satisfy three types of validity: construct (i.e., theoretical validity), content (i.e., face validity), and predictive (i.e., criterion-referenced empirical validity), it is not always clear whether this arises from the method itself or from the manner in which it is applied. This means that care needs to be taken before embarking on any application of methods to make sure that one is attempting to use the method in the spirit for which it was originally designed.

Prior to embarking on any kind of intervention (be it an analysis, design or evaluation of a system), an Ergonomist needs to have a strategy for deciding what methods to use in and how to adapt to the domain context [2]. Determining an appropriate set of methods (because individual methods are rarely used alone), requires some planning and preparation. Stanton and Young (1999) [25] proposed a process model to guide the selection of methods, as shown in Fig. 1. As Annett (2005) [2] points out, care and skill is required in developing the approach for analysing the problem, formulating the intervention, implementing the intervention, and determining the success of the intervention. Complex systems may require the Ergonomist to have a flexible strategy when approaching the problem. This can mean changing the nature of the analysis and developing a new approach as required. Thus, pilot studies are often helpful in scoping out the problem, before a detailed study is undertaken. This may mean that there can be several iterations through the criteria development and methods selection process. Of course, from a practitioner perspective, the time taken to carry out pilot studies might simply be unavailable. However, we would argue that there is no harm in running through one's selection of methods as a form of 'thought-experiment' in order to ascertain what type of output each method is likely to produce, and deciding whether or not to include a method in the battery that will be applied. While it is important not to rely too heavily on a single approach, nor is there any guarantee that simply throwing a lot of methods at a problem will guarantee useful results.

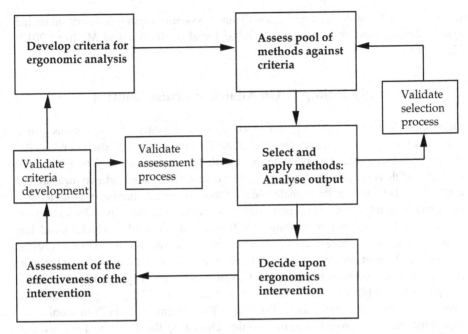

Fig. 1. Validating the methods selection and Human Factors intervention process (adapted from Stanton & Young, 1999 [25])

As shown in Fig. 1, method selection is a closed loop process with three feedback loops. The first feedback loop validates the selection of the methods against the selection criteria. The second feedback loop validates the methods against the adequacy of the ergonomic intervention. The third feedback loop validates the initial criteria against the adequacy of the intervention. There could be errors in the development of the initial criteria, the selection of the methods, and the appropriateness of the intervention. Each should be checked. The main stages in the process are identified as: determine criteria (where the criteria for assessment are identified), compare methods against criteria (where the pool of methods are compared for their suitability), application of methods (where the methods are applied)), implementation of Human Factors intervention (where an Human Factors programme is chosen and applied) and evaluation of the effectiveness of the intervention (where the assessment of change brought about by the intervention is assessed).

Two case studies are presented to demonstrate the added-value of Human Factors to system design and engineering. They also demonstrate some aspects of the requirements specification process. The first case study is based on the development of the drivers interface for a Stop and Go Adaptive Cruise Control system. Further information on the system development and evaluation may be found in Stanton et al (2011) [20]. The second case study is based on the development of the pilots interface for a Mission Communication Planning system. Further information on the system development and evaluation may be found in Stanton and McIlroy (2012) [22].

2   Case Study 1: Stop & Go Adaptive Cruise Control

Stop & Go Adaptive Cruise Control (S&G-ACC) is a system that maintains cruise speed in the same way as a conventional cruise control system, but also maintains the gap to the vehicle ahead by operating the throttle and brake systems. The S&G-ACC control module is mounted at the front of the vehicle, which uses radar to measure the gap and closing speed to the vehicle ahead. Once the vehicle has become stationary, the driver must intervene. This can be achieved by pressing the resume button, which will reactivate S&G-ACC providing a sufficient distance to the vehicle ahead has been attained, or by depressing the throttle, which will always override the system. The system is immediately cancelled by either the cancel button or driver braking. S&G-ACC is an extension to regular ACC, which has previously only operated above 26 kph. The capability of S&G-ACC over ACC is achieved by adding radar that can operate at slow speeds over short distances. The system has a built-in monitoring capability and so the speed is limited to that chosen by the driver, and the level of deceleration is also limited by the designers of the system. The system will not undertake emergency braking and under such conditions the driver will be required to intervene. When the driver is required to operate the brakes, i.e. the maximum S&G ACC brake level is reached, the system warns the driver by an audible warning. Due to the limited braking of the system, the driver may be called upon to intervene when approaching a slow moving or stationary object. The likelihood of the driver needing to intervene increases with the speed of the vehicle. The S&G-ACC system had also been designed for assistance in queuing scenarios, to keep a set distance behind slow moving vehicles.

The original system to be tested presented an amber follow icon when the vehicle enters follow mode and the icon is extinguished when the vehicle leaves follow mode. This is the simplest interface, as shown in Fig. 2a. A re-development of this interface was to indicate the presence of a new in-path target (e.g., a new vehicle) by flashing the icon red at first (as shown in Fig. 2b), before assuming steady state of the amber icon. The third interface represented a departure from the follow icon design. This interface encapsulated the driver requirements on temporal, spatial and mode information, by mapping the in-path target data onto a representation of the radar display (as shown in Fig. 2c). This offered a direct relationship between the position of the in-path target in the world (i.e., the position of another road user) and its representation on the driver interface (i.e., the highlighted ball in the centre of the display at 21 metres).

Fig. 2a. The standard icon display

Fig. 2b. The flashing red icon (left) followed by the standard icon (right) display

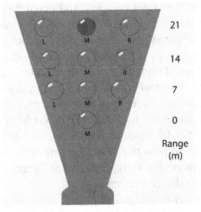

Fig. 2c. The radar display analogy

The mapping between the different interface designs and the elements of Situation Awareness (SA) is indicated in Table 1. As Table 2 shows, all three interface designs support mode awareness but only the radar display supports spatial awareness and, to a limited extent, temporal awareness. Cognitive mismatch is a general problem for automated systems [5], so design needs to focus on communication of the appropriate modal, spatial and temporal information. It was therefore anticipated that performance of drivers, in detecting new in-path targets that had been acquired by the S&G-ACC system, would be superior with the radar display. Seppelt & Less (2007) [19] argue that interface design needs to communicate the system limits in a continuous manner to the driver. The radar display analogy offers continuous information on modal, spatial and temporal changes (which the driver can compare to information in

Table 2. Mapping interface design and the SA elements

Interface Design	Modal Awareness	Temporal Awareness	Spatial Awareness
Standard Icon	████		
Flashing Icon	████		
Radar Display	████	▓▓▓▓	████

the world) whereas the two other iconic displays only communicate discrete information on modal changes.

The dark shaded area in Table 2 indicates that the interface supports the type of SA. For example the standard and flashing icons only support mode awareness, because they are only lit if a target vehicle is being tracked by the S&G-ACC system, which changes the vehicle from 'cruising' mode to 'following' mode. As well as mode awareness, the radar display can also communicate spatial awareness information, i.e., the range and direction of the target vehicle. Some limited temporal awareness information may also be communicated via the radar display (shown by the lighter shading) as the target gets closer to or further on away from the host vehicle, i.e., the rate of approach of the target vehicle. Additional time-to-contact information would need to be provided to better support time situation awareness. For the driver of a car with S&G-ACC, spatial relevance of other vehicles (e.g., longitudinal and lateral position of in-path target), temporal relevance of other vehicles (e.g., time to impending contact), and modal relevance of other vehicles (e.g., acquisition of a new in-path target or not) are extremely important. Integration of all this information should help to ensure that the driver responds appropriately to the dynamic road-vehicle environment. Bookhuis et al (2008) [7] report high driver acceptance of a congestion assistant that was functionally similar to the S&G-ACC system. Further Bliss and Acton (2003) [6] propose that drivers are more likely to accept systems that have greater operational reliability in reporting of information about the state of the world as well as optimizing driver responses.

As shown in Fig. 3, far fewer changes in in-path target were detected with the icon interfaces. This suggests that driver's were more likely to commit mode errors in these conditions, as they were less able to detect the fact that the S&G-ACC system had acquired a new in-path target and was no longer tracking the old one. With multiple in-path targets present, it would seem to be important that the driver should know which one is being tracked by the S&G-ACC system. In summary, drivers were more able to detect the change of an in-path target with the radar display than the two icon displays (based on data from in-path, multiple-target, test - to simulate a vehicle queuing scenario where other road users (such as cyclists, pedestrians and motorcyclists) might pass between the host vehicle and the tracked vehicle). This means that, in a situation with multiple vehicles, drivers were more likely to mistake the target vehicle being tracked by the automatic S&G-ACC system when using the iconic interfaces.

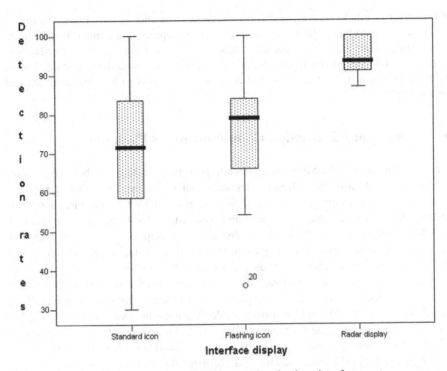

Fig. 3. Detection rates by drivers using the three interfaces

The finding that drivers in the iconic display conditions were less able to identify changes of the in-path targeting by the system, raises the idea that mode errors were more prevalent in iconic conditions, as the drivers' reports of system status departed from its actual status. Mode errors are of particular interest, because they are the result of people's interaction with technology. In his classification of human errors, Norman (1981) [16] singled this error type out as requiring special attention in the design of technological systems. The misclassification of the mode of the automatic S&G-ACC system could lead to driver errors which might have serious effect. Mode awareness by the driver should be of utmost importance. A measure of the success of the design will be the extent to which drivers are aware which mode the system is in, and how that relates to the behaviour of the vehicle in any given situation. The mode errors in this study were related to the drivers' failure to appreciate that the automatic system had changed its in-path target vehicle. This means that the driver thought that the S&G-ACC system was tracking one target whilst, in fact, it was tracking another. Other studies have shown that mode errors can have potentially disastrous outcome on system performance [17][18][27]. In the case of S+G-ACC, one can imagine a scenario where the host vehicle is tracking a leading vehicle when a motorcycle pulls between the host and tracked vehicle. The question for the driver of the host vehicle is whether the S&G-ACC system had acquired the motorcycle as the new in-path target, or is still tracking the original vehicle. This judgment becomes even more important if the original tracked vehicle increases its speed, as the host vehicle will similarly increase speed in order to maintain the gap between the two vehicles [19].

If the driver is able to determine that the S&G-ACC has not acquired the motorcycle as the new in-path target, then they will be able to prepare for a manual intervention. The findings from the study reported in this paper suggest that the radar display will be more useful to the driver in the scenario described above than the iconic displays in reducing cognitive mismatch [5] and these effects are likely to become more marked over time [14].

3   Case Study 2: Mission Communications Planning

The main function of the MPS communications software is to allow helicopter pilots to load a collection of radio frequencies such that when airborne, pilots have easy access to all of the frequencies they will require, and that each of these frequencies is properly labelled with regards to where and with whom that frequency is associated. The MPS software contains a visual display of a map of the United Kingdom displaying the boundaries of all major controlled airspaces, including military danger zones and minor and major air fields and airports. By studying the proposed route, marked on the map by a solid black line, pilots must decide what frequencies they will need for their mission. These frequencies must then be looked up in one of the Royal Air Force (RAF) Flight Information Publications, for example the British Isle and North Atlantic en-route supplement (BINA). A detailed description of the process of planning communications in MPS can be found in McIlroy, Stanton and Remington (2012) [15] and in Stanton and McIlroy (2012) [22].

In its present guise, the communication planning software interface is perceived as difficult to use, which has implications for training and mission planning, as indicated by the following quotes from experienced pilots who also train others:

> "The AH has an incredibly capable communications suite. However, it is regularly under-utilised by the front-line as the planning and setup process is overly complicated and error prone."

> "Training aircrew to configure the wide variety of voice, data and frequency agile encrypted radios on the Helicopter is an overly intensive task for both staff and students - primarily due to the overly complex tools used to configure various radio, channels & Nets."

Some of the complexity is due to the inherent complexity of the system components (e.g., there are 4 radios, 60 call-signs, 10 presets, 4 boot-up channels – all doubled for a two day communications plan) coupled with the constraints acting on communications planning (e.g., the standard operating procedures for communications settings, the mission timings, changes in airspace authority and so on). Helander (2007) [11] notes that computerisation of systems is making the coupling of systems even more complex, and that uncoupling of system elements may make interaction design more achievable. Although the current generation of communications planning starts with the presentation of a map with a route, communications planning resorts to a series of tables, fields and buttons (as shown in Fig. 4). We suspect that this results in a disconnection between how pilots think about planning their communications and what the software requires of them to prepare a communications plan. This line of reasoning was explored in the research presented within the current paper.

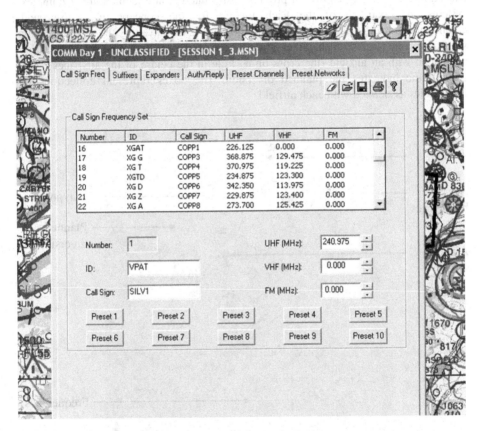

Fig. 4. The call-sign frequency list for the communications planning

At the beginning of the project, two full day meetings were held with a subject matter expert (SME) in which the analysts were introduced to military communications in general and to the current software technology in particular. The analysts were supplied with a version of the MPS software to inform analyses. Across a further six days, the analysts worked with the SME to further their understanding of the mission planning process and the MPS software through SME walkthroughs of different communications planning tasks. During these meetings the SME produced a number of Rich Pictures [8] of the communications planning task. A Rich Picture is graphical representation of a problem, concept, situation or work domain. It can include any kind of figure or text and has no prescribed rules or constraints. The Rich Picture has its origins in Soft Systems Methodology [8][9] and its primary purpose is to describe a system in such a way that is useful to both individuals external to, and actors within that system; it serves to organise and structure the body of information provided by the expert. Rich Pictures are commonly used in information systems education [12], as they can often provide easily interpretable depictions of complex systems. An example of the Rich Picture for the concept of air-to-ground communications is presented in Fig. 5. In the route is displayed by the solid line with waypoints and circles on the line. The dashed circles indicate airspace boundaries associated with an airfield (the cross on a circle in the centre of the airspaces). The dashed line indicates the planned diversion. The boxes represent collections of frequencies associated with each airfield.

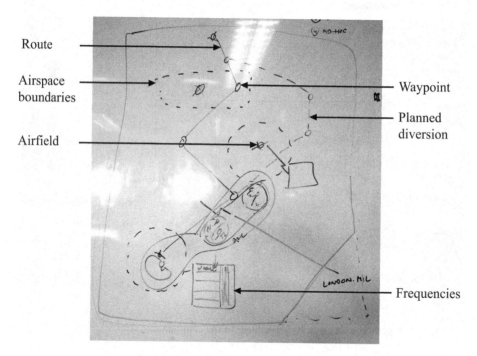

Fig. 5. Rich Picture of air-to-ground communications

One of the most significant problems with MPS was the lack of correspondence between the user's mental model and the system model. A mental model is an internal, mental representation of the way things exist or work in the real world. A mismatch between system model and user mental model results in a system that is unintuitive; the way the user thinks about the task is not reflected in the way the user must interact with the system. Rather than relying on a mental representation of the task to guide behaviour the user must use a learnt sequence of actions to progress through the system. For the air-to-ground communications planning stage of the task, results from a think-aloud study (reported in McIlroy, Stanton, & Remington, 2012 [15]) suggested that thought processes are map based. The expert explicitly stated that he was using the map to not only guide the decision making process (when deciding which frequencies to include in the plan) but also when getting an overview of the plan so far and when reviewing the completed plan. The Rich Picture presented earlier underlines this mismatch. In this diagram the SME graphically represented his concept of the air-to-ground communications process. The route is presented in such a way as to draw attention to those airspaces that are passed through, and those that are close by. Furthermore frequencies are directly linked to an airspace (indicated by the boxes in Fig. 5); they are not in a separate table only identified by ICAO (International Civil Aviation Organisation) codes (as is the case with the current version on the system and the frequencies are in a separate window shown in Fig. 4, which covers the map).

Another significant issue pertaining to the volume of information requiring management was relatively straightforward to address. In the current system the user must refer to a reference document (BINA) in order to get the frequencies associated with each airspace controlling authority. They must refer to a different reference document (RAF flight information handbook) to find out the name of an airport, airfield or special user airspace from the ICAO code given in the CSF or preset channels list, as these names are not contained within MPS. All of this information, although currently used from a paper-based format, is also held within an electronic database, the Digital Aeronautical Flight Information File (DAFIF). The information held in this file covers the entire globe, and all authorities contained within the file have both frequencies and coordinates associated with them. By taking advantage of this information it is possible to directly link frequency data with map data. In addition, the name of each airspace controlling authority can be displayed with the ICAO code. By linking communications data to the map, the problems of both task organisation and mental model mismatch are addressed, at least for air-to-ground communications.

Fig. 6 displays a screenshot of the proposed interface; on it, a map with a route marked on it is displayed as it would be in MPS, with the exception that there are communication symbols and frequency tables included. The symbols indicate that there is some communications information associated with that position on the map whilst the tables display that information. The symbols were designed and refined in an iterative process via repeated meetings with a subject matter expert. The symbol is displayed on a white background on the so that even if the map is predominately a dark colour, the symbols will still be clear to the user. The symbols are displayed just off centre of the airspace such that runway information is not obscured. The distance of the icon from the centre of the airspace is based on distance on the screen, not map-based geographical distance.

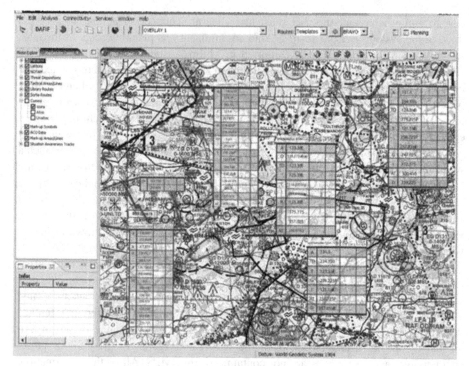

Fig. 6. Example new communications planning interface

For each airspace a label displaying all associated frequencies is presented alongside a number of options for selection. This presentation of frequencies is largely based on the depiction of frequencies in the Rich Picture for air-to-ground communications, in Fig. 5. To compare the proposed system with the current MPS software tool two simulations were created; a simple one comprising 4 contactable airspace authorities and a complex on containing 8 contactable airspace authorities. The simulations, based on a series of possible screenshots, were constructed such that the amount of mouse travel, number of mouse clicks and number of keystrokes necessary to complete the plan could be recorded (see Table 3). Although the sequence of actions was fixed for each simulation, the method for advancing through the simulated plans was a realistic one. By moving the mouse cursor to the relevant area on the screen and only then clicking to progress it was possible to estimate the amount of mouse travel and number of mouse clicks necessary to complete the plan. The number of keystrokes was estimated from the amount of information requiring insertion by typing.

To verify the validity of the proposed system a focus group with a number of SMEs was arranged. During the focus group, which lasted for approximately 6 hours, four Helicopter pilots (responsible for training new recruits in MPS) and two software engineers were present along with the researchers. A presentation was given in which the research conducted, and the resulting proposed system were explained at length. Comments, suggestions and criticisms were encouraged, and although a number of minor

Table 3. Results for simple and more complex communications plan

	Findings for simple plan			Findings for more complex plan		
	Current system	Proposed system	Percent decrease	Current system	Proposed system	Percent decrease
Mouse travel (m)	19	9	52	26	22	17
Mouse clicks	206	86	58	283	120	58
Keystrokes	291	32	89	534	116	78
Time (mins)	22	5	77	32	10	69

changes and additions were recommended, the proposed system was accepted as a vast improvement on the MPS software tool. All of the recommendations to come from the focus group were implemented, and all are contained within the proposed system.

4   Conclusions

In the first case study of Stop and Go Adaptive Cruise Control, the relative merits of different approaches to in-car display design, several conclusions may be drawn from the work presented in this paper to do with design of the driver interface and testing of that interface on drivers. The interface need only capture the essential features to enable the driver to make direct mappings between the world and the representation of it. In terms of the dynamics of S&G-ACC, this would include the representation of the leading vehicle, its spatial reference to the host vehicle (i.e., spatial situation awareness), an indication of whether or not the leading vehicle has changed (i.e., modal situation awareness), and leading headway of the in-path target vehicle (i.e., temporal situation awareness). Spatial representation is perhaps the easiest to design, and the radar display design attempted to show the relation between the in-path target vehicle and the host vehicle. Modal awareness is more difficult, as it requires representation of a change in state of the system. The flashing of the 'ball' in the radar display (and flashing icon in the icon display) is one way of drawing the driver's attention to the fact that a new target has been detected. Whatever representation is chosen, it needs to be able to communicate the information quickly and effectively to the driver [5][19]. Temporal awareness is even more difficult to display. None of the interfaces in the study communicated this information completely effectively. A digital time-to-contact displaying 'seconds' could communicate this information, but it would increase workload dramatically.

In the second case study, the Rich Pictures [8][9] were constructed by an SME primarily to the researchers gain a fuller understanding of the communications planning task independent of MPS. Not only did the pictures gave a valuable insight into the way in which the expert conceives the task, they also proved an invaluable tool in designing the interface for the proposed communications planning system. The air-to-ground Rich Picture was particularly useful in inspiring the design of the new system; it outlined the SME's representation of the task, showing that the arrangement of frequencies is not list-based but organised into groups of frequencies, each relating to an airspace controlling authority on the map of the ground. The representation of the aircraft's route as it travels through and around airspaces was similar to representation of the route on the map display in MPS; the major difference being that the selection of frequencies, i.e. who will need to be contacted, is done while studying the route, not after studying the route. This has been capitalised on in the proposed system; frequencies are directly tied to the map and can be selected from that view. Mapping the structure of the system interface and interaction design to the user's conceptual models of communications planning has increased the usability of the mission planning software for the communications planning task.

In conclusion, the aim of this paper has been to demonstrate the valuable contribution the Human Factors has to make in the specification and design of systems. The unique insights that arise from the application of Human Factors theories, models and methods appear to result in a deeper understanding of the interactions between people, the tasks they are performing and the requirements for interactions and technological interfaces. Human Factors approaches are both system-oriented (i.e., focusing on the interactions) and systematic (i.e., structured and holistic). The value they add, over and above traditional software engineering, seems self-evident in the two case studies presented. Both projects were undertaken with engineers and subject matter experts who had been involved in the previous design solutions. The role that Human Factors played in these projects was to translate the user requirements into meaningful design representations (i.e., graphical rather than textual) that the engineers could readily code into a prototype interface. It is apparent that this did not occur to the same extent in previous iterations of the interfaces. The benefits were demonstrated in the evaluation, which show improvements of between 20-70 percent over the more traditional design approaches. These benefits are typical of Human Factors interventions.

References

1. Annett, J.: A note on the validity and reliability of ergonomics methods. Theoretical Issues in Ergonomics Science 3(2), 229–232 (2002)
2. Annett, J.: Conclusions. In: Wilson, J.R., Corlett, E.N. (eds.) Evaluation of Human Work, 3rd edn., pp. 1009–1013. CRC Press, Boca Raton (2005)
3. Annett, J., Stanton, N.A.: Task Analysis. Taylor and Francis, London (2000)
4. Baber, C.: Evaluating Human-Computer Interaction. In: Wilson, J.R., Corlett, E.N. (eds.) Evaluation of Human Work, 3rd edn., pp. 357–388. CRC Press, Boca Raton (2005)
5. Baxter, G., Besnard, D., Riley, D.: Cognitive mismatches in the cockpit: Will they ever be a thing of the past? Applied Ergonomics 38, 417–423 (2007)
6. Bliss, J.P., Acton, S.A.: Alarm mistrust in automobiles: how collision alarm reliability affects driving. Applied Ergonomics 34, 499–509 (2003)
7. Brookhuis, K.A., van Driel, C.J.G., Hof, T., van Arem, B., Hoedemaeker, M.: Driving with a congestion assistant: mental workload and acceptance. Applied Ergonomics 40, 1019–1025 (2008)
8. Checkland, P.: Systems Thinking, Systems Practice. John Wiley & Sons, Chichester (1981)
9. Checkland, P., Scholes, J.: Soft systems methodology in action. John Wiley & Sons, Chichester (1990)

10. Diaper, D.: Task Analysis in Human Computer Interaction. Ellis Horwood, Chichester (1989)
11. Helender, M.G.: Using design equations to identify sources of complexity in human-machine interaction. Theoretical Issues in Ergonomics Science 8(2), 123–146 (2007)
12. Horan, P.: A new and flexible graphic organiser for IS learning: The Rich Picture. In: Proceedings of Informing Science Conference & IT Education Conference, Cork, Ireland, pp. 133–138. Informing Science Institute (2002)
13. Karwowski, W.: International Encyclopaedia of Ergonomics and Human Factors, vol. I-III. Taylor & Francis, London (2001)
14. Lai, F., Hjalmdahl, M., Chorlton, K., Wiklund, M.: The long-term effect of intelligent speed adaptation on driver behaviour. Applied Ergonomics 41, 179–186 (2010)
15. McIlroy, R.C., Stanton, N.A., Remington, B.: Developing expertise in military communications planning: Do verbal reports change with experience? Behaviour and Information Technology 31(6), 617–629 (2012)
16. Norman, D.A.: Categorisation of action slips. Psychological Review 88, 1–15 (1981)
17. Norman, D.A.: The "problem" with automation: Inappropriate feedback and interaction, not "overautomation". Philosophical Transaction of the Royal Society of London, B 327, 585–593 (1990)
18. Reason, J.: Human error. Cambridge University Press, Cambridge (1990)
19. Seppelt, B.D., Lee, J.D.: Making adaptive cruise control (ACC) limits visible. International Journal of Human Computer Studies 65, 192–205 (2007)
20. Stanton, N.A., Dunoyer, A., Leatherland, A.: Detection of new in-path targets by drivers using Stop & Go Adaptive Cruise Control. Applied Ergonomics 42(4), 592–601 (2011)
21. Stanton, N.A., Hedge, A., Salas, E., Hendrick, H., Brookhaus, K.: Handbook of Human Factors and Ergonomics Methods. Taylor & Francis, London (2005)
22. Stanton, N.A., McIlroy, R.C.: Designing mission communication planning: the role of Rich Pictures and Cognitive Work Analysis. Theoretical Issues in Ergonomics Science 13(2), 146–168 (2012)
23. Stanton, N.A., Salmon, P.M., Walker, G.H., Baber, C., Jenkins, D.: Human Factors Methods: A Practical Guide for Engineering and Design, 1st edn. Ashgate Publishing Ltd., Aldershot (2005)
24. Stanton, N.A., Salmon, P.M., Walker, G.H., Baber, C., Jenkins, D.: Human Factors Methods: A Practical Guide for Engineering and Design, 2nd edn. Ashgate Publishing Ltd., Aldershot (2013)
25. Stanton, N.A., Young, M.: A Guide to Methodology in Ergonomics: Designing for Human Use. Taylor & Francis, London (1999)
26. Wilson, J.R.: A framework and context for ergonomics methodology. In: Wilson, J.R., Corlett, E.N. (eds.) Evaluation of Human Work, 2nd edn., pp. 1–39. Taylor & Francis, London (1995)
27. Woods, D.D., Johannesen, L.J., Cook, R.I., Sarter, N.B.: Behind Human Error: Cognitive Systems, Computers and Hindsight. CSERIAC, Ohio (1994)

Improving Software Effort Estimation Using an Expert-Centred Approach

Emilia Mendes

School of Computing, Blekinge Institute of Technology, SE-371 79 Karlskrona, Sweden
Emilia.Mendes@bth.se

Abstract. A cornerstone of software project management is effort estimation, the process by which effort is forecasted and used as basis to predict costs and allocate resources effectively, so enabling projects to be delivered on time and within budget. Effort estimation is a very complex domain where the relationship between factors is non-deterministic and has an inherently uncertain nature, and where corresponding decisions and predictions require reasoning with uncertainty. Most studies in this field, however, have to date investigated ways to improve software effort estimation by proposing and comparing techniques to build effort prediction models where such models are built solely from data on past software projects - data-driven models. The drawback with such approach is threefold: first, it ignores the explicit inclusion of uncertainty, which is inherent to the effort estimation domain, into such models; second, it ignores the explicit representation of causal relationships between factors; third, it relies solely on the variables being part of the dataset used for model building, under the assumption that those variables represent the fundamental factors within the context of software effort prediction. Recently, as part of a New Zealand and later on Brazilian government-funded projects, we investigated the use of an expert-centred approach in combination with a technique that enables the explicit inclusion of uncertainty and causal relationships as means to improve software effort estimation. This paper will first provide an overview of the effort estimation process, followed by the discussion of how an expert-centred approach to improving such process can be advantageous to software companies. In addition, we also detail our experience building and validating six different expert-based effort estimation models for ICT companies in New Zealand and Brazil. Post-mortem interviews with the participating companies showed that they found the entire process extremely beneficial and worthwhile, and that all the models created remained in use by those companies. Finally, the methodology focus of this paper, which focuses on expert knowledge elicitation and participation, can be employed not only to improve a software effort estimation process, but also to improve other project management-related activities.

Keywords: Software Effort Estimation, Expert-centred Approach, Process Improvement, Cost Estimation, Project Management.

M. Winckler, P. Forbrig, and R. Bernhaupt (Eds.): HCSE 2012, LNCS 7623, pp. 18–33, 2012.

1   Introduction

The purpose of estimating effort is to predict the amount of effort (person/time) required to develop an application (and possibly also a service within the Web context), often based on knowledge of 'similar' applications/services previously developed. The accuracy of an effort estimate can affect significantly whether projects will be delivered on time and within budget; therefore effort estimation is taken as one of the main foundations of a sound project management. However, because effort estimation is a complex domain where corresponding decisions and predictions require reasoning with uncertainty, there are countless examples of companies that underestimate effort. Jørgensen and Grimstad [1] reported that such estimation error can be of 30%-40% on average, thus leading to serious project management problems.

Fig. 1 provides a general overview of an effort estimation process [2]. Estimated characteristics of the new application/service to be developed, and its context (project), are the input, and effort is the output we wish to predict. For example, a given software company may find that to predict the effort necessary to implement a new e-commerce Web application, it will need to estimate early on in the development project the following characteristics:

- *Estimated number of new Web pages.*
- *The number of functions/features (e.g. shopping cart, on-line forum) to be offered by the new Web application.*
- *Total number of developers who will help develop the new Web application*
- *Developers' average number of years of experience with the development tools employed.*
- *The choice of main programming language used.*

Of these variables, *estimated number of new Web pages* and *the number of functions/features to be offered by the new Web application* characterise the **size** of the new Web application; the other three, *total number of developers who will help develop the new Web application, developers' average number of years of experience with the development tools employed,* and *main programming language used,* characterise the project - the context for the development of the new application, and are also believed to influence the amount of effort necessary to develop this new application. The project-related characteristics are co-jointly named 'cost drivers'.

No matter what type of development it is (of an application or of a service), in general the one consistent input found to have the strongest effect on the amount of effort needed to develop an application or service is size (i.e. the total number of server side scripts, the total number of Web pages), with cost drivers also playing an influential role.

Evidence also shows that for most part of existing software & service projects, effort estimation is based on past experience, where knowledge or data from past finished applications & projects are used to estimate effort for new applications & projects not yet initiated [1]. The assumption here is that previous projects are similar to the new projects to be developed, and therefore knowledge and/or data from past projects can be useful in estimating effort for future projects. This process is also illustrated in Fig. 1. Those steps (some or all) can be executed more than once throughout a given software development cycle, depending on the process model adopted by the company. For example, if the process model adopted by a company complies with a waterfall model this means that most probably there will be an initial effort estimate for the project, which will remain unchanged throughout the project. If a company's process model complies with the spiral model, this means that for each cycle within the spiral process a new/updated effort estimate is obtained, and used to update the current project's plan and effort estimate. If a company uses an agile process model, an effort estimate is likely to be obtained for each of a project's iterations (e.g. sprints). In summary, a project's process model drives at what stage(s) an effort estimate(s) is/are obtained, and whether or not these estimates are revisited at some point throughout a project's development life cycle.

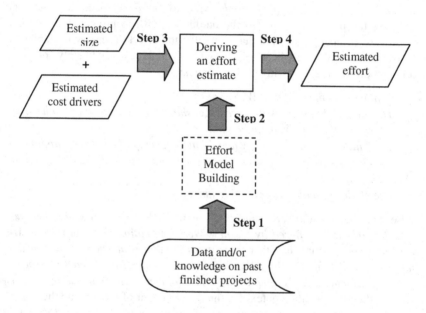

Fig. 1. Effort Estimation process [2]

Note that cost and effort are often used interchangeably within the context of most effort estimation literature since effort is taken as the main component of project costs. However, given that project costs also take into account other factors such as contingency and profit [3] we will use the word "effort" and not "cost" throughout this paper.

The remaining of this paper is organised as follows: the next Section provides a motivation for using an expert-centred approach to improving software effort estimation, followed by another two Sections where first the approach we propose is briefly introduced and second explained in more detail using the experience from eliciting six different expert-centred real models. Finally, our last two Sections discuss our experience building six expert-centred models to improve effort estimation, and lessons learnt, respectively.

2   Motivation to Employing an Expert-Centred Approach

Most research in software & Web effort estimation has to date focused on solving companies' inaccurate effort predictions via investigating techniques that are used to build formal effort estimation models, in the hope that such formalisation will improve the accuracy of estimates.

They do so by assessing, and often also comparing, the prediction accuracy obtained from applying numerous statistical and artificial intelligence techniques to datasets of completed software/Web projects developed by industry, and sometimes also developed by students. Recent literature reviews of software and Web effort estimation studies are given respectively in [4] and [5].

The variables characterising such datasets are determined in different ways, such as via surveys [6], interviews with experts [7], expertise from companies [8], a combination of research findings [9], or even a researcher's own consulting experience [10]. In all of these instances, once variables are defined, a data gathering exercise takes place, obtaining data (ideally) from industrial projects volunteered by companies. Except when using research findings to inform variables' identification, invariably the mechanism employed to determine variables relies on experts' recalling, where the subjective measure of an expert's certainty is often their amount of experience estimating effort.

However, in addition to eliciting the important effort predictors (and optionally also their relationships), such mechanism does not provide the means to also quantify the uncertainty associated with these relationships and to validate the knowledge obtained. Why should these be important?

Our experience developing and validating single-company expert-centred Software and Web effort prediction models that incorporate the uncertainty inherent in this domain [11] showed that the use of an expert-centred structured iterative process in which factors and relationships are identified, quantified and validated [12][13][14] leads the participating companies to a much more thorough and deep understanding of their mental processes and their decisions when estimating effort, when compared to just the recalling of factors and their relationships. The iterative process we use employs Bayesian inference, which is one of the techniques employed in root cause analysis [15]; therefore it aims at a detailed analysis and understanding of a particular phenomenon of interest.

In all the case studies we conducted, the original set of factors and relationships initially elicited was always modified as the model evolved; this occurred as a result of applying a root cause analysis approach comprising a Bayesian inference mechanism and feedback into the analysis process via a model validation. In addition, post-mortem interviews with the participating companies showed that the understanding they gained by being actively engaged in building those models led to both improved estimates and estimation processes [11][12][13][14].

We therefore contend that the use of an expert-centred structured iterative process provides the means to elicit a more robust set of predictors and relationships, when compared to other means of elicitation. We argue that the recalling mechanism used in surveys and interviews to elicit the important factors (and also occasionally their relationships) when estimating effort does not provide any means for experts to understand thoroughly their own decision making processes via the quantification of the uncertainty part of that decision process, and the validation of the factors they suggested during the elicitation. This means that the list of factors elicited is most likely based on a superficial process.

3   An Overview of the Expert-Centred Approach

3.1   Technique Used

The expert-centred approach proposed herein is based on a technique called Bayesian Networks (BN). This technique and corresponding process are briefly introduced in this Section, and further details are given in [14].

A BN is a model that enables the characterisation of a knowledge domain in terms of its factors, their relationships, and the uncertainty inherent to that domain. It has two parts [15]. The first part, known as the BN's qualitative part, results in a graphical structure comprising the factors and causal relationships identified as fundamental in the domain being modelled. This structure is depicted by a Directed Acyclic Graph (DAG) (see Fig. 2(a)). In addition to identifying factors and relationships, this part also includes the identification of the states (values) that each factor should take (e.g. Small (1 to 5), Medium (6 to 15), or Large (16+) in Fig. 2(a)).

The second part, known as the quantitative part, represents the relationships identified in the qualitative part, and their quantification, done probabilistically. This quantification represents the uncertainty in the domain being modelled, and in order for it to be accomplished, a Conditional Probability Table (CPT) is associated to each node in the graph. A parent node's CPT describes the relative probability of each state (value) (Fig. 2(b) CPTs for nodes 'Total Number of Web pages' and 'Total Number of Images'); a child node's CPT describes the relative probability of each state conditional on every combination of states of its parents (Fig. 2(b) CPT for node 'Total Effort'). Each row in a CPT represents a conditional probability distribution and therefore its values sum up to one [8]. Such probabilities can be attained via expert elicitation, automatically from data, from existing literature, or using a combination of these. However, within the context of this research all probabilities were obtained via expert elicitation. Once both qualitative and quantitative parts are specified, the BN is validated using data on past finished projects, where one project at a time is entered as evidence (see Fig. 2(d)) and used to check whether the BN provides the highest probability to a value (range of values) that includes the real actual effort for that project, which is known. If not, then the BN is re-calibrated.

The building of a BN model is an iterative process where one can move between the three different steps of this process – building the BN's structure, or qualitative part, building the CPTs, or the quantitative part, and validating the model. Once a BN is validated (see Fig. 1(c), evidence (e.g. values) can be entered into any node, and probabilities for the remaining nodes automatically calculated using Bayes' rule [8] (see Figs. 2(d) and 1(e). This was the validation method employed herein.

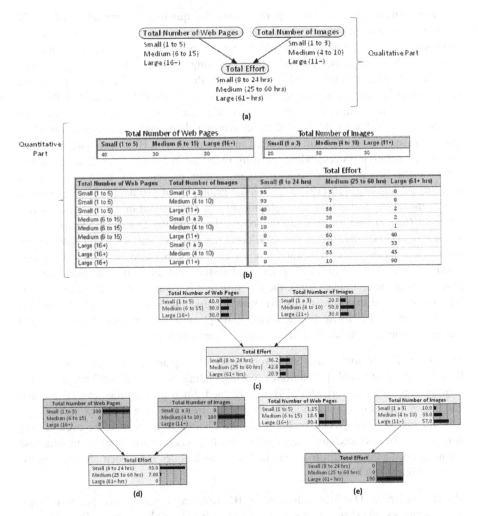

Fig. 2. Parts of a Bayesian Network an Types of Reasoning

In summary, BNs can be used for different types of reasoning, such as predictive (see Fig. 2(d)), diagnostic (see Fig. 2(e)), and "what-if" analyses to investigate the impact that changes on some nodes have on others [15].

3.2 Process We Employed to Building the Expert-Centred Models (BNs)

The process that was used to build and validate the expert-centred models focus of this research is an adaptation of the Knowledge Engineering of Bayesian Networks (KEBN)

process proposed in [16] (see Fig. 3). As shown in Fig. 3, this process iterates over three steps - Structural Development, Parameter Estimation, and Model Validation, until a complete BN is built and validated. Each of the steps is detailed next:

Structural Development: This step represents the qualitative component of a BN, which results in a graphical structure comprised of, in our case, the factors (nodes, variables) and causal relationships identified as fundamental for effort estimation of software & Web projects. In addition to identifying variables, their types (e.g. query variable, evidence variable) and causal relationships, this step also comprises the identification of the states (values) that each variable should take, and if they are discrete or continuous. In practice, currently available BN tools require that continuous variables be discretised by converting them into multinomial variables, also the case with the BN software used in this study. The BN's structure is refined through an iterative process where existing literature in the field can also be used as input to the process. This structure construction process has been validated in previous studies (e.g. [16][17]) and uses the principles of problem solving employed in data modelling and software development [18]. Throughout this step the Kowledge Engineer (responsible for eliciting the knowledge from the Domain Expert(s) (Des)) also evaluates the structure of the BN, checking whether variables and their values have a clear meaning; all relevant variables have been included; variables are named conveniently; all states are appropriate (exhaustive and exclusive); a check for any states that can be combined. Once the BN structure is assumed to be close to final the KE may still need to optimise this structure to reduce the number of probabilities that need to be elicited or learnt for the network. If optimisation is needed, techniques that change the causal structure (e.g. divorcing [19]) are employed.

Parameter Estimation: This step represents the quantitative component of a BN, where conditional probabilities corresponding to the quantification of the relationships between variables [19] are obtained. Such probabilities can be attained via Expert Elicitation, automatically from data, from existing literature, or using a combination of these. When probabilities are elicited from scratch, or even if they only need to be revisited, this step can be very time consuming. In order to minimise the number of probabilities to be elicited some techniques have been proposed in the literature (e.g. [16][17]).

Model Validation: This step validates the BN resulting from the two previous steps, and determines whether it is necessary to re-visit any of those steps. Two different validation methods are generally used - Model Walkthrough and Predictive Accuracy. Model walkthrough represents the use of real case scenarios that are prepared and used by DEs to assess if the predictions provided by the model correspond to the predictions experts would have chosen based on their own expertise. Success is measured as the frequency with which the model's predicted value for a target variable (e.g. quality, effort) that has the highest probability corresponds to the experts' own assessment.

Predictive Accuracy uses past data (e.g. past project data), rather than scenarios, to obtain predictions. Data (evidence) is entered on the model (see example in Fig. 2(d)), and success is measured as the frequency with which the model's predicted value for a target variable (e.g. quality, effort) showing the highest probability corresponds to the actual value from past data.

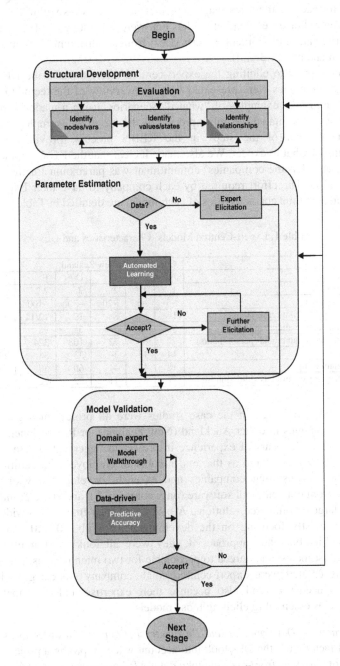

Fig. 3. KEBN, adapted from [16]

4   Detailing the Expert-Centred Approach

This Section revisits the adapted KEBN process (see Fig. 3), detailing the tasks carried out for each of the three main steps part of that process within the context of six expert-centred effort estimation models that were separately elicited by the author with the participation of Domain Experts (Des) from six different Companies (five in New Zealand and one in Brazil).

In all cases, prior to eliciting the expert-centred effort models, the DEs from all participating companies were presented with an overview of the technique that was going to be used, and examples of "what-if" scenarios, using a made-up BN model. This, we believe, facilitated the entire process as the use of an example, and the brief explanation of each of the steps in the KEBN process, provided a concrete understanding of what to expect. We also made it clear that the KE was a facilitator of the process, and that the companies' commitment was paramount for the success of the collaboration. The effort required by each company to have their Expert-centred models created and the characteristics of each model are detailed in Table 1.

Table 1. Expert-Centred Models' Characteristics and DEs

Characteristics	Companies in New Zealand					Co. Brazil
	A	B	C	D	E	F
Number of DEs	1	1	2	2	7/2	1
Number of Employees	~5	~5	~20	~30	~100	~30
Number of 3-hours elicitation sessions	12	6	8	12	12/12	20
Total hours to elicit & validate model	36	18	24	36	98	60
Effort to elicit & validate model (person/hours)	72	36	72	108	324	120
Number of factors	14	13	34	33	38	19
Number of relationships	18	12	41	60	50	37
Number of past projects used as validation set	22	8	11	22	22	9

The DEs who took part in the case studies were all project managers of well-established companies in either Auckland (New Zealand), or Rio de Janeiro (Brazil), each with at least 10 years of experience in project management. These companies varied in their size, measured as the total number of employees. In addition, all six companies were consulting companies and as such, developed a wide range of applications, from conventional software (only company E), and static & multimedia-like to very large e-commerce solutions. All six companies employed a wide range of technologies, mostly focusing on the development of Web 1.0, 2.0 and Web 3.0 applications. Finally, when approached, they were all looking at improving their current effort estimates, and agreed to participate for two main reasons: i) because the models being created were expert-centred single-company models geared towards their specific needs; ii) and also because their expertise and participation were acknowledged as essential to eliciting those models.

Detailed Structural Development and Parameter Estimation: In order to identify the fundamental factors that the DEs took into account when preparing a project quote we used the set of variables from the Tukutuku dataset [6] as a starting point (see Table 2).

We first sketched them out on a white board, each one inside an oval shape, and then explained what each one meant within the context of the Tukutuku project. Our previous experience eliciting expert-centred models in other domains (e.g. ecology, resource estimation) suggested that it was best to start with a few factors (even if they were not to be reused by the DE), rather than to use a "blank canvas" as a starting point [16].

Table 2. Tukutuku Variables

	Variable Name	Description
Project Data	TypeProj	Type of project (new or enhancement).
	nLang	Number of different development languages used
	DocProc	If project followed defined and documented process.
	ProImpr	If project team involved in a process improvement programme.
	Metrics	If project team part of a software metrics programme.
	DevTeam	Size of a project's development team.
	TeamExp	Average team experience with the development language(s) employed.
Application	TotWP	Total number of Web pages (new and reused).
	NewWP	Total number of new Web pages.
	TotImg	Total number of images (new and reused).
	NewImg	Total number of new images created.
	Num_Fots	Number of features reused without any adaptation.
	HFotsA	Number of reused high-effort features/functions adapted.
	Hnew	Number of new high-effort features/functions.
	TotHigh	Total number of high-effort features/functions
	Num_FotsA	Number of reused low-effort features adapted.
	New	Number of new low-effort features/functions.
	TotNHigh	Total number of low-effort features/functions

Within the context of the Tukutuku project, based on collected data, a new high-effort feature/function and a high-effort adapted feature/function require respectively at least 15 and 4 hours to be developed by one experienced developer.

Once the Tukutuku variables had been sketched out and explained, the next step was to remove all variables that were not relevant for the DEs, followed by adding to the white board any additional variables (factors) suggested by them. This entire process was documented using digital voice recorders and also text editors. We also documented descriptions and rationale for each factor proposed by the DEs. The factors proposed were indeed influenced by DEs' hunches and insights; however DEs decisions and choices were also very much influenced by their solid previous experience managing Web projects, and estimating development effort.

Next, we identified the possible states that each factor would take. All states were discrete. Whenever a factor represented a measure of effort (e.g. Total effort), we also documented the effort range corresponding to each state, to avoid any future ambiguity. For example, to one of the participating Web companies, 'very low' Total effort corresponded to 4+ to 10 person hours, etc. Once all states were identified and thoroughly documented, it was time to elicit the cause and effect relationships. As a starting point to this task we used a simple medical example from [19] (see Fig. 4).

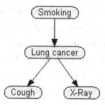

Fig. 4. An example of a cause and effect relationship

This example clearly introduces one of the most important points to consider when identifying cause and effect relationships – timeline of events. If smoking is to be a cause of lung cancer, it is important that the cause precedes the effect. This may sound obvious with regard to the example used; however, it is our view that the use of this simple example significantly helped the DEs understand the notion of cause and effect, and how this related to Web effort estimation and the BNs being elicited. Once the cause and effect relationships were identified, we worked on the elicitation of probabilities to quantify each of the cause and effect relationships previously identified. In all four cases, there was an iterative process between the structural development and parameter elicitation steps.

Detailed Model Validation: Both Model walkthrough and Predictive accuracy were used to validate all six expert-centred models, where the former was the first type of validation to be employed in all cases. DEs used different scenarios to check whether the node Total_effort would provide the highest probability to the effort state that corresponded to the DE's own suggestion. However, it was also necessary to use data from past projects, for which total effort was known, in order to check the model's calibration. Table 1 details the number of projects used by each company as validation set. In all cases, DEs were asked to use as validation set a range of projects presenting different sizes and levels of complexity, and being representative of the types of projects developed by their companies.

For each project in a validation set, evidence was entered in the expert-centred model, and the effort range corresponding to the highest probability provided for 'Total Effort' was compared to that project's actual effort. Whenever actual effort did not fall within the effort range associated with the category with the highest probability, there was a mismatch; this meant that some probabilities needed to be adjusted. In order to know which nodes to target first we used a Sensitivity Analysis report, which provided the effect of each parent node upon a given query node. Within our context, the query node was 'Total Effort'. Whenever probabilities were adjusted, we re-entered the evidence for each of the projects in the validation set that had already been used in the validation step to ensure that the calibration already carried out had not been affected. This was done to ensure that each calibration would always be an improvement upon the previous one. Once all projects were used to calibrate a model, the DE(s) assumed that the Validation step was complete.

Each of the five New Zealand expert-centred models has been in production for at least 18 months, and the Brazilian model has been in production since May 2011. Due to shortage of space we cannot show the models; however, more details about these six expert-centred models are given in [11].

5   Further Gains from Eliciting Expert-Centred Models

Except for Company E, where the expert-centred model is also used to estimate effort for non-Web-based projects, all the five remaining models represent solely the knowledge elicited from domain experts relating to their previous experience estimating effort for Web development projects; therefore we believe that by aggregating their knowledge we can obtain a wider understanding on the fundamental factors affecting effort estimation (mainly Web effort estimation) and their causal relationships.

The type of aggregation mechanism we are suggesting herein applies solely to the qualitative parts of the expert-centred models elicited (factors and relationships only), as aggregating their quantitative parts and also the different categories used to measure each factor would prove to be a herculean (if not impossible) task; in addition, our goal is not to obtain a cross-company expert-centred model.

Some of the advantages of such type of aggregation are as follows [20]:

- The aggregation from different experts of knowledge relating to the same phenomenon has the obvious advantage of providing an opportunity to amplify and broaden our overall understanding of that phenomenon.
- The graph (map) resulting from the aggregation mechanism uses as input factors and relationships from models that were built and validated using a process based on a root cause analysis technique [15]; such technique, by requiring a thorough and deep understanding of experts' mental processes and their decisions when estimating effort, provides the means to truly portray the phenomenon focus of this research, i.e. effort estimation.
- The introduction of more structure into the effort estimation process, as such map can be used as a checklist to help improve judgment-based effort estimates [1].
- Anecdotal evidence we obtained throughout the elicitation process and post-mortem meetings with several companies revealed that the use of a map aggregating companies' expert knowledge with regard to factors and relationships relevant for Web effort estimation would be extremely useful to help them elicit factors and relationships when building their own Web effort prediction models; therefore they would like to use such aggregated map at the start of their elicitation process.
- Our aggregated map shows graphically not only the set of factors and relationships from the input models, but also a way to identify visually the most common factors and relationships resulting from the aggregation. Such knowledge may also be useful to project managers to revisit the factors they consider when estimating effort for new projects.

- The aggregated map can be used to provide companies with a starting point to building a single-company expert-based Web effort estimation model. This is also an approach suggested in [1][21].

Herein we will just present the main patterns observed from aggregating those six expert-centred models [11]; however, further details on the aggregation mechanism employed and an example of the sort of aggregated map we are focusing herein is given in [20].

The main patterns observed from aggregating the six expert-centred effort estimation models are presented below.

Apart from total effort, which was identified by all participating companies, there were three factors that were chosen by five of the six Companies:

- Average Project Team Experience with Technology
- Effort to Program Features
- Project Management Effort

The next set of factors selected by four Companies were the following:
- Adaptation Effort of Features off the shelf
- Development Effort of New Features
- Effort to Develop User Interface
- Project Risk Factor
- Effort Production testing

Except for Project Risk Factor and Average Project Team Experience with Technology, all the remaining factors were related to the effort to accomplish certain tasks, such as adapting or developing a new feature, testing and interface design. Note that these factors are very much related to more dynamic Web applications, which offer a large set of features (this requiring more detailed testing). It is also interesting that the effort to develop the user interface was also chosen by four of the six companies. Nowadays, with the plethora of Web technologies and possibilities available, good interface design and usability can also add very much so to a company's competitive advantage on the global market.

All six expert-centred models presented several effort-related factors as predictors of Total effort. Note that these factors represent tasks that are part of an effort estimation process and therefore, their relationship with Total effort has an associative nature, however not of type cause&effect.

6   Lessons Learnt

The elicitation of expert-centred models, and their aggregation has provided numerous lessons, as follows:

First: engaging with industry. At the start of this research, in order to reach out to industry, we invited the local NZ IT industry to attend a seminar about software & Web effort estimation and how to improve their estimates. The seminar provided an introduction to using expert-centred models, their value as estimation tools, and their capability for running "what-if" scenarios. Many of the participating companies saw the immediate value in such an approach, in particular because it enabled the very close and fundamental participation of in-house domain experts while building and validating the company-specific model. Several companies sign up to collaborate.

Second: Time constraints. Depending on the complexity of the expert-centred model, the elicitation of probabilities can be very time consuming. Motivated by this issue, we have also made a preliminary attempt at investigating mechanisms to enable the automatic generation of probability tables. An attempt was devised and used with two NZ companies that participated more recently in this research. This solution comprised the comparison between different probability generation algorithms and expert-driven probabilities. A tool was implemented as a result of this work [22]; however, further work is needed to validate the proposed solution.

Third: Value for a company. Except for the company in Brazil, the other participating companies were contacted for post-mortem interviews. The main points highlighted were the following:

- The elicitation process enabled experts to think deeply about their effort estimation process and the factors taken into account during that process, which in itself was considered advantageous to the companies. This has been pointed out to us by all the DEs interviewed.
- Once a company's expert-centred model was validated, DEs started to use their model not only for obtaining better estimates than the ones previously prepared by subjective means, but also sometimes as means to guide their requirements elicitation meetings with prospective clients. They focused their questions targeting at obtaining evidence to be entered in the model as the requirements meetings took place; by doing so they basically had effort estimates that were practically ready to use for costing the projects, even when meetings with clients had short durations. Such change in approach proved to be extremely beneficial to the companies given that all estimates provided using the models turned out to be more accurate on average than the ones previously obtained by subjective means.
- Clients were not presented the models due to their complexity; however by entering evidence while a requirements elicitation meeting took place enabled the DEs to optimise their elicitation process by being focused and factor-driven.
- One of the participating companies, the largest company in total number of employees, and also the one that built the largest BN model, provided the following feedback: The DEs who participated in the causal structure and probabilities' elicitation changed completely their approach to estimating effort as follows: they presented the BN model to all of their development teams, and asked that from that point onwards every estimate for any task should be based on the factors that had been elicited. This means that an entire team started to use the factors that have been elicited, as well as the BN model, as basis for their effort & risk estimation sessions. In addition, the

DEs presented the model at a meeting with other company branches, so to detail how the Auckland branch was estimating effort and risk for their healthcare projects. The other branches were so impressed, in particular the one from the US, that they increased the number of Healthcare software projects outsourced to the NZ Branch, as they recognised the benefits of using a model that represented factors and uncertainties. Overall, such change in approach provided extremely beneficial to the company.

All the companies remained positive and very satisfied with the results. We believe that the successful development of these six expert-centred models was greatly influenced by the commitment of the participating companies, and also by the DEs' experience estimating effort.

Acknowledgments. We thank all the Web companies who participated in this research. This work was sponsored by the Royal Society of New Zealand (Marsden research grant 06-UOA-201), and by CAPES/PVE (Brazil).

References

1. Jørgensen, M., Grimstad, S.: Software Development Effort Estimation: Demystifying and Improving Expert Estimation. In: Tveito, A., Bruaset, A.M., Lysne, O. (eds.) Simula Research Laboratory - by thinking constantly about it, ch. 26, pp. 381–404. Springer, Heidelberg (2009)
2. Mendes, E.: Cost Estimation Techniques for Web Projects. IGI Global Publishers (2007)
3. Kitchenham, B.A., Pickard, L.M., Linkman, S., Jones, P.: Modelling Software Bidding Risks. IEEE Transactions on Software Engineering 29(6), 542–554 (2003)
4. Jørgensen, M., Shepperd, M.J.: A Systematic Review of Software Development Cost Estimation Studies. IEEE Transactions Software Engeneering 33(1), 33–53 (2007)
5. Azhar, D., Mendes, E., Riddle, P.: A Systematic Review of Web Resource Estimation. In: Proceedings of PROMISE 2012 (accepted for publication, 2012)
6. Mendes, E., Mosley, N., Counsell, S.: Investigating Web Size Metrics for Early Web Cost Estimation. Journal of Systems and Software 77(2), 157–172 (2005), doi:10.1016/j.jss.2004.08.034
7. Ruhe, M., Jeffery, R., Wieczorek, I.: Cost estimation for Web applications. In: Proceedings ICSE 2003, pp. 285–294 (2003)
8. Ferrucci, F., Gravino, C., Di Martino, S.: A Case Study Using Web Objects and COSMIC for Effort Estimation of Web Applications. In: EUROMICRO-SEAA, pp. 441–448 (2008)
9. Mendes, E., Mosley, N., Counsell, S.: Web metrics - Metrics for estimating effort to design and author Web applications. IEEE MultiMedia, 50–57 (January-March 2001)
10. Reifer, D.J.: Web Development: Estimating Quick-to-Market Software. IEEE Software, 57–64 (November-December 2000)
11. Mendes, E.: Using Knowledge Elicitation to Improve Web Effort Estimation: Lessons from Six Industrial Case Studies. In: Proceedings of the International Conference on Software Engineering (ICSE 2012), track SE in Practice, pp. 1112–1121 (2012)
12. Mendes, E.: Knowledge Representation using Bayesian Networks A Case Study in Web Effort Estimation. In: Proceedings of the World Congress on information and Communication Technologies (WICT 2011), pp. 310–315 (2011)

13. Mendes, E.: Building a Web Effort Estimation Model through Knowledge Elicitation. In: Proceedings of the International Conference on Enterprise Information Systems (ICEIS), pp. 128–135 (2011)
14. Mendes, E., Polino, C., Mosley, N.: Building an Expert-based Web Effort Estimation Model using Bayesian Networks. In: 13th International Conference on Evaluation & Assessment in Software Engineering (2009)
15. Ammerman, M.: The Root Cause Analysis Handbook: A Simplified Approach to Identifying, Correcting, and Reporting Workplace Errors (1998)
16. Woodberry, O., Nicholson, A., Korb, K., Pollino, C.: Parameterising Bayesian Networks. In: Australian Conference on Artificial Intelligence, pp. 1101–1107 (2004)
17. Druzdzel, M.J., van der Gaag, L.C.: Building Probabilistic Networks: Where Do the Numbers Come From? IEEE Trans. on Knowledge and Data Engineering 12(4), 481–486 (2000)
18. Tang, Z., McCabe, B.: Developing Complete Conditional Probability Tables from Fractional Data for Bayesian Belief Networks. Journal of Computing in Civil Engineering 21(4), 265–276 (2007)
19. Jensen, F.V.: An introduction to Bayesian networks. UCL Press, London (1996)
20. Baker, S., Mendes, E.: Aggregating Expert-Driven Causal Maps for Web Effort Estimation. In: Kim, T.-H., Kim, H.-K., Khan, M.K., Kiumi, A., Fang, W.-C., Ślęzak, D. (eds.) ASEA 2010. CCIS, vol. 117, pp. 264–282. Springer, Heidelberg (2010)
21. Montironi, R., Whimster, W.F., Collan, Y., Hamilton, P.W., Thompson, D., Bartels, P.H.: How to develop and use a Bayesian Belief Network. Journal of Clinical Pathology 49, 194 (1996)
22. Baker, S., Mendes, E.: Evaluating the Weighted Sum Algorithm for Estimating Conditional Probabilities in Bayesian Networks. In: Proceedings of the Software Engineering and Knowledge Engineering Conference (SEKE 2010), pp. 319–324 (2010)

A Compositional Model for Gesture Definition

Lucio Davide Spano[1], Antonio Cisternino[2], and Fabio Paternò[1]

[1] ISTI-CNR Via G. Moruzzi 1, 56127 Pisa
{lucio.davide.spano,fabio.paterno}@isti.cnr.it
[2] Università di Pisa, Dipartimento di Informatica, Largo Bruno Potencorvo 3, 56127 Pisa
cisterni@di.unipi.it

Abstract. The description of a gesture requires temporal analysis of values generated by input sensors and does not fit well the observer pattern traditionally used by frameworks to handle user input. The current solution is to embed particular gesture-based interactions, such as pinch-to-zoom, into frameworks by notifying when a whole gesture is detected. This approach suffers from a lack of flexibility unless the programmer performs explicit temporal analysis of raw sensors data. This paper proposes a compositional, declarative meta-model for gestures definition based on Petri Nets. Basic traits are used as building blocks for defining gestures; each one notifies the change of a feature value. A complex gesture is defined by the composition of other sub-gestures using a set of operators. The user interface behaviour can be associated to the recognition of the whole gesture or to any other sub-component, addressing the problem of granularity for the notification events. The meta-model can be instantiated for different gesture recognition supports and its definition has been validated through a proof of concept library. Sample applications have been developed for supporting multitouch gestures on iOS and full body gestures with Microsoft Kinect.

Keywords: Input and Interaction Technologies, Model-based design, Software architecture and engineering, Gestural Interaction.

1   Introduction

In recent years a wide variety of new input devices has changed the way we interact with computers. Nintendo Wii in 2006 has broken the point and click paradigm with the Wiimote controller, based on gestures in a 3D space; iPhone has shown better usability by means of multitouch in 2007, while Microsoft introducing Kinect in 2010 has expressed a way of interaction without wearing sensors of any kind. All these new devices exploit gestures performed in different ways, such as moving a remote, touching a screen, or through whole-body movements.

The introduction of these novel interaction techniques in the mass market has not affected current user interface programming frameworks yet: the underlying model is still bound to the observer pattern, where events occur atomically in time and gets notified through messages or callbacks. Indeed, the support for gestures has been mostly forced in the same paradigm by hiding the gesture recognition logic under the

M. Winckler, P. Forbrig, and R. Bernhaupt (Eds.): HCSE 2012, LNCS 7623, pp. 34–52, 2012.

hood, which usually means providing high-level events when the gesture is completed, and leaving the possibility to provide intermediate feedback to the handling of low-level events that are not correlated with the high-level ones. The drawback of this approach is twofold: on the one hand the temporal extension of a gesture is significant with respect to the time scale of a system, a gesture may require in fact seconds to complete; on the other hand the set of recognizable gestures is fixed and inaccessible to the system unless the programmer hooks the low level events generated by sensors and re-implements the full gesture-recognition logic.

Moreover, gesture interfaces exploit the movement evolution in space and time as argument for the interaction, therefore their effect on the UI usually changes according to the movement speed or the space covered, and the program has to perform these calculations. To better handle these problems, a framework must offer an extended vision of how to handle gestures allowing for sub-gesture recognition and concurrent recognition of multiple gestures (i.e. pinch-to-zoom and drawing with another finger). The state of the art tools leave the programmer with the choice between pre-cooked recipes and do-it-yourself with handling low level events. The problem with this paradigm arises when we need intermediate feedback during the gesture execution. With a single event notification, the developer is forced to re-implement the low-level tracking, because it is not possible to separate the complex gesture in smaller constituents. In addition, it is not also possible to compose two or more predefined gestures. For instance, if we want to create a view that can be zoomed and panned at the same time for the iPhone, we have again to track the low-level events, and hard-code the gesture composition.

In this paper, we address such granularity problem by defining a gesture description meta-model that allows constructing complex gestures from a well-defined set of building blocks and composition operators. Moreover, composition semantics is defined using Petri Nets and can be efficiently implemented in a framework. Using our model, developers can associate the UI behaviour either to simple or complex gestures, enabling gestures reuse and composition, which is not currently supported in user interface frameworks. The implementation of a proof-of-concept library for the recognition of the modelled gestures is also described. Finally, we discuss two application prototypes that exploit such library, based on two different recognition supports: iOS devices and Microsoft Kinect.

2   Related Work

The attempt to create compositional representations of different event sources into higher-level events, have a very long research history [1] and the need of a structured approach is exacerbated by the new interaction devices available nowadays. In [3], the analysis of the various interaction techniques considered different dimensions of languages (lexical, syntactical, semantic and pragmatic), in order to provide designers with a theoretical foundation when creating interfaces based on gestures. Through the years, such work evolved in order to include sensors that started to be pervasively included in consumer devices, supporting the advancement towards the *Reality-Based*

Interaction [5]. For instance, in [14] the authors characterized the physical actions that users need to perform to enter a command through accelerometer-based devices. While such categorization is useful to define how and why the user should perform an action rather than another, the following step is to ease the development of such kind of interfaces. In this regard, the support offered by frameworks has to be effective and uniform across the different operating systems and devices [8]. Therefore, we want to focus on generic and machine-understandable gesture descriptions, such as the Gesture Definition Markup Language (GDML) [9], which allows a declarative description of the sequence of events that the device senses for recognizing a custom touch gesture, raising a single event when the gesture completes. We overcome this approach supporting the association of UI behaviour also to gesture sub-parts and parallel gesture recognition. In [7], Kammer et al. described GeForMT, a formalization language for multitouch gestures defined by four components: pose function, atomic gestures, composition operators and the focus on a user interface object. We propose a more general solution that is suitable for devices different from touch screens.

Model-based approaches for user interfaces included gesture descriptions limited to specific supports (e.g. multitouch [12], 3D interaction [4] etc.). In our work, we attempt to overcome the main limitation of these description languages, which is the focus on a single gesture recognition support. Our paradigm aims to be more abstract while allowing concurrent gesture recognition, preserving composition and independence from concrete sensor values: our meta-model allows describing gestures for different recognition devices with a uniform vocabulary.

The definition of a compositional model for complex multitouch gestures has been defined in [6]. The authors use regular expressions for describing gestures, where literals are identified by triples containing the touch event type (start, move, end), the touch identifier and the concerned UI object. The operators are the usual ones for regular expressions. Our work shares with this approach the possibility to create composite expressions for describing gestures, separating them from the UI control. However, we overcome the single gesture recognition assumption in [6], providing the possibility to define parallel gestures. In order to do this, we use Petri Nets for the definition of a gesture meta-model, a notation that has been proved to be effective for the description of event-driven interactive interfaces [2].

In addition, we provide a general solution that is applicable not only for touch devices, but also for different recognition supports by creating an abstract representation of the different features that can be observed, as happens in existing descriptions of multimodal interaction [15].

3   Gesture Description Meta-model

In this section, we theoretically define our gesture description meta-model. Such meta-model is abstract with respect to a specific gesture recognition support, which means that it is possible to instantiate it for different devices (e.g. multitouch screens, body tracking devices, remotes etc.). We start from the definition of the basic building blocks (ground terms), which represent the set of basic features observable through a specific device. Composed terms represent complex gestures (that can be further decomposed) and they are obtained connecting ground or composed terms through a well-defined set of composition operators.

The definition of the UI behaviour can be associated to the recognition of basic or composed gesture definition. As we will better explain in the following sections, we used Non Autonomous Petri Nets [13] in order to describe the recognition process, since they ease the description of parallel computations driven by external events, such as the reaction of the user interface according to the notifications coming by the gesture recognition device. Once the Petri Nets for a basic building block and for all the composition operators have been defined, the designer can create complex gestures through expressions of basic building blocks and/or complex gestures composed through the set of operators. The actual Petri Net for the complex gesture is derived visiting bottom-up the complex gesture expression definition and can be executed by the library (see section 4.1).

3.1   Basic Building Blocks: Ground Terms

Ground terms of our language are the basic building blocks of our gesture description model, since they cannot be further decomposed. They are defined by the events that developers currently track in order to recognize gestures. Ground terms do not have a temporal extension, though their values may be obtained by computing a function of the raw sensor data (the current gesture support).

For instance, if we are describing a gesture for a multitouch application, the ground terms are represented by the low-level events that are available for tracking the finger positions, which are usually called touch start, touch move and touch end. Besides, for creating full body gestures, the current recognition devices and libraries offer means for tracking specific skeleton points, such as hands, head, shoulders, elbows etc. As happens for multitouch gestures, also full body ones are recognized tracking the skeleton points positions over time.

Here, we define an abstract building block that can be instantiated for different gesture recognition supports. In order to do this, we have to consider that a gesture support provides the possibility to track a set of features that change through the time. As said before, the meaning of each feature (and the associated low-level event) depends on the concrete gesture recognition support.

A feature is a n-dimensional vector (e.g., the position of a finger is a vector with two components, the position of a skeleton joint has three components, etc.). A set of features can be also represented with a vector with a number of components equals to the sum of the dimensions of its elements. A set of features is the abstract representation of a gesture recognition support at a given time, since it describes the data provided by a given hardware and software configuration. We will provide examples for the definition of a gesture recognition support in the following sections. The state of a gesture support at a given time is represented by the current value of each feature. The state of a gesture recognition support over time can be represented by a sequence of such states, considering a discrete time sampling. Equation 1 defines a feature f, a gesture recognition support G_S, a gesture recognition support state G_{S_i} and a gesture recognition support state sequence S.

$$f \in \mathbb{R}^n \tag{1}$$

$$G_S = [f_1, f_2, \dots, f_m] \qquad G_S \in \mathbb{R}^k \quad f_i \in \mathbb{R}^{n_i} \quad \sum_{i=1}^{m} n_i = k$$

$$G_{S_i} = [f_1(t_i), f_2(t_i), \dots, f_m(t_i)] \qquad t_i \in \mathbb{R}$$

$$S = G_{S_1}, G_S, \dots, G_{S_n} \qquad n \in \mathbb{N}$$

A gesture building block notifies a change of a feature value between t_i and t_{i+1}. Such notification can be optionally associated to a condition, which can be exploited for checking properties of the gesture state sequence such as trajectories for hand movements. For instance, it is possible to checks whether the path of a tracked point is linear or not, avoiding the notification of different movements.

The feature change notification is accomplished by the gesture support, and it is external with respect to the current state of the gesture recognition.

We define the basic traits and the composition operators using Non-Autonomous Petri Nets. A Petri Net is a bipartite graph consisting of two types of nodes: transitions (represented as black rectangles) and places (represented as circles), which are connected by directed arcs. A place contains a positive number of tokens and the state of the net is represented by the distribution of the tokens among the places. When all the places that are connected to a given transition contain at least one token, the transition fires, withdrawing a token from all the incoming places and adding one token to all the outcoming ones. In this work, we consider a particular type of Petri Net called Non-Autonomous, in which the firing of a transition is enabled not only by the presence of the tokens, but also by the occurrence of an event that does not depend on the considered Net. Therefore, in Non-Autonomous Petri Net, the transition fires only if the incoming places contain a token *and* if an event of a given type occurs (see [13] for a more detailed description). We need such kind events in order to model the notification of a feature change by the considered gesture support.

We define an event type for each observed feature and each optional gesture state sequence constraint. It is possible to model the external notification with the definition of a function $raise$, which establishes if the Petri Net external event will be raised at a time t as defined in equation 2.

$$raise\big(E_{f_i, P(S)}, t\big) \Leftrightarrow \big(f_i(t) \neq f_i(t-1)\big) \wedge p(S) \qquad p: S \longrightarrow \{true, false\} \tag{2}$$

It states that the event $E_{f_i, P(S)}$ at time t is raised if the value of the feature f is changed and if the property on the gesture support state sequence $p(S)$ is verified. In order to avoid a cumbersome representation, we will identify the events simply specifying the related feature and optionally giving a name to the gesture state sequence property. If no constraint has to be verified on the state sequence, we will simply omit it. For instance we will identify the event in Fig. 1 with $f_i, p(S)$. If $p(S)$ is true for all S, the event will be identified as f_i.

In order to model the current progress in the gesture recognition, we use a control state token (Cs) on the Petri Net. The recognition of a basic block will be enabled by the presence of such token, and it will be inhibited by its absence. As we explain better in the following sections, the parallel recognition of different gestures in a composed Net is possible managing multiple instances of such control state token. The Petri Net in Fig. 1 defines a basic building block for gesture recognition.

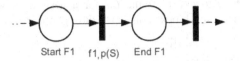

Fig. 1. Gesture recognition building block

The two dotted arrows connect this subnet to transitions that are "externals" with respect to the building block, namely the previous and the following parts of the gesture net. The place $Start\ F1$ receives the control state token from its incoming transition. If it is the first one in the recognition net, it will contain the token associated with the entire recognition process. The transition after this place fires only when the event $f1, p(S)$ occurs. Finally, the control state token will reach the place $End\ F1$, concluding the basic gesture recognition. The actions to be performed in order to react to the basic gesture recognition are associated to the latter place. The out coming arrow starting from the $End\ F1$ place connects the considered block with the next part of the gesture net.

In order to represent a basic building block we use the notation $F_i[p]$: we assign a name to the considered feature (F_i in this case) and also to the boolean function (p), which is omitted if it is true for every gesture support state.

3.2 Composition Operators

A gesture description model is based on the composition of the aforementioned ground terms. The connection is performed through a set of operators, which express different temporal relationships among them. Such set has as starting point those defined in CTT [11], which has been proved effective in defining the temporal relationship for task modelling. Some of them (sequence and choice) have been already defined through Petri Nets in [10]. We provide here a complete definition together with the support for conditions on device feature that is peculiar to gesture modelling. Table 1 lists the composition operators that we will describe in the next sections. All binary operators are associative, therefore the n-ary version of a binary operator (e.g. choice) is defined applying such property.

Table 1. List of composition operators

Operator	Notation	Arity
Iterative	G^*	1
Sequence	$G1 \gg G2$	2 (n)
Parallel	$G1 \parallel G2$	2 (n)
Choice	$G1 [] G2$	2 (n)
Disabling	$G1 [> G2$	2 (n)
Order Independence	$G1 \mathbin{|=|} G2 \mathbin{|=|} ... \mathbin{|=|} Gn$	n

During the discussion in the following sections, we need also the definition of two different sets of ground terms, given a complex gesture definition. The first one is the set that containing all its ground terms. We refer such set as GS (Ground terms Set).

Equation 3 defines how to construct the GS for a gesture G, which consists of a recursive set union on the sub-blocks connected through the composition operators.

$$G = F_i[p] \Rightarrow GS_G = \{F_i[p]\} \tag{3}$$
$$G = G1^* \Rightarrow GS_G = GS_{G1}$$
$$G = G1 \; op \; G2 \Rightarrow GS_G = GS_{G1} \cup GS_{G2} \qquad op \in \{\gg, ||, [], [>\}$$
$$G = G1 \mathrel{|=|} G2 \mathrel{|=|} \ldots \mathrel{|=|} Gn \Rightarrow GS_G = \bigcup_{i=0}^{n} GS_{Gi}$$

The second set we need to define contains only the ground terms not appearing as the right operand in a sequencing temporal relation, so they are immediately recognizable when the gesture execution starts. The operators that express such relation are *sequence* and *disabling*. We will call such set starting ground terms set, or SGS and it is defined in Equation 4. Obviously $SGS \subseteq GS$.

$$G = F_i[p] \Rightarrow SGS_G = \{F_i[p]\} \tag{4}$$
$$G = G1^* \Rightarrow SGS_G = SGS_{G1}$$
$$G = G1 \; op \; G2 \Rightarrow SGS_G = SGS_{G1} \qquad op \in \{\gg, [>\}$$
$$G = G1 \; op \; G2 \Rightarrow SGS_G = SGS_{G1} \cup SGS_{G2} \qquad op \in \{||, []\}$$
$$G = G1 \mathrel{|=|} G2 \mathrel{|=|} \ldots \mathrel{|=|} Gn \Rightarrow SGS_G = \bigcup_{i=0}^{n} SGS_{Gi}$$

3.2.1   Iterative Operator

The iterative operator repeats the recognition of gesture subnet for an indefinite number of times. In order to avoid an infinite gesture definition, each iterative basic block should also be coupled with a disabling operation. As already specified in Table 2, we will use the $*$ symbol in order to represent the iterative operator (e.g. F^* recognizes an infinite number of value changes for the feature one). It is possible to define this operator simply creating a cycle from the ending transition of a gesture subnet to its starting place. In this way, the recognition subnet will be fed again with the control state token, immediately after the gesture has been recognized. Fig. 2 shows the Petri Net definition of the iterative operator. The thicker arrow represents the operator definition.

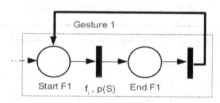

Fig. 2. The iterative operator

3.2.2   Sequence Operator

This operator simply defines that two gesture subnets should be performed in sequence. We use the $\gg$ symbol in order to represent this operator. It is possible to define such operator connecting the last transition of the first gesture with the starting place of the second one. Fig. 3 shows a gesture consisting of the sequential composition of two basic feature recognizers. The thicker arrow represents the sequence operator.

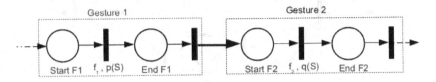

Fig. 3. The sequence operator

3.2.3   Parallel Operator

The parallel operator defines the recognition of two or more different gestures at the same time. We use the ‖ symbol in order to represent the parallel operator.

From the Petri Net definition point of view, the blocks representing the parallel gestures should be simply put in different recognition lines. In order to do this, we assign a different control state token to each line. This can be obtained, as shown in Fig. 4, inserting a transition that "clones" the control state token and dispatching a copy to the starting place of each different recognition lines. We add a place at the end of each recognition line that forwards the "cloned" control state token to the last transition that, once all gestures terminated, restores only one token in the net.

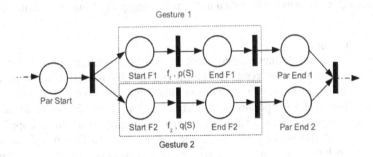

Fig. 4. The parallel operator

3.2.4   Choice Operator

The choice operator defines a gesture that is recognized if exactly one between its first and its second component is detected (either one or the other). We use the symbol [] for representing it. The net can be defined as it is shown in Fig. 5, and its construction is similar to the parallel operator. The transition after the *Choice Start* place splits the control state token between two subnets, each one representing a component involved in the choice. The two lines cannot evolve independently as happens for the parallel operator. Therefore, when one subnet starts its recognition, the other one should be interrupted. In order to do this, it is sufficient to connect the first place of the first gesture subnet with the first transition of the second one and vice versa. In this way, once one of the two feature events is raised, the control state token from the other gesture subnet is deleted.

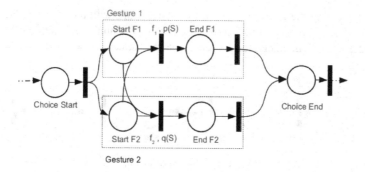

Fig. 5. The choice operator

More precisely the steps to be followed for constructing a Petri Net for $G1[\ ]G2$ in the general case are the following:

1. Calculate SGS_{G1} and SGS_{G2}
2. Connect the first place of each element of SGS_{G1} with the first transition of each element in SGS_{G2}
3. Connect the first place of each element of SGS_{G2} with the first transition of each element in SGS_{G1}

The last transition of each gesture subnet is connected to the *Choice End* place, which forwards the control state token to the following part of the recognition net.

3.2.5   Disabling

The disabling operator defines a gesture that stops the recognition of another one, thus "disabling" it. The operator symbol is [>. It is typically needed when a gesture is iterative, in order to define the condition that stops the loop. Fig. 6 shows the definition of the disabling operator using Petri Nets for $G1[> G2$. The basic idea is to connect the first place of each basic component belonging to $G1$ to a "copy" of the first transition of the starting blocks of the second one. In Fig. 6 we can see an example of this kind of net, where the first gesture is composed by only one building block. This gesture can be disabled by the second one, which starts with an event related either to the feature $f2$ or $f3$. In order to obtain the desired effect, we connect the *Start F1* place with a copy of both the transitions after the *Start F2* and *Start F3*. In order to construct the net for $G1[> G2$ in the general case, we need to perform the following steps:

1. Calculate the sets GS_{G1} and SGS_{G2}
2. Connect the starting place of each element of GS_{G1} with a copy of the first transition of each element in SGS_{G2} , possible duplicates (transitions that have the same incoming places and the same external event) are merged. In case of order independence operator, a transition duplicate is added also to each *OI Flag* and *OI End* (see section 3.2.6)
3. Connect the second place of each element in SBS_{G2} with the transitions generated at step 2. Such connection has to preserve the single control state token property

for each sub-gesture, so we need to collapse recursively the recognition lines with an ad-hoc net in the case $G1$ sub-components contain the parallel or the order independence operator.

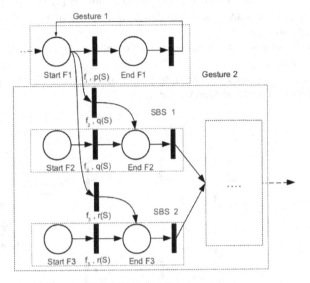

Fig. 6. The disabling operator

3.2.6   Order Independence

The order independence operator is used when two or more gestures can be performed in any order. The composed gesture is recognized when all of its subcomponents have been recognized. We will use the symbol $|=|$ for this operator. It is worth pointing out that such operator is not strictly needed, because it is possible to derive it according to the following property in Equation 5.

$$G1 |=| G2 = (G1 \gg G2)[\,](G2 \gg G1) \qquad (5)$$

In general, we can define an order independence composition of a set of n gestures as a choice between all the permutations of its elements. Inside each permutation the gesture set elements are connected through the sequence operator. Obviously, such kind of definition creates $n!$ options for the choice that makes it too expensive both from the space and time point of view. It is possible to provide a more compact net for defining this operator, which is shown in Fig. 7. The idea is to create a Petri Net that repeats n times the choice between the composed subnets, removing one option at each iteration.

The steps to construct this net for $G1|=|G2|=|\ldots|=|Gn$ are the following:

1. Calculate $SGS_{Gi} \forall i \in [1, n]$
2. Create an *OI Flag* place for each Gi and connect it with its last transition.
3. Create an *OI End* place for each Gi and connect it with the same transition at the end of the net.

4. Connect the transition after the *OI Start* place with each starting place of all elements in SGS_{Gi} and with all the *OI Flag* places.
5. For each $i \in [1, n]$, connect the starting places of each element of SGS_{Gi} with all the starting places of each element in $\bigcup_j SBG_{Gj}$, with $j \in [1, i-1] \cup [i+1, n]$
6. For each $\in [1, n]$, connect the event-driven transitions of each element of GS_{Gi} with *OI Flag*$_i$ and vice versa.
7. For each $i \in [1, n]$ connect the ending transition of the net associated to G_i with all the elements in SGS_{Gi}
8. For each $i \in [1, n]$, connect the starting places of each element of SBS_{Gi} with the last transition of the order independence net.

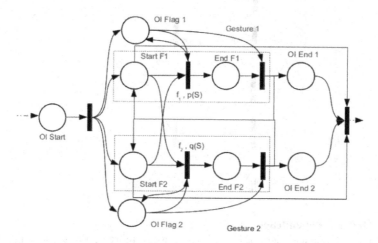

Fig. 7. The order independence operator

4   Library Support

In this section we detail the implementation of GestIT[1], a proof of concept library that allows the development of gesture interfaces according to our meta-model definition. The library class diagram is shown in Fig. 8. It has a core independent from the actual gesture recognition support (*core* package), plus a set of extensions, which deal with the actual devices that currently are iOS devices (*multitouch* package) and Microsoft Kinect (*fullBody* package). The library core contains the classes for the defining gesture expressions (either ground terms or composed ones), represented by the abstract class *TmpExp*. The *SimpleTmpExp* class implements the Petri Net for recognizing a generic basic building block, and it is a refinement of *TmpExp*. The actual feature changes and the optional conditions on them (see section 3.1) are defined by a delegate object associated to the *SimpleTmpExp* instances, which is obviously device-dependent.

Therefore, the library contains an abstract interface (*ExpContent*) that defines the protocol for the generic delegate. It consists of two instance methods: *accept* and *consume*. The first one receives the current gesture recognition support state

---

[1]   The GestIT library is available at http://gestit.codeplex.com/

(represented by the abstract class *ExpEventArgs*) and the Petri Net *Token* that, for convenience, contains the information on the previous gesture recognition support state sequence. A concrete implementation of the delegate returns a boolean value indicating whether the feature change is recognized or not, according to the parameter values. The *consume* method allows the developer to specify the amount of gesture data to be maintained during the gesture recognition, since it is not feasible to maintain the entire sequence of feature values because of memory space. We better detail this point in section 4.1. The possibility to combine building blocks and composed gestures is provided by other two *TmpExp* subclasses: *BinaryTmpExp* and *ComplexTmpExp*. The first one implements all Petri Nets representing binary operators (sequence, parallel, choice, disabling). Obviously, an instance of this class behaves differently according to the *operator* property and its *left* and *right* operands, which belong to the *TmpExp* class (thus it is possible to connect both building blocks and complex gestures). The N-ary versions of such operators can be obtained associating the operands, exploiting the aforementioned associative property. The second *TmpExp* subclass implements the Petri Net for the order independece and contains a list of *operands* (again belonging to the *TmpExp* class). The iterative operator is represented by a boolean flag on the *TmpExp* class.

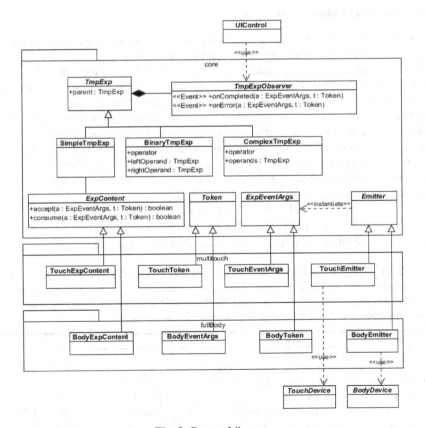

Fig. 8. Gesture Library

A gesture definition is represented by a *TmpExp* tree, where all leafs are *SimpleTmpExp* instances, while the other nodes belong either to the *BinaryTmpExp* or the *ComplexTmpExp* class. At runtime, the tree is managed by a device dependent implementation of the *Emitter* class. Its responsibility is to listen to device updates and to forward them to the leafs that currently contain a token. For each one of them, the *Emitter* will invoke the *accept* method. If the return value is true, the *Emitter* will invoke the *consume* method. Then, the *SimpleTmpExp* will notify the recognition to its parent expression that, according to the Petri Net semantics, will move the *Token*, propagating the notification up to the tree hierarchy and proceeding with the gesture recognition. In section 4.1 we provide a concrete example of this mechanism.

It is possible that the device raises an update that is not *accept*ed by any leaf. In this case, the gesture recognition should be interrupted, and the developer should have the possibility to define how the interface should react to the interruption. The library offers the possibility to associate a handler not only for the successful recognition of a gesture (either basic or composed), but also for the recognition failure. The recognition failure is also propagated to the upper levels of composition tree as in the successful case.

4.1   Modelling Multitouch Gestures

A multitouch screen can detect a maximum number of touches. For each touch, the device can detect its screen position (usually expressed in pixel). In addition, it is possible to detect the current time. According to our abstract meta-model, we will have n features related to the touch positions (one for each detectable touch) and a feature related to the current time. If a touch is not currently detected on screen, we say that its current position is the point $(\bot, \bot)$. We identify the feature related to the i-th touch with p_i, while we will use the *time* symbol for the time. In order to have a uniform terminology with the current multitouch toolkits, we define the simplest set of multitouch gestures in Equation 6. Starting from these building blocks, it is possible to define complex gestures using the composition operators. A set of common multitouch gestures is defined in Table 2.

$$\begin{aligned} Start_i &= p_i \left[p_i(t-1) = (\bot, \bot) \wedge p_i(t) \neq (\bot, \bot)\right] \\ Move_i &= p_i \left[p_i(t-1) \neq (\bot, \bot) \wedge p_i(t) \neq (\bot, \bot)\right] \\ End_i &= p_i \left[p_i(t-1) \neq (\bot, \bot) \wedge p_i(t) = (\bot, \bot)\right] \end{aligned} \tag{6}$$

Table 2. Modelling of common multitouch gestures. In expression 2, the condition *pos* checks if the sequence of touches are almost in the same position, while *timeDiff* checks if they are close in time. In expression 5, the path has to be *linear* with a certain *speed*. In expression 6, the c condition checks whether the finger movement is circular or not.

	Gesture name	Expression
1	Tap	$Start_1 \gg End_1$
2	Double Tap	$Start_1 \gg End_1 \gg Start_1 \left[pos \wedge timeDiff \right] \gg End_1$
3	Pan	$Start_1 \gg Move_1^* \left[> End_1\right.$
4	Slide	$Start_1 \gg Move_1^*[linear \wedge speed] \left[> End_1\right.$
5	Pinch	$(Start_1 \mathbin{|=|} Start_2) \gg ((Move_1^* \| Move_2^*) \left[> (End_1 \mathbin{|=|} End_2)\right)$
6	Rotate	$(Start_1 \mathbin{|=|} Start_2) \gg (Move_1^*[c] \| Move_2^*[c]) \left[> (End_1 \mathbin{|=|} End_2)\right.$

In order to recognize multitouch gestures described with this formal definition with our library, we need to define the concrete implementation of the abstract classes discussed in section 4, represented as the *multitouch* package in Fig. 8. The first one is *TouchEventArgs*, an *ExpEventArgs* subclass, which contains the information about a device feature update (touch identifier, touch point, time). The instances of this class are created by a *TouchEmitter,* an *Emitter* subclass, which translates the OS touch screen updates into a format manageable by the library. The *TouchEventArgs* instances are forwarded to the leafs of the *TmpExp* tree that, as already discussed in section4, are *SimpleTmpExp* instances. These leafs are connected with *TouchExpContent* instances, which are *ExpContent* refinements. The *TouchExpContent* class has two instance variables, which represent the touch identifier and the type of a basic building block for touch gestures (start, move, end).

Therefore, the *accept* method checks the conditions defined in Equation 6, according to the specified type. Further conditions to be checked can be defined by developers sub-classing *TouchExpContent* and overriding the *accept* method. The *TouchToken* class contains the information on the gesture sequence, and represents the concrete implementation of a *Token*. Obviously, it is not possible to store in memory each single feature update especially when programming for mobile devices. Therefore, it is possible to specify the maximum number of updates to be buffered and, for convenience, if the starting point of each touch should be maintained or not.

We better clarify how a developer can use the library for providing multitouch gesture support for a UI control with an example. We consider a pinch gesture (defined in Table 2, expression 5) and the following are the steps that have to be followed by the UI control initialization code.

1. Construct the tree of *TmpExps* represented by the UML object diagram in Fig. 9, starting from the leafs, and then associate each *SimpleTmpExp* to the delegate for recognizing the desired feature. This initialization code is generated starting from an XML description of the gesture through an XSLT. However it is possible to code it without the XML description. In addition, it is possible to store such code in a separate class (e.g. *PinchTmpExp*) and reusing it for different UI controls.

2. Create a *TouchToken* instance, specifying the number of updates to be buffered and whether the initial position of each touch has to be stored or not.

3. Create an instance of the *TouchTmpEmitter* class, passing the token created at step 2, and the current UI control (that will be used in order to receive the touchscreen updates from the OS).

4. Attach the handlers to the completion and/or error event of the entire gesture and/or its subparts, represented by the instances of *TmpExps* created at step 1.

The flow of notifications that allows the library to manage the recognition and to raise the appropriate intermediate events is shown in Fig. 9. We suppose that it has already recognized a touch start with id 1. Therefore, the net is waiting for another touch start, this time with id 2. Such "waiting" is defined by the token position (represented as a circle-enclosed T on the *s2* object in Fig. 9). When the touch screen senses a new touch, the *TouchEmitter* forwards such notification to *s2*, the tree leaf that currently contains the token (arrow 1). After that, *s2* tries to recognize the touch, invoking the *accept* method of its *TouchExpContent* delegate, which will return *true* (arrow 2).

Then *s2* notifies its successfully completion to its parent, *c1*, which represents the expression   .

All the building blocks enclosed in this expression are recognized, thus the order independence expression is completed. Therefore, the event handler attached to *c1* is executed. In our example, it paints two circles on the currently visualized image in correspondence of the touch points (A square in Fig. 9), providing intermediate feedback to the user while executing the gesture.

This is the point where our approach break the standard observer pattern: the gesture recognition is not already finished, but it is possible to define UI reactions to the completion of its sub-parts, without re-coding the entire recognition process, as happens for instance when a viewer has a built-in pinch for zoom gesture recognition. After that, *c1* notifies the completion to its parent, *pinch* (arrow 4), which represents an enabling expression. Having completed its left operand, *pinch* passes the token to its right operand *b2* (arrow 5), which represents a disabling expression, and *b2* passes the token to both its operands (arrow 6), which both duplicate it (arrow 7) at next step. The left one represents a parallel expression, while the right one represents an order independence (see section 3.2.3 and 3.2.5). Finally, we have four different basic gestures that can be recognized as next ones: touch 1 move, touch 2 move, touch 1 end or touch 2 end. The dotted circles in Fig. 9 represent the new token positions.

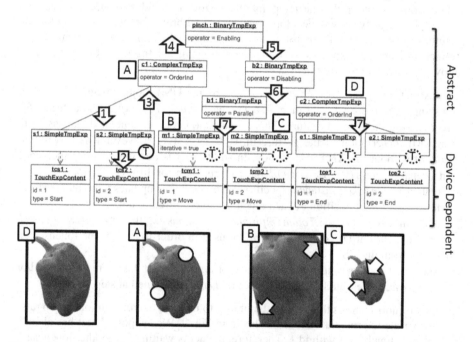

Fig. 9. Recognition of a pinch gesture. The numbered arrows represent the sequence of notifications when the user touches the screen with the second finger, the squares represent the handlers attached to gesture sub-components, while the circle represents the position of the token before the second touch, and the dotted circles the position of the token after the second touch. The lower part shows the effects of the attached handlers on the UI.

It is worth pointing out that the device dependent part of the recognition support is concentrated on delegates for the *SimpleTmpExp* object (represented at the bottom of the tree in Fig. 9). Therefore, the remaining part of the support is implemented by classes that are not bound to a specific device (identified by the "Abstract" label in Fig. 9) and can be exploited not only for multitouch, but also for full body gestures and other recognition supports. The example discussed here is a part of an iOS proof of concept application that allows zooming the current view through the pinch gesture and drawing with a pan gesture. The application gives intermediate feedback during the pinch, showing two divergent arrows while zooming in and two convergent arrows while zooming out (respectively square B and C in Fig. 9). The two gestures are composed through the parallel operator, so it is possible to draw and to zoom the view in at the same time (e.g. using one hand for zooming and one for drawing). From the developer point of view, the difference in handling them at the same time or separately is a matter of selecting the choice or the parallel operator for the composition. No further code is required, which is not the case for current multitouch frameworks. In addition, both gestures have been defined separately from the application (they are contained as samples in the iOS library implementation) and nevertheless the developer can associate UI reactions at different levels of granularity (to the whole gesture, or part of it).

4.2   Modelling Full-Body Gestures

The devices that enable the recognition of full-body gestures (e.g. Microsoft Kinect), are able to sense the 3D position of the complete skeleton joints for up to two users, while they can sense the body centre position of up to four more users, in meters. The SDKs provide facilities for projecting the position on the image space of the RGB camera or depth sensor, obtaining the corresponding coordinates in pixels (obviously, without considering the depth axis). In addition, some of them (e.g. Primesense NITE) are also able to track the joint orientations. Finally, it is also possible to have more information using Computer Vision techniques. For instance, it is possible to detect fingertips if the user is really close to the sensor, or to detect if a hand is open or not at intermediate distances (e.g. calculating the convex hull and convexity defects).

From the point of view of our abstract meta-model, we consider as a feature the user identifier, the 3D position of each skeleton joint (both in meters and in pixels), the orientation of each joint (represented as 3D vectors) the time and, if present, any additional information on the hands state (either fingertip position or a hand open or closed flag). As should be clear from the discussion in sections 4 and 4.1, it is possible to extend the library with an *Emitter* subclass (*BodyEmitter*) and a set of *ExpContent* subclasses for recognizing each feature (see Fig. 8, *fullBody* package).

We implemented the library extension in C# with the Kinect for Windows SDK, together with a sample application based on it. The application visualizes a 3D car model, which can be moved and rotated by the user. In order to avoid unwanted interactions, we specified that the user has to stand with the shoulders in a plane (almost) parallel to the sensor, before starting the interaction with the car. Thus, if the user is not in front of the device (which means most of the times in front of the screen), the interface will not give any response. The car position can be changed with a "on air grab" gesture (closing the right hand, moving and reopening it). In addition, the car can be rotated performing the on air grab gesture with two hands, which means closing two hands, moving them maintaining almost the same distance in between, and then reopening them. We want also to display the 2D projected hand position on the screen, in order to provide an immediate feedback to the user for each hand movement. The resulting gesture model is defined Equation 7. The *Front* and *NotFront* gestures respectively activate and deactivate the UI interaction. When a change in the feature associated to the left and right shoulder (indicated as S_l and S_r) occurs, they respectively check if the sensor parallel plane property (p) is true or false.

The UI interaction consists of three gestures in parallel. The first and the second one are simply a hand position change. The UI will react to their completion moving a correspondent (left or right) hand icon. The *Move* gesture is the one associated to the car position change, and consists of a sequence of a right hand close (represented cH_r) and a unbounded number of right hand moves (mH_r^*), interrupted by the opening of the right hand (oH_r). The *Rotate* gesture is represented by the same sequence, performed with both hands in parallel, almost maintaining the same distance (the d condition).

$$
\begin{aligned}
&Front \gg (mH_r^* \,\|\, mH_l^* \,\|\, (\,Move\,[\,]\,Rotate))^*[> NotFront \\
&Front = (S_l[p]\|S_r[p]) \\
&NotFront = (S_l[!\,p]\|S_r[!\,p]) \\
&Move = cH_r \gg (mH_r^*\,[> oH_r) \\
&Rotate = (cH_r\|cH_l) \gg ((mH_r[d]\|mH_l[d])^*[> (oH_r\|oH_l))
\end{aligned}
\tag{7}
$$

The intermediate feedback associated to different sub-parts of the composed gestures is shown in Fig. 10. When the correct pose is detected (the *Front* gesture is completed), the car passes from a grayscale to a full-colour visualization, indicating that it is possible to start the interaction (the B square in Fig. 10). When the user "grabs" the car with one hand (completes cH_r), a 4 arrow icon is shown on top of the car (C square). The change of the car position is associated to the following hand movements (mH_r^*). When the user closes two hands in parallel (completes ($cH_r\|cH_l$)), a circular arrow is displayed (D square), suggesting the gesture function. The car rotation is associated to the parallel movement of the two hands (the completion of $(mH_r[d]\|mH_l[d])^*$). The car returns inactive when the user is not in the front position any more (A square).

Writing such application with the support of our library has a set of advantages, which is possible to notice also in this simple case. First of all, the defined gestures are separated from the UI control. Indeed, the car viewer is a standard WPF 3D viewport, enhanced with full body gestures at the application window level. Second, the possibility to inspect the gesture definition and to attach handlers at the desired level of granularity allowed us to define easily when and how to react to the user input, without mixing the logic of the reactions with the conditions that need to be satisfied for executing them. Finally, we do not define any additional UI state for maintaining the gesture execution. Indeed, if we created such application simply with the Kinect for Windows SDK, we would have needed at least a state variable for maintaining what the user has already done and, consequently, for deciding what s/he is allowed to do next (e.g. when the user closes the right hand the state has to change for moving the car at next hand movement). Most of the times, this ends with the implementation of a state machine inside the handler of the skeleton tracking update, which mixes the management of all gestures together. Especially when we want to support parallel gestures, mixing the different gestures leads to code difficult to understand and maintain. Our approach helps the developer to separate the temporal aspect and the UI reaction and to reuse gesture definition in different applications, while maintaining the possibility to define fine-grained feedback.

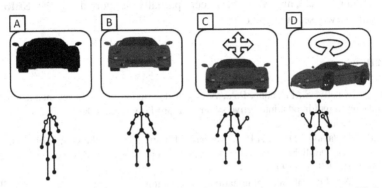

Fig. 10. The car viewer application. The upper part of the figure shows the UI feedback provided while performing the gestures represented in the lower part.

5   Conclusions and Future Work

The lack of proper programming models for defining gestures is a major issue in defining gesture-based interfaces and it limits significantly the ability to fully exploit the new multitouch and 3D input devices, now becoming widely available. The observer pattern underlying the traditional event-based programming is largely inadequate for tracking gestures made of multiple inputs over time, forcing the programmer to choose between handling the complexity of this process or picking one of a pre-defined gestures recognized by the framework used.

In this paper we have proposed a declarative, compositional meta- model for defining gestures, addressing this key issue allowing for simultaneous recognition of multiple gestures and sub-gestures under control of the programmer rather than the framework. The meta-model elements contain ground terms and composition operators that have been theoretically defined using Non Autonomous Petri Nets. It allows reusing and composing the definition of gestures in different applications, providing the possibility to define UI reactions for the recognition not only for the entire gesture, but also for its sub-components. Moreover, we reported a proof-of-concept library, which has been exploited for managing two different gesture recognition supports (iOS and Microsoft Kinect), showing the flexibility and the generality of the approach. We developed two sample applications for demonstrating the advantages of the proposed modelling technique in reusing gesture definitions, which can be exploited at the desired level of granularity.

Now that we have a well-define model we will continue our research by studying both implementation efficiency and effectiveness in real world scenarios. Moreover we will use the ability of the model to recognize many gestures at once to study what we call *posturing*, which is the analysis of user postures while interacting with a system in order to adapt the interface without explicit commands.

In addition, we also plan to provide an authoring environment for the gesture definition, providing testing and simulation capabilities, in order to ease the development of gestural interfaces based on our model and library.

Acknowledgements. This work has been partially supported by the SERENOA project, http://www.serenoa-fp7.eu/.

References

1. Accot, J., Chatty, S., Palanque, P.A.: A formal description of low level interaction and its application to multimodal interactive system. In: 3rd DSVIS EUROGRAPHICS, pp. 92–105. Springer (1996)
2. Bastide, R., Palanque, P.A.: A Petri-Net based Environment for the Design of Event-driven Interfaces. In: DeMichelis, G., Díaz, M. (eds.) ICATPN 1995. LNCS, vol. 935, pp. 66–83. Springer, Heidelberg (1995)
3. Buxton, W.: Lexical and pragmatic considerations of input structures. SIGGRAPH Comput. Graph. 17(1), 31–37 (1983)
4. González-Calleros, J.M., Vanderdonckt, J.: 3D User Interfaces for Information Systems based on UsiXML. In: Proc. of 1st Int. Workshop on User Interface Extensible Markup Language, UsiXML 2010, Berlin, Germany. Thales Research and Technology, France, Paris (2010)
5. Jacob, R.J.K., Giroaud, A., Hirshfield, L.M., Horn, M.S., Shaer, O., Solovey, E.T., Zingelbaum, J.: Reality-based interaction: a framework for post-WIMP interafaces. In: CHI 2008, Florence, Italy, pp. 201–210. ACM Press (April 2008)
6. Kin, K., Hartmann, B., DeRose, T., Agrawala, M.: Proton: multitouch gestures as regular expressions. In: CHI 2012, Austin, Texas, U.S., pp. 2885–2894 (May 2012)
7. Kammer, D., Wojdziak, J., Keck, M., Groh, R., Taranko, S.: Towards a formalization of multi-touch gestures. In: ITS 2010, ACM International Conference on Interactive Tabletops and Surfaces, Saabrucken, Germany, pp. 49–58. ACM Press (November 2010)
8. Luyten, K., Vanacken, D., Weiss, M., Borchers, J., Izadi, S., Wigdor, D.: Engineering patterns for multi-touch interfaces. In: EICS 2010, Proceedings of the 2nd ACM SIGCHI Symposium on Engineering Interactive Computing Systems, Berlin, Germany, pp. 365–366. ACM Press (June 2010)
9. NUI Group, Gesture Recognition, http://wiki.nuigroup.com/ Gesture_Recognition (Website retrieved: May 27, 2012)
10. Palanque, P.A., Bastide, R., Sengès, V.: Validating interactive system design through the verification of formal task and system models. In: EHCI 1995, Yellowstone Park, USA, pp. 189–212. Chapman & Hall (1995)
11. Paternò, F.: Model-based design and evaluation of interactive applications. Applied Computing (2000)
12. Paternò, F., Santoro, C., Spano, L.D.: MARIA: A Universal Language for Service-Oriented Applications in Ubiquitous Environment. ACM Transactions on Computer-Human Interaction 16(4), 1–30 (2009)
13. René, D., Alla, H.: Discrete, Continuous and Hybrid Petri Nets. Springer (2005)
14. Scottidi, A., Blanch, R., Coutaz, J.: A Novel Taxonomy for Gestural Interaction techniques based on accelerometers. In: IUI 2011, Proceedings of the 16th International Conference on Intelligent User Interfaces, Palo Alto, CA, USA, pp. 63–72. ACM Press (February 2011)
15. Vanacken, D., Boeck, J.D., Raymaekers, C., Coninx, K.: NIMMIT: A notation for modeling multimodal interaction techniques. In: GRAPP 2006, Setubal, Portugal, pp. 224–231 (2006)

A Design Process for Exhibiting Design Choices and Trade-Offs in (Potentially) Conflicting User Interface Guidelines

Llúcia Masip[1], Célia Martinie[2], Marco Winckler[2], Philippe Palanque[2], Toni Granollers[1], and Marta Oliva[1]

[1] DIEI (Universidad de Lleida)
c/Jaume II, 69, Lleida 25001, Spain
{lluciamaar,tonig,oliva}@diei.udl.cat
[2] IRIT, Université Paul Sabatier
118 route de Narbonne, 31062 Toulouse Cedex 9, France
{winckler,martinie,palanque}@irit.fr

Abstract. In the last decades a huge amount of knowledge about user interface design has been gathered in the form of guidelines. Quite often, guidelines are compiled according to user interface properties (e.g. usability, accessibility) and/or application domains (e.g. Web, mobile). In many situations designers have to combine several guideline sets in order to address the specific application domain and the desired set of properties corresponding to the application under consideration. Despite the fact that the problems related to the selection of guidelines from different sources are not new, the occurrence and management of conflicting guidelines are poorly documented leaving designers with little help in order to handle conflicts in a rationale and consistent way. In this paper we revise the questions related to selection and management of conflicting guidelines and we propose a systematic approach based on design rationale tools and techniques for exhibiting choices and trade-offs when combining different guidelines sets. This paper illustrates how such as an approach can also be used to deepen the knowledge on the use of user interface guidelines recording decisions across projects in an iterative way.

Keywords: user interface guidelines, guidelines management, design rationale.

1   Introduction

The design of usable interactive systems is a complex task which requires knowledge and expertise both on human factors and software development. User interface guidelines represent a technical solution for organizing recommendations and best practices which are aimed at providing guidance throughout the development process of interactive systems [1]. User interface guidelines are widely available but, quite often they are in many different formats with contents varying both in terms of quality and level of details. Recommendation for User Interface development appear in the literature under various names including principles for user interface design, heuristics,

M. Winckler, P. Forbrig, and R. Bernhaupt (Eds.): HCSE 2012, LNCS 7623, pp. 53–71, 2012.
© IFIP International Federation for Information Processing 2012

guidelines, user interface design patterns and standards. Whilst principle and heuristics (such as "*give appropriate feedback*") tend to be the least prescriptive and general, design standards (such as ISO [16]) are very specific, though also very restrictive and prescriptive. User interface guidelines and design patterns lie in between these extremes. Design patterns, in particular, offer invariant solutions to a recurrent problem within a given context [2]. In general, such recommendations (either standards, guidelines…) appear together in the literature as a set of interlinked recommendations for a specific domain [3][4]. For the sake of simplicity, this paper exploits the term 'user interface guidelines' with its most generic meaning but our approach can also be used so resolve conflicts with the other kinds of recommendations.

The Human-Computer Interaction (HCI) community has been prolific in the development of guidelines for interactive systems [5]. These recommendations are usually gathered in compilations which are often organized by user interface properties (e.g. usability, accessibility, user experience) and/or by application domains (e.g. Web, mobile applications, tabletops). Currently there is a wide range of sources of guidelines available including many HCI areas such as web-based systems [6], safety critical systems [7], cooperative interaction [8], ubiquitous computing [3], interactive TV [8], web accessibility [9], UX patterns [3]…

In many situations designers have to combine different guidelines sources in order to address the specific application domain and the desired set of properties corresponding to their project [5]. For instance in the Ubiloop project we make use of mobile and Web technology for allowing citizens to report urban incidents. As there is no user interface guideline compilation covering Web and mobile technology, incident reporting systems, usability, security, and user experience, we had to combine different guideline sources. The combination of different guidelines ended-up with a huge list of entries containing duplicated entries, similar statements using different terms, guidelines that refer to elements that are not relevant to the project, and potentially conflicting guidelines (for example, security guidelines recommending validation steps that contradicts with usability guidelines that recommend minimal actions). In order to design a user interface meeting both usability and security in such context, a cleaning-up selection process was required to provide reliable, consistent and usable set of guidelines.

These problems related to the selection of guidelines from different sources have been previously reported in the literature (such as in [10] and [11]) and motivated the development of tools for working with guidelines [12] and [5]. Nonetheless, the inner problems related to the occurrence of potentially conflicting guidelines have been poorly documented so far. The resolution of conflicts is a daunting and demanding task that often requires taking into account the trade-offs associated with alternative design choices. Therefore, whenever a good solution for solving conflicts between guidelines is found, it is worth the effort recording and documenting it for further reuse. This is the contribution of this paper which proposes a systematic approach for selecting guidelines and documenting the conflicts managements. Hereafter, design rationale is proposed as a complimentary technique that can be ultimately included as an integral part of the tools for working with guidelines. Our ultimate goal is to integrate the design process presented in the current paper into a tool (in line with the

Open-HEREDEUX project [13]) for supporting the detection of conflicts between guidelines, the resolution of conflicts and the reuse of previously defined solutions.

The paper is organized as follows: section 2 provides an overview of existing approaches and tools for working with guidelines; section 3 describes the how design rationale can be used to solve conflicting guidelines; section 4 provides an overview of our design process including the integration of support for design rationale; section 5 illustrates the approach through a case study involving conflicting guidelines. Lastly, section 6 concludes the paper and identifies directions for future work.

2   Overview of User Interface Guidelines Management

This section points out the main questions related to user interface guidelines management. For a full survey please refer to [5] and [37].

2.1   Organization of Guidelines Sources

One of the major issues for the effective use of user interface guidelines is the fast access to the appropriate design solutions [4]. Guidelines must be organized in such a way that they are easy to locate, that they are grouped when appearing in common cases, that they provide different viewpoints, and that they permit to generate new solutions from the ones proposed. Several works focus on the organization of guidelines for improving search of guidelines in large datasets [30] and many others try to organize guidelines in a way they can become easier to understand and apply along the different phases of the development process [14]. Some works [3][15] propose XML-based languages for structuring the description of guidelines.

Currently, there are many sources of user interface guidelines which are organized by the intended use of guidelines (e.g. support design, development and/or testing phases in the development process), the level of formalization of guidelines sets (user interface design guidelines/design patterns, standards...) and/or the scope (ex. generic guides, platform-specific, corporation-specific style guides, etc.) [5].

Participants on the development process (i.e. task analyst, the project leader, the human factors expert, graphical designers, the designers, the programmers and the user interface evaluators) might be interested in particular sub-sets of guidelines. Furthermore, some years ago, the only factor which was considered when a designer or evaluator wanted to design or evaluate an interactive system was the usability [16]. But to now factors such as accessibility [9], communicability [17], cross-cultural [18], plasticity [19], playability [20], security [21] and user experience [22][23], become important elements for deciding the quality of use of the interactive systems.

2.2   Tools for Working with Guidelines

Many studies in the literature report tools for working with guidelines. These tools can be classified in two main categories: tools for automating user interface inspection and tools for managing guidelines sources. In the first category we will find tools such as EvalIris [3] that encode guidelines into algorithms for inspecting the user interface automatically. Very often, tools supporting inspection are used with Web applications where the code source (HTML/CSS) can be easily parsed [23][24].

Tools such as SIERRA [26], SHERLOCK [27] and GUIDE [30] are some examples of tools dedicated to the collection and maintenance of guidelines sets. These tools are able to manage usability guidelines in a more or less sophisticated way and permits to use in the design or evaluation of the specific interactive system. Most of these tools support the organization of several guidelines sources by adding specific metadata that facilitate searching of guidelines according to multiple criteria (ex. desired properties such as usability, application domain, etc.). Nonetheless, the presentation of guidelines remains a textual description.

A very few tools provide features for the management of user interface guidelines and the automated inspection of the user interface. In this category there is DESTINE [3] which can perform the assessment of guidelines formally expressed in a XML-compliant specification language called Guideline Definition Language (GDL). DESTINE includes a database for recording guidelines from diverse sources, however, not all guidelines can used for automated inspection.

2.3   Management of Potentially Conflicting Guidelines

Several works report [11][28] problems associated to the management of guidelines sets. Vanderdonckt [5] discusses the potential occurrence of conflicting problems when selecting guidelines from diverse sources, for that those authors propose a dedicated process for selecting the best set of guidelines for a specific interactive system. Vogt [11] extends that work by proposing taxonomy of 11 types of problems associated to conflicting guidelines. Abascal et al. [28] explicitly mention that a step for the resolution of conflicting guidelines should be performed when selecting guidelines in an educational context (i.e. teaching guidelines); nonetheless they do not describe how conflict resolution can be specified. In [34] a set of unresolved problems are presented for the tools for working with guidelines. One of these specified problems is the maintenance of the guidelines. And the authors points to the conflicting guidelines as an examples of unresolved problem [29]. Finally, the state of the art about the process to get the most adequate set of guidelines is done and the most highlighted research in the definition of a process to get guidelines is [5]. In this research, a process to develop a set of guidelines is described using as the main point five milestones to get a tool for working with guidelines. Another work is [38] where defines a generic framework for the collaborative development of guidelines and standards involving many experts in the usage of guidelines.

To sum up, despite the fact that several works agree on the existence of potential conflicting user interface guidelines, there is not any research so far proposing a methodological approach for dealing with such conflicts. Existing tools for working with guidelines can handle diverse guidelines sources but they are not able to exhibit if conflicts between guidelines. Moreover, even if designers are able to solve the conflicts between guidelines, they have no support to document their arguments leading to the solution, which can be lost in future projects.

2.4   Traceability of Conflicting Guidelines

As far as we know, there is no work in the literature describing how systematically dealt with such conflicts. The resolution of conflicting guidelines requires the systematic exploration of design options. In previous work [32][33] we propose the Design Rationale TEAM (Traceability, Exploration and Analysis Method) and the support tool called DREAM (Design Rationale Environment for Argumentation and Modeling) to support the systematic exploration of design options during the development process of interactive systems. Hereafter we illustrate the main concepts of the TEAM notation for describing guidelines. The combination of guidelines and the resolution of potential conflicts are described in section 4.

2.4.1   The TEAM Notation and Tool Support

TEAM notation is an extension of MacLean and al.'s QOC (Question Option Criteria) [32] which allows the description of available options for a design question and the selection of an option according to a list of criteria. The TEAM notation extends QOC to record the information produced during design meetings, including:

- Questions that have been raised,
- Design options that have been investigated and the ones that have been selected,
- Criteria that have been used for evaluating the options considered,
- Requirements for the system and how they are supported by design options,
- Factors that have been taken into account and how they relate to criteria,
- Arguments and documents used to explain the design options,
- Task models corresponding to options,
- Scenarios that are used to compute, for each option the value of the criteria.

Fig. 1 shows a simple TEAM model that contains all elements require to describe guidelines. In the example below, the requirement for the web site *"provide access to data"* is represented by a square. The question raised during the web site design (represented by a square with rounded-corners) indicates two possible design options (represented by circles) to grant users with access to a Web site: *"provide direct access"* and/or *"ask first for login and password"*. The measurable criteria associated to design options are presented by isosceles triangles. The clip-shaped icon next to the item *"reach record in less than 20s"* links this criterion to the arguments and documents that can be used to measure it. The criteria can be directly connected to factors and sub-factors (represented by equilateral triangles) such in the case of the factor *security* and the sub-factors *efficiency* and *effectiveness* that are connected to the factor *usability*. The different types of lines between the criteria and options represent the fact that a given option can support (favour) a criterion (the line is bold) or not support it (the line is dotted). Thus, the option *"provide direct access"* supports *effectiveness* and *efficiency* but it does not support user data protection. The option *"ask for login and password"* strongly supports user data protection (bold line) but has an impact on *effectiveness* and *efficiency* (thin lines). TEAM supports more precise connection between elements (including absolute and comparative values) but this is not presented here due to space constraints.

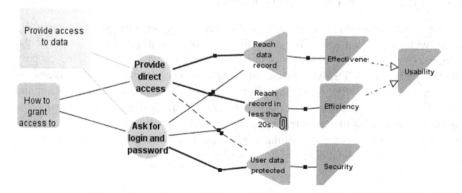

Fig. 1. Simple model showing the main elements supported by the notation TEAM

TEAM models can leverage the design rationale process by helping designers to document their decisions and choices with respect to the many options available. Moreover, TEAM models can also help to decide to reuse (or not) design choices when facing an already experienced issue. TEAM notation is supported by the tool DREAM which supports the edition, recording and analysis TEAM diagrams [33].

2.4.2   Mapping Individual Guidelines to Design Rationale Elements.

Guidelines sources often provide information that can easily matched to factors and criteria that can be used to measure factors as illustrated in Fig. 2. Hereafter an example based on the *"WCAG guideline 1.1 text alternatives" is provided*, as bellow:

Description of the guideline: *"Guideline 1.1 Text Alternatives: Provide text alternatives for any non-text content so that it can be changed into other forms people need, such as large print, braille, speech, symbols or simpler language".*
Source: (WCAG) 2.0 (see [9])
Factor: *Accessibility*
Criteria: *Perceptibility*

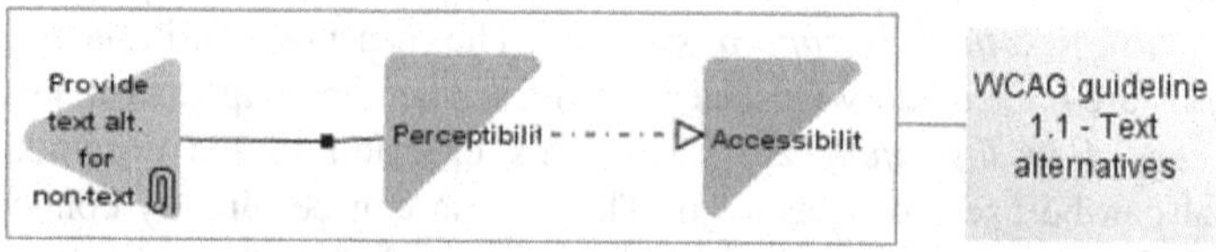

Provide text alt. for non-text — Perceptibilit - - - - - ▷ Accessibilit — WCAG guideline 1.1 - Text alternatives

Fig. 2. Representation of individual guidelines using the notation TEAM

It is noteworthy that the overall description of the guidelines is mapped to a non-functional requirement (represented by a square). Moreover, the guideline is connected through a box embedding the criteria *"provide text alt. for non-text"*, the factor *accessibility* and the sub-factor *perceptibility*; such as composition shows that all these elements are part of the guideline description. The clip in the diagram indicates that there are additional documents explaining how the criteria can be assessed.

3   A Process for the Management of Guidelines Selection

Our approach assumes that design rationale methods can help in two ways: i) to select guidelines that can help to decide on the design options; and ii) to support the decision-making processing leading to the resolution of conflicting guidelines. Such hypotheses imply that the description of guidelines can be extended to represent design rationale elements.

3.1   Overview of Process

Fig. 3 presents our approach for dealing with guidelines management. It encompasses three phases: the *organization of the guidelines* which is concerned by how relevant sources of guidelines are identified (step **①**), how guidelines are collected (step **②**), systematically described (step **③**) using a design rationale notation (**R**) and then stored into a database included in a database; the second phase describes how designers search into the database (step **④**) for suitable guidelines, which requires the selection of a guidelines subset that fulfil the needs of guidance for a given project (step **⑤**). At this point conflicting guidelines are detected and solved (step **⑥**); conflict resolution is then recorded **CR** into the database; the final phase describes how guidelines subsets can be effectively used (step **⑦**) during the development process as help for the design and/or evaluation of user interfaces.

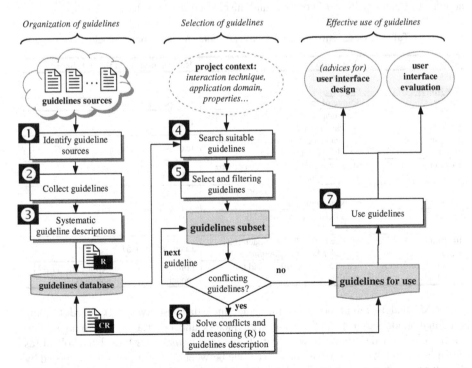

Fig. 3. Overview of a process for rationalizing the management of user interface guidelines

Although the process can run independently, it is (partially) included in the Open-HEREDEUX project [13]. Open-HEREDEUX (short name of Open HEuristic REsource for Designing and Evaluating user experience) considers the wide concept of the user experience and includes four components: the Open Repository which stores all the needed information, the Adviser who lists the most adequate guidelines for a specific interactive system, the Scorer who helps to carry out the evaluation, and finally, the Results Analyzer where quantitative and qualitative results can be achieved. Currently, three tools developed in the context of the Open-HEREDEUX project support (partially) this process: the *open repository* tool that stores the set of guidelines, the Adviser which implement searching and filtering functions allowing to browse the open repository an select a sub set of guidelines (steps ❹ and ❺), and the tool *Scorer* which is dedicated to presented previously selected guidelines during the evaluation phases (step ❼).

3.2   Systematic Guidelines Description

In order to provide a seamlessly association of user interface guidelines, design rationale process and guidelines storage an appropriate schema for representing guidelines in a database is needed. It is worthy of notice that guidelines descriptions can include diverse attributes as discussed in [33]. However in Table 1 just a small subset of attributes that are relevant for understanding of the contribution aimed for this paper is provided. This information is stored in the guideline database (handled by the Open Repository tool) to facilitate the later detection of conflicts and the extraction of results.

Table 1. Description of the database attributes for describing guideline

Attribute	Description	Representation in the database
Guidelines description	Statement describing the guideline	text
Source	Source of the guidelines	text, pointers to documents
Application domain(s)	Known applications domain where the guideline is used	text
User interface components	User interface that can affected by the guideline (e.g. text, images)	text
Keywords	Metadata and keywords that can be improve searching	text
Factors	List of factors and sub-factors covered by the guidelines	TEAM model
Criteria	List of criteria that should be measured	
Importance of factors	A value that tells the impact of a particular factor to the guideline	Likert scale (1-5)
Potential conflicting guidelines	List of known conflicts and the solutions	pointers to other guidelines and TEAM model resolution of conflicts

TEAM models might occur in the guidelines database twice: i) for describing individual guidelines (in combination with factors and criteria as shown in section 2.4.2); and ii) for describing how *potential conflicting guidelines* have been solved (as shown in section 3.4). In order to help to decide between recommendations proposed by potentially conflicting guidelines, it is import to know each guideline is related to factors. For this purpose, the proposed schema also allows to define the *importance of factors* in a given guidelines in Likert scale of 1 to 5. Table 2 provides a view at glance on what could be the impact of factors/sub-factors with respect to the guideline "*WCAG guideline 1.1 text alternatives*". As we shall see, this guideline is considered to have little impact on usability sub-factors and as far as accessibility is a concern, the perceptibility for blind and blind-deaf is more important that just for perceptibility for deaf. However, this guideline is not addressing security factors, which remain blank.

Table 2. Weights of factors for the guideline "*WCAG guideline 1.1 text alternatives*"

		lowest	←	priority	→	highest
Factor	**Sub-Factor**	1	2	3	4	5
Usability	Effectiveness	x				
	Efficiency	x				
	Satisfaction	x				
Accessibility	Perceptibility (for blind)					x
	Perceptibility (for deaf)	x				
	Perceptibility (for blind-deaf)				x	
	Perceptibility (cognitive disabilities)			x		
Security	User data protection					

3.3   Select and Filtering Guidelines

Ideally, guidelines databases should contain exhaustive set of guidelines covering diverse sources and application domains. Nonetheless, huge entries of guidelines are difficult to handle. So quite it is often useful to create a subset which contains only guidelines that are really relevant to the development of a given applications. In Fig. 3, the selection and filtering of guidelines is made in the step 5. In the Open-HEREDEUX approach this is done be the tool called Adviser will pre-select appropriate guidelines for a specific interactive system by taking into account the functionalities of the system, its features and its components.

The sets of guidelines could include guidelines by different authors, for different users, for different factors, for different applications domains, etc. All these elements can be used as inputs for searching and selecting guidelines. So that our approach not only supports searching but it also allows the definition of weight that factors might have for a project. For that designers must select the list of factors and then determine the priority of each factor and/or sub-factors. The priority for each factor can be defined using a form that is build using a Likert scale similar to that presented in Table 2. For example, a designer can choose that the security is the most important property for a specific system or that the accessibility for blind people is the priority. It also possible to remove factors and/or sub-factors that are not relevant for the project, for example one can decide that perceptibility for deaf is not going to be taken into account. In a first moment, the selection of factors and sub-factors will help to retrieve the list of entries in the databases and then select only those guidelines that treat those factors. As we shall see latter on, the weight given to factor will help to decide the resolution of conflicting guidelines when then occurs. Once a sub-set of guidelines has been selected, then it is time to check for potential conflicts, as described below.

3.4   Conflict Management and Guidelines Cleaning

The combination of different guidelines sources into a single database will eventually end-up with entries that might contain similar statements employing different terms (which might be confusing), duplicated entries, guidelines that refer to design elements that are not relevant to the project, and potentially guidelines which are strongly conflicting i.e. proposing contradictory recommendations. In all these cases a cleaning process is required together with a resolution process in case of strong conflicts.

In our approach, the guideline database is supposed to contain all necessary information for helping designers to detect conflicts between guidelines. However, (as listed above) not all conflicts look alike and many types of connections between guidelines might occur. For example, considering the existence of two guidelines (**G1** and **G2**) the following scenarios and types of connections can be defined:

- Equal (E): guidelines can be considered very similar or equal.
  Ex. The website guideline G1: "Is user provided with the essential information to carry out each task?" is the same as G2: "Only show essential information" for mobiles.

- More general (MG): G1 is more general than G2.
  Ex. The website guideline G1: "Are the same elements grouped and located in the same place?" is more general than G2: "When designing an application, optimize edit view for data entry, grouping related items and prioritizing more commonly edited items at the top of the screen" for mobiles.

- More specific (MS): G1 is more specific than G2.
  Ex. The guideline G1: "Are the required values always marked using the same method?" is more specific than G2: "Required fields are marked".

- Conflict (C): There is a clear contradiction between both guidelines.
  Ex. The website guideline G1: "Is there in the top and the bottom of the page information about where are the users and the last page visited?" is conflicted with G2: "Do not repeat the navigation on every page" for mobiles.

- Superseded (S): One guideline presents a superseded of the other one.
  Ex. The guideline G1: "Use Audio CAPTCHA to prevent spam" is a superseded version of the guideline G2: "Use graphic CAPTCHA to prevent spam."

In all the scenarios above, the set of guidelines should be cleaned-up before use. The cleaning is part of the selection and filtering process described in the step 5 of Fig. 3. If the conflict is of type E, the solution could be use either G1 or G2, without distinctions but one of them should be removed to avoid redundancy in the subset. If the conflict is an MG, the solution is to choose G2 and then to remove G1 from the subset of selected guidelines. In this case, it is better to use the most specific one so, the guideline *"When designing an application, optimize edit view for data entry, grouping related items and prioritizing more commonly edited items at the top of the screen"* is chosen. If the conflict is of type MS, the solution is to choose G1. Otherwise, the selected guideline will be *"Are the required values always marked using the same method?"* The scenarios (E), (MG) and (MS) are relatively simple to detect and to treat. However, when a guideline is superseded (S) by another or it is in conflict (C) with other guideline, further analysis is required. The goal of our approach is to help designers to specify systematically arguments and decisions.

In our approach, the first step to solve the conflict is to align the two (or more) guidelines. The way to get the design rationale is to construct a TEAM diagram from the individual TEAM diagrams that have be stored in the database as part of the guideline definition. The element question in the TEAM notation should be provided by the designer as it is a factor dependent of the context of the project. The options can be provided either but the recommendations in the guidelines description or manually provided by the designers. Finally, the weights associated to factors and each guideline is depicted in the diagram. The rest of the resolutions of the conflict are done by the designers with the help of the tool DREAM. When a solution is found, a diagram containing the solution is recorded. Moreover, every guideline considered 'in conflict" is tagged in the database. So in the future it would be possible to retrieve the solutions found in previous projects.

When a solution is finally found, the appropriate guideline (G1 or G2) becomes part of the subset of guidelines going to be used in the project (Fig. 3, step 7). To sum up, the main aim of the first stages to manage clashes is to save all the needed information about the whole sets of guidelines, the interactive system and the context of use. If this information is saved properly, the next steps will be done and will be easier to get. The next section illustrate the whole proceed in a concrete case study.

4   Case Study

The example provided in this section is issued from the application of our approach in the context of the Ubiloop project. Hereafter we only illustrate a few guidelines addressing the design of *captchas* which, as we shall see, are obviously conflicting. This example was deliberated chosen for focusing the discussing on the process of selecting and describing conflicts between the guidelines rather than improve the knowledge of conflicts of this particular element of the design. Due to space reasons, we don't describe the preliminary steps required for creating the database of guidelines. We assume that guidelines are already stored into a database but there is conflicting guidelines have not been reported (yet).

4.1   Informal Description of the Case Study

The Ubiloop is concerned by the development of solutions for improving the quality of the environment of the city using mobile and information technologies. The approach proposed by Ubiloop is to offer an incident reporting systems that allows citizens to report incidents in their neighbourhood that might affect the quality of life, such a potholes, broken street lamps, graffiti, etc. The requirements for this application include the use Web technology. Moreover, the application should run in whatever platform/or devices citizens might have at their disposal, which might include smartphones. In our working scenario, mobile technology is an essential ingredient because it allows users to make a report just after problems have been detected when all the details about the incidents are still fresh in users' mind.

We also have identified some factors that are important for this kind of application including the usability, as everyone should be able to use the application and perform a report in a minimal time. Accessibility is an important factor enhanced by regulations. Security becomes an important factor as the kind of application we have in mind can suffer attacks from spambots tools that can shutdown Web servers with massive spams and/or reduce the trust on the information collected.

Based on these requirements, we have searched the guidelines database for the three applications domains that are concerned by our project: Web applications, mobile and incident reporting. The selection process is described below.

4.2   Selection of Guidelines

There is huge set of reference in the guideline database that can provide suitable recommendation for dealing with the design of application domains. A first search reveals as many as 117 entries for guidelines including: 82 guidelines for Websites, 84 guidelines for mobile phones and 11 guidelines for incident reporting forms.

A first analysis of these 177 entries reveals several overlaps and conflicts between guidelines. For example, there are 16 clashes between guidelines for building Web applications and guidelines for building incident reporting systems. As many as 138 conflicts concern guidelines for the development of Web and mobile applications. Finally, 19 clashes are detected between guidelines for incident reporting forms and guidelines for mobile applications. These numbers are better presented in Fig. 4.

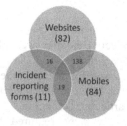

Fig. 4. Overlapping of guidelines issues from three guidelines sets: Web sites, Incident reporting systems and mobile applications

Therefore, designers should compare if it is possible to apply all these guidelines or, in a contrary way, they detect clashes and they have to choose one or other. So, the next step was to clean the list of guidelines by removing duplicated entries.

4.3   Management of Guidelines Related to Captchas

In our scenario, designers' goal is to develop an interactive system and for that they need advices which in our case are provided by guidelines. The first question designers have to answer is how users will have access to the data on the Web site so that they will be able complete the incident report form. The user should insert all the information of the incident and the system should assure the security of the transmission and the privacy of the personal information. In addition, the interface should be able to control that only real users fill in the form. It means that the interface should present the needed security restrictions to prevent spam or robot messages.

A possible solution to the questions above is to introduce in the user interface a new component to cover the requirement of the security: a captcha. A captcha stands for "Completely Automated Public Turing test to tell Computers and Humans Apart"[1]; it is a type of challenge-response test used in computing as an attempt to ensure that the response is generated by a person. Captchas help in ensuring that all reports have been inserted by citizens and not by bots because humans can read distorted text and or sound but current computer programs can't. By asking users to fill in a form field the letter shown as distorted text/sound, it is possible to infer that the other fields in a form were duly completed by a human. Several possible implementations of captchas exist. Fig. 5 shows some examples of design options for captchas including visual, audio and visual-audio captchas.

a) visual captcha   b) audio captcha   c) visual-audio captcha

Fig. 5. Examples of design options for captchas

Whilst captchas help to ensure security, they can reduce usability and accessibility as pointed by the guidelines in Table 3.

Table 3. Main conflicts between guidelines related to Captcha

Design Questions	G1(Captcha guidelines) Sources: [35] [36]	Type of conflict	G2(Website guidelines) Sources: [12][36]
	Visual Captcha		
How do we can access to the complete meaning of the graphic?	Do not add alternative text for protecting user data.	C	Add alternative text to images
How is the text presented in graphic captcha?	Present distorted text to difficult the text recognition.	C	Present text clearly.
	Audio Captcha		
How do we can access to the complete meaning of the audio?	Do not add any alternative information	C	Add Braille information.
How is the information presented in audio captcha?	Noisy should be added deliberately.	C	Use clear messages
How can users understand the language of the captcha?	The audio should speak in a specific language	C	The multi-language option appears
	Text Captcha		
Is the text easy to read?	Use easy and understandable questions	MG	Text can be resized inside the browser.

---

[1] Further details at : http://www.captcha.net/

One of the most striking conflicts can be translated as follows:

- G1: Prevent spams from bots.
- G2: Provide text alternative for non-textual elements.
- Type of clash (G1 in respect to G2): Conflict (C)
- Rational for describing the conflict: as providing a text alternative for non-visual element captcha (as it is done with the attribute *alt* for images) will remove the security protection as programs can also read the *alt* attribute from HTML pages.
- Question: How is the text presented in the graphic captcha?
- Rational for deciding the conflict: importance of security versus accessibility and usability should help to decide if we keep (or not) captcha as a design option, and is so, which is the most appropriate design option for implementing captcha (for this is necessary to describe with which kind of accessible issues we are dealing with: visual impairments, audio, etc.).

The solutions for these conflicting guidelines requires a deep analysis of the associated trade-offs and the weight given to each factor can help designers to make a decision. For example, as security is very important in our case study, captchas should be implemented even if they can reduce the usability of the final user interface. If accessibility for blind people is important, then should go for a visual-audio captcha instead of a simpler visual captcha. It is important to note that whatever is the decision, it will represent an infringement of some guidelines. In order ensure that the decision explicitly represents trade-offs, a design rationale is necessary. When conflicts between guidelines occur, designers resolve it and document the solution. For that our approach proposes the use of design rationale. In Fig. 6 how designers can create a TEAM model for help the decision-making process leading to the best design options for using captchas in the context of the Ubiloop project is illustrated.

The constructions of such TEAM models must be done by designers with the help of the tool DREAM. However, assuming that we already have in our guideline database the design rationale used to describe a set of individual guidelines using the TEAM notation (see section 2.4.2), it is possible to automatically retrieve these individual models and insert them automatically in that TEAM model used to analyse the trade-offs and conflicts between guidelines. This situation is illustrated in Fig. 6 by the two guidelines "*WCAG guideline 1.1- text alternative*" [9] and "*Usable security: prevent spams from bots*" [9][35].

As we see in Fig. 6, the TEAM notation supports the observation of the relationships between guidelines and factors, thanks to its simplicity and readability, intended to be understandable by most of the actors involved during design (graphic designers, developers, customers,...),. The weights (visible through the connecting lines) suggest that the option *provide direct access* to the application does not comply with the security (dashed line in the connection) so this solution should be selected. The many alternative implementations of captchas do favour security but only visual and audio-visual captchas are accessible for blind users, so that one on these options can be selected. This diagram explicitly shows the compromises that have been made between the guidelines for deciding the final solution to the problem. Once a decision

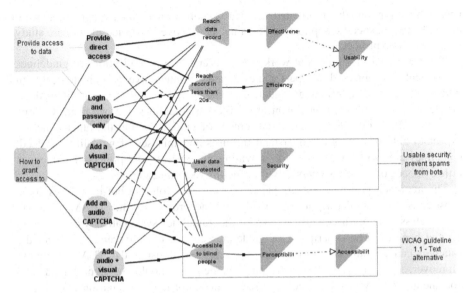

Fig. 6. TEAM model describing the rationale for analysing trade-off between captchas with respect to the requirements of the Ubiloop projects and potentially conflicting guidelines

was made for the Ubiloop project, it is recorded into our guidelines database so that it will become available for the next time when designers are confronted to a similar problem. The solution of this conflict also becomes accessible when browsing the guidelines in the database, so that it would be possible to explore trade-offs and known conflict with other guidelines.

Conflicting guidelines can be perceived at a glimpse at TEAM diagrams by looking at the lines connecting guidelines and design options. Our claim on "easier to observe" is based on the fact that a glimpse at a TEAM diagram allows to detect the divergent 'favouring lines' when some paragraph of text to would be required to explain the same thing. When diagrams are getting larger (in case of multiple conflicts only) visualization techniques such as bi-focal browser have been proposed [39] as well as colour matrixes [33].

5   Discussion

In this paper some of most striking questions related to selection and management of conflicting guidelines have been revised. Moreover, we have shown how a design rationale approach can help for dealing with trade-offs and design choices associated to guidelines. The same approach can also be used to trace the rationale behind the evolution of guidelines recommendations that are updated to reflect changes in either user behaviour or improvements of the technology.

Whilst the existence of potentially conflicting guidelines is almost common sense, as far as we know these problems are barely documented in the HCI literature. Nowadays the problems of conflicting guidelines become more important because new applications are being created using a combination of technologies that were before known in specific application domains; as we have illustrated in our case study for the Ubiloop project.

The main goal of the present work is help users of large collections of guidelines (in particular designers, developers and evaluators of interactive systems) to deal with trade-offs between conflicting guidelines. The present work puts at light these problems related to the management of conflicting guidelines. On one hand we hope to deepen the knowledge on the management of guidelines. On the other hand we expect to help designers to understand the uses and misuses of guidelines. Indeed, guidelines are world-wide used for providing guidance to the projects but there is little evidence on how designers solve conflicting recommendations.

The approach presented in this paper is a possible solution but it imposes some constraints for the description of guidelines according to the TEAM notation. Nonetheless, it is not necessary to have all the guidelines systematically described to get the benefits. The description of guidelines can be done incrementally and the database can contain entries that are not represented using the TEAM notation. Moreover, we suggest that conflicting guidelines should be represented and documented only when they occurs in real projects for two main reasons: first of all because we need the contextual elements given by the real project to decide the best option; secondly because the modelling activity can be time-consuming so it is better to make an effort when we can have an immediate benefit.

It is noteworthy that our approach for describing guidelines can be triggered either if we need guidelines for the design and/or evaluation of interactive systems. However, in some cases, the solution of conflicting guidelines will be achieved after several iterations in the development process of the application. For example, if we are in a design phase, we can select the guidelines, we can provide a TEAM model to complete the description of individual guideline and, possible detect that guideline might be in conflict with other guidelines. However, it might happen that the resolution of the conflict could not be done at design time as it might require some user testing to decide the trades-offs and the arguments allowing to solve the conflict. Thus only when evaluations have been performed we can go back and record the solutions for the conflicts identified previously. Whilst the decision making process leading to the resolution of the conflicting guidelines is done by designers in an ad hoc manner, the description of the solution should be systematic and exhaustive. In this paper we advocate for a systematic approach to guidelines conflict management using a supporting method and framework for the reuse of solutions to common recurrent conflicts.

This work also brings some questions that might influence the development of new tools for working with guidelines. Indeed most of the tools for working with guidelines can be described as a simple catalogue or database with searching facilities [10]. In fact there is little room in these tools for an active support of the decision-making process that occurs when building new applications. Indeed, our approach cannot only benefits designers with advices for the user interface but also call them for providing feedback about their decisions.

6   Future Work

Currently we are working to fully implement our approach in the Open-HEREDEUX project [13] that includes, among other components, the Open Repository, the Adviser and the Scorer. So, all the information about the conflicts will be stored in the Open database of guidelines. Moreover, the Adviser would be the processor who will detect the conflicts and, using the design rationale notation, who will send the solutions to the Open Repository to save them. Up to now, the Open Repository, the Adviser and the Scorer are available to get the most suitable set of guidelines for designers and evaluators. The next step is the implementation of the Result Analyzer and the methodology presented here to detect conflict between guidelines.

This paper illustrates the feasibility of our approach; however it has only been applied in a single real-world project. Further studies are necessary to investigate the potential of adoption of our approach by a larger community of designers and developers of interactive systems. With this respect, we want to explore in the future the participation of online communities that could help by creating individual TEAM models for guidelines and reporting the potential conflicting guidelines. The motivation of providing these feedbacks is that one can also get benefits of information provided by other members of the community. That is an alternative for creating a collective intelligence around the management of conflicting guidelines. In such context, design rationale because even more important because it can help the contributors to provide the right arguments for solving the conflicts. As the trades-off and design options are systematically exhibited by TEAM models, it might reduce the ambiguities associated with the interpretations of comments send by contributors.

The approach is aimed at recording the solutions for conflict resolutions so that they become available for future use. Thus a database is enriched with knowledge about the conflicts. Such information can be exploited in the future for understanding how conflicts have been solved. We can also envisage using such information with recommender systems that could provide real time advices when selecting guidelines sources, for example.

Future work will include usability and scalability studies based on empirical studies with designers and larger cases studies employing a larger set of guidelines.

Acknowledgements. The work has been supported by Universitat de Lleida for pre-doctoral fellowship to Llúcia Masip and the EU project FEDER Ubiloop.

References

1. Tidwell, J.: Designing interfaces. O'Reilly, Sebastopol (2005)
2. van Welie, M., van der Veer, M.: Pattern languages in Interaction Design: Structure and Organization. In: Proc. of INTERACT 2003, pp. 527–534. IOS Press, IFIP (2003)
3. Abascal, J., Arrue, M., Fajardo, I., Garay, N., Tomás, J.: The use of guidelines to automatically verify Web accessibility. Univers. Access Inf. Soc. 3(1), 71–79 (2004)

4. Winckler, M., Bernhaupt, R., Pontico, F.: Challenges for the Development of User Interface Pattern Languages: A Case Study on the e-Government Domain. Int. Journal on WWW/INTERNET, IADIS Digital Library 8(2), 59–84 (2010)
5. Vanderdonckt, J.: Development milestones towards a tool for working with guidelines. Interacting with Computers 12(2), 81–118 (1999)
6. Van Duyne, D.K., Landay, J.A., Hong, J.A.: The Design of Sites: Patterns, Principles, and Processes for Crafting a Customer-Centered Web Experience. Addison-Wesley, Reading (2002)
7. Grill, T., Blauhut, M.: Design Patterns Applied in a User Interface Design (UID) Process for Safety Critical Environments (SCEs). In: Holzinger, A. (ed.) USAB 2008. LNCS, vol. 5298, pp. 459–474. Springer, Heidelberg (2008)
8. Kinert, T.: User-Centered Interaction Design Patterns for Interactive Digital Television Applications, 315 p. Springer, London (2009) ISBN 978-1-84882-274-0
9. W3C. Web Content Accessibility Guidelines 2.0. W3C Candidate Recommendation (April 2008), http://www.w3.org/TR/WCAG20/
10. Vanderdonckt, J., Farenc, C. (eds.): Tools for Working with Guidelines. Springer, London (2001)
11. Vogt, T.: Difficulties in Using Style Guides for Designing User Interfaces. In: Vanderdonckt, J., Farenc, C. (eds.) Tools for Working with Guidelines, pp. 197–208. Springer, London (2001)
12. Martin, D., Rouncefield, M., Sommerville, I.: Applying Patterns of Cooperative Interaction to works (Re)Design: E-Government and Planning. In: Proceedings of ACM CHI 2002, Minneapolis, USA, April 20-25, pp. 235–242 (2002)
13. Masip, L., Oliva, M., Granollers, T.: OPEN-HEREDEUX: OPEN HEuristic REsource for Designing and Evaluating User eXperience. In: Campos, P., Graham, N., Jorge, J., Nunes, N., Palanque, P., Winckler, M. (eds.) INTERACT 2011, Part IV. LNCS, vol. 6949, pp. 418–421. Springer, Heidelberg (2011)
14. Pontico, F., Winckler, M., Limbourg, Q.: Organizing User Interface Patterns for e-Government Applications. In: Gulliksen, J., Harning, M.B., van der Veer, G.C., Wesson, J. (eds.) EIS 2007. LNCS, vol. 4940, pp. 601–619. Springer, Heidelberg (2008)
15. Beirekdar, A., Keita, M., Noirhomme, M., Randolet, F., Vanderdonckt, J., Mariage, C.: Flexible Reporting for Automated Usability and Accessibility Evaluation of Web Sites. In: Costabile, M.F., Paternó, F. (eds.) INTERACT 2005. LNCS, vol. 3585, pp. 281–294. Springer, Heidelberg (2005)
16. ISO. International Standard. ISO 13407. Human-centered design, processes for interactive systems (1991)
17. Prates, R., de Souza, C., Simone, D.J.: Methods and tools: a method for evaluating the communicability of user interfaces. Interactions, 31–38 (2000)
18. Jiang, Y., de Bruijn, O., De Angeli, A.: The Perception of Cultural Differences in Online Self-presentation. In: Gross, T., Gulliksen, J., Kotzé, P., Oestreicher, L., Palanque, P., Prates, R.O., Winckler, M. (eds.) INTERACT 2009, Part I. LNCS, vol. 5726, pp. 672–685. Springer, Heidelberg (2009)
19. Thevenin, D., Coutaz, J.: Plasticity of User Interfaces: Framework and Research Agenda. In: Conference on Human-Computer Interaction, INTERACT 1999, vol. 1, pp. 110–117 (1999)
20. González Sánchez, J.L., Padilla Zea, N., Gutiérrez, F.L.: From Usability to Playability: Introduction to Player-Centred Video Game Development Process. In: Kurosu, M. (ed.) HCD 2009. LNCS, vol. 5619, pp. 65–74. Springer, Heidelberg (2009)

21. Avizienis, A., Laprie, J.C., Randell, B., Landwehr, C.: Basic Concepts and Taxonomy of Dependable and Secure Computing. IEEE Trans. Dependable Secur. Comput. 1(1) (2004)
22. Blackwell, A.F., Fincher, S.: PUX: patterns of user experience. Interactions 17(2), 27–31 (2010)
23. Xiong, J., Winckler, M.: An investigation of tool support for accessibility assessment throughout the development process of Web sites. Journal of Web Engineering (JWE) (Special Issue about Web Usability and Accessibility) 7(4), 281–298 (2008)
24. Xiong, J., Farenc, C., Winckler, M.: Analyzing Tool Support for Inspecting Accessibility Guidelines During the Development Process of Web Sites. In: Weske, M., Hacid, M.-S., Godart, C. (eds.) WISE 2007 Workshops. LNCS, vol. 4832, pp. 470–480. Springer, Heidelberg (2007)
25. http://www.evengrounds.com/es/node/120
26. Vanderdonckt, J.: Accessing guidelines information with SIERRA. In: Proc. 5th IFIP TC 13 INTERACT 1995, pp. 311–316. Chapman & Hall, London (1995)
27. Grammenos, D., Akoumianakis, D., Stephanidis, C.: Integrated support for working with guidelines: the Sherlock guideline management system. Interacting with Computers 12(3), 281–311 (2000)
28. Abascal, J., Nicolle, C.: The application of USERfit methodology to teach usability guidelines. In: Vanderdonckt, J., Farenc, C. (eds.) Tools for Working with Guidelines, pp. 209–216. Springer, London (2001)
29. Abascal, J., Nicolle, C.: Why Inclusive Design Guidelines. In: Nicolle, C., Abascal, J. (eds.) Inclusive Design Guidelines for HCI, pp. 3–13. Taylor & Francis, London (2001)
30. Henninger, S.: A methodology and tools for applying context-specific usability guidelines to interface design. Interacting with Computers 12(3), 225–243 (2000)
31. Partarakis, N., Mourouzis, A., Doulgeraki, C., Stephanidis, C.: A Portal-Based Tool for Developing, Delivering and Working with Guidelines. In: Stephanidis, C. (ed.) UAHCI 2007, Part I. LNCS, vol. 4554, pp. 507–516. Springer, Heidelberg (2007)
32. Lacaze, X., Palanque, P., Barboni, E., Bastide, R., Navarre, D.: From DREAM to Reality: Specificities of Interactive Systems Development With Respect to Rationale Management. In: Dutoit, A.H., McCall, R., Mistrík, I., Paech, B. (eds.) Rationale Management in Software Engineering: Concepts and Techniques, Rationale Management in Software Engineering, pp. 155–170. Springer (2006)
33. Martinie, C., Palanque, P., Winckler, M., Conversy, S.: DREAMER: a Design Rationale Environment for Argumentation, Modeling and Engineering Requirements. In: Proceedings of the 28th ACM International Conference on Design of Communication (SIGDOC 2010), September 26-29, pp. 73–80. ACM Press, São Carlos (2010)
34. Cranor, L.F., Garfinkel, S. (eds.): Security and Usability: Designing Secure Systems that People Can Use, 744 pages. O'Reilly Media, ISBN-10: 0596008279
35. http://www.evengrounds.com/es/node/120
36. http://www.evengrounds.com/es/node/584
37. Mariage, M., Vanderdonckt, J., Pribeanu: State of the Art of Web Usability Guidelines. In: The Handbook of Human Factors in Web Design, pp. 688–700. Lawrence Erlbaum Associates (1999), doi:10.1.1.58.4494, ISBN: 080584612
38. Dearden, A., Finlay, J.: Pattern languages in HCI: A Critical Review. Journal of Human-Computer Interaction 21(1), 49–102 (2006)
39. Palanque, P., Lacaze, X.: DREAM & TEAM: A Tool and a Notation Supporting Exploration of Options and Traceability of Choices for Safety Critical Interactive Systems. In: Baranauskas, C., Abascal, J., Barbosa, S.D.J. (eds.) INTERACT 2007. LNCS, vol. 4663, pp. 525–540. Springer, Heidelberg (2007)

A Development Process for Usable Large Scale Interactive Critical Systems: Application to Satellite Ground Segments

Célia Martinie, Philippe Palanque, David Navarre, and Eric Barboni

ICS-IRIT, University of Toulouse 3, 118 route de Narbonne,
31062 Toulouse Cedex 9, France
{martinie,palanque,navarre,barboni}@irit.fr

Abstract. While a significant effort is being undertaken by the Human-Computer Interaction community in order to extend current knowledge about how users interact with computing devices and how to design and evaluate new interaction techniques, very little has been done to improve the reliability of software offering such interaction techniques. However, malfunctions and failures occur in interactive systems leading to incidents or accidents that, in aviation for instance, are [22] 80% of the time attributed to human error demonstrating the inadequacy between the system and its operators. As an error may have a huge impact on human life, strong requirements are usually set both on the final system and on the development process itself. Interactive safety-critical systems have to be designed taking into account on an equal basis several properties including usability, reliability and operability while their associated design process is required to handle issues such as scalability, verification, testing and traceability. However, software development solutions in the area of critical systems are not adequate leading to defects especially when the interactive aspects are considered. Additionally, the training program development is always designed independently from the system development leading to operators trained with inadequate material. In this paper we propose a new iterative design process embedding multiple design and modeling techniques (both formal and informal) advocated by HCI and dependable computing domains. These techniques have been adapted and tuned for interactive systems and are used in a synergistic way in order to support the integration of factors such as usability, dependability and operability and at the same time in order to deal with scalability, verification and traceability.

Keywords: Software engineering, formal methods, task modeling, safety management, model-based design, training.

1   Introduction

Currently, most of the contributions in HCI are related to innovative interaction techniques, reports on User-Centred Design products and systems, prototyping techniques, usability evaluation and user experience. Most of the proposed techniques and methods are usually targeting mass market applications. When dealing with

M. Winckler, P. Forbrig, and R. Bernhaupt (Eds.): HCSE 2012, LNCS 7623, pp. 72–93, 2012.
© IFIP International Federation for Information Processing 2012

usability they focus on ensuring that the user will accomplish her/his goals in an efficient way, without error and with a maximum satisfaction while when user experience is concerned, they focus on flow, emotions, ... In safety-critical contexts, effectiveness and efficiency to accomplish user tasks are also very important but there are additional constraints to be accounted for on the system being used such as reliability and operability. Additionally, beyond these constraints on the final products, constraints also apply to the development process itself. Requirements for designing and developing safety-critical systems (as defined in standard such as DO-178B [16] or ESARR 6 [15] widely used in aeronautics) aim at ensuring that the various steps of the process are traceable (and have been traced) and that risk analysis has been carried out carefully demonstrating that risk of failure or malfunctions remains at a tolerable level. On the human side, users of such systems are trained to use the system, being required to follow operational procedures and behaving in an appropriate way according to both safety regulations and mission constraints.

This paper proposes a new development process able to address interactive systems issues, safety critical concerns in system development as well as human factors issues. To this end, we integrate in this process, methods, techniques and tools which aim at taking into account usability, reliability and operability. This process is centred on models which are the only way to deal with large systems and complex operator activities. In previous work we have a set of tool-supported notations that can be used to design reliable, usable and operable interactive critical systems [26]. This process enables seamless integration between formal behavioural models of the system components and informal behaviours expressed in standard programming languages. Beyond this computer science view it integrates formal and informal techniques (such as prototyping and usability evaluation) which are necessary when dealing with human factors aspects.

The first section of the paper highlights the key issues that need to be addressed to design and develop interactive safety-critical systems. This section highlights expected properties of the systems to be built (usability, operability, safety and reliability) as well as requirements on the process itself (support for verification, traceability, scalability and to support construction of associated material such as training programme of operators). The second section presents existing design processes that support the development of interactive system. The third section presents the new development process and explains how this process produces usable, dependable and safe interactive systems and how it meets process requirements in the area of safety critical systems. The last section exemplifies how this process has been implemented to design and develop a satellite ground segment application and presents why and how requirements identified in section 2 are met.

2   Requirements for Design and Development of Interactive Systems in Safety Critical Contexts

We propose to analyze two kinds of concerns that are still open issues in the safety-critical domain: nonfunctional requirements for the system, but also requirements on the development process. These two types of requirements are detailed in the next paragraphs.

2.1 Requirements for the System to Be Produced

This sub-section details which properties have to be taken into account during the development process of a safety-critical interactive system and the reasons why.

2.1.1 Usability and Operability

Safety critical systems aim at achieving safety-critical missions (e.g. controls a spatial aircraft, carry people from a destination to another, monitoring a power plant...). Humans that interact with such systems operate the system, i.e. they use it according to predetermined procedures, predetermined tasks and predetermined behaviors they have been trained to master, in contexts that have been analyzed during the system design.

Usability term usually refers to effectiveness, efficiency and satisfaction. But, designed safety-critical interactive systems are also required being operable, i.e. they are required providing all of the needed functionalities so that the user is able to control the system and to accomplish all the possible tasks she/he can be requested to perform. Additionally, designed system has also to be error-tolerant and safe. Since a few years, these properties have been tackled by consolidated cross-domain taxonomies of usability, generally from a software perspective. Operability, Error tolerance [2] and software safety [45] have been added to the usability definition.

2.1.2 Reliability

It is now widely agreed upon that in order to easier to use systems, generic and specific functionalities have to be offered to the users of such systems. However, increasing the number of functionalities by adding, for instance, undo/redo mechanisms, WYSIWYG facilities increases the likelihood of system crashes. In particular, the current reliability level of software suites proposed by main software companies clearly show that building reliable interactive software is still a challenge for software development teams. While rebooting the systems is the most reasonable action in order to recover from a software crash, this is totally unacceptable in real-time safety critical systems where people life is at stake.

2.1.3 Safety

This property aims at classifying systems which *will not endanger the human life or the environment* [46]. Current User-Centred Design approaches and model-based design methods do not explicitly account for potential erroneous human and technical behaviour. But, particular attention is paid to the design and development of a safety-critical system, especially with the transversal activity of safety management. Goal is to ensure that the risk associated with the use of the system is tolerable. And risks are usually quantified and classified to provide a common understanding of tolerance. Safety integrity levels (SIL) enable to characterize the effects of a failure condition in the system. The failure conditions are usually categorized by their effects on the system, users and environment. Table 1 presents a classification of safety integrity levels for space systems 16420-1 [20]. Another example is the classification for aircraft software DO178-B [16], which identify 5 safety integrity levels (Catastrophic, Hazardous, Major, Minor, No effect).

The safety expert has to analyse incidents and accidents that occurred on similar systems, in order to prevent accidents from re-occurring. Identification of system functions or boundaries, together with hazards and risks analysis enables to determine required safety integrity levels for each system function. Hazards and risks analysis are part of the safety assessment process and consists in examining the effect of a failure condition in the system. A safety integrity level is associated to each part of the system after that a safety analysis has been performed by an expert.

Table 1. Severity of identified hazards (ISO 16420-1)

Severity	Consequence
1) Catastrophic hazards	i) loss of life, life-threatening or permanently disabling injury or occupational illness, loss of an element of an interfacing manned flight system;
	ii) loss of launch site facilities or loss of system;
	iii) severe detrimental environmental effects.
2) Critical hazards	i) temporarily disabling but not life-threatening injury, or temporary occupational illness;
	ii) major damage to flight systems or loss or major damage to ground facilities;
	iii) major damage to public or private property; or
	iv) major detrimental environment effects.
3) Marginal hazards	minor injury, minor disability, minor occupational illness, or minor system or environmental effects.
4) Negligible hazards	less than minor injury, disability, occupational illness, or less than minor system or environmental damage.

2.2   Requirements for the Design-and-Development Process

This section details the concerns taken into account for the development process of a safety-critical interactive system including support to handle scalability, verification and traceability and training.

2.2.1 Scalability

The complete specification of interactive application is now increasingly considered as a requirement in the field of software for safety critical systems due to their increasing use as the main control interface for such systems. As the user interface as a part of command and control systems may represent a huge quantity of code, User Interface Tools must provide ways to address this complexity. Support only dealing with code management is not enough and there is thus a critical need for addressing this complexity at a higher level of abstraction. This paper argues that one possible way to deal with these issues is to follow the same path as in the field of software engineering where modeling activities and model-based approaches take the lead with standards like UML. Several contributions argue for this approach [38], and especially when new interaction techniques have to be addressed during the development process (such as the so-called Post-WIMP [21] or animations [14]).

2.2.2 Verification

Verification techniques aim at providing ways for ensuring systems reliability prior to implementation. User Interface Tools that would provide such capabilities would empower developers by offering means for reasoning about their systems at a higher level of abstraction.

Formal description techniques support verification and make it possible to assess properties such as: whatever state the system is in, at least one interactive object is enabled, mutual exclusion of actions, reachability of specific states [36]. Testing activities also support verification and model-based approaches [8] featuring formal description techniques can provide support to developers in the later phases of the development process where the intrinsic nature of interactive systems makes them very hard to address properly otherwise. For instance, the event-based nature of interactive systems makes them impossible to test without tool support for the generation of the possible test cases. Work in this field is still preliminary but contributions are available for WIMP interaction techniques providing means for regression testing [29] and coverage criteria [30].

2.2.3 Traceability

Traceability of requirements throughout the whole design and development process is explicitly required for safety-critical systems, from system requirements to all source code or executable object code. DO-178B [16] requires the use of methods and techniques for systematically exploring design options and for supporting the traceability of design decisions. Similarly, ESARR [15] on Software in Air Traffic Management Systems explicitly requires traceability to be addressed in respect of all software requirements. However, such standards only define what must be done in terms of traceability but provide no information on how such goals can be reached by analysts and developers.

2.2.4 Training

Human operating a safety-critical system has to be trained and qualified [26]. Users of such systems have to also to be "adapted" (or prepared) to use the system. Indeed, training is the mean to achieve this goal and is therefore mandatory for users of critical systems. Related work presented in [1] and [43] argue that training enables:

- Ensuring that operators have reached a required level of skill and knowledge before using the system.
- Enhancing and maintaining users' performances.
- Decreasing the number of human errors while using the system.

Training programs of safety critical systems have to be designed in such a way that the future user has been evaluated as being able to operate the system she/he has be trained to use. To achieve this goal, Systematic Approaches to Training are widely used across application domains of safety-critical systems [23] [26]. Unfortunately, users of interactive critical systems have not always been trained on the system they are going to use. In best cases, they have been trained on simulators of real systems that mimic the expected system's behavior. The development process should provide a way to ensure that users are prepared to the complete system's behavior.

3   Limitations of Existing Design Processes for Interactive Systems

Proposing processes for the development of software systems has been a recurring activity of researchers and practitioners in the area of software engineering. Indeed, managing large scale software systems requires structured and systematic approaches for coping with the complexity.

3.1   Legacy Software Development Processes

The early waterfall model proposed in the 70s [43] is made up of eight steps ranging from "system requirement" phase to "operation" phase. While such structured processes (and the following versions such as the V model from [28]) promote the construction of reliable software by building the "system right", they have also demonstrated their difficulty in building the "right system" i.e. a system corresponding to the needs of the various stakeholders especially in the context of unstable and evolving requirements. To try to address such concerns the spiral development process promoted by Boehm [9] has introduced the production of specific artifacts called prototypes in order to first identify the adequacy of the current version of the software with clients' requirements, and second provide a framework for handling explicitly iterations. It took nearly 10 years (and a significant increase in software size and complexity) to understand that such iterative processes were not delivering as expected, as demonstrated by a thorough study of more than 8000 project in 382 companies reported by the same Barry Boehm [10] in 2006. As identified in this study, the main drawback of these early software development processes (beyond the inherent difficulty of building large and complex system products) was the difficulty to identify user needs and to produce software meeting both those needs and to encompass ever evolving new technologies.

3.2   User Centered Software Design Processes

Even though it took a long time to make its way in the area of software engineering, the necessity of designing software compliant with user need and user capabilities has been recognized as critical in the area of Human-Computer Interaction much earlier. The User Centered Design approach (introduced in [33]) has promoted to place user-related consideration at the center of the development processes. Several processes have since been proposed to take into account usability while designing an interactive system. Hartson et al. [18] and Collins [12] identified mandatory steps to design usable system. Curtis & Hefley [13] first tried to match software development processes with usability engineering and techniques. Rauterberg [40] identified more precisely design steps to involve end-users in an iterative-cyclic development process. Goränsson et al. [17] proposed a design process centered on usability: *"The usability design process is a UCSD approach for developing usable interactive systems, combining usability engineering with interaction design, and emphasizing extensive active user involvement throughout the iterative process"*. This work highlights that design processes for interactive systems are required to be highly iterative and to promote multiple designs through evolvable prototypes in order to accommodate requirements changes and results from usability evaluations. However, such processes have put too much emphasis on the user side forgetting the complex reality of software development.

3.3   Agile Approaches to Software Development

Iterative or agile approaches, such as Scrum [47], advocate that requirements tuning is performed by means of rapid and systematic iterations. However, including the last version of Scrum released end of 2011 there is still no reference to end user. Validation of prototypes by clients will not provide feedback to developers about compatibility with users' tasks and activities for instance. This has been clearly stated and identified in [48] where User Centered and Agile approaches where compared and assessed. Beyond that, task/artifact lie cycle as identified in [11] adds a new dimension to user needs evolution. Indeed, as described in the studies reported in that paper, the fact of providing users with new tool (even if the tools are perfectly in line with their needs) will change the needs as the work and practice of users will evolve due to this particular new tool. This demonstrates the need to involve end users throughout the development process to test, validate the systems and redefine their needs, as promoted by several research contributions [19].

Another very different problem lays in the iterative nature of the agile and spiral processes. Indeed, (as advocated by the early development processes such as waterfall or V) without identified phases gathering in one same location all the information required, software development will be chaotic resulting in hard to manage, test and modify software that has been built adding regularly new functionalities without following a global and thorough design. While this might not be a big problem when small and rather simple applications are considered, when it comes to large scale and complex systems (as satellite ground segments) this might have significant impacts both in term of development costs and resources but also in terms of reliability and dependability. To handle such complexity model-based approaches such as UML or [37] provide abstraction and domain specific notations. However, approaches such as Scrum or the Spiral model reject the use of models due to the cost in terms of effort and time.

Table 2 presents a synthetic view on coverage of requirements by types of development processes, which have been presented in this section. It highlights the absence of appropriate development processes for interactive critical systems, as no one of them is covering all of the requirements. During, the past 20 years, various contributions issued by the authors targeted to create, evaluate and enhance scalable techniques, methods, notations and tools to support the design of interactive systems which could fulfill usability, reliability and safety properties. These contributions support the creation of a new development process which takes into account requirements for the system to be produced, but also requirements for the design and development process.

Next section presents the new development process which is iterative (to support incremental developments and evolution of needs and requirements) integrating task models and end-user evaluation (to handle the always evolving users' needs and to ensure usability) while proposing extensive use of models (to ensure reliability of the software). In this next section, at each stage of the development process, one or more references are cited to indicate the technique, notation, tool and/or method used to support this development process.

Table 2. Synthesis of coverage of requirements by types of software development processes (TIA= Taken Into Account – NA= Not Addressed)

	Requirements for the interactive critical system to be produced			Requirements for the design and development process			
	Usability	Reliability	Safety	Scalability	Verification	Traceability	Training
Legacy development processes	NA	TIA	TIA	TIA	TIA	TIA	NA
User Centered Design processes	TIA	NA	NA	NA	NA	NA	NA
Agile approaches	NA	NA	NA	TIA	TIA	NA	NA

4   A Development Process for Safety Critical Interactive Systems

The proposed process takes into account previously presented system properties and previously presented development process constraints. It leverages informal HCI techniques (including mock-ups, low-fidelity prototyping, field studies…) and formal HCI techniques (including formal description techniques, formal analysis, performance evaluation…) to address usability, reliability and operability properties that generally not targeted simultaneously.

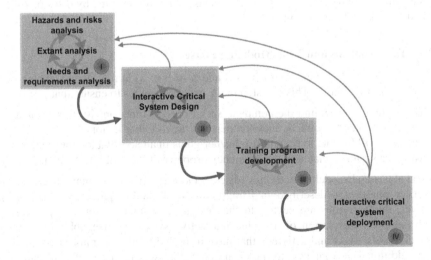

Fig. 1. Abstract view of the development process

Fig. 1 presents an abstract view of an iterative development process for critical interactive applications. As stated in the introduction the models makes explicit the design and construction of a training program and the required iterative aspect (doted arrows) for addressing users' needs and required changes following a usability evaluation. It also exhibits:

- The required activity of traceability of choices and decisions throughout this development process (by the large arrow on the right-hand side of the diagram).
- The required activity of safety management (by the large arrow on the left-hand side of the diagram), which is also a transversal activity that starts in the early stage of the design project with hazards and risks analysis activities and that will end when the system will not be in use anymore.

The first phase (disc I in Fig. 1) includes safety analysis activities such as incident and accidents analysis, existing systems analysis (or extant analysis), hazards and risks analysis. At the end of this first phase, needs and requirements for the system have been set, including safety integrity levels for each part of the system. The next step of interactive critical system design (disc II in Fig. 1) is triggered and will issue a very high-fidelity prototype as well as several types of models and descriptions for the next phases of training program development (disc III in Fig. 1) and system deployment (disc IV in Fig. 1).

4.1   Interactive Critical System Design

Fig. 2 presents a more detailed view of this development process making explicit the three specific sub-phases of the interactive critical system design process:

- Task analysis and modeling phase (under discs 3 and 7 in Fig. 2, detailed in §4.2)
- Low-fidelity prototyping iterative phase (loop represented by discs 2, 3 4 and 5 in Fig. 2, detailed in §4.3)
- Very-high fidelity prototyping iterative phase (loop represented by discs 6, 7, 8, 9 and 10 in Fig. 2, detailed in §4.4)

4.2   Task Analysis and Task Modeling Phase

Task analysis and task modeling (discs 3 and 8 in Fig. 2) aim at understanding and describing user activities. This key step in the process enables to ensure that:

- The system is providing the complete set of needed functionality to support user activities (related to effectiveness property of the usability factor).
- The user will be able to accomplish his/her goals in an acceptable timeframe while using the system (related to the efficiency property of the usability factor).

Task analysis and modeling activities (discs 3 and 8 in Fig. 2) may have been started in earlier phases (as described in paragraph "Needs and requirements analysis"), however, this activities are central to the design phase of the proposed process. It highly supports the design of a usable interactive system as it enables to identify precisely goals, tasks and activities that have to be led by the operator. Task models bring additional advantages to task analysis: the structuration of the gathered information about operators' activities and the possibility to use software tools to compute, analyze and simulate these models. When supported by a task modeling notation and tool featuring human tasks refinement (cognitive, motor, perceptive tasks) and complex activities edition and simulation, this step enables qualitative analysis of user or operator tasks (disc 4 and 9 in Fig. 2).

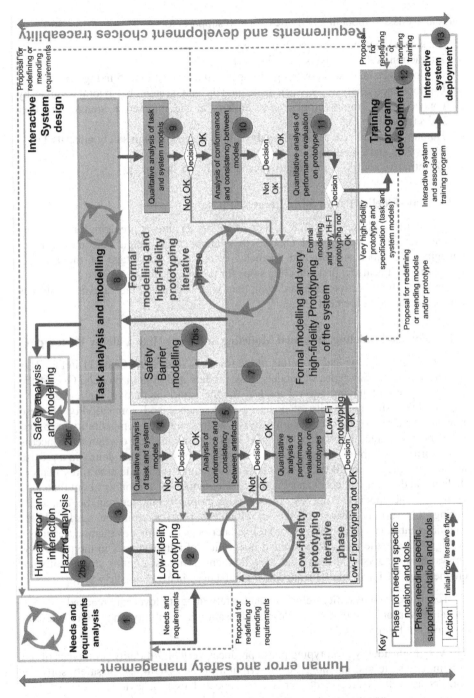

Fig. 2. Detailed view of the development process

Task analysis and modeling activities are also supports for:

- Task deviation analysis (disc 2bis in Fig. 2)
- Interactions safety analysis (disc 3ter in Fig. 2)
- Conformance analysis between prototypes and user task (disc 5 in Fig. 2)
- Conformance analysis between task models and system behavioral models by connecting the input/output event handlers to the interactive input/output user tasks (disc 10 in Fig. 2).
- Human error and task deviation analysis [35] in case of high safety integrity levels (discs 2bis and 2ter in Fig. 2).
- Quantitative analysis of user performances (disc 11 in Fig. 2).

4.3   Low-Fidelity Prototyping Iterative Phase

Low-Fi iterative phase (discs 2, 3, 4, 5 and 6 in Fig. 2) aims at preparing first versions of the interactive system and enables to evaluate first design outcomes without engaging too much human and financial resource at this stage of the process. Furthermore, it is also a first detection steps for potential safety issues.

Once low-fidelity prototypes are compliant with user tasks, the validated materials can be forwarded to the next phase.

4.4   Formal Modeling, Informal Modeling and Very High-Fidelity Prototyping

Very Hi-Fi prototyping and modeling phase (discs 7, 7bis, 8, 9, 10 and 11 in Fig. 2) is heavily based on two types of models: task models and system models. One of the critical aspects of having several models for the same interactive application is to support the resulting activity of ensuring conformance and compatibility of these models. We already proposed several ways of addressing such compatibility in [6] but it has been extended in order to deal also with the training and operational concerns [26]. Formal description techniques are the only means for both modeling in a precise and unambiguous way all the components of an interactive application (presentation, dialogue and functional core) and to propose techniques for reasoning about (and also verifying) the models. Applying formal description techniques can be beneficial during the various phases of the development process from the early phases (requirements analysis and elicitation) to the later ones including evaluation (testing).

Fig. 3 details the task allocation and integration of competencies in the process. It shows how analysis, design and development artifacts coming from software engineering, HCI and safety management can be used in a synergistic way to:

- Test if required usability, reliability and safety integrity levels are reached.
- Identify problems if required levels of usability, reliability and safety integrity have not been reached.

The very high-fidelity prototyping phase produces very high-fidelity prototypes of the system, complete and unambiguous description of the system and of safety software barriers as well as precise description of expected user behaviors. It enables fine tuning of these prototypes, descriptions and models to ensure that system's behavior will be fully compatible with user tasks and will prevent human error to endanger the system and its environment. All of these materials are the inputs of the next phase.

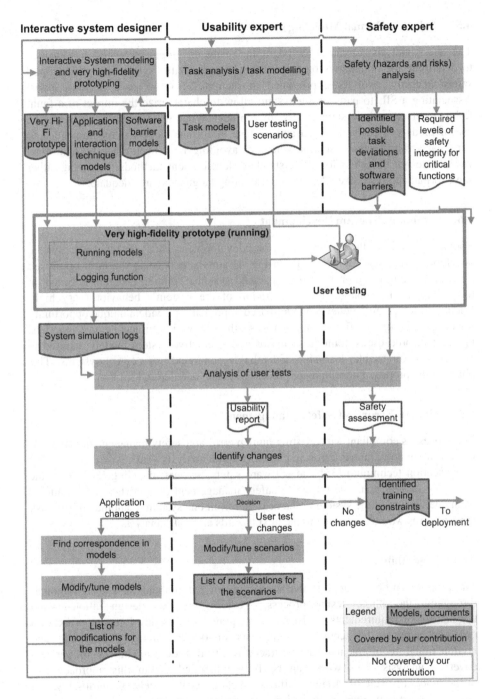

Fig. 3. Task allocation and integration of competencies in the process

4.5   Selective Formal Modeling

The safety analysis activity at the beginning of the development process has enabled to determine the boundaries between different parts of the system and the required safety integrity level (SIL, presented in section 2.1.3) for each of these parts. Associating a SIL to parts of the system allow to characterize the impact of a fault, failure or error on the system and its environment. When the required SIL is high, the use of models is easily justified and the use of formal models is recommended to verify and validate the system's behaviour avoiding fault occurrence by additional work at design time. For low SIL, standard development methods (involving either semi-formal approach like UML or programming languages) are adequate.

4.6   Training Program Development

The integration of the training program development as a phase of the system development process itself (disc III in Fig. 1) aims at producing the most optimized possible training program w.r.t. the designed system. Training program is based on the complete and unambiguous description of the system's behavior (very high-fidelity prototype and models). Model-based approaches provide a unique opportunity for integrating, in a unified iterative process, the four main artifacts i.e. tasks models, operational procedures, training scenarios and interactive system models required to be designed for usable, learnable and reliable command and control systems. This phase of the proposed development process has been detailed in [26].

4.7   Human Error and Safety Management

The process is compliant with existing human error and safety management activities. Indeed, it supports human error and task deviation analysis (Task Analysis for Error Identification technique) [35] and software safety barriers modeling [20]. And, the task error models could be reused as safety management artifact (task error pattern) from one version of the system to the next and from one system to another. These task error patterns would contribute to the next hazards and risks analysis.

4.8   Traceability

The proposed process supports the traceability of requirements and design choices throughout the whole design process. Previous work on design rationale and traceability of requirements [25] can be integrated to this development process in order to support the record and analysis of design choices. Functional and nonfunctional requirements can be traced w.r.t. this design choices to perform coverage analysis. This work can be fully integrated within this approach and furthermore, as well as design artifacts (such as task models, scenarios, system models) can be bound to design choices, task models with error patterns and software safety models can also be bound to requirements and design choices.

4.9   Tools Supporting the Development Process

As we mentioned in sections 2 and 3, supporting notation and tools for user tasks and system behavior are needed to handle usability within large-scale systems. In order to apply the development process we used two existing notations, one for task modeling and one for system behavior modeling.

An expressive and scalable task modeling notation is required to support the design of a usable interactive application. HAMSTERS [24] (Human-centered Assessment and Modeling to Support Task Engineering for Resilient Systems) is a task modeling notation designed for representing the decomposition of human goals into activities (perceptive, cognitive, motor, interactive...). It supports the description of large-scale and complex tasks and its associated software tool (also called HAMSTERS) enables to edit task models and simulate their execution.

A formal notation is required to support the design of a dependable system, especially when high safety integrity levels have to be reached. ICO formalism [32] and associated Petshop IDE also provides support for specifying entirely an interactive system behavior (scalability) and for integrating software components to ICO formal models and then enabling:

- The integration of low safety integrity level components with high safety integrity level components.
- The integration of models of software safety barriers [20].

The last element highlighted by the development process is the need for performance evaluation for assessing the actual performance of the application (and the interaction techniques, disc 10 on Fig. 2). Here again the Petri net based description technique of ICOs is very useful as Petri nets are one of the very few formalism providing both verification and performance evaluation supports as demonstrated by [34].

Furthermore, the two tools, HAMSTERS and Petshop have been integrated in a software development framework, which provides support for correspondence matching between the two types of models and co-execution of the very high-fidelity prototype with the underlying system and task models [3].

5   Application of the Development Process to Satellite Monitoring and Control Applications

In order to ensure its feasibility, the proposed development process has been applied to large scale ground segment applications. This section summarizes the results from the application of this process and highlights how requirements for designed product and for design and development process have been met.

5.1   Context in Which the Process Has Been Applied

This case study is part of the work that has been done for the TORTUGA[1] research and technology initiative, which aims at improving the reliability of both ground

---

[1] http://www.irit.fr/recherches/ICS/projects/tortuga/

segment systems and users involved in the operation of such systems. Many models and prototypes have been produced for different industrial case studies accomplished within this research project but only a few are shown, due to space constraints. Different entities are involved in the satellite application domain: the *space segment* (including the spacecraft) and the *ground segment* (made up of antennas for communication and the mission control system). Our focus is the operation control system. This system is in charge of maintaining the spacecraft in operation. During early validation phases of various ground segment applications, operators have encountered usability issues. CNES (French National Space Studies Center) Ground segment products department and Operations department agreed to study the feasibility of approaches developed within Tortuga project on a monitoring and control application of a ground segment. For this purpose, we applied the development process exposed in previous section to design and develop a very high-fidelity prototype for a new ground segment application and associated training sessions. We only provide here the excerpt necessary to discuss the application of the proposed development process. Indeed, tasks and operations of a mission control system are more numerous than what is presented here.

5.2   Artifacts Produced During the Application of the Process

The first steps in applying this process have been to analyze existing documentation about the procedures operators have to follow, about the system they were using and their associated user manuals. Several observations of operators in command and control rooms have been conducted (for two different satellite missions). Operators have been interviewed and have been filled in questionnaires. The analysis of these artifacts led to produce a list of user needs as well as scenarios and task models. A human error analysis also led to produce task models of operators' potential interaction errors. Fig. 4 a) presents an extract of the task model describing the setup of a redundant solar panel of the satellite (SADA2) if a failure on the in charge solar panel (SADA1) has occurred. It indicates that the operator has to select a particular procedure "Switch ON SADA2" while using the ground segment application. Then, the operator has to activate the procedure. This will send a particular *Telecommand* to the satellite, which will start to rotate the solar panel. Then the operator will have to confirm the stop of the solar panel rotation. In this example, we focus on one type of error but an example of a complete case study of task analysis for error identification can be found in [35]. Human errors can occur while accomplishing this procedure to setup the redundant solar panel. For example, Fig. 4 b) presents the task model of erroneous actions performed by the operator in that case. From the Human Error Reference Table [35], an interference error [41] or associative-activation error [39] can occur if the operators click on "YES" while they had decided not to confirm stop or if they click on "NO" while they had decided to confirm stop (confirmation pop up in Fig.6).

Five low-fidelity prototypes have been produced and confronted to task models and to operators, then very-high fidelity prototyping phase started. This phase led to produce formal models (11 ICO models) of the ground segment application prototype and presentation part of the user interface (a screenshot of the UI is presented in Fig. 6), but also formal behavioral models (15 ICO models) of the procedures executed by the operators. Fig. 5 shows an excerpt of the ICO model corresponding to the procedure of switching to the redundant solar panel. This excerpt describes the system's behavior when it displays the message pop up to confirm that solar panel rotation will be stopped.

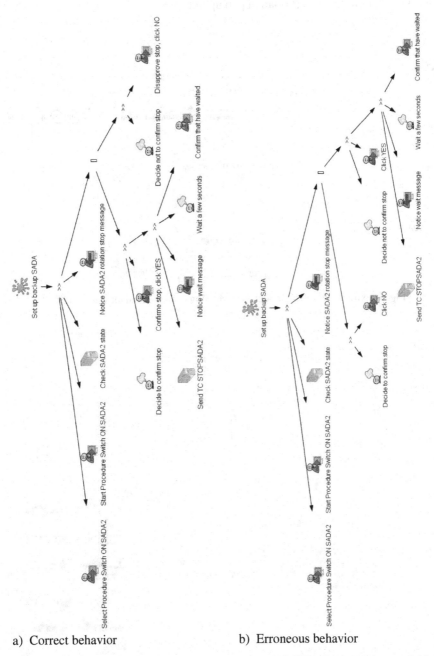

a) Correct behavior   b) Erroneous behavior

Fig. 4. Task models of the operational procedure to switch ON redundant solar panel driver

The presented notation and tool framework enables the binding of task models, system models and very Hi-Fi prototype. For example, task "Confirm stop, click YES" in Fig. 4 a) corresponds to transition "msgYES_stopSADA2Rotation" in Fig. 5 and to "Yes" button of the confirmation pop up in Fig. 6.

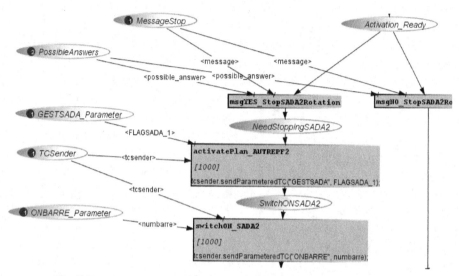

Fig. 5. Extract of the ICO model for switching to the redundant solar panel

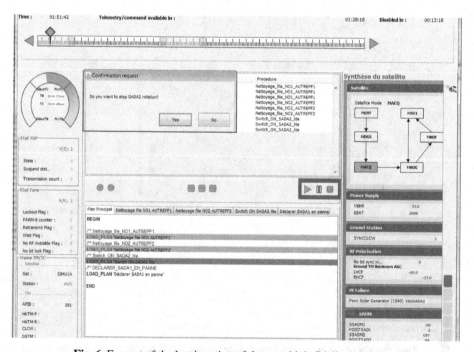

Fig. 6. Excerpt of the last iteration of the very high-fidelity prototype

Formal behavioral models of the system and of the procedures are put in correspondence with task models in the HAMSTERS-Petshop IDE. These models co-execute with the presentation part of the user interface (Fig. 6). Conformance and consistency between operators' tasks and prototype has been validated and training sessions have been developed and executed thanks to these produced artifacts.

Table 3 presents statistics about the artifacts produced while applying the development process. It is important to note that we only addressed in the project the most common functions in the ground segment applications deployed at CNES. We consider here neither mission-related functions nor specific aspect of the ground segments related to a specific satellite.

Table 3. Artifacts produced during the application of the development process

Artifacts of the ground segment application		Numerical values
Number of task models		20
Number of tasks per task model		12 to 20
Number of Low-Fi prototypes		5
Number of Hi-Fi prototypes		2
Number of ICO behavioral models		26
ICO models	places per model	15 to51
	transitions per model	10 to 36
	arcs per model	35 to 233
Number of training sessions		2
Number of scenarios per training session		3 to 5

5.3   How Requirements Are Met throughout the Development Process

5.3.1   Presented in this Article

The application of the development process to industrial projects proves the **scalability** of the proposed tool-supported approach. Task analysis and modeling supports the **usability and operability** of the designed and developed applications. Formal descriptions of the application behavior and of the operational procedures provide support for **reliability**. **Safety** concerns are addressed through the identification of human errors and tasks deviations (represented in the tasks models).

5.3.2   Not Presented in this Article

Going further in supporting **usability**, fine logging techniques, introduced in [34], enables quantitative analysis of user performance while using the system. These logging techniques can support in a very efficient way standard usability evaluation techniques especially when new and complex interaction techniques (such as multimodal ones) are considered [7].

Training is integrated as first class citizen in the development process. A detailed case study describing the training program development process and underlying concepts (such as Systematic Approach to Training), as well as the way our model-based approach can be used to leverage this process is described in [26]. Tasks models and system models are extremely useful for assessing the coverage of the training program and its adequateness to both the operators' tasks and system behavior.

Safety management phases are not described in details in this case study but complete examples can be found in previous work [35] [4] and can be fully integrated in the proposed process. In particular, hazards and risk analysis techniques as well as safety integrity levels identification techniques [46] can be used within the proposed process. Additionally, It has been demonstrated in previous work that safety modeling [4] and software barrier modeling [5] phases can be plugged-in directly in the proposed process, as part of an integrated framework. **Training** is also linked to those aspects as many operations are defined for managing incidents and failures that by definition have a low probability of occurrence and thus require regular re-training in order not to be forgotten.

Traceability of the needs and requirements throughout the whole development process and design choices can be achieved [25] using adequate notations and tools which are complementary to those presented in this article.

Verification of the application can be achieved through applying formal techniques related to Petri nets (which are the underlying formalism of ICO) [36].

6   Conclusion

This paper proposed a development process for the design, implementation and evaluation of safety critical interactive systems. It deals explicitly with requirements that target interactive critical systems (requirements for the system and requirements for the development process). Beyond that it integrates the training program within the process providing a unique opportunity to deliver timely and with a perfect match both a system and its training material. It also explicitly describes the articulation between high-level SILs and low-level ones and thus provides integration for formal and informal approaches.

The excerpts from the industrial application of the process are presented to show what the various products of the development process are and do not aim at being comprehensive. While it is very difficult (not to say impossible) to demonstrate the validity of a development process we have tried to report at each step its advantages and its limitations. To go beyond this case study we would like to emphasize the fact that this contribution is built upon several contributions and comes from the outcomes of the implementation of these contributions in several critical application domains such as space ground segments applications, interactive cockpits of large civil aircrafts and air traffic control management.

Future work is directed towards multi-users interactions and activities as well as computer mediated communication with remote users thus handling explicitly the issues related to team work both in a local setting and remote. We also focus our work on the issues related to automation and more precisely at providing means for designing automation in a user-centered way and to ensure that safety critical requirement are taken into account throughout the development process.

Acknowledgments. This work has been partly funded by R&T CNES (National Space Studies Center) Tortuga R-S08/BS-0003-029 and Airbus under the contract CIFRE PBO D08028747-788/2008.

References

1. Aguinis, H., Kraiger, K.: Benefits of Training and Development for Individuals and Teams, Organizations, and Society. Annual Review of Psychology 60, 451–475 (2009)
2. Alonso-Rios, D., Vasquez-Garcia, A., Mosqueira-Rey, E., Morey-Bonillo, V.: Usability: A Critical Analysis and Taxonomy. Intl. Journal of Human–Computer Interaction 26(1), 53–74 (2010)
3. Barboni, E., Ladry, J.-F., Navarre, D., Palanque, P., Winckler, M.: Beyond Modelling: An Integrated Environment Supporting Co-Execution of Tasks and Systems Models. In: Proc. of EICS 2010, pp. 143–152. ACM (2010)
4. Basnyat, S., Chozos, N., Johnson, C.: Incident and Accident Investigation Techniques to Inform Model-Based Design of Safety-Critical Interactive Systems. In: Gilroy, S.W., Harrison, M.D. (eds.) DSV-IS 2005. LNCS, vol. 3941, pp. 51–66. Springer, Heidelberg (2006)
5. Basnyat, S., Palanque, P., Schupp, B., Wright, P.: Formal socio-technical barrier modelling for safety-critical interactive systems design. Safety Science 45(5), 545–565 (2007)
6. Bastide, R., Navarre, D., Palanque, P.: A Tool-Supported Design Framework for Safety Critical Interactive Systems in Interacting with Computers 15(3), 309–328 (2003)
7. Bernhaupt, R., Navarre, D., Palanque, P., Winckler, M.: Model-Based Evaluation: A New Way to Support Usability Evaluation of Multimodal Interactive Applications. In: Maturing Usability: Quality in Software, Interaction and Quality, series on HCI. Springer (April 2007)
8. Bodart, F., Hennebert, A.-M., Leheureux, J.-M., Vanderdonckt, J.: Encapsulating Knowledge for Intelligent Automatic Interaction Objects Selection. In: Human Factors in Computing Systems INTERCHI 1993, pp. 424–429. Addison Wesley (1993)
9. Boehm, B.: A spiral model of software development and enhancement. ACM SIGSOFT Software Engineering Notes 11(4), 14–24 (1986)
10. Boehm, B.: A View of 20th and 21st Century Software Engineering. Invited talk. In: IEEE Int. Conf. on Software Engineering (2006), http://www.isr.uci.edu/icse-06/program/keynotes/boehm.html
11. Carroll, J.M., Kellogg, W.A., Rosson, M.B.: The Task-Artifact Cycle. In: Carroll, J.M. (ed.) Designing Interaction: Psychology at the Human-Computer Interface. Cambridge University Press, Cambridge (1991)
12. Collins, D.: Designing Object-Oriented user interfaces. Benjamin/Cummings Publishing, Inc., Readwoods City (1995)
13. Curtis, B., Hefley, B.: A WIMP no more: the maturing of user interface engineering. Interactions 1(1) (1994)
14. Esteban, O., Chatty, S., Palanque, P.: Whizz'Ed: a Visual Environment for building Highly Interactive Software. In: INTERACT 1995, Lillehammer, Norway, pp. 121–127 (1995)
15. Eurocontrol, ESARR 6, Eurocontrol Safety Regulatory Requirement 6, Software in ATM Functionnal Systems, version 2.0 (2010)
16. European Organisation for Civil Aviation Equipment. DO-178B, Software Consideration in Airborne Systems and Equipment Certification. EUROCAE (1992)

17. Göransson, B., Gulliksen, J., Boivie, I.: The Usability Design Process - Integrating User-Centered Systems Design in the Software Development Process. Software Process: Improvement and Practice 8(2), 111–131 (2003)
18. Hartson, H., Hix, D.: Human-computer interface development: concepts and systems for its management. ACM Computing Surveys 21(1) (1989)
19. Hussain, Z., Slany, W., Holzinger, A.: Investigating Agile User-Centered Design in Practice: A Grounded Theory Perspective. In: Holzinger, A., Miesenberger, K. (eds.) USAB 2009. LNCS, vol. 5889, pp. 279–289. Springer, Heidelberg (2009)
20. International Standard Organisation. Space systems safety requirements. Part 1: System safety. ISO 16420-1 (April 2004)
21. Jacob, R.: A Software Model and Specification Language for Non-WIMP User Interfaces. ACM Transactions on Computer-Human Interaction 6(1), 1–46 (1999)
22. Johnson, C.: On the over emphasis of human error as a cause of aviation accidents: systemic failures and human error in US NTSB and Canadian TSB aviation reports 1996–2003, Ergonomics (2006)
23. Martinie, C., Palanque, P., Navarre, D., Winckler, M.: A formal approach supporting effective and efficient training program for improving operators' reliability. In: Safety and Reliability for managing Risk (ESREL 2010), pp. 234–243 (2010)
24. Martinie, C., Palanque, P., Winckler, M.: Structuring and Composition Mechanisms to Address Scalability Issues in Task Models. In: Campos, P., Graham, N., Jorge, J., Nunes, N., Palanque, P., Winckler, M. (eds.) INTERACT 2011, Part III. LNCS, vol. 6948, pp. 589–609. Springer, Heidelberg (2011)
25. Martinie, C., Palanque, P., Winckler, M., Conversy, S.: DREAMER: a design rationale environment for argumentation, modeling and engineering requirements. In: SIGDOC 2010, pp. 73–80 (2010)
26. Martinie, C., Palanque, P., Winckler, M., Navarre, D., Poupart, E.: Model-Based Training: An Approach Supporting Operability of Critical Interactive Systems: Application to Satellite Ground Segments. In: Proc. of EICS 2011, pp. 53–62 (2011)
27. Mayhew, D.J.: The Usability Engineering Lifecycle, A practitioner's handbook for User Interface Design. Morgan Kaufmann Publishers, San Francisco
28. McDermid, J., Ripken, K.: Life cycle support in the Ada environment. ACM SIGAda Ada Letters III (1) (1983)
29. Memon, A.M., Soffa, M.L.: Regression testing of GUIs. In: 9th European Software Engineering Conf., pp. 118–127 (2003)
30. Memon, A.M., Soffa, M.L., Pollack, M.E.: Coverage criteria for GUI testing. In: 8th European Software Engineering Conference, pp. 256–267 (2001)
31. Navarre, D., Palanque, P., Martinie, C., Winckler, M., Steere, S.: Formal Description Techniques for Human-Machine Interfaces - ModelS-Based Approaches for the Design and Evaluation of Dependable Usable Interactive Systems. In: Handbook of HMI, A Human-Centered Approach, USA, Ashgate
32. Navarre, D., Palanque, P., Ladry, J., Barboni, E.: ICOs: A model-based user interface description technique dedicated to interactive systems addressing usability, reliability and scalability. ACM Trans. Comput.-Hum. Interact. 16(4), 1–56 (2009)
33. Norman, D., Draper, S. (eds.): User Centered System Design: New Perspectives on Human-Computer Interaction. Lawrence Erlbaum Associates, Hillsdale (1986)
34. Palanque, P., Barboni, E., Martinie, C., Navarre, D., Winckler, M.: A model-based approach for supporting engineering usability evaluation of interaction techniques. In: EICS 2011, pp. 21–30. ACM SIGCHI (2011)

35. Palanque, P., Basnyat, S.: Task Patterns for Taking Into Account in an Efficient and Systematic Way Both Standard and Erroneous User Behaviours. In: HESSD 2004, Toulouse, France, pp. 109–130 (2004)
36. Palanque, P., Bastide, R.: Verification of an Interactive Software by analysis of its formal specification. In: INTERACT 1995, Lillehammer, Norway, pp. 191–197 (1995)
37. Palanque, P., Bernhaupt, R., Navarre, D., Ould, M., Winckler, M.: Supporting Usability Evaluation of Multimodal Man-Machine Interfaces for Space Ground Segment Applications Using Petri net Based Formal Specification. In: Ninth International Conference on Space Operations, Rome, Italy, June 18-22 (2006) CD-ROM proceedings
38. Paternò, F., Santoro, C., Spano, L.D.: MARIA: a universal, declarative, multiple abstraction-level language for service-oriented applications in ubiquitous environments. ACM Transactions on Computer-Human Interaction 16(4), article n. 19 (2009)
39. Preece, J., Rogers, Y., Sharp, H., Benyon, D., Holland, S., Carey, T.: Human-Computer Interaction. Addison-Wesley, UK
40. Rauterberg, M.: An Iterative-Cyclic Software Process Model. In: International Conference on Software Engineering and Knowledge Engineering. IEEE, Capri (1992)
41. Reason, J.: Human Error. Cambridge University Press
42. Rettig, M.: Prototyping for tiny fingers. Commun. ACM 37(4), 21–27 (1994)
43. Royce, W.: Managing the Development of Large Software Systems. In: IEEE Wescon, pp. 1–9 (1970)
44. Salas, E., Cannon-Bower, J.: The Science of Training: A Decade of Progress. Ann. Review of Psychology, 471–499 (2001)
45. Seffah, A., Donyaee, M., Kline, R.B., Padda, H.K.: Usability measurement and metrics: A consolidated model. Journal of Software Quality Control 14(2) (June 2006)
46. Storey, N.: Safety-critical computer systems. Addison-Wesley (1996)
47. Schwaber, K.: Agile Project Management with Scrum. Microsoft Press (February 2004)
48. Sy, D., Miller, L.: Optimizing Agile User-centred design. In: CHI 2008 Extended Abstracts on Human Factors in Computing Systems (CHI EA 2008), pp. 3897–3900. ACM, New York (2008)

Agile User Experience Development in a Large Software Organization: Good Expertise but Limited Impact

Kati Kuusinen, Tommi Mikkonen, and Santtu Pakarinen

Tampere University of Technology, Tampere Finland
{kati.kuusinen,tommi.mikkonen,santtu.pakarinen}@tut.fi

Abstract. While Agile methods were originally introduced for small, tightly coupled teams, leaner ways of working are becoming a practical method to run entire enterprises. As the emphasis of user experience work has inherently been on the early phases before starting the development, it also needs to be adapted to the Agile way of working. To improve the current practices in Agile user experience work, we determined the present state of a multi-continental software development organization that already had a functioning user experience team. In this paper, we describe the most prevalent issues regarding the interaction of user experience design and software development activities, and suggest improvements to fix those. Most of the observed problems were related to communication issues and to the service mode of the user experience team. The user experience team was operating between management and development organizations trying to adapt to the dissimilar practices of both the disciplines.

Keywords: User experience (UX), Agile development, human-centered design (HCD), human-computer interaction (HCI).

1   Introduction

User experience (UX) plays a significant role in the success or failure of contemporary software-centric products and services, as well as the companies producing them [15]. The fundamental goal of UX work is to create software that is highly usable and fulfills user needs. UX, standardized as a "person's perceptions and responses resulting from the use and/or anticipated use of a product, system or service," is inherently based on the iterative model of human-centered design (HCD) [16], where context of use and user requirements are specified, and software is developed to meet those requirements. Yet, most prevailing Agile software development methodologies do not give clear guidance on how to incorporate user experience design activities in the software engineering practices. For instance, the Agile Manifesto [1] itself ignores UX-related activities.

In general, Agile development [1] refers to using iterative and incremental approach that emphasizes collaboration, feedback and working software over

M. Winckler, P. Forbrig, and R. Bernhaupt (Eds.): HCSE 2012, LNCS 7623, pp. 94–111, 2012.

processes, documentation and strict plans. By Agile UX we refer to work that systematically results in desired user experience of the outcome and is conducted according to Agile principles.

This paper describes the state-of-the-practice of Agile UX work in a large software organization that provides specialized software systems, mainly for internet service provider (ISP) markets. The company, one of the front-runners in the Agile transformation on the global scale, has several sites on various continents, and these all work together in an Agile manner. While their software development is aligned with Agile practices, the company has had problems in integrating UX work with Agile development. Our aim is to improve the current situation in Agile UX work within the company, and more generally to reveal good practices in Agile UX. Moreover, the goal is to uncover impediments and issues (both organizational and methodological) that support Agile UX inside the company. The study consisted of a web survey with 50 questions and 76 respondents which was followed by 13 face-to-face semi-structured interviews. We also studied internal documentation and compared it with the results of the interviews and the survey.

The rest of the paper is structured as follows. Next, in Section 2, we provide some related work and background on user experience and Agile development. In Section 3, we introduce the ways of working in the organization in which the study has been carried out. In Section 4, we discuss how the actual study was implemented, and in Section 5, we list the main lessons we have learned from the study. In Section 6, we give an extended discussion of the study and possible future actions. Towards the end of the paper, in Section 7, we draw some final conclusions.

2 Background and Related Work

Previous research has indicated there is a clear need for further studies of UX work in the field of Agile development [12, 25]. Silva da Silva et al. [25] conducted extensive literature research regarding HCD (including UX) and Agile methods. They presented 58 research articles found relevant in their study, and pointed out that most studies have been descriptions and conclusions of experiments. Therefore, they conclude that further studies are needed to understand the best practices in Agile UX work.

2.1 Practicing Agile UX Work

There is no clear consensus on best practices in Agile UX work – in other words, UX work that is conducted in accordance with Agile principles and methods, thus integrating (or merging) UX work and HCD practices with Agile development practices. There is clear evidence that some or little design upfront (SDUF or LDUF, respectively) is needed also with an Agile approach; this is recommended in 31 papers analyzed by Silva da Silva et al. However, the reason those papers recommended LDUF is that big design upfront is against Agile principles, and these articles present no recommendations on which design practices should be used during design upfront. Besides the need for SDUF, another evident finding is that integrating UX design and other development activities improves communication and collaboration between the functions; this is reported in 26 articles presented by Silva da Silva et al. Common practices in Agile HCD work include low fidelity prototypes, user tests, and user stories. However, ways of utilizing these practices vary. User testing on paper prototypes and on working software were equally recommended [25].

Common problems in Agile UX work include power struggles, differences in schedules between HCD and implementation, communication issues, unwillingness to understand project needs, and failure to achieve the right amount of user involvement [6]. Budwig et al. [4] report problems in understanding the big picture. UX work conducted within a development sprint caused confusion and problems in communication and off-shore coordination [4]. Petrovic et al. [22] state that in many cases, UX specialists are those who end up in quality assurance work. The above issues still remain unsolved, since they are considered as too expensive or difficult to improve. In addition, design vision and information architecture ought to be understood before starting implementation, and their realization assured in development. Such practices prevent the situation in which problems are discovered only after implementation [22].

Ferreira et al. [11] observed that upfront design improves user satisfaction and product consistency. Upfront design assisted in finding affordable design solutions. It also supported project-level estimation and prioritization, and thus led to savings in time and costs. Federoff and Courage [10] report that Agile UX work has been improved by parallel development and design, working one sprint ahead, interactive prototypes for communicating design, and design studios. Budwig et al. [4] report that a UX team benefitted from close collaboration with a broad cross-functional team since issues were found earlier and addressed faster. They also recommend that the UX team should work one to two sprints ahead of development teams in their own sprints, and should be co-located with development teams. The UX team should also work with business people to define requirements before starting UX work. Moreover, the UX team should already be involved in roadmap work. Working closely together helps in sharing information, and starting UX work early enables recognizing and considering user expectations in time, that is, when UX still is affordable and leads to optimal savings in development time and costs.

Chow and Cao [7] conducted multiple regression analysis on 48 common hypotheses of success factors in Agile software development and determined that only 10 were supported. From those, the authors found that the truly critical success factors were these: correct delivery strategy, proper practice of Agile techniques, and a competent team. The second set of important factors included good Agile project management process, a cooperative orally communicating team, and strong customer involvement.

Currently, one of the most recommended process models for applying UX work in an Agile context seems to be the "one sprint ahead" approach (Figure 1) originally proposed by Miller [21] and Sy [27], later applied or modified by Fox et al. [13], Silva da Silva et al. [25], and many others.

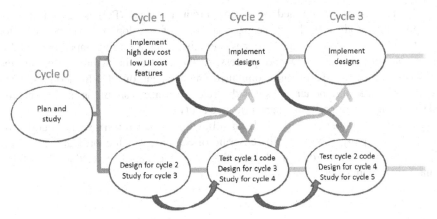

Fig. 1. One sprint ahead approach. Redrawn from [27]

The process model of Miller [21] and Sy [27] has been in use at Autodesk, but no recent experience reports were available. One sprint ahead is also recommended by Budwig [4] and Federoff and Courage [10]. Indeed, as by definition, UX design is iterative [16], working at least one sprint ahead gives an opportunity for iterations. Sy [27] observed the approach helped to complete the design just in time, which resulted in less design waste. The approach helped to gain a shared vision; through daily contact developers could be aware of design progression and give their input early enough [21]. Miller found the close cooperation and daily interaction between developers and UX designers to be an essential success factor. She reported savings in design and development time and improvements in user satisfaction [21].

3 Way of Working in the Organization

In the following, we introduce the ways of working within the software development organization we have studied. First, we discuss research and development, where Agile practices play a major role. Then, we address certain other functions of the company, where other practices exist.

3.1 Research and Development

As the company being investigated is one of those that have been spearheading the Agile transformation, it is only expected that Scrum [24, 26] is extensively used in research and development. Scrum (Figure 2) is a simple, iterative framework for project management. When using Scrum, incoming requirements to be implemented are stored in Product Backlog (PB). They are implemented in terms of Sprints – iterations of a fixed length of two to four weeks. For each Sprint, a collection of Product Backlog items are selected and refined into Sprint Tasks. Then, these are implemented in tasks of the Sprint. After each Sprint, a complete system is available, that can be delivered to clients, at least in principle.

Only three roles are defined in Scrum: Product Owner (PO) is responsible for managing the Product Backlog; Team, consisting of developers, is responsible for executing the Sprint; and Scrum Master will eliminate any emerging impediment and is responsible for enforcing the Scrum process. At the heart of the Scrum process are the self-organized Scrum Team and committed involvement of PO. In addition, team stability is of crucial importance, as it is the Team that takes care of the implementation tasks as a single, high-performing and effective entity.

The company being studied has been following Scrum for six years. Due to the size of the company, they also utilize Scrum-of-Scrums, which coordinates the effort of all Scrum teams towards a single goal that is more comprehensive than that of any of the Scrum teams themselves.

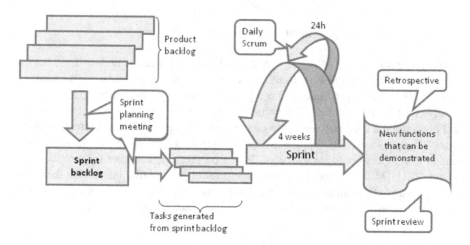

Fig. 2. Scrum process

3.2   User Experience

The company has an established UX team with about 15 UX professionals. The team has existed for four years. The majority of the team is physically co-located in Finland, but some of the team is located in Asia. Organizationally, the majority of the UX team is allocated to product management, which is responsible for developing a concept of software before starting a project. Hence, UX specialists are usually involved in development early on. The UX team members have specialized roles. One is specialized in research activities, another is responsible for official communication inside the organization, and some are interaction or graphic designers. The UX team rarely works together as a team. Instead, members have certain projects or tasks they are working with as individuals or sometimes as pairs.

Fixed quarter and yearly plans structure product management's work whereas R&D is following Scrum in their work. In general, product management is responsible of defining the product and making early concepts. R&D implements the products. As the UX team members operate between R&D and product management, their ways of working have characteristics of both product management and R&D – in general, the UX team's iterative practices do not follow Scrum. While the UX team members usually have some design upfront time, in some cases they start design work as implementation sprints begin. Generally, they adapt the practices of the function or team with which they are cooperating with.

Generally, UX issues are not in PB as such, and there are no acceptance criteria for UX work. However, UX team members working in projects follow PB. Usually developers get the design outside PB as wireframe or high-fidelity images. The UX team has earlier tried Agile working methods inside the team, too, but they were unable to stay one sprint ahead of development. Therefore, the trial was cancelled.

3.3   Other Parts of the Organization

Inside the organization, the use of Scrum is limited to R&D. In contrast, when delivering complete system-level solutions, for example, commonly composed out of the parts that are developed using Scrum, the process resembles a more conservative iterative approach, where releases are planned in advance according to the needs of the most important customers. The approach is iterative but it has fixed scope and time frame. In addition, there are certain management activities that do not follow Agile principles. Such topics fall beyond the scope of this paper.

4   Research Method

The explorative case study [18, 23] described in this paper was conducted by two researchers from a university research organization over a ten-month period from February to October 2011. The main research question was 1. How can the present state of Agile UX work be improved in the case organization. Other research questions were 2. What are the significant challenges in Agile UX work in the organization and how those can be resolved, and 3. What are the current good practices in Agile UX work. Since the case study was explorative, we did not have a hypothesis. We are also studying other companies with similar approach, e.g. [17].

4.1   Main Themes of the Case Study

The present state analysis was conducted in two parts: In the first part, a survey concentrated on collaboration and interaction, processes and tools, and respondents' knowledge about UX and usability; in the second part, a series of interviews concentrated on processes, collaboration, and acquiring and using user feedback. Processes and tools included both official and unofficial practicalities and working methods in the organization, such as the official development process and how employees follow it in practice. The collaboration and interaction section concentrated on how employees communicate with each other, which collaboration methods they would prefer, and what is hindering their cooperation. Knowledge was measured by how respondents defined UX and usability and how they would rate their own expertise.

4.2   Survey

The web survey was designed to reveal the present state of UX work in Agile organizations in general (in this paper we focus on one particular organization). It consisted of 50 questions (31 open and 19 closed-ended) on collaboration and interaction, processes and tools, and concepts and knowledge. The questions were generated iteratively by two researchers, based on a variety of studies [3, 5, 7, 9, 14, 20, 28, 29, 31]. References were studied to determine significant areas and common problems to generate appropriate questions. Questions and concerns were collected from the mentioned studies and iterated into a survey by the two researchers. The survey was piloted in two companies and iterated based on the feedback before starting the data gathering for the study presented in this paper.

The survey was open for answers for three weeks in February 2011. Invitations to participate in the survey were sent to members of the R&D organization and to its interfaces, such as marketing and management, including the UX team. Interviews were conducted two months later, after the survey had been analyzed. Interview questions were generated to go deeper in the focus areas, and from topics that remained unclear upon analyzing the survey responses.

Open-ended questions of the survey were analyzed by two researchers with a qualitative, theory-bound analysis method with an emergent coding approach [18] as follows. First the researchers separately read the material and classified the data per question. After that the researchers discussed the categories and formed classes. Then the data were coded into classes individually by two subjective coders to quantify them. An inter-rater reliability analysis using the Cohen's kappa statistic was performed to determine the consistency among coders. Quantified data were analyzed with SPSS to find statistical significances. Theory was bounded to data in the analysis phase when linking findings with Agile and UX methodologies.

4.3   Interviews

Semi-structured interviews were conducted as individual or pair interview by one or two interviewers. About 70 to 80 minute interviews were recorded and analyzed from written transcripts. Interview questions covered the job content and tasks of each interviewee: which tasks are their responsibility, who they are working with, and how they communicate with UX specialists and users of their work output. Additionally, questions about utilized Scrum roles and practices were asked.

Interviewees were selected to cover the most focal roles in software development. The company contact person helped in arranging the interviews. Questions were grouped based on the respondents' role. Some of the questions were aimed at all the respondents, but each role also had role-specific questions.

The interviews were analyzed by using the affinity wall method as instructed by Beyer and Holtzblatt [2]. The data-driven method utilizes theory-independent coding on a physical wall. Transcribed interview data were worked into 1126 notes each containing one piece of information. Three researchers (two subjective and one objective coder) categorized notes either including one into an existing category or creating a new one if no suitable category was available. If the note was considered irrelevant to the study, it was excluded from the analysis. Later we labeled and revisited the existing categories, and grouped those under new upper-level categories.

5   Findings

Over the course of the study, it quickly became apparent that although the original goal was to study the relation between Agile development and UX design, the findings would also reveal numerous other organizational aspects. In the following, we introduce the sample and our main findings organized into four categories (understanding UX, UX team, and cooperation). While listed separately, the issues are often intertwined with each other, and improving the situation requires considering them all.

5.1   Survey Participants and Interviewees

Table 1 describes the job roles of the 76 survey respondents. They had been working for the company 2 to 16 years, mean 7 years. Total work experience varied between 4 and 24 years, mean 14 years. Thirty-three respondents (developers, architects, scrum masters, and POs) were from R&D, whereas the rest (38) were from other functions such as management and UX. We calculated Cohen's kappa for coding open-ended answers. The inter-rater agreement was found to be kappa = 0.885 with p < 0.001 (almost perfect).

Table 1. Survey respondents' job categories (open-ended question)

Job	N	Job	N
Developer	20	UX specialist	6
Management	19	Scrum master	4
Product manager	7	Product owner	3
Architect	6	No answer	5
Quality assurance	6		

Table 2 presents office locations of the respondents. All the interviewees and 56.9% of the survey respondents work at the head office in Helsinki, Finland, and thus the core of the findings is strongly linked with that site. Different sites have their own ways of working; there is no general process that all the sites would follow.

Table 2. Office locations of survey respondents (closed-ended question)

Office location	N	Office location	N
Helsinki	37	Kuala Lumpur	7
Bordeaux	9	St Petersburg	3
Oulu	7	Paris	2

Altogether 13 persons with different roles in development were interviewed. Table 3 presents interviewee roles and codes that are used in this paper when presenting results to reveal which of the interviewees are behind each finding. The interviewees had total work experience from 9 to 31 years, mean 15.1 years. They had been working for the company from 3 months to 17 years, mean 5.2 years. And they had working experience of Scrum from 2 to 5.5 years, mean 3.4 years.

Table 3. Interviewees' work roles and codes used in this paper

Code	Role	Code	Role
H1, H2	Product owner	H8, H9	Scrum master
H3, H4	UX designer	H10	Quality engineer
H5, H6	Architect	H12	UX manager
H7	Developer	H11, H13	Product manager

5.2   Overview of the Results

The survey revealed that problems in Agile UX work were mostly process and communication related. The expertise both in Scrum and UX was generally good. Of the survey respondents, 85.7% evaluated their expertise in UX on a six-level scale from inadequate (1) to adequate (6) to successfully complete their assignments four or higher, N=70. On a six-level scale from novice (1) to expert (6), 63.0% evaluated their expertise in UX four or higher. Scrum masters (75.0%), quality engineers (50.0%), product managers (42.8%), and managers (38.9%) considered their expertise in UX low most often. The biggest problems in Agile UX work were considered to be lack of cooperation between UX specialists and developers, lack of time for designing UX / getting UX designs for implementation too late, and balancing the amount of early concept creation work for understanding the big picture before starting a development project.

Interviews concentrated on the process, communication, and acquiring and utilizing user information and feedback. Both the survey and interviews indicated problems in communication due to lack of face-to-face time. In interviews we discussed through the development process and found improvable issues from every phase, such as lack of common practice for early UX work and verifying the implementation of UX design. It was also hoped that UX work should be more agile.

5.3   Understanding UX

We asked in the beginning of the questionnaire how the respondents understand UX in general. UX was understood to be a feeling (28.6%) a user gets when interacting with a product; and the feeling is built on usability (22.9%) (i.e., ease of use and efficiency). Also 22.9% of the 70 respondents emphasized the holistic nature of UX and described it as a whole-life cycle from buying to end of life and said that it includes many aspects. Especially product managers (42.9% of them) and UX specialists (33.3%) referred to the holistic nature, whereas managers (36.8%) and developers (35.0%) described UX as a feeling the user gets while using the product.

Later in the questionnaire we asked what good UX means in the applications or services the participants were developing and got 49 responses. Traditional usability factors were ranked high (Figure 3). Ease of use (34.7%) and efficiency (22.4%) were seen as the most important: 14.3% of respondents thought the service should satisfy user needs, and 14.3% described mainly non-negative user feelings – *"user does not get frustrated."* Only three respondents (6.2%) described positive feelings, such as *"good UX means that user is happy or likes the application."* However, more ambitious UX goals are set in the beginning of a project. There is a strong feeling that these goals do not spread in the organization effectively and that people both in the R&D and outside of it are unaware of them. On the other hand, for most of the applications and services the company produces, the product strategy emphasizes invisibility and ease of use.

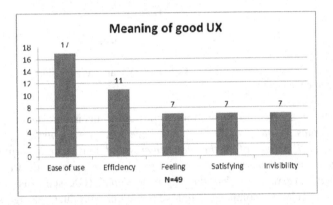

Fig. 3. Good UX in our applications (open-ended question)

The company had not defined how they understand UX. Good UX may have various forms depending on context and service. When asked "how does 'company name' define user experience," 37.5% said they do not know; 33.3% described some definition such as ease of use, *"the UX team has defined it,"* or *"no customer complaint means it is ok"*; and 6.3% answered there was no common definition.

5.4   Tasks of the UX Team

The UX team was partly operating as a service organization where product managers or developers could order some design work. It seems that service mode was causing many of the observed problems related to UX work, such as inability to constantly deliver design in time for development or doing UX work too late. Lund [19] claims service mode is the biggest threat to viable UX work. In the survey, 33.3% of respondents answered that one of UX team's most important tasks is consulting or helping development teams (Figure 4). A UX team member clarified this: *"When a project has remembered they need some specs or screens, then they have ordered those and we made them."* On the contrary, the UX team told in interviews that their biggest responsibilities are making designs and understanding the big picture. Six interviewees wanted to see UX specialists giving guidelines and making high-level designs whereas the developers would solve design details and trivial cases by themselves with help from UX team when needed (H1, H3, H4, H9, H11, H12).

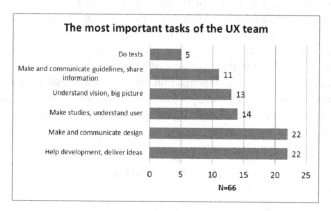

Fig. 4. In the survey, the most important tasks of the UX team were considered to be to consult and design (open-ended question)

The UX team seemed to have limited power of decision: *"One of the most challenging issues in our work is that we have lots of responsibility, we should manage the overall picture of all the requirements and how it can be captured in the UI level. And on the other hand, we have no power of decision at all; we need to be diplomatic with everyone to find the happy medium"* (UX specialist). When we presented the results to company employees (mainly product managers, product owners, UX specialists, and architects), they considered understanding vision, the overall picture, and user should be more important.

5.5   Cooperation with UX Specialists

In general, the UX team operates as a link between R&D and product management. When asked *'what is expected from you in your job?'* an interviewed UX specialist told *"it is mostly communication, acting as a link between development and product managers. And to visualize both business and technical requirements and try to transfer those into pleasant, easy-to-use user interfaces."* Physically the majority of UX specialists are co-located with product management and apart from R&D. Survey respondents considered in an open-ended question that at its best UX cooperation is started early (18.6%), and communication happens face-to-face (15.3%). However, 11.9% reported cooperation would be at its best as long as it actually happened, or if they just had a UX specialist available. It seems there are problems with availability of UX resources.

In contrast, unsuccessful cooperation (Figure 5) is conducted too late (26.7%), there is too little or no communication (18.3%), or the design the UX team delivers is unsuitable or not implementable (18.3%). Unclear responsibilities or disagreement on who can make decisions hinders cooperation (13.3%). Too little communication between organizational units may lead to such non-Agile practices as working separately and communicating ready-made work between units (e.g. between UX and R&D). In general, more agile approach for UX work was hoped for (H1, H2, H3, H4, H7, H8, H9, H10, H13).

Participants from R&D generally wished for more face-to-face time with the UX team (Figure 6), as observed both in the survey and interviews. Synchronizing R&D and UX work was seen as a major problem as UX and R&D frequently work on different schedules. Interviewees from R&D mentioned getting contributions from the UX team (e.g., for design) takes too much time. In addition, UX and R&D should cooperate more frequently in an iterative manner. The interviewed architects hoped that architecture and UX design could be done in iterative cooperation.

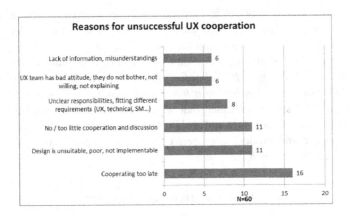

Fig. 5. Unsuccessful UX cooperation happens too late (open-ended question)

Often developers are introduced to the design only when implementation starts. Typically, product management outlines the first draft of a concept, and often the UX team is involved, whereas a development team usually joins the work later. *"When the development team gets involved, they just say 'no!' We should have discussed earlier."* Similar problems occur when product management makes first drafts with developers and without UX team, *"Sometimes all parties are involved (from the beginning), but sometimes product managers work directly with developers and we (UX team) are like 'no,no,no! UX suffers'."* Interviewees described there is no guidance on cooperation available; individual product managers decide if they want to include UX issues, and UX work can be easily cut out (H1,H3, H5, H6, H10, H12).

106   K. Kuusinen, T. Mikkonen, and S. Pakarinen

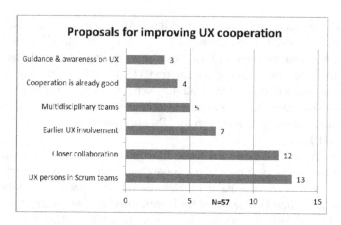

Fig. 6. Respondents hoped for more constant and frequent cooperation with UX specialists (open-ended question)

In many cases, architecture designs are made without feedback from the UX team and architects have to "guess" how it should be: *"It's better to have some UX input before final design."* Interviewees said that the UX team gives feedback on ready-made architecture design and says that this should have been done differently. The same occurs with UX design: *"It kind of feels that we just get some ready-made (UX) design at some point and this is how it looks, and there's no chance to affect that."* Both interviews and survey indicated that when there are incompatibilities between UX and architectural design, UX and architects discuss changes to architecture with the product owner and product manager. Changes are made if there is time, but usually architecture stays as it is.

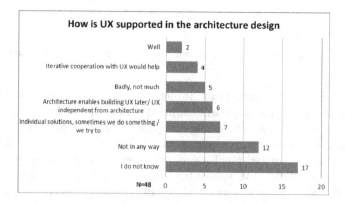

Fig. 7. UX is not present in architecture design (open-ended question)

Architecture may be designed without the UX team's contribution even in those cases where contribution would be needed. Over third of survey respondents (35.4%) did not know how UX is supported in architecture design (Figure 7). One fourth

(25.0%) of respondents say it is supported minimally or not at all; 14.5% describe their own informal solution; 12.5% believe good architecture enables building good UX later on or that UX is not affected by architecture; and 8.3% hope to have iterative cooperation between UX specialists and architects in the future.

There are no commonly agreed-upon practices in, for example, communicating design or documenting user requirements. Depending on the development team, the UX team may deliver design e.g. as wireframes or highly detailed Photoshop images. Again, at worst, ready-made UX designs may be communicated via email to developers. User requirements may be communicated as user stories or use cases (34,5%), or by various other means. Of the survey respondents, 54.5% told user requirements are documented informally, poorly, or not at all. Interviewed architects and developers hoped user requirements would be incorporated and explained in user stories. Interviewed UX specialists told they would prefer doing wireframe that developers would complete by following the style guide. Doing detailed Photoshop images was seen as waste of time since the details can be seen from the style guide. However, currently it is not ensured that UX will be implemented according to the style guide, or as designed. The interviewed UX specialists hoped that developers or quality assurance would ensure the UX implementation.

6   Discussion

In general, the company had a functioning and competent UX team with established practices. However, the company had divergent ways of working, and UX work was not included in the development process and practicalities sufficiently enough. There were many unofficial practices concerning UX work. Individuals could have made their own decisions whether to follow those practices in their work. Especially decisions made by individual product managers and product owners had a significant effect on the impact of UX work in the company.

Currently, UX specialists had an iterative way of working where they did the design work based on an existing product backlog. They were rarely involved before the PB was created. In some cases UX specialists had some design upfront time. But regularly they also had to start the design work only after implementation work had been started, which they considered stressful. UX design was communicated to developers with various methods depending on developers and the skills of the UX specialist. The UX team also had the role of quality assurance in UX issues as no one else ensured that implementation follows the style guide or the UX design. One explaining issue might be that half of the quality engineers who participated in the survey considered their expertise in UX issues low.

6.1   Identified Problems and Potential Solutions

Table 4 presents problems the organization had with UX issues and suggests solutions to fix those. The solutions are based on related work and the development and business models utilized in the organization. Thus, suggestions from literature are compounded with the present state of the organization. The organization used the suggested solutions to evolve their current practices and to create new better ones. Mainly, the issues presented in the table are due to unclear practices and responsibilities, and the service-organization approach that was prevalent in the company. The organization already has a functioning and efficient UX team; the majority of UX work already leads to a good outcome. These practices are part of continuous improvement activities and a means to further systematize UX work.

Table 4. Suggestions for observed UX challenges

Problem	Solution
UX work is started too late	UX specialist involving roadmap concept creation and UX related decisions (early involvement suggested by e.g. [4, 8, 10, 25])
UX design does not match architecture design	Both UX and architecture design made iteratively with both disciplines involved [4, 22]
Developers misunderstand design, UX team does not notice technical limitations	A developer participating in UX design [4, 22]. The participating developer as the first contact person for other developers
UX specialists have to hurry with design	Design made in UX sprints with the help of an architect or developer [4, 22], one sprint ahead of development [4, 10, 21, 27]. Some design upfront [11, 25]
UX design is not ensured during development	Acceptance criteria for UX issues; team owns UX implementation, PO or quality engineer approves [22]
UX work is bypassed because of tight timeline	Criteria for minimum/desired UX at project start [30]
UX elements dropped arbitrarily during implementation	Plan for minimum UX design realization; essential and optional parts or solutions [29]. Power of decision for UX people [6, 11]
UX team doing lots of reactive work	UX team involved earlier [4, 8, 10, 25]. UX specialist involved in decisions when and where UX work is needed [6, 11]. UX team not a service organization [19]

6.2   Implementing Results in the Organization

A workshop reviewing the study results was arranged in the company after the study period during fall 2011. The 14 participants were from different areas of product development, both from R&D and outside of it (3 product owners, 2 architects, a scrum master, a quality engineer, 3 product managers, 3 UX specialists, and a director responsible of R&D methods). The workshop aimed at generating ideas for concrete actions that could be taken to improve the current situation. The participants worked in three groups of four to five persons, and they were instructed to create seven realizable ideas and select three of them to present to others. All the groups wanted to ensure that UX design is realized during development, and therefore suggestions were limited to seven. Finally, the presented ideas were ranked by voting. The ranked actions were as follows:

1. Product Backlog items will be groomed for UX before development starts.
2. Product, architecture and UX roadmaps will be synchronized regularly.
3. UX target will be set in the beginning.
4. Release UX quality will be fast-checked during development.
5. Design version control will be improved.
6. UX resources will be increased.
7. UX stakeholder will be in action during project.

Later, a UX review method was implemented in the official development process. With help of others, the UX team created the method to tackle the most severe issues found in the study presented in this paper: The company started a monthly practice where a user study is arranged to examine a selected feature or product. The participant roles are usually two UX specialists, UX manager, a product manager, a product owner, an architect or developer, and a user. The user has pre-defined tasks to perform, and the others are observing and making notes of certain issues. After the user test part of the meeting, the test is revisited task by task and everyone marks on a whiteboard the biggest flaw they observed. The observations are discussed and ordered. The product owner and architect or developer orders the list by business value and developer effort. The product owner selects how many of the list items they can commit to within the next release cycle. The first experiences of the method show that the method helps to reveal UX flaws and increases the participants' understanding of UX. However, the fixed release plans strongly limit the agility of R&D. In one UX review meeting that a researcher was observing during spring 2012, the product owner said they are able to welcome none of the items to the product backlog since they are already too busy with the release.

7   Summary and Conclusions

In the study described in this paper, we conducted a present state analysis concentrating on UX within Agile software development in a large software organization.

76 employees participated in a large, mainly qualitative survey and 13 persons with different work roles were interviewed. The data were analyzed with a qualitative content analysis method, and with SPSS. Results were divided into categories based on the survey structure, that is, into process, cooperation, and understanding of UX. Another category, the UX team, was generated during analysis mainly to describe the team's current working mode and position in the organization.

The organization is advanced both in Scrum and UX work; they have a competent UX team and knowledge about both Agile and UX development is at high-level in the organization. However, the organization has a separate product management (including the UX team) which operates by yearly and quarter plans, and R&D which follows Scrum. Differences in schedules and ways of working make cooperation more challenging. The most pervasive challenges were related to communication problems, too late UX work, and issues in power relations and in areas of responsibility.

Communication issues, caused mostly by too little face-to-face time, led into misunderstandings and time wasting. UX specialists' insufficient power of decision enabled e.g. product owner, product manager or development team to cut out UX issues generally at any point. Responsibility issues seem to be common in Agile UX as the role of UX specialists is unclear in many cases.

The results are not conclusive in the sense that they are to a great extent addressing organizational rather than methodological issues. Consequently further research in this field is needed in order to refine Agile methodologies to better support UX related issues.

Acknowledgment. We want to thank all the participants of the study: the interviewees and survey respondents, and persons who read this paper and gave their valuable comments. In particular, special thanks go to our contact person in the company for the commitment to our study. Finally, the financial support of the Finnish Funding Agency for Technology and Innovation (TEKES) is gratefully acknowledged.

References

1. Agile Alliance. Manifesto for Agile Software (2001),
   http://agilemanifesto.org
2. Beyer, H., Holtzblatt, K.: Contextual Design: Defining Customer-Centered Systems. Morgan Kaufmann (1998)
3. Boivie, I., Gulliksen, J., Göransson, B.: The lonesome cowboy: A study of the usability designer role in systems development. IWC 18(4), 601–634 (2006)
4. Budwig, M., Jeong, S., Kelkar, K.: When Usability met Agile: A case study. In: Proc. of the 27th International Conference Extended Abstracts on Human Factors in Computing Systems (CHI EA 2009), pp. 3075–3084. ACM (2009)
5. Bygstad, B., Ghinea, G., Brevik, E.: Software development methods and usability: Perspectives from a survey in the software industry in Norway. Interacting with Computers 20(3), 375–385 (2008)
6. Chamberlain, S., Sharp, H., Maiden, N.: Towards a Framework for Integrating Agile Development and User-Centred Design. In: Abrahamsson, P., Marchesi, M., Succi, G. (eds.) XP 2006. LNCS, vol. 4044, pp. 143–153. Springer, Heidelberg (2006)
7. Chow, T., Cao, D.B.: A survey study of critical success factors in Agile software projects. Journal of Systems and Software 81(16), 961–971 (2008)
8. Coplien, J.O., Bjørnvig, G.: Lean Architecture: For Agile Software Development, 376 pages. John Wiley and Sons (2011)
9. Earthy, J.: Usability maturity model: Processes (1999),
   http://www.idemployee.id.tue.nl/g.w.m.rauterberg/
   lecturenotes/Usability-Maturity-Model[2].pdf
10. Federoff, M., Courage, C.: Successful User Experience in an Agile Enterprise Environment. In: Smith, M.J., Salvendy, G. (eds.) HCII 2009, Part I. LNCS, vol. 5617, pp. 233–242. Springer, Heidelberg (2009)
11. Ferreira, J., Aumann, Y., Biddle, R.: Up-Front Interaction Design in Agile Development. In: Concas, G., Damiani, E., Scotto, M., Succi, G. (eds.) XP 2007. LNCS, vol. 4536, pp. 9–16. Springer, Heidelberg (2007)

12. Ferreira, J., Sharp, H., Robinson, H.: User experience design and Agile development: Managing cooperation through articulation work. Software Practice and Experience 41(9), 963–974 (2011)

13. Fox, D., Sillito, J., Maurer, F.: Agile methods and user-centered design: How these two methodologies are being successfully integrated in industry. In: Proc. AGILE 2008 Conference, pp. 63–72. IEEE Press (2008)

14. Hussain, Z., Slany, W., Holzinger, A.: Current State of Agile User-Centered Design: A Survey. In: Holzinger, A., Miesenberger, K. (eds.) USAB 2009. LNCS, vol. 5889, pp. 416–427. Springer, Heidelberg (2009)

15. Innes, J.: Why Enterprises Can't Innovate: Helping Companies Learn Design Thinking. In: Marcus, A. (ed.) HCII 2011, Part I. LNCS, vol. 6769, pp. 442–448. Springer, Heidelberg (2011)

16. ISO 9241-210:2010. Ergonomics of human-system interaction. Part 210: Human-centered design for interactive systems (2010)

17. Kuusinen, K., Väänänen-Vainio-Mattila, K.: How to Make Agile UX Work More Efficient: Management and Sales Perspectives. Accepted to NordiCHI (2012)

18. Lazar, J., Feng, H.F., Hochheiser, H.: Research Methods in Human-Computer Interaction. John Wiley and Sons (2010)

19. Lund, A.M.: Creating a user-centered development culture. Interactions 17(3), 34–38 (2010)

20. Marcus, A., Ashley, J., Knapheide, C., Lund, A., Rosenberg, D., Vredenburg, K.: A Survey of User-Experience Development at Enterprise Software Companies. In: Kurosu, M. (ed.) HCD 2009. LNCS, vol. 5619, pp. 601–610. Springer, Heidelberg (2009)

21. Miller, L.: Case Study of Customer Input for a Successful Product. In: Proc. of AGILE 2005, Agile Alliance (2005)

22. Petrovic, K., Siegmann, M.: Make Space for the Customer: The Shift towards Customer Centricity. In: Marcus, A. (ed.) HCII 2011, Part I. LNCS, vol. 6769, pp. 485–490. Springer, Heidelberg (2011)

23. Runeson, P., Höst, M.: Guidelines for conducting and reporting case study research in software engineering. In: Empirical Software Engineering, vol. 14(2) (2009)

24. Scrum Alliance, http://scrumalliance.org/

25. da Silva, T.S., Martin, A., Maurer, F., Silveira, M.: User-centered design and Agile methods: a systematic review. In: Proc. of the International Conference on Agile Methods in Software Development, AGILE 2011 (2011)

26. Sutherland, J., Schwaber, K.: The scrum papers: Nut, bolts, and origins of an Agile framework (2011), http://jeffsutherland.com/ScrumPapers.pdf

27. Sy, D.: Adapting usability investigations for Agile user-centered design. Journal of Usability Studies 2(3), 112–132 (2007)

28. Venturi, G., Troost, J.: Survey on User Centred Design integration in the industry. In: Proc. of the Third Nordic Conference on Human-Computer Interaction. ACM International Conference Proceeding Series, vol. 82 (2004)

29. Venturi, G., Troost, J., Jokela, T.: People, organizations, and processes: An inquiry into the adoption of user-centered design in industry. International Journal of Human Computer Interaction 21(2) (2006)

30. Viikki, K., Palvainen, J.: Integrating Human-Centered Design into Software Development - An Action Research Study in Automation Industry. In: Proc. of (SEAA 2011). IEEE Computer Society (2011)

31. Zhou, R., Huang, S., Qin, X., Huang, J.: A survey of user-centered design practice in China. In: IEEE International Conference on Systems, Man and Cybernetics, pp. 1885–1889 (2008)

Can GUI Implementation Markup Languages Be Used for Modelling?

Carlos Eduardo Silva and José Creissac Campos

Departamento de Informática, Universidade do Minho & HASLab, INESC TEC
Braga, Portugal
{cems,jose.campos}@di.uminho.pt

Abstract. The current diversity of available devices and form factors increases the need for model-based techniques to support adapting applications from one device to another. Most work on user interface modelling is built around declarative markup languages. Markup languages play a relevant role, not only in the modelling of user interfaces, but also in their implementation. However, the languages used by each community (modellers/developers) have, to a great extent evolved separately. This means that the step from concrete model to final interface becomes needlessly complicated, requiring either compilers or interpreters to bridge this gap. In this paper we compare a modelling language (UsiXML) with several markup implementation languages. We analyse if it is feasible to use the implementation languages as modelling languages.

Keywords: User Interfaces, Modelling, Markup languages.

1 Introduction

With the current plethora of available devices, applications need to migrate and adapt between those different devices. This is particularly the case for Web applications, which might be run in a diversity of browsers and form factors. We are particularly interested in the possibility of automatically performing the adaptation of user interfaces (UI). For example, in the context of interactive kiosks or public screens.

Model-based User Interface Development (MBUID) is a basis for the solution to this problem. Models (and model transformations) provide a means to both, reason about the design of the user interface, independently from concrete implementation details, and to refine the models to concrete user interfaces. Work in MBUID is based on the existence of adequate modelling languages, known as User Interface Description Languages (UIDLs) [1,2]. A typical UIDL will support describing an interface at several levels of abstraction, and performing transformations between those levels. The Cameleon Reference Framework for model-based development of multi-target user interfaces [3] identifies four such levels:

M. Winckler, P. Forbrig, and R. Bernhaupt (Eds.): HCSE 2012, LNCS 7623, pp. 112–129, 2012.

- Concepts and Task model — describes the tasks to be performed and the entities users manipulate in their fulfilment;
- Abstract User Interface (AUI) — describes the UI independently of any concrete interaction modality and computing platform;
- Concrete User Interface (CUI) — describes an instantiation of the AUI for a concrete set of interaction modalities;
- Final User Interface (FUI) — corresponds to the UI that is running on a computing platform either by being executed or interpreted.

A diversity of UIDLs has been proposed over the years, using different language paradigms, and covering a variety of applications areas and interaction styles. In [2] a number of proposals is described, with foci as diverse as user interfaces for safety critical systems [4], tangible interaction [5], or 3D user interfaces [6]. Notations used are a mix of textual markup languages and graphical notations. Markup languages, in particular, have gained considerable popularity (see [1] for a survey). Relevant languages in this category include: UIML, which supports both device independent and modality independent UI descriptions [7]; XIML, currently in development by Redwhale Software [8]; MariaXML, the successor of TeresaXML, supports Rich Internet Applications (RIAs), multi-target user interfaces, and applications based on the use of Web services [9]; and UsiXML, a UIDL that aims to cover all aspects of a user interface, for instance, portability, device independence, multi-platform support, amongst others [10]. Moreover, UsiXML is structured according to the Cameleon reference framework.

Typically these languages will cover some or all the abstraction levels in MBUID, from the Concepts and Task to the CUI models. The FUI will be obtained either by interpretation of the CUI models, or by compilation into some target implementation language. Since the interpreters are themselves developed in some specific implementation technology, FUIs are in any case expressed in a different technology from the more abstract models.

Implementation languages, however, have also been evolving from the typical imperative languages like C or Java into declarative markup languages such as HTML or XAML. Although markup languages are usually associated with Web applications, other platforms are also adopting them, for example, Android.

Implementation technologies are therefore moving towards solutions that are closer to what is used for modelling. This begs the question of whether a clear separation between modelling and implementation languages still exists, or whether it will be possible to bridge the gap between a FUI and its models. Hence, in this paper we analyse the feasibility of using declarative markup implementation languages at higher levels of abstraction for MBUID.

In order to carry out this analysis, we will compare UsiXML against a number of implementation languages. UsiXML was choosen since it follows the Cameleon Reference Framework. The implementation languages we chose to analyse are: MXML (Flex), XAML (Silverlight) and HTML5 (three of the most used languages in Web applications development); Android XML (to cover mobile applications); and the LZX Markup language from OpenLaszlo, an industry framework that generates Flash and HTML.

The remainder of the paper is structures as follows: Section 2 presents an overview of the different markup languages we are analysing in this paper. Section 3 compares the different languages. Section 4 presents a case study with the markup languages. The paper ends with discussion and conclusions in Section 5.

2   Markup Languages Overview

Markup languages are declarative languages, where the code is written in the form of annotations called tags. Building UIs with declarative languages is a paradigm shift when comparing to imperative languages. Instead of defining how to build the interface, we define what the interface is. For example, in order to build, imperatively, a UI with a window and a button, we would first build a window, then build a button, and afterwards define that the button is inside the window. Building the same UI declaratively we would define a window, and a button inside the hierarchy of the window. Another aspect that made these languages prosper is their easier understandability, especially by non programmers.

This section presents an overview of each of the markup languages chosen for this analysis: UsiXML, MXML, XAML, HTML5, Android XML and LZX. These are all XML-based markup languages, providing tags for describing different input/output controls (buttons, labels, input fields, etc.) and containers, supporting the definition of a UI in terms of the components that it contains. Usually they will be associated with some technological framework, responsible for rendering the interface and for more advanced features such as expressing behaviour (typically through a scripting language). Since some of these markup languages have more than one technology available to create the UI, we chose one of them to analyse. For example, for XAML we considered Silverlight.

2.1   Modelling Languages — UsiXML

The USer Interface eXtensible Markup Language (UsiXML) [10] is a UIDL that supports the description of user interfaces at the different levels of abstraction identified in the Cameleon reference framework. In particular, it supports the creation of domain models, task models, AUI models and CUI models.

The language supports multi-context and multi-target UI development through transformations either between abstraction levels (reification/abstraction), or through changes of context at the same abstraction level. The notion of context is dependent on the specific details of a given development, but might include the users, the technological platform, and/or the environment in which the interaction takes place.

Available tags change between the different models, as their concepts are different. For example, a control tag in a AUI model might correspond to a button tag in a CUI model.

2.2   Implementation Technologies

MXML (Adobe Flex). In 2004 Macromedia introduced its framework to develop RIAs, named Flex. Flex can be seen as a developer driven framework to produce Flash content. Flex applications produce as output Flash files (*.swf*) and thus run just like Flash applications. In November 2011, Flex became open-source as Adobe donated it to the Apache Software Foundation.

Flex is composed of a scripting language (ActionScript) and of an XML markup Language (MXML). Their relationship is similar to the relationship between JavaScript and HTML. MXML contains the tags expected of an implementation declarative language.

XAML (Silverlight). In order to merge the benefits of the Windows Presentation Foundation (WPF), Microsoft's desktop application user interface framework, with the RIAs' benefits, Microsoft developed Silverlight. It brings applications similar to the ones developed in WPF to all major platforms through their Web browsers. Silverlight applications run in an ActiveX browser plug-in that is installed in the local machine similarly to the Flash plug-in to run Flash based applications.

The user interface is written in a markup language called eXtensible Application Markup Language (XAML). XAML, although originally developed for WPF, was also adopted as the user interface modelling language of Silverlight and Windows 8 Metro interfaces. XAML has tags for the most common widgets in UI development.

HTML5. HTML5 is the fifth major revision of HTML, the main language of the Word Wide Web. It succeeds the previous version (HTML4), which became a W3C Recommendation in 1997, and aims to improve over that version in order to enable more complex Web pages to be built.

Despite the fact that the HTML5 specification is still under development, the language has gained increased acceptance and support. One of the major driving factors behind its development and acceptance was the increase in the Internet quota of mobile phones.

New features in HTML5 include:

- New semantic elements to better describe a Web page (such as: *nav*, *aside*, *section*, *article*, *header*, and *footer*), in order to diminish the use of the generic *div* tag.
- New multimedia tags have been added, *audio* and *video*, replacing the *object* tag. These tags enable the quick integration of videos from other resources into a Web page. Moreover, multimedia can now be set to preload or to autoplay and can also have integrated controls.
- New attributes were added. For example, the *draggable* and *dropzone* attributes enable support for native drag-and-drop functionality. Another new attribute is *hidden* indicating that the element is not yet/no longer relevant.
- The *canvas* tag was added, which supports bitmap graphics. Most browsers currently support 2D canvas, but there are some experimental builds with 3D canvas support.

Android XML. Android is an Open Source platform (Apache License) targeting mobile devices. It is released by Google under the Open Handset Alliance and is based on the GNU/Linux operating system. Android applications are written in the Java programming language. However, instead of using the Java Virtual Machine (JVM), Android uses the Dalvik Virtual Machine, which is optimized for mobile devices.

Unlike the other languages analysed in this document, which require a markup language to develop the UI, or other languages in which the UI is built programmatically, Android allows the UI to be built both ways. The use of markup for development is recommended since it has the advantage of separating presentation from behaviour, thus making the user interface implementation easier to understand. Nevertheless, it is always possible, even for interfaces defined via markup, to build interface objects programmatically at runtime.

OpenLaszlo (LZX). OpenLaszlo is an Open Source platform which enables the development of interfaces using a specific markup language called LZX. It can then generate applications in either Flash or HTML. The goal is to, in the future, enable the platform to produce applications in other languages, for example, Silverlight. Thus, a user interface description in LZX can be seen as a CUI. This makes it relevant to compare it with UsiXML since in both cases concrete languages are intend to be used as a basis to generate UI description in other languages.

The LZX language is an XML-based language, with JavaScript as the scripting language. It was developed to be similar to HTML and JavaScript. However, the declarative language includes some object-oriented programming features such as: inheritance; encapsulation; and polymorphism. Therefore, LZX can have objects, attributes, events and methods like any object-oriented programming language. Moreover, LZX eases data manipulation by allowing data binding to XML elements.

3   Comparing the Languages

When comparing the languages, we were interested in assessing to what level the implementation languages provide features that are similar to the modelling language in question. The goal was not to assess the quality of each language *per se*, but to compare their expressive power and usefulness.

With this goal in mind, two orthogonal dimensions can be considered: the level of abstraction at which it is possible to use a language, and the coverage provided by the language for modelling the different architectural layers of a user interface (Presentation, Dialogue and Functional core — cf. the Arch/Slinky model [11]). Additionally, from a more practical perspective, we were interested in analysing the technological availability and applicability of the languages.

Regarding the level of abstraction, by definition UsiXML covers all levels, while the implementation languages are used to develop actual user interfaces.

For the current analysis we will mainly focus on the CUI level. The most obvious candidate for an intersection between the two worlds.

Regarding user interface layers, markup languages are typically used to describe structure. In this case, the presentation layer. Hence, that will be the focus of the analysis. Nevertheless, we mention other aspects where relevant. In particular, support for expressing behaviour. Hence, in comparing the languages the following criteria were considered:

- Behaviour: This criterion captures the different actions that can be performed using the declarative language only, with no scripting involved.
- Style: This criterion defines the type of styling associated with the technology.
- Vector graphics: In the last few years, the availability of a canvas to enable drawing vector graphics has become increasingly important.
- Tags: A comparison of the tags available in each language, taking UsiXML as the reference. The tags we chose to analyse were the ones present in the CUI examples of the FlashiXML tool (a UI renderer for UsiXML).

Regarding technological availability and applicability we choose to consider:

- License type: Depicts the accessibility of the technology.
- Tools: This criterion considers the different tools associated with the languages.
- Targets: These technologies can be available in a single or in several platforms.

Table 1 compares the different languages according to these criteria.

In terms of license, although some of these technologies started as proprietary software, currently the only proprietary one is Silverlight. The tools criterion is the one that differs most from language to language. The only language that simply requires a Web browser to run is HTML5. Flex and Silverlight both require a plug-in to be installed. UsiXML and LZX have tools that either compile the models to other languages, or perform runtime interpretation and rendering. Target technologies include Flash and DHTML in the case of LZX; and Flash (FlashiXML [12]), Flex (FlexiXML [13]), OpenLaszlo (UsiXML2OpenLaszlo), Tcl/Tk (QTKiXML [14]), and Java (InterpiXML [15]), amongst others, in the case of UsiXML. Android applications are the only ones that do not run as, or compile to, Web applications, they run in the Android OS. Therefore, Android is the only analysed technology that is single platform.

Regarding styling capabilities, all the technologies either have CSS styling, or a specific styling done exclusively using markup. UsiXML has a *stylesheet* tag in its specification. There are tools, such as FlexiXML that support CSS for styling. However, the tool we used, FlashiXML does not support styles. All the languages analysed had Vector graphics support.

Table 1. Markup Languages Comparison

Languages	UsiXML	Flex	Silverlight	HTML5	Android	LZX
License	OpenSource	OpenSource	Proprietary	OpenSource	OpenSource	OpenSource
Tools	Interpreters and compilers	Flash plug-in	Silverlight plug-in	Web Browser	Android OS	Compiles Flash and DHTML
Targets	Multiplatform	Multiplatform	Multiplatform	Multiplatform	Singleplatform	Multiplatform
Behaviour	Multimedia, Transitions	Multimedia	Multimedia	Multimedia	Multimedia	Multimedia
Styles	Stylesheet	CSS	Markup	CSS	Markup	CSS
Vector Graphics	Yes	Yes	Yes	Yes	Yes	Yes
Tags	box	Group	StackPanel	div	LinearLayout	view
	gridBagBox	Grid	Grid	table	TableLayout	grid
	textComponent	Label	TextBlock	label	TextView	text
	output:Text	Label	Label	label	TextView	text
	input:Text	TextInput	TextBox	input type="text"	EditTex	edittext
	imageComponent	Image	Image	img	ImageView	image
	comboBox	ComboBox	ComboBox	select	Spinner	combobox
	item		ComboBoxItem	option	item	textlistitem
	button	Button	Button	button	Button	button
	radioButton	RadioButton	RadioButton	input type="radio"	RadioButton	radiobutton
	behavior					
	event					
	action					
	methodCall					
	methodCallParam					
	transition					
	graphicalTransition					

Regarding supported tags, the first conclusion when looking at Table 1 is that, unlike UsiXML, the implementation markup languages are not prepared to handle behaviour tags. They handle behaviour by using a non-markup scripting language. On the contrary, UsiXML does not have an associated scripting language. However, UsiXML's behaviour tags handle basic generic behaviour situations, like window transitions, only. Therefore, if more complex behaviour is needed, it falls to the developer of the interpreter or compiler to choose whether or not to support a scripting language. For example, FlashiXML uses Action-Script as the scripting language.

Moreover, the layout tags are the ones that are prone to having most differences between the languages. Languages like HTML do most layout by using CSS, while other languages have styling options and different layout options. For instance, Android has tags for Linear Layout, Relative Layout, Table Layout, Grid View, Tab Layout and List View.

Aside from the behaviour tags, all other tags have correspondence between the markup languages. The only exception is the *item* tag in Flex, which handles *comboboxes* by binding to data collections only, and does not allow the explicit declaration of single items. Therefore, we can do a direct and easy translation between the different markup languages. Such translation would also need to have in consideration the different attributes of the tags.

However, the translation between the languages is not always unidirectional. For instance, the *box* tag in UsiXML corresponds better to the *div* tag in HTML5. Nevertheless there are other tags, specifically since HTML version 5, that also correspond to a box in UsiXML but have specific semantic meanings such as the *nav*, *aside*, *section*, *article*, *header*, and *footer* tags.

Moreover, some tags can be changed according to the styling they are given. For example, the *span* tag in HTML5 is an inline element whereas a *div* tag is a block-level element. By changing the styling, we can have a *span* tag behaving as a *div* tag and vice-versa. This aspect is quite difficult to address in these languages translation.

4 Case Study

Since in theory the translation seemed to be feasible, we decided to investigate the issue further by developing a small example application in each of the languages. The goal was to evaluate the markup languages' strengths and weaknesses through a case study. The example application simulates a Web store that sells CDs, called Music Store, and is based on a similar application from the FlashiXML examples suite. The customer is able to add CDs to a shopping cart, by selecting them from a list of available CDs, and afterwards fill his/hers personal details to buy the chosen CDs.

The application is composed of two main frames (see Figure 1). The initial frame (*Shop Frame*), depicted in Figure 1-a), comprises a list of the albums in the music store (left), and a basket (another list) to keep track of the customer's selected items (right). Each album has a preview button which enables a small

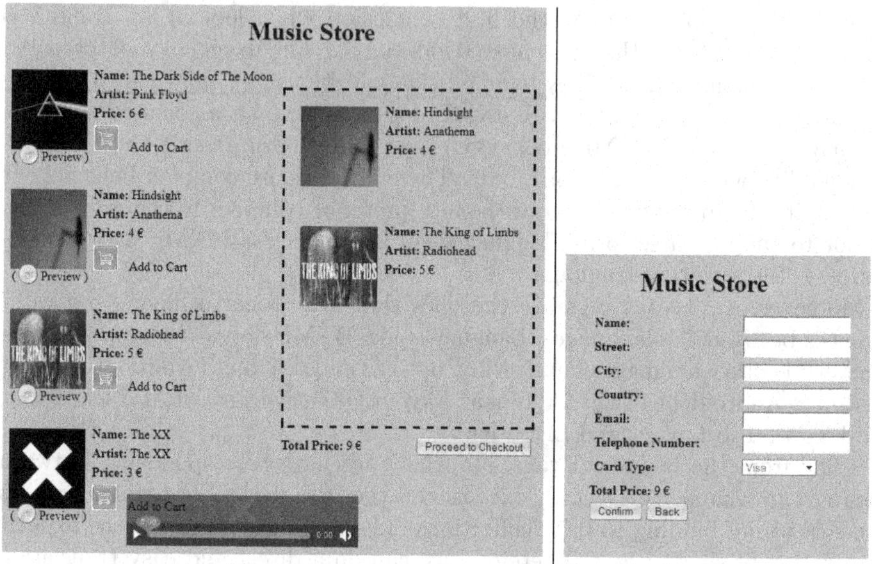

a) Shop frame   b) Checkout frame

Fig. 1. Music Store Application

preview of the album to be played. The customer can buy an album either by clicking on the *"Add to Cart"* button next to the album, or by dragging and dropping the album cover into the basket area. When an album is added to the basket, the total value of the shopping cart is updated accordingly.

Once the desired alguns have been selected, the customer can move on to *Checkout* by clicking on the *"Proceed to Checkout"* button. This button replaces the *Shop* frame with the *Checkout* frame, depicted in Figure 1-b).

The *Checkout* frame comprises several text boxes and a listbox, which enable customers to fill in their details, specifically, the name, address and credit card type. Afterwards, the user can confirm the transaction or go back to the previous frame, where he can rebuild the basket list again.

The application screen size is kept small so that the example can also cover mobile applications. This is relevant because we are considering Android XML, which is used for applications running on smartphones and tablets.

With this example we intend to analyse both the languages' capabilities in the context of developing traditional Web applications, with buttons and forms to interact with the user, but also some more advanced RIAs features. RIAs, in comparison to traditional Web applications, present a number of improvements: no page refreshing; shorter response times; drag-and-drop capabilities; multimedia animations. From these improvements, we chose to implement in our application two frames without page refreshing, drag-and-drop, and multimedia, by allowing previewing an album by playing a small audio sample. Next we will present the main aspects that differ in building the application for each language.

4.1 UsiXML

Regarding UsiXML, we developed a CUI model, taking as a basis the original Music Store application. The final user interface will have to be generated using an appropriate renderer. In this case, we chose to use FlashiXML.

UsiXML has several types of layouts for CUI modelling, such as: *box*, *group-Box*, *flowBox*, *gridBox*, *gridBagBox*, and *listBox*. However, the FlashiXML renderer seems to work with only a few of them, therefore, we built the entire application with the *box* tag. This tag is flexible since it has an attribute called type that defines the orientation of the child elements.

FlashiXML cannot handle styling, which is aggravated as in this language every element requires quite a few attributes. For example, the labels for the name and street in the *Checkout* frame were coded as follows:

```
<textComponent id="name" defaultContent="Name:" width="100"
    height="25" borderWidth="0" fgColor="000000" isBold="true"
    textSize="16" textHorizontalAlign="right" numberOfLines="1"/>
<textComponent id="address" defaultContent="Street:" width="100"
    height="25" borderWidth="0" fgColor="000000" isBold="true"
    textSize="16" textHorizontalAlign="right" numberOfLines="1"/>
```

By looking at the code it is noticeable that style sheets would make a significant impact in the coding. Moreover, the same pattern is repeated throughout the whole application.

In terms of behaviour, UsiXML does not have tags for drag-and-drop. Therefore, the drag-and-drop was implemented entirely using ActionScript. The transition between the *Shop* frame and the *Checkout* frame, however, was entirely implemented through the declarative language, as depicted in the following code (that models the *Checkout* button in the *Shop* frame):

```
<button width="100" height="25" isEnabled="true" isVisible="true"
    defaultContent="Checkout" id="button_go" name="button_go">
    <behavior id="behavI8">
        <event id="evtI8" eventType="depress" eventContext="button_go"/>
        <action id="actI8">
            <transition transitionIdRef="Tr1"/>
            <transition transitionIdRef="Tr2"/>
            <transition transitionIdRef="Tr3"/>
            <transition transitionIdRef="Tr4"/>
        </action>
    </behavior>
</button>
```

Four transitions are used (see the *transition* tags): Tr1 and Tr2 are fade-out transitions (of the *Shop* frame and of the background) and TR3 and TR4 are fade-in transitions (of the *Checkout* frame and of the new background). These transitions are defined elsewhere in the model.

Another issue is that UsiXML has a *videoComponent* tag but not a *audioComponent* one. Thus, we assumed that like some other languages, the *videoComponent* is used in both cases. Nevertheless, the tag was not tested since

FlashiXML does not handle these components. A possibility to add multimedia in FlashiXML is to use ActionScript to do the entire process. However, in that case we are relying in a specific implementation technology. Arguably, we would have something closer to a FUI.

4.2 MXML (Flex)

In Flex layout is defined using containers: *Group* behaves like a simple box, *HGroup* arranges the elements horizontally, and *VGroup* arranges the elements vertically. Elements can also be arranged according to relative or absolute coordinates. The code bellow shows the coding of the two labels and the button below the drop area in the *Shop*.

```
<s:HGroup x="444" y="491">
    <s:Label  text="Total Price" styleName="labelS"/>
    <s:Label  id="totP" text="0 €" styleName="labelT"/>
</s:HGroup>
<s:Button x="578" y="486" label="Proceed to Checkout"
          click="button1_clickHandler(event)"/>
```

In terms of multimedia elements, these can be handled with tags if using the Flash library which has a *Sound* and a *Video* tag for audio and video respectively. Drag-and-drop is supported exclusively through ActionScript.

4.3 XAML (Silverlight)

Layout design in Silverlight is very flexible. There are built-in layouts like grids, stackpanels or listboxes, but there is also the option of controlling the elements' position by using margin, padding or horizontal and vertical alignments.

Adding multimedia is very straightforward. We add a media element in the XAML, as follows:

```
<MediaElement x:Name="media" AutoPlay="False"
              Source="Sounds/05LotusFlower.mp3" />
```

Afterwards, the event handler uses the following C# code to start playing the audio.

```
media.Position = TimeSpan.Zero;
media.Play();
```

This example also shows that to access a XAML element in C# we just need to invoke his name.

Silverlight drag-and-drop has some disadvantages. For instance, only a few elements can have drag-and-drop action controls. Specifically there are the following controls (the names identify their purpose):

- ListBoxDragDropTarget,
- TreeViewDragDropTarget,
- DataGridDragDropTarget, and
- DataPointSeriesDragDropTarget.

Thus, for an element to be draggable, it has to necessary be a child element of one of the previous layouts. A second option would be to achieve drag-and-drop by manually implement the click handlers. A third option would require the use of an external library called Drag and Drop Manager. In our implementation we chose to use the *ListBoxDragDropTarget* control, as follows:

```
<toolkit:ListBoxDragDropTarget AllowDrop="True"
                               AllowedSourceEffects="Copy">
    <ListBox x:Name="Listbox">
        <StackPanel Name="spPF">
        ...
```

Therefore, every album is a *StackPanel* inside a *Listbox*. A difference between this implementation and the applications from the other languages is that instead of dragging just the image, it is possible to drag anywhere in the album area.

4.4 HTML5

The layout in HTML5 is clearly more difficult to define than in most other languages tested in this document. By using CSS, developing the layout feels less natural than using boxes and predefined layouts.

On the contrary, drag-and-drop is easy to implement in HTML5. Just by adding the *draggable* attribute to an element, that element can be dragged across the application. Nevertheless, in order to define where the elements could be dropped (in this case, the shopping basket) a small amount of JavaScript was required.

The new multimedia tags, in this case the audio tag, are very useful. Just by adding the following code:

```
<audio controls="controls" hidden>
    <source src="sounds/05LotusFlower.ogg" type="audio/ogg"/>
    <source src="sounds/05LotusFlower.mp3" type="audio/mpeg"/>
</audio>
```

the audio file is available in the application, and playback and volume controls are added. The controls are depicted in Figure 1, in the black box at the bottom of the main frame. Controls are browser specific. In this particular case the Firefox browser controls are being shown.

A problem with building an application in HTML is the different browsers' reactions to the same code. Furthermore, with HTML5, the browsers have even more differences. For example, in the previous audio tag, both an *ogg* and an *mp3* file were added, since neither the current version of Opera nor of Firefox play *mp3* files. Moreover, browsers are still updating to add the new HTML elements. For example, in Internet Explorer the *hidden* tag does not set the elements to invisible, thus, both frames and controls appear when the application starts. This is expected to improve with time.

4.5 Android XML

Despite mobile phones' screen sizes being much smaller than a traditional computer's screen, we opted to keep the application exactly the same. To compensate for the screen size, we added vertical scrollbars to navigate up and down the albums list, the shopping basket list, and the entire form in the second frame. Another development decision was to keep the layout as the default Android light layout. The major difference from the applications modelled in the other languages is the form, which now has a different look, more appropriate for mobile systems.

The Android XML seems to be more verbose than all the other markup languages analysed in this document. As an example, a simple label would be defined as follows:

```
<TextView android:id="@+id/nameLabel1"
          android:layout_width="50dp"
          android:layout_height="wrap_content"
          android:text="@string/namelabel" />
```

Another interesting characteristic in Android development is that it encourages keeping an XML file name strings.xml where all the strings should be stored. For instance, the string for the label in the above example (*namelabel*) is stored in that file as follows:

```
<string name="namelabel">Name:</string>
```

This separation between the strings and the actual interface's source code, enables one to easily change the strings' contents in the future.

In terms of multimedia, Android doesn't have a tag for audio. Nevertheless it has a tag for video called *VideoView*.

Drag-and-drop in Android is achieved by using the *setOnTouchListener* method in the elements that should be dragged, and then using the method *startDrag()* to enable the drag. The elements that are expecting drops should implement the *onDragListener*. This listener uses a method called *getAction()* which retrieves the current action of the drag. This action can be whether the drag element has entered or exited the drop area, or whether the drag element has been dropped in the drop area. This last action is the one we are interested in in this particular application.

4.6 LZX

The layout and design process in Laszlo is easy both to accomplish and to learn. The main component is called "*view*" which visually is a rectangular container. Obviously there can be nested views, and they are used to organize the elements on the rendered application. Moreover, application elements can be arranged easily on the page, by using layouts. For instance:

```
<simplelayout axis="x" spacing="6"/>
```

arranges all elements according to the "*x*" axis and with a spacing value of 6 between them. Furthermore, elements can also be placed with relative and absolute positioning like in HTML. Nevertheless, using the boxes for arrangement is more understandable.

OpenLaszlo has a multimedia tag for both audio and video called *videoview*. Moreover, we can also add video and audio as resources of regular views. However, in the current version, multimedia only works when the application is compiled to Flash.

The drag-and-drop of the albums was hard to implement. In Laszlo, we had to implement the methods to start and stop the dragging and also the methods to check if the element where we dropped the image was the correct one. For example, the code for the last method was the following:

```
<method name="droppedInView" args="theView">
    <![CDATA[
        var absX = theView.getAttributeRelative( "x", canvas );
        return (this.x > absX && this.x < absX+theView.width);
    ]]>
</method>
```

The method determines whether the place where an object has been dropped is inside the view sent as a parameter. In this particular case this is calculated by looking at the absolute coordinates of the X axis. The <![CDATA[and]]> tags allow us to write characters that would otherwise not be possible in XML files (for example the '<' and '>' signs).

4.7   Applications' Comparison

After all the applications were built, we analysed them according to a number of metrics. The results are depicted in Table 2. The first criterion was the number of different tags present in each applications. UsiXML is clearly the one with a greater diversity of tags. Nevertheless, that greater number can be related to having behaviour tags also, which can also be seen in Table 1. HTML5's high value is related to this new version featuring new tags to bring more expressiveness to the language.

Table 2. Application Comparison

Languages	UsiXML	Flex	Silverlight	HTML5	Android	LZX
Number of Different Tags	23	14	12	18	12	17
Total Number of XML lines	215	139	182	182	189	187
Total Number of Scripting lines	70	102	128	85	98	33
Total Number of styling lines	0	6	0	93	0	0
Total Number of lines	285	247	310	360	287	220
Percentage of Scripting lines	24,56	41,3	41,29	23,61	34,15	15
Total Number of Tags	141	107	139	106	132	146
Total Number of Attributes	653	236	646	121	572	186

The second criterion defines the total number of XML lines. The two outliers are UsiXML with the biggest number of lines, and Flex with the lowest number.

The third criterion is the total number of scripting lines. In this criterion LZX is clearly the language that requires less scripting. Mostly due to the fact that the scripting code in LZX is greatly embedded with the XML code. For instance, the code for the Back button in the *Checkout frame* is the following:

```
<button onclick="back();">
    Back
    <method name="back">
        shop.setAttribute('visible',true);
        payment.setAttribute('visible',false);
    </method>
</button>
```

This code shows that not only is the script written inside the method tag but also that the elements (shop and payment) are easily invoked and altered.

The forth criterion shows the total number of styling lines. We decided to do styling only when needed. HTML5 is the language that normally requires styling, mostly for layout purposes. It is also interesting to notice that, although such a high number of lines were used in styling, the XML file size is still similar to that of Silverlight, Android and LZX which had no styling in this implementation.

This leads to the fifth criterion, total number of lines, where HTML5 is clearly the one that requires more lines. While LZX and Flex took the least amount of coding.

The percentage of scripting lines criterion show us how much imperative programming we need comparing with the whole application. Both Flex and Silverlight require a high amount of imperative programming comparing with the rest of the technologies analysed.

In terms of the total number of tags, UsiXML and LZX have more tags than the rest. It is interesting to note HTML5's behaviour since it was one of the languages with most XML lines, but is the one with less total number of tags.

The last criterion is the total number of attributes. In this criterion, UsiXML, Silverlight and Android clearly use many more attributes than the other languages. HTML5, although the language with the higher total number of lines, is in this criterion the one with lowest number of attributes, reflecting the styling effect in these metrics.

While the above numbers do not provide a objective measure of quality of the different languages, they are useful in showing that no obvious differences can be seen between the model developed in UsiXML and the applications developed in the other languages. This corroborates our belief that it is possible to use markup implementation languages as modelling languages at (at least) CUI level.

Another important aspect regards which language to choose. For that choice, aspects such as the learnability of the languages are relevant. The Cognitive dimensions of notations proposed by Green and Petre [16] would be useful to make such analysis. That however was not the specific aim of our study. In any case, if we had to choose an implementation language for modelling, LZX and HTML5 look the most promising since when comparing the percentage of scripting lines required they had even better results than UsiXML.

5 Conclusions

In this paper we have compared different declarative GUI implementation languages with a declarative modelling language. The motivation behind the work is the possibility of performing adaptation of web applications' user interfaces to different devices and form factors. Given that the implementation technology has moved towards declarative markup languages, we were interested in analysing the viability of using the interfaces expressed in those languages as models of the user interfaces.

Looking at the results, we see that not all aspects of a user interface can be handled declaratively. In particular, implementation languages are not prepared to handled behaviour declaratively. This limits the specification of the interface we can perform using declarative languages only. To be fair, this is an issue also in terms of the modelling language, as UsiXML provides few behaviour specific tags too (e.g. transitions). In fact markup languages are, in general, geared towards describing the structural aspects of the user interface.

Some of the languages have several tags to define the same concept. Although this increases the expressiveness of the language, it also decreases the level of abstraction of an hypothetical model. For instance, in HTML5 we can have *div*, *nav*, *aside*, *section*, *article*, *header*, and *footer* tags, all corresponding to a box at a higher level of abstraction. Nevertheless, regardless of the lager number of tags in a language, it still falls to the developer the decision to use them or not. Hence, we can think of defining profiles or dialects of the language for CUI (AUI) modelling. It can be decided, for example, that a box should always be modelled by a *div* tag. This will allow us to embed a modelling language inside a implementation language, taking advantage of all the tool support that is available.

This embedding of a modelling language inside an implementation language is particularly relevant when it comes to animating the models. As the analysis has shown, the fact that specific players are needed for modelling languages, raises a number of issues in terms of support for specific languages features and language versions. While this also happens for the implementation languages, the industry and community support behind languages such as HTML means that evolution of those technologies will be much faster. However, it must be noted that regarding aspects as model transformation and context adaptation, the tool support provided by UsiXML related tools will be lost.

Another aspect that might create difficulties, in particular if we consider deploying the models to different languages, relates to managing layout and expressing behaviour. The languages are very different in terms of these aspects. In fact, the amount of layout options differ significantly from language to language, and while they all resort to scripting to express behaviour, the scripting languages used differ. The answer here might be to look for behaviour oriented languages to complement the models with behavioural information.

In terms of limitations of the analysis, it must be recognised that our analysis was focused mainly in CUIs. The capabilities of implementation languages at higher levels of abstraction, like AUIs, requires further consideration. Moreover, our analysis was targeted specifically at graphical user interfaces (i.e. we have not considered what issues might be raised by other interaction technologies such as the use of multimodality). This happens because the notion of context that interests us the most relates to the form factor of the device displaying the interface.

Another aspect is that nowadays a relevant number of Web applications is built dynamically. That is, the markup used to generate the interface is not written directly by the developer. Instead, code is written that generates (or, at least, manipulates) the markup. This means the markup will only be available at run time, which in turn means that we need dynamic code analysis techniques to be able to obtain and transform the user interface.

Hence, as future work we intend to, on the one hand further develop the notion of embedding a modelling language in a implementation language, and on the other hand, study techniques for the dynamic analysis of the interface in order to extract and transform the models.

Acknowledgments. This work is funded by the ERDF – European Regional Development Fund – through Programme COMPETE, and by the Portuguese Government through FCT – Foundation for Science and Technology, project ref. FCOMP-01-0124-FEDER-015095. Carlos Eduardo Silva is further funded by the Portuguese Government through FCT, grant SFRH/BD/71136/2010.

The authors wish to thank the anonymous reviewers for their helpful comments on an earlier version of this paper.

References

1. Guerrero-Garcia, J., Gonzalez-Calleros, J.M., Vanderdonckt, J., Munoz-Arteaga, J.: A theoretical survey of user interface description languages: Preliminary results. In: Proc. of the 2009 Latin American Web Congress, LA-WEB 2009, pp. 36–43. IEEE Computer Society, Washington, DC (2009)
2. Shaer, O., Jacob, R.J.K., Green, M., Luyten, K. (eds.): ACM Transactions on Computer-Human Interaction Special issue on UIDL for next-generation user interfaces 16(4) (November 2009)
3. Calvary, G., Coutaz, J., Thevenin, D., Limbourg, Q., Bouillon, L., Vanderdonckt, J.: A Unifying Reference Framework for Multi-target User Interfaces. Interacting with Computers 15, 289–308 (2003)
4. Navarre, D., Palanque, P., Ladry, J.F., Barboni, E.: ICOs: A model-based user interface description technique dedicated to interactive systems addressing usability, reliability and scalability. ACM Transactions on Computer-Human Interaction 16(4), 18:1–18:56 (2009)
5. Shaer, O., Jacob, R.J.: A specification paradigm for the design and implementation of tangible user interfaces. ACM Transactions on Computer-Human Interaction 16(4), 20:1–20:39 (2009)

6. Wingrave, C.A., Laviola Jr., J.J., Bowman, D.A.: A natural, tiered and executable uidl for 3d user interfaces based on concept-oriented design. ACM Transactions on Computer-Human Interaction 16(4), 21:1–21:36 (2009)

7. Helms, J., Schaefer, R., Luyten, K., Vermeulen, J., Abrams, M., Coyette, A., Vanderdonckt, J.: Human-Centered Engineering of Interactive Systems With the User Interface Markup Language. In: Seffah, A., Vanderdonckt, J., Desmarais, M. (eds.) Human-Centered Software Engineering. Human-Computer Interaction Series, pp. 139–171. Springer, London (2009)

8. Puerta, A., Eisenstein, J.: XIML: a common representation for interaction data. In: Proceedings of the 7th International Conference on Intelligent user Interfaces, pp. 214–215 (2002)

9. Paternò, F., Santoro, C., Spano, L.D.: MARIA: A universal, declarative, multiple abstraction-level language for service-oriented applications in ubiquitous environments. ACM Transactions on Computer-Human Interaction 16(4), 1–30 (2009)

10. Limbourg, Q., Vanderdonckt, J., Michotte, B., Bouillon, L., López-Jaquero, V.: USIXML: A Language Supporting Multi-path Development of User Interfaces. In: Feige, U., Roth, J. (eds.) DSV-IS-EHCI 2004. LNCS, vol. 3425, pp. 200–220. Springer, Heidelberg (2005)

11. Gram, C., Cockton, G. (eds.): Design Principles for Interactive Software. Chapman & Hall (1996)

12. Berghe, Y.V.: Etude et implémentation d'un générateur d'interfaces vectorielles à partir d'un langage de description d'interfaces utilisateur. Master's thesis, Université catholique de Louvain (2004)

13. Campos, J.C., Mendes, S.A.: FlexiXML - A portable user interface rendering engine for UsiXML. In: User Interface Extensible Markup Language - UsiXML 2011, pp. 158–168. Thales Research and Technology (2011)

14. Denis, V.: Un pas vers le poste de travail unique: QTKiXML, un interpréteur d'interface utilisateur à partir de sa description. Master's thesis, Université catholique de Louvain (2005)

15. Goffette, Y., Louvigny, H.: Development of multimodal user interfaces by interpretation and by compiled components: a comparative analysis between InterpiXML and OpenInterface. Master's thesis, Université catholique de Louvain (2007)

16. Green, T.R.G., Petre, M.: Usability analysis of visual programming environments: a 'cognitive dimensions' framework. Journal of Visual Languages and Computing 7, 131–174 (1996)

Constraining and Creating Solutions – Reflections on the Analysis of Early Design

Chris Roast

Culture, Communication and Computing Research Institute
Sheffield Hallam University
Sheffield, S1 1WB
United Kingdom
c.r.roast@shu.ac.uk

Abstract. This research explores how an existing analytic framework (the cognitive dimensions framework) for interactive digital design reflects knowledge relevant to exploring the design space. The work examines this idea through the analysis of the transcripts of three digital design collaborative workshops run as part of "Studying Professional Software Design"[1]. Expert deliberation within these workshops is assessed and related to the analytic framework. The cognitive dimension framework has not been applied to observational data of this sort before. However, the approach described in this paper appears to provide a viable means of analysis. In conclusion we demonstrate that approaching observational data in this manner is not highly complex but is sufficient to provide useful insights. Reflections from the resulting analysis shed light on the interests and tensions evident in early stages of digital product design.

Keywords: user centred development, early design decisions, cognitive dimensions.

1 Introduction

This paper describes an exploration of the design process for digital systems, motivated by the analysis of data taken from three professional digital design workshops illustrating early concept formation [1] and collaborative research with professional developers on a live commercial project [2]. We are particularly interested in the design space of interactive digital design and how well that space is navigated and understood during the process of developing a conceptual design. The motivation for this work is based on an interest in understanding expertise in the domain of interactive digital design, exploring the implications for how design might be improved or supported.

Here we consider design expertise to reveals itself in terms of being able to short-circuit what would otherwise be time consuming problem-solving expeditions. It is

---

[1] For more information on these resources the reader is directed to:
http://www.ics.uci.edu/design-workshop/videos.html

M. Winckler, P. Forbrig, and R. Bernhaupt (Eds.): HCSE 2012, LNCS 7623, pp. 130–145, 2012.
© IFIP International Federation for Information Processing 2012

very common for large scale design problems to be addressed through tackling components with them. Hence managing complexity is achieved through structures that modularize or scope specific challenges [3]. However the digital design space embodies a massive range of complexities. Jackson [4] provides a rich account of how abstractions and perspectives are core to managing complexity in contemporary software projects. Despite that, working with and effectively using such structures is non-trivial. The mechanisms to cope with the complexity are not comprehensive and they thus fail to deal adequately with some design requirements. One significant contributory factor is the persistent opacity of digital artefacts. The structures employed to manage complexity are intrinsically abstract and poorly understood by non-technical stakeholders. In addition, while abstractions and structures can enable constructive development they can always be usurped both technically and by the emergent user needs. System requirements of interactive devices are frequently realized via their behaviours and these are hard to both specify and comprehend prior to encountering them via experience. A sample of research in the area of the psychology of digital programming shows that the ambition of wishing to engineer digital systems can be undermined by the fact that even simple digital programs can be difficult to comprehend [5]. In particular specific highly promoted techniques aimed at addressing some elements of perceived complexity have been shown to undermine their overall rationale [6].

The view taken here is that the need to structure and manage the complexity of the digital design space can be interpreted as a means of representing the space in a manner that is amenable for navigation and exploration. As such the manner in which the structure is imposed is attempting to serve to two purposes: (i) to make it easier for human designers to work with, and (ii) make it appropriate for technically meeting the requirements of a particular design problem. We are interested in the first of these - the fact that human factors plays a role in determining the way in which the design space is explored. Hence, when faced with a range of technical approaches in a design process, the choice of approach will not only be governed by the technical quality but also by the ease with it can be understood and applied. The quality of the representations employed and the experience and expertise of the designers will inform such a choice. It is interesting to see whether: expertise applied in a design setting demonstrates insights into the digital design space, thus reducing the likelihood of poor choices; how a design representation supports that process; and, the extent to which choices address the technical requirements or client needs.

1.1   An Analytic Framework

The chosen analytic framework for considering human factors and the exploration of digital design space is that of "cognitive dimensions" [7]. The cognitive dimensions framework provides a set of concepts that have been used as a means of capturing generic aspects of human interaction with complex information structures, with aim of emphasizing recurring factors pertinent to design quality [8]. This framework is unique in that: (i) it has been developed from the examination of the hard problems that arise with information systems such as the use of representations to define and comprehend complex behaviours, and (ii) it has been articulated in terms that do not presuppose human factors expertise. In doing so, the framework appears to be appeal as a means of easily capturing important observations about concepts are expressed and developed.

To illustrate this point we briefly introduce one of elements of framework - **"hidden dependencies"**. As its name suggests, this refers to the fact that digital artefacts can manage masses of inter-related data items which means changing one item can influence many others. Despite users and developers being fully aware of such dependencies, they can still manifest themselves un-expectedly. Tools and notations used when designing and/or using a system can be judged in terms of how they form, expose and manage such dependencies. Design often uses diagrams and structures to capture and circumscribe both data and functional dependencies. While these make explicit some dependencies others can be hidden and still need to managed by, say, cross-checking design changes in each of a number of views. Our proposal in this paper is that digital design experts are likely to have experienced re-current issues arising from working with concepts such as hidden dependencies and will therefore be prepared for dealing them. Designers with greater expertise may be more attentive to managing dependencies.

To date the concepts from cognitive dimensions framework have been used constructively to frame or drive reflections, hence "hidden dependencies" provides a way of seeing a particular problem [2]. By contrast, the work reported faces two challenges. First, whether the interesting features captured by the dimension framework relate to professional design expertise and experience, and second, whether such a relationship is evidence in "raw" observational data. To address the first of these, for this study, we are pre-supposing that expert experience based design behaviour will, in part, match the insights that the framework is designed to encourage. While this premise is speculative, it is not unrealistic especially since the framework is based on extensive research experience examining human behaviour in relationship to technology supported development. However, we'd not claim that such a match is a basis from assuming the framework reflects expert mental processes. The second challenge is to employ the dimension concepts in the analysis of observational data, and our approach is described below, see sections 3 and 4.

1.2   The Workshop Data

The data used for this work is from expert developers engaged in common a design task. This was developed as part of project aimed at generating an open research resource based upon collecting a foundational set of observations and insights into software design[2]. The task examined was to develop a preliminary user interface

---

design and also data model and architecture for a given "brief". The brief was for a traffic simulation system explicitly for use in an education context. The simulation would used by tutors and students to explore the influence of different traffic signal protocols upon traffic flow. Rich contextual detail was provided regarding what can be assumed of the simulated traffic system and what functionality could be assumed to already exist. In addition, the set task required both the completion of technical and design details in limited time.

Three separate pairs of professional developers worked on the given task for between one to two hours with limited additional support. They were required to manage their own activities while completing the task and thus had to balance between technical concerns and those of design. Their discussion and use of a whiteboard was recorded and transcribed - this data is freely available from the project coordinators and other research exploring the same data sets is the subject of a special issue on Design Studies [1]. In summary: the workshops lasted between one hour and two hours and the transcripts of discussions being between 6,000 and 12,000 words long.

2   The Cognitive Dimension Framework

The Cognitive Dimensions Framework is a relatively informal means of examining the space of design alternatives from the perspective of exploring the factors that can influence utilization of an artifact - one such factor "hidden dependencies" was introduced earlier. The framework arose primarily from the fields of human factors and human-computer interaction, and the examination of users working with digital languages, notations and representations. This is of relevance to examining design and development since it has been motivated by the examination of languages and representations by which digital systems are themselves are defined. A common feature of the representation examined has been their use for defining activities in the future, such as: (i) expressing code that subsequently operates autonomously; or (ii) developing, say a, set of rules that subsequently auto-process unwanted emails. Unlike many more traditional user interface assessment and analysis approaches, the framework focuses upon important factors related to effective use, without presupposing their relative importance. This enables its use as a basis for discussion and reflection in a wide range of contexts. Hence, while the framework was initial motivated by examples taken from structured visualisations, it has developed to be applied to a broader range of information artifacts. Topics examined using the framework, include: textual and visual programming languages; APIs [9]; specification notations [10]; spreadsheets [11]; musical notations [12]. Green et al. [8] provides a summary of the range of work employing the framework and its development. Recently we have employed a simple tabular format for reporting based on the framework that has been successfully used to facilitate co-operative assessment of complex systems [2].

The dimensions of the framework are discussed and illustrated thoroughly in [13], below we outline some of the dimension concepts and suggest their potential role in design. It will be clear from these brief introductions the concepts are closely associated and to some extent overlap.

Premature commitment – this concerns the idea that systems and notations can demand that users make decisions before they are ready to. Although this behavior may be "demanded" it might not in fact be technically necessary. By contrast while such behavior might be seen as unsuitable, it might be purposefully designed to promote a greater diligence or responsibility on the part of the user. An example of premature commitment might be in a formatting rule for inserting an image in a document, using the rule might demand that the image file is specified and exists, when in fact a placeholder could be provided.

Viscosity – this concerns the relative complexity of changing information represented in a system. This relates closely to common notions of efficiency in usability. However a key reflective point promoted by the concept is that while a notation tends to make some changes easy, others may be purposefully made complex or hard. In the example of formatting rules, a relative positioning rule (align A with B) can be compared with an absolute positioning rule (find the position of B and set A to that position). Assessing their viscosity would encourage the consideration of what changes to rule uses are most likely to be supported by these two alternatives and whether they are both needed.

Visualisation and juxtaposition – this concerns information outputs that the user may use in combination, and the difficulty or ease of combining them. In the simplest chase information needs are met by presenting information juxtaposed making human perceptual inferences easy, such as comparing values on a histogram. More often than not all possible information needs can be satisfied and the user might then have to navigate between sources, possible even switching between applications. Using the example of formatting rules, we can envisage the benefit of being able to see the rules that influence the same element juxtaposed with one another.

Abstraction – this concerns the potential to employ abstractions within a systems and the ease with which they can be used. Abstraction normally supports working with general classes or groups of entities and not specific individuals. It is used productively in many settings within software engineering. By contrast some systems impose pre-defined abstractions that users then have to assimilate. As with viscosity, the concept of abstraction is used as a means of reflecting on the nature of support that is provided. An example of abstraction with formatting rules would be how groups of rules serving a collective purpose might be managed as a single composite entity.

Hard mental operations – this concept has close associations with Abstraction, it is concerned with whether the operations available to users of a representation are easy or hard to understand. For this it is necessary to envisage the manner in which a user will think about achieving a particular objective and whether the operations provided by the system match them. In the case of a set of formatting rules a hard mental operations would reveal themselves when updating a single rule rarely serves a meaningful purpose. One can envisage a number of updates to different rules being needed in order to achieve a required effect.

Provisionality – this concept focuses upon how speculative or incomplete work is supported. In system supported activity it is frequently the case that the user is constrained to completing specific operations or procedures, while this can be helpful, it can impair speculative activity or experimentation. Provisionality thus promotes the consideration of what might benefit from being transient or incomplete in order to encourage effective use. In the case of formatting rules, high provisionality could mean ill-formed, incomplete or inconsistent rules do not "break" the system but are worked with.

3   Applying the Framework

To employ the concepts from the cognitive dimensions framework in examining observational data, it is necessary to identify how features of the observational data related to the concepts of interest. To achieve this we rely upon the premise that points in the workshop discussions where decisions are made are likely to provide explicit indications of participants' expertise. Such "decision points" were urged to be locations where expertise and insight are most likely to reveal themselves and thus be appropriate candidates for finding relating to dimension concepts. Hence, specifics of deliberations at these points would be mapped to concepts provided a focus for the more detailed assessment of the data.

Following a preliminary assessment of the workshop resources a prior assessment of the dimensions was conducted mapping them to rationale topics that likely to be directly evidenced in design deliberations. In summary, table 1 indicates the relative relevance of factors for each of dimensions considered. This provides a means of relating what is being discussed during design deliberations to the dimensions that are potentially applicable.

Table 1. Relating deliberation topics to the framework concepts (*** = highly relevant; **=relevant; *=possibly relevant)

		Viscosity	Visibility	Hidden Dependencies	Hard mental operations	Provisionality	Premature Commitment	Abstraction
Mental effort		*		**	***	***	***	**
Physical effort		***	***	*		***	**	**
Actively – doing things	Creating		*	***	**	**	**	*
	Modifying	***	*	***	**			*
Non active (ie. navigating)		**	***	*				*
Meaningfulness				**	***	*	**	***

The different strengths of mapping shown in table 5 were determined from the critical assessment of cognitive dimensions framework and its prior use. For instance, the dimension of 'Viscosity' focuses upon the complexity of making changes and thus we'd expect this to be evidenced in discussions of the physical effort required to when making changes for specific purposes. Thus discussions focused upon the modification of application data are likely to also be highly relevant. Less relevant will be user navigation since changing data in realistic setting can incur navigation. Similarly, when assessing 'Abstraction' it can be argued that it is predominantly concerned with support for managing aggregates and groupings. Evidence of this concept in design discussions would include: discussion of the meaningfulness of categories; discussion of the physical and mental effort associated with operations upon and navigating abstractions especially user created abstractions; less closely related is the influence of abstraction when acting on or navigating application data. This type of assessment was conducted for each of the dimensions, linking them to broad topic categories that are more likely to be evidenced in design discussions.

The rationale for creating and using the mapping in table 2 is predominantly to provide a method for managing unstructured observational data. This benefit is qualified by the fact that the mapping could itself weaken the association between observed data and its interpretation. Although this mapping may serve as a guide as to what dimensions are "evidenced", the key indicator of expertise relates to the extent to which a discussion embodies some reflection upon alternatives and an awareness of the longer term consequences of particular decisions.

4   Analysis and Outcomes

Following the initial review of the resources, a strategy to identify significant points in the workshop was developed. The primary rationale for this was to provide a focus for more detailed assessment. The approach taken was to read through the workshop transcriptions and highlight segments of the discussion at which it appeared that constructive decisions were made – i.e. decisions add detail or substance to the design based upon rational assessment. Key points in the transcripts where explicit alternatives were being articulated and assessed were taken to be of highest potential relevance; followed by, points involving the implicit assessment of alternatives (these might even be where workshop participants make unilateral assertions about a design option).

Selected foci were each assessed in terms of the reflective depth of the consideration of the topics. This involved reading the relevant section of transcript and also viewing the video record of the same section. At this stage of the analysis it became clear that the motivation for the decisions fell into two broad categories based upon the primary intended beneficiary of the decision: 'external users' - the intended users of the final design (tutors and students using the simulation tool for educational purposes); 'internal users' – those involved in subsequent technical development (software developers and designers). These two categories were used to factor the initial assessment of decision points.

Table 2. Assessment of workshop 1 focused upon discussions at selected key points

Locus of decision timestamp	What participants discussed and basis for their argument	User focus
[12:01.1]	Participants agree on there being no need to model road traffic lanes. Argument based on avoiding complexity, dependencies and whether lanes are required by the brief. Rationale: avoiding **physical effort** and implicit **mental effort**, making code **creation** easier. Dominant framework concepts: **Provisionality** and **Premature Commitment**	Internal
	The implications for tutors and student users discussed. Rationale: **mental effort** and **physical effort**, especially when **creating** a configuration. Dominant framework concepts: **Provisionality** and **Premature Commitment**	External
[23:02.8]	Revisiting the modelling of the lanes with a focus upon the integrity of the simulation (e.g. traffic queuing). Rationale: reducing **mental effort** and **physical effort** and **meaningfulness** Dominant framework concepts: **Abstraction** and **Premature Commitment**	Internal
	Rationale: **meaningfulness** for the tutor Dominant framework concepts: **Abstraction**	External
[49:33.4]	Revisiting more details about the operation of the lanes model. Rationale: the "perfect" simplification reducing **mental effort**. Dominant framework concepts: **Premature commitment**	Internals

The outcome of the assessment of the decision points and their mapping to cognitive dimension concepts is summarized in tables 2, 3 and 4. Linking this assessment back to the cognitive dimensions framework the rationale supporting decisions has been assessed in terms the relevant topics used in table 1. Working backwards from that mapping, it is possible to associate specific decision points with the dimensions of most relevance. This has been an analytic process based upon the assessment of the workshop discussions at the point of interest and the relevance to the dimensions. Where possible a single dominant dimension has been identified, though on occasions the mapping and the workshop transcript could not be used to effectively to identify a single dimension. However as we have pointed out the potential for overlaps between the different concepts is high, and when necessary critical judgment was applied to identify a dominant dimension in specific cases. The outcome is indicated in Table 5.

Table 3. Assessment of workshop 2 focused upon discussions at selected key points

Locus of decision timestamp	What participants discussed and basis for their argument	User focus
[0:47:49]	Debating how best to implement the propagation of traffic flow information. Rationale: referring to patterns of processing, **meaningful** software engineering concepts. Dominant framework concepts: **Abstraction**	Internals
	Rationale: an architecture offering users an easy link between **changing** configurable elements and **seeing** the consequences. Dominant framework concepts: **Viscosity**	External
[1:01:10]	Discussion of where best to position behavioural rules in the data model. Rationale: size and complexity of alternative options imposing **mental effort** making **modifications** hard to manage. Software pattern approaches considered as **meaningful** concepts. Dominant framework concepts: **Hidden dependencies**	Internal
[1:17:36]	Discussing a conflict between cars initiated with a behavior when in that behavior might get **modified**. [Unresolved due to time limitations]	Internal
[1:26:45]	User interface design discussed, considering providing: pause, fast forward and re-set style controls, and showing actual cars and their movement. Rationale: prior decisions regarding technical model dominate considerations. [Unresolved]	External
[1:31:56]	Discussing various other interaction design options. Rationale: **mental** and **physical effort** when a viewing simulation (**passively** exploring simulation as it runs). Dominant framework concepts: **Visibility**	External
[1:41:44]	Discussing how intersections can inferred from overall road grid (and the implications) of that. Rationale: **mental** and **physical effort** when **creating** the tool to cope with the problem. Dominant framework concepts: **Hidden dependencies**	Internal

Table 4. Assessment of workshop 3 focused upon discussions at selected key points

Locus of decision timestamp	What participants discussed and basis for their argument	User focus
[0:21:09]	Discussion how junctions are created and configured by users. Rationale: reducing **physical** and **mental effort** when **creating** a road layout. Dominant framework concepts: **Premature commitment** and **Provisionality**	External
	Discussion how junctions might be manipulated by users. Rationale: reducing **physical effort** and **mental effort** when **manipulating** and when **viewing** a road layout. Dominant framework concepts: **Hidden dependencies** and **Visibility** and **Viscosity**	External
[0:41:13]	Discussing junction behaviour in detail with an emphasis upon the representation and configuration of traffic light behaviour Rationale: **Modifying** and **passively** viewing configurations considered, as well as **meaningfulness** for users and the **physical effort** involved. Dominant framework concepts: **Hidden dependencies**	External
[1:14:03]	Discussing how to show and edit junction details (popping-up versus in side bar). Rationale (as above) some choices deferred to "prototype".	External
[1:27:48]	Discussing differentiating modes of use: configuring; experimenting and running. Rationale: High level concepts of purpose (**meaningfulness**). Dominant framework concepts: **Abstraction**	External
[1:31:05]	Discussion of feedback and visualising feedback and providing tabular results. Rationale: reducing **mental effort** and allowing results to be **navigated** with little **physical effort** Dominant framework concepts: **Visibility**	External
[1:33:49]	Considering the potential of real-time configurable simulation and value of seeing immediate cause and effect. Rationale: allowing **modifications** and **passively** interpreting the results to infer **meaningful** relationships Dominant framework concepts: **Visibility** and **Hidden dependencies**	External
[1:47:53]	Summarise points requiring clarification	Internal

5   Findings

An overall reflection on this the analysis shows that each workshop tended to have a predominant focus upon either "internal users" or "external users", and that the focus tends to relate to different cognitive dimensions. Design discussions focused upon the needs and requirements of end users appeared to be assessed in terms concerned with the immediate complexity of seeing information and working with it. This lead to a focus upon issues concerning: Visibility, Viscosity and Hidden dependencies. By contrast considerations of the internal issues, such as the suitability of a design decision for subsequent technical development, appeared to emphasize: Provisionality; Premature Commitment and Abstraction. This grouping of the dimension concepts is similar to that found in a earlier study conducted in which professional developers were engaged in co-operative assessment of one of their software application's with motivating questions derived from the same framework [2].

5.1   General Observations

The briefing for the workshop asked for the development of both technical details (such as a data model) and a user interface design within a limited time frame. This created a tension in the workshop of meeting both aims. Despite this, the interplay between the technical and user perspective was only rarely considered. In particular there was one occasion of an unforeseen conflict between technical design and probable user needs. The technical design provided an abstract model of traffic flow, while user needs were judged to demand a fine grain simulation.

Table 5. Outline mapping of cognitive dimensions to workshop data indicating the focus upon internal or external user needs

	Workshop 1	Workshop 2	Workshop 3
Viscosity		e	e
Visibility		e	e e e
Hidden Dependencies		i i	e e e
Mental operations			
Provisionality	i i		
Premature commitment	i i i		e
Abstraction	i i	i	e

With the discussions in two of the workshops focusing mainly upon the internal requirements, it is of interest that the participants frequently referred to themselves as engaging in future work on the project. They were positioning themselves as "developers". It appears that participants in these cases had a mutual understanding of the implications of a number of decisions — in-depth discussions were not common and summary justifications appeared to be adequate. For instance, on occasions there was consensus that a particular decision would "simplify" a solution, without a need for further explanation. Hence, it seems that workshops with a good common knowledge of technical possibilities pursued that route, and in doing so did not need to openly deliberate about specific technical choices. This can approach also go hand-in-hand with a reticence to explore factors that are unfamiliar or not well understood.

Hence, the openness of the brief could be seen as providing too much freedom. In particular the lack of a detailed user perspective meant the workshop was more reliant upon speculatively envisaging users. A dominant illustration of this for the workshop was the response to the lack of detail about the educational context set-up in the brief. The specific teaching and learning style to be used is not articulated, and hence the brief does not promote design decisions impinging on teaching and learning. Expertise in that area may breed the innovative exploration of learning styles, however pedagogic factors were only addressed partially and indirectly. This is an illustration how design options are not thoroughly explored.

Another distinction between workshops and their user focus are the apparent development styles. Those who focused upon internal user requirement worked consistently with the attitude that: (i) the right technical decisions are needed to ease future work; (ii) subsequent technical develop would follow good practice. By contrast the opportunity for adopting an "agile" or iterative development approach to refining a solution was only alluded to in the externally focused workshop (workshop 3).

5.2   Framework Based Assessment

The relationship between the cognitive dimensions identified in our analysis and the design deliberations can be examined in more detail. In particular we can assess the extent to which factors implied by the dimensions are evident in the discussions in the workshops.

Internal Assessment. Premature commitment, provisionality, hidden dependencies and abstraction are significant in the internal requirements discussions.

The workshop requirement of developing a data model was clearly considered as a point of high commitment, and significant effort went into getting it right. There were a few occasions when the technical details were in effect deferred by embodying a general structure in the model - an example of this is the adoption of a software engineering patterns. In terms of the cognitive dimensions framework this suggests that a data model in itself is too committing, promoting technical deliberation prior to full understanding overall needs.

Hidden dependencies appear in the discussion of technical decisions when the discussion uses mini-scenarios to illustrate complexity. The features of hidden dependencies and ways of managing them were not explored directly by the participants. Were this style of justification by illustration not adopted, the discussion could easily be classed as being focused upon premature commitment as opposed to hidden dependencies.

Abstraction stands out as being a moderating force when considering "simple" models - a key factor being the "meaningfulness" of a proposed alternative. In the data analysed two domains of meaningfulness are employed: meaningful in terms of external requirements (such as the realisation of "traffic queues") and meaningfulness in terms of familiar software engineering approaches (such as data models and software engineering patterns).

In conclusion the demands of developing a data model appear to be highly committing and potentially disruptive to the balancing of internal and external considerations. On the basis that a data model is needed it appears that concepts such as software engineering patterns provide a means of delaying commitment to technical details. While this could have provided a solid technical approach from which external factors could be explored but this opportunity was not taken.

External Assessment. Visibility, Viscosity and Hidden dependencies are the dominant dimensions mapped to when considering external users needs. The inter-relationship between viscosity and visibility is close with the main distinguishing factor being whether the requirement concerns users passively examining information or actively engaged in changing data or configurations. In the majority of cases the discussion focused upon possible user interface options, to ensure particular tasks are easily performed and required data is visualised usefully. What these two dimensions would bring to such discussions is a focus upon the side effects of particular solutions in order to encourage critical reflection. So in the case of visualising data, screen area is a limiting factor which naturally promotes the consideration of exactly what, and how much, information can be realistically be simultaneously displayed in a coherent manner. On a few occasions the consideration of such side effects are evidence. This is most obvious in workshop 3 where the whiteboard was used to draw a composite of display design details and application data. In this case the board provided a limiting factor of sorts.

The mapping to hidden dependencies arises in one case from the domain topic of the workshop. The simulation system being envisaged serves an educational purpose, and the workshop participants recognize that learning in that setting often arises from finding inter-relationships.

The other case of hidden dependencies is related to other dimensions and arises when the configuration of a simulation is being considered. Here the motivation was to ease the management of the data structure needed to define a simulation. The visual approach to addressing this problem, by using the whiteboard extensively, encourages the consideration of solutions where the complexity is visually evident and thus potentially less hidden.

5.3   Recommendations

Having examined early stage software design workshops and identified potential links with the cognitive dimensions framework. A number of conclusions can be drawn about the exploration of the design space. Some arise from reflections on the workshops themselves while others are the consequence of examining how the cognitive dimensions framework could inform this type of design activity.

Get into problems. Early stages of development suffer from often being too open. This lack of constraints means that design details can be proposed and agreed with little consideration. Only when enough detail is established do decisions demand a more thorough and careful examination and justification.

Approaches to avoiding decisions in a vacuum encourage inherent problems to be confronted early. Two examples of this in the workshops studied are: (i) to promote the consideration of the problems arising from different perspectives (such as internal and external); (ii) exaggerate factors to constrain the problem space, such as requiring a specifically small screen size.

Feed creativity. Initial design concepts lack details. For a design team to work effectively with them they must be confident to work creatively in order explore a design space. This requires the setting to be one in which the ethos is to find interesting ideas and avoid "solutions".

Design representations should enable provisonality or variablity so as to limit their treatment as definitive representations. Similarly representations should be understood as being part of a process of iterative exploration, and hence they are best viewed as transient representations.

Too much common knowledge within a team can discourage the exploration of alternatives. This is exacerbated if they are exploring aspects of system use and operation outside their collective expertise.

Less selectivity. One of the factors that appears to limit effective exploration of the design space is a tendency to focus on some facets of a problem and ignore others. The potential to provide support for exploration that discourages this can be considered. This could include techniques such as systematically reviewing decisions and their implications from different stakeholder perspectives.

Visualising. The use of visual sketching is a useful means of implicitly managing and experimenting with design alternatives. This appears to be particularly valuable when considering user activity at the device, as it goes some way towards bringing competing issues together in a single representation. Other low fidelity prototyping methods such as paper prototyping serve a similar purpose.

In general we cannot claim these points to be in any way comprehensive, since the focus of analysis within the workshops has been selective, and similarly there is no claim regarding the adequacy of the dimensions examined.

6   Conclusions

We have argued that the early stages of software design have distinctive features that are not supported by a wide range of software engineering practices which focus upon development once a design concept is well established. As such early concept design is a process that is complicated by its openness and the unbounded opportunities and promises associated with it. Establishing sufficient details for design decisions and technical assessment to be grounded is core to exploring the design space. Hence, it is valuable to understand how effective exploration takes place, and thus how productive design arguments and development proceed.   This problem has been addressed by endeavoring to apply the cognitive dimensions framework as a means of analysing how the design space is explored in three software design workshops involving professional developers engaging with the same given design brief.

The cognitive dimensions framework has generated a lot of interest as a tool for analysis and assessment of complex interactive systems. The frameworks, and derivations of it, have predominantly been the instruments to conduct analysis. By contrast, in this work we have employed the framework for assessment of observation data gathered with no specific analytic setting. Our approach has been to develop a rational basis for focusing upon and interpreting specific points in the data from the workshops and thus map observed data to concepts in the framework. Future work in the area would hope to develop this analysis approach further. One particularly interesting direction would be to focus more on the visual representations used to articulate and support the design deliberations.

Reflecting upon this interpretation of the data and what appear to be common features of the analysis as a whole we have been able to develop some recommendations for improving the productiveness of early stage software design. The recommendations while based upon the research and analysis identify features of productive design and development that not uncommon to inter-disciplinary group work. Thus while the use of the cognitive dimension framework in this manner is novel the resulting insights are closely reflect elements of good practice.

Acknowledgements. The author is grateful for being able to access to the workshop resources that served as a basis for this paper. It should be noted that the results described in this paper are based upon videos and transcripts initially distributed for the 2010 international workshop "Studying Professional Software Design", as partially supported by NSF grant CCF-0845840. For more information on these resources the reader is direct to: http://www.ics.uci.edu/design-workshop/videos.html. The author is also indebted to reviewers' comments on earlier drafts of this paper.

References

1. Petre, M., van der Hoek, A., Baker, A.: Editorial in Design Studies 31(6), 533–544 (2010), Special Issue Studying Professional Software Design, http://dx.doi.org/10.1016/j.destud.2010.09.001
2. Roast, C., Uruchurtu, E., Dearden, A.: The programming-like-analysis of an innovative media tool. In: Psychology of Programming Interest Group Annual Conference, University of York (2011)
3. Simon, H.A.: The Sciences of the Artificial. MIT Press, Cambridge (1979)
4. Jackson, M.: Representing structure in a software system design. Design Studies 31(6), 545–566 (2010), Special Issue Studying Professional Software Design, doi:10.1016/j.destud.2010.09.002
5. Ramalingam, V., Wiedenbeck, S.: An empirical study of novice program comprehension in the imperative and object-oriented styles. In: Wiedenbeck, S., Scholtz, J. (eds.) Papers presented at the Seventh Workshop on Empirical Studies of Programmers (ESP 1997), pp. 124–139. ACM, New York (1997), http://doi.acm.org/10.1145/266399.266411

6. Khazaei, B., Roast, C.: The influence of formal representation on solution specification. Requirements Engineering 8(1), 69–77 (2003), doi:10.1007/s00766-002-0146-9
7. Green, T.R.G., Petre, M.: Usability analysis of visual programming environments: a 'cognitive dimensions' framework. J. Visual Languages and Computing 7, 131–174 (1996)
8. Green, T.R.G., Blandford, A.E., Church, L., Roast, C.R., Clarke, S.: Cognitive dimensions: Achievements, new directions, and open questions. Journal of Visual Languages and Computing 17(4), 328–365 (2006), doi:10.1016/j.jvlc.2006.04.004
9. Clarke, S., Becker, C.: Using the cognitive dimensions framework to measure the usability of a class library. In: Proceedings of the First Joint Conference of EASE & PPIG (PPIG 15) (2003)
10. Triffitt, E., Khazaei, B.: A Study of Usability of Z Formalism Based on Cognitive Dimensions. In: Kuljis, J., Baldwin, L., Scoble, R. (eds.) Proceedings of the Fourteenth Annual Meeting of the Psychology of Programming Interest Group, pp. 15–28 (2002)
11. Hendry, D.G., Green, T.R.G.: Creating, comprehending, and explaining spreadsheets: a cognitive interpretation of what discretionary users think of the spreadsheet model. Int. J. Human-Computer Studies 40(6), 1033–1065 (1994)
12. Blackwell, A.F., Green, T.R.G., Nunn, D.J.E.: Cognitive Dimensions and musical notation systems. Paper Presented at ICMC 2000: Workshop on Notation and Music Information Retrieval in the Computer Age, Berlin (2000)
13. Green, T.R.G., Blackwell, A.: Cognitive Dimensions of Information Artefacts: a tutorial Version 1.2 (October 1998), http://www.ndirect.co.uk/~thomas.green/workStuff/Papers/

Smartphone Applications Usability Evaluation: A Hybrid Model and Its Implementation

Artur H. Kronbauer[1], Celso A.S. Santos[2], and Vaninha Vieira[3]

[1] PMCC – UFBA, Av. Adhemar de Barros s/n sala 138,
Salvador – BA, Brazil
arturhk@gmail.com
[2] DI – CT – UFES, Av. Fernando Ferrari s/n sala 8,
Vitória – ES, Brazil
saibel@inf.ufes.br
[3] DCC – UFBA, Av. Adhemar de Barros s/n sala 234,
Salvador – BA, Brazil
vaninha@ufba.br

Abstract. Evaluating the usability of smartphone applications is crucial for their success, so developers can learn how to adapt them considering the dynamicity of mobile scenarios. The HCI community recommends considering different requirements when evaluating those applications, such as quantitative data (metrics), subjective evaluation (users' impressions) and context data (e.g. environment and devices conditions). We observed a lack in the literature of approaches that support those three requirements combined into a single experiment; generally one or a pair of them is used. Besides, performing usability evaluation on real mobile scenarios is hard to achieve and most proposals are based on laboratory-controlled experiments. In this paper, we present our proposal for a hybrid usability evaluation of smartphone applications, which is composed by a model and an infrastructure that implements it. The model describes how to automatically monitor and collect context data and usability metrics, how those data can be processed for analysis support and how users' impressions can be collected. An infrastructure is provided to implement the model allowing it to be plugged into any smartphone Android-based application. To evaluate our proposal, we performed a field experiment, with 21 users using three mobile applications during a 6-month period, in their day-to-day scenarios.

Keywords: Usability Evaluation, Smartphone Application, Remote Usability Evaluation, Usability Testing.

1 Introduction

In recent years, the introduction of several technologies has revolutionized society's methods of communication, entertainment, and the execution of daily tasks. Simultaneously, the process of digital convergence has generated a great number of devices (PDAs, smartphones, tablets) capable of gathering different forms of user-computer interaction in an integrated way and with reasonable processing power.

M. Winckler, P. Forbrig, and R. Bernhaupt (Eds.): HCSE 2012, LNCS 7623, pp. 146–163, 2012.

Considering that the interaction of the user with this kind of device is extremely sensitive to the context in which the application is running, what constitutes the most adequate scenario for executing usability tests is a topic of great discussion. The central question is whether these experiments should be performed in the field, or in the laboratory [1].

Another important question has to do with the kind of data that must be present in a usability evaluation. Besides quantitative data used to determine the quality of the interfaces and the usability of the applications, subjective data should also be considered in order to draw conclusions about the users' satisfaction.

The main problem when evaluating mobile applications is the development of approaches whose evaluations integrate quantitative, subjective and context data in the same experiment. Nowadays, those three points of interest are investigated in isolation, which makes the relationship between those results difficult to determine [2].

Faced with this challenge, the objective of this study is to assess the new applications usability, their functionalities, how the users adapt to them to do their daily tasks, the satisfaction level provided and the level of external interferences.

In order to achieve evaluations with different kinds of information, we propose an approach to support the evaluation of smartphone applications based on the Android platform. This approach blends two strategies for data capture: the first one, known as Logging [3], is based on the data collection related to the user interaction with an application, allowing statistical analysis regarding usability; it allows the use of sensors available in the smartphones for contextual data collection, such as luminosity intensity and the device´s position [4]. The second one, known as Experience Sampling Method (ESM) [5], is based on the collection of users' feelings towards a specific product through questions.

The main contribution of this work is to propose a new approach that is able to relate different types of data to evaluate the usability of embedded applications on smartphones. The proposed approach can contribute to the implementation of field and laboratory experiments, whether they are supervised or not.

The remainder of this article is divided into six sections. Section 2 describes the proposed model. Section 3 presents an infrastructure that implements the model, to capture and evaluate usability data from Android applications. Section 4 presents a case study performed to evaluate the proposal and analyzes the results found on the experiments. Section 5 discusses related works to reinforce our contributions. Finally, in Section 6, we present conclusions and future work.

2   The UEProject: A Model for Usability Evaluation on Smartphone Applications

In our work, we propose the Usability Evaluation Project (UEProject), which is composed by a model and an infrastructure to support a hybrid approach for usability evaluation on Smartphone Applications. The proposed model enhances the capture of quantitative and subjective data, contextualized within the evaluation scenario and in conjunction with the identification of the users' profiles.

The intention is to go beyond the collection of statistical data, such as identifying the frequency of use, the error count or speed of execution of a task. The goal is to provide an infrastructure that enables the contextual factors associated with usability problems, and identify the user perception regarding the application.

The model uses a component-based architecture to support the reuse of the implemented resources and its redefinition according to evaluators' needs. Figure 1 presents the three high level components that represent the model and their relations: Mapping Unit, Traceability Unit and Assessment Unit. Arrows indicate information transfer between the components.

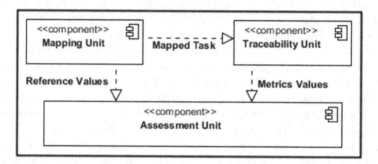

Fig. 1. Main components of the model

The Mapping Unit is responsible to provide the necessary resources for mapping the tasks that will be investigated later in the application under evaluation. It generates the Mapped Tasks and Reference Values that provide information about the context in which the task was mapped and the perceptions of the person responsible for mapping it. The Traceability Unit provides a library of metrics that uses the mapped tasks, enabling an instrumentation of the application's source code with metrics for the capture of quantitative, contextual, and subjective data concerning the user profile. The values obtained during user interactions are sent to the Assessment Unit. The Assessment Unit is responsible for receiving the transmitted data, transferring it to a database and enabling evaluations. Next subsections present the internal components of the model's units.

2.1   Mapping Unit

This unit is subdivided into three components responsible for providing the task-mapping functionalities. In Figure 2 the components diagram can be seen, with its interfaces and doors for data transfer from one component to another.

Initially it has been planned that the applications' source code be made available. The objective of this action is to allow the Source Code Analyzer component to identify which classes refer to the treatment of users' interactions. These classes are identified and provided as a requirement for the Mapping Code Generator component so that it can attach information that enables the identification of tasks to the original source code. The result of this component's action is to perform the instrumentation of the application's original code, thereby allowing the tasks to be mapped. After the source code is prepared for mapping, it must be forwarded to the Mapping Device component where the tasks will be mapped. This device must enable the mapping of tasks and make them available to be used by other units in the model.

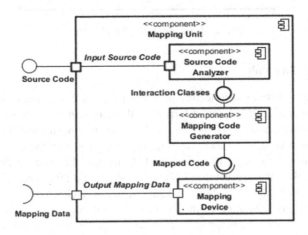

Fig. 2. Mapping Unit Architectural Overview

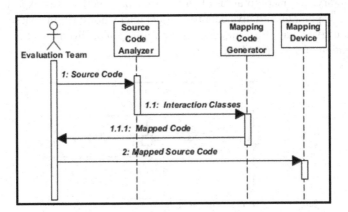

Fig. 3. Steps for application instrumentation for task mapping

In Figure 3, the diagram portrays the sequence that enables the exchange of messages and data between the Mapping Unit components.

In Figure 4 the diagram of a simplified use case is presented, where the only two existing interactions are shown. In the first interaction, the Evaluation Team is responsible for providing the application's source code and, in the second, for performing the tasks' mapping for later assessment. It is worth noting that the tasks' mapping can be done by a test engineer, an experienced user, or even average users who are chosen according to their profile, thereby allowing future comparisons.

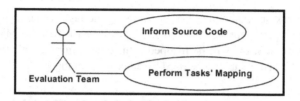

Fig. 4. Use Case of the Mapping Unit

2.2   Traceability Unit

This unit is responsible for collecting different types of information: (i) user profile (e.g. education and age); (ii) data referring to the user's interaction, such as hits and time to complete a task; (iii) contextual data like luminosity and noise; and (iv) subjective data, related to the users' feelings regarding the applications' usage.

For the instrumentation of the source code to include the code for capture metrics and data collection, the Traceability Unit was divided into three internal components, as can be seen in Figure 5: Metrics Library, Metrics Generation and Interaction Device. The Metrics Library is the component that provides the structure to all capture metrics. It uses the mapped tasks to bring together the structure of the metrics with information about the application source code. It generates, as result, the metrics' structures adapted to the application under evaluation. In the development of the Metrics Library, the incorporation of three types of structure was expected: (i) the ones used to capture quantitative data from users interactions; (ii) the ones responsible for the subjective data (direct interactions with users) and; (iii) the metrics that allow instrumentation of the available sensors.

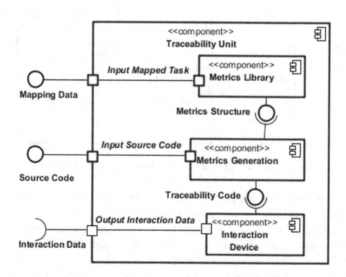

Fig. 5. Traceability Unit Architectural Overview

The Metrics Generation component receives as input the application's source code and the adapted metrics structure to be attached to this code. As result it provides a new source code with the inserted metrics, the Traceability Code. The component Interaction Device requires the installation of the application's new code containing the metrics that will be used for data capture. This device should enable the user's interaction while allowing data to be captured.

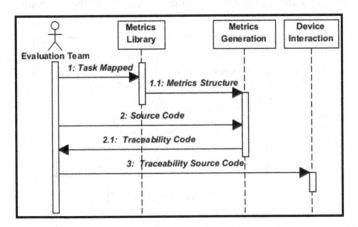

Fig. 6. Steps for the instrumentation of an application with the metrics for capturing data

In Figure 6, the diagram presents the sequence of actions that permits the exchange of messages and data between the Traceability Unit components.

Figure 7 presents two use case diagrams concerning the Traceability Unit. The first actor (Evaluation Team) is responsible for providing files with the mapped tasks and the application's source code, enabling the creation of a new application with metrics for capturing data. The second actor (User) uses the application while data concerning usability, context, profile, and feeling about application usage are captured.

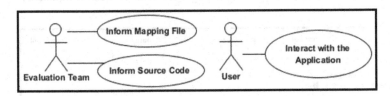

Fig. 7. Use Cases Diagram of the Traceability Unit

2.3   Assessment Unit

This unit was structured in four different components that are responsible for infrastructure where data to be evaluated will be stored over time. Figure 8 presents an architectural overview of its components. To illustrate better its behavior, the sequence diagram in Figure 9 presents the exchange of messages and data between the components.

Initially, the Data Receiver component collects the data captured during the execution of the user's interactions within the application under evaluation. A second component, the Populate Database, performs the verification of new data arrival and populates it into the database. The Database component represents a Database Management System (DBMS) that stores persistent data. The Analysis Component has the responsibility to access existing data in the database and to provide resources that enable the extraction of usability information relevant to the evaluators.

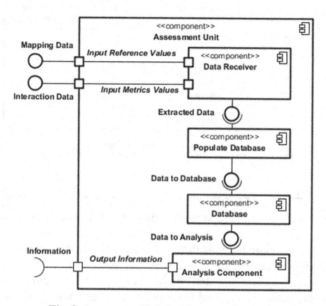

Fig. 8. Assessment Unit Architectural Overview

To make the Assessment Unit easier to understand, the diagram that follows (Figure 9) illustrates the exchange of messages and data between components.

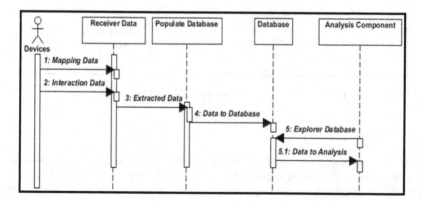

Fig. 9. Actions performed by the components of the Assessment Unit

The only direct interaction of an actor with the devised components in this unit is at the moment of the assessments done by the Evaluation Team. This team is responsible for defining data, parameters, and configurations so the information can be extracted according to their needs.

3   The UEProject Infrastructure

In this section, we describe the infrastructure implemented to verify the feasibility of the UEProject model. The technological aspects and techniques used in the implementation of the infrastructure are discussed. Additionally, the section describes the tools created, or used from the market, to cover all the components according to the model proposal.

We defined four premises related to how technical choices will be made when planning the construction of the infrastructure, as follows.

1) To propose that the data can be collected anywhere the user is interacting. To facilitate this, the technique Logging was chosen. This strategy consists of automatically monitoring and gathering data concerning the applications' use.

2) To define that all used software licenses should be free. To this end, we decided to develop the components using the Java Language, since it is platform-independent and free. The components obtained from the market were also chosen according to this premise. The objective is to make the project economically feasible.

3) To determine that all collected data might be gathered from smartphone applications. For this reason, the Android platform was chosen because it uses Java and Android is widely used nowadays.

4) To suggest that the applications' source code to be instrumented should not be modified. Therefore the Aspect Oriented Program (AOP) [6] was chosen. AspectJ[1], an AOP plugin for Java is used to instrument the applications with codes considered as transversals. In this case, the codes are needed to map the tasks and the code related to the metrics for data gathering.

In this implementation of the infrastructure, the proposed way for task mapping was to capture the methods executed in the application after the interaction of the Evaluation Team. The group of interactions for a task execution is translated into a group of methods executed in the application. The mapped methods are used as Join Points so the metrics can be introduced in an application, without modifying the original source code. In this sense, Point Cuts are used to define the rules that validate the execution of the metrics built in the Advices.

The following subsections describe the tools used to implement the components of the three units defined in the Model.

3.1   Tools Used in the Mapping Unit

The first developed tool looks at the Source Code Analyzer and the Mapping Code Generator. This tool was called the Mapping Aspect Generator (MAG). Figure 10 presents a workflow showing all the necessary steps for the preparation of an application to be mapped.

---

[1] Available in http://www.eclipse.org/aspectj/

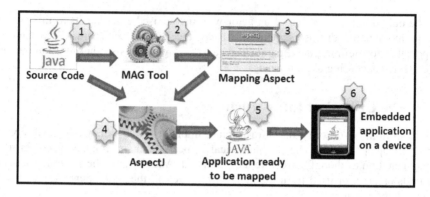

Fig. 10. Workflow for the insertion of mapping aspects into an application

Initially the MAG tool must receive the application's source code to be mapped (step 1). After that, the tool goes through all the classes and creates a list of the classes that deal with users' interactions (step 2). Afterwards the tool uses the list of classes and generates an Aspect to implement the *onUserInteraction*[2] method in the classes that do not yet have it (step 3). This action enables the detection of users' interactions. The next action is to compile the application's source code with the generated Aspect, using AspectJ (step 4). The result will be that the application is ready to be mapped (step 5). To end the process, the application will be embedded on a device that allows the interactions to take place (step 6).

To allow the task mapping and the association of reference values and context during the interaction of the Evaluation Team, another tool was developed, called the Automatic Task Description (ATD). This tool must be embedded on the device on which the application will be mapped and executed simultaneously with the application (Device Mapping component). Therefore, as the Evaluation Team interacts with the application, the executed methods are automatically captured as the concluding steps of a task.

The main point of this tool is to act as a filter that identifies when a user interaction occurs. Also, the filter identifies which classes, methods, and application parameters were used.

3.2   Tools Used in the Traceability Unit

The tool proposed to implement the Metrics Library and the Metrics Generation components was named Usability Metrics Generation. This tool contains a library that has the structure of the metrics that are available to perform measurements. Figure 11 shows a workflow of necessary actions for the automatic generation of the Aspects and its association with the source code of the application.

---

[2] Available in `http://developer.android.com/reference/android/app/Activity.html`

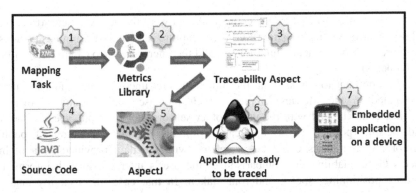

Fig. 11. Workflow for the insertion of the aspects of traceability in an application

The tool receives as input the XML file generated in the Mapping Unit (step 1). Next, the existing methods in the XML, along with the information contained in the Metrics Library (step 2), will be used to generate the Aspects responsible for the capture, transmission, and persistency of the data (step 3). Afterwards, the source code of the application (step 4) and the generated Aspect (step 3) must be compiled using AspectJ (step 5). The result is the generation of an application with the metrics (step 6). Later, the Application will be loaded onto the device with which the user will interact.

The efficiency and effectiveness of the users' interactions are measured through usability metrics described in Table 1. All the measurements take into consideration the mapping of a task, where all the steps to its conclusion are described. Thus, the errors, for instance, are identified every time the user interacts with the application that is not in the previous mapping.

Table 1. Usability Metrics

Usability Metrics	Objectives
Metrics for the capture of assertiveness	
Actions in conformity	Quantify the difficulty of interaction for the user in a task using the interface.
Actions in violation	
Metrics for the search and use of tasks	
Unfinished task	An unfinished task can mean that the user is lost or searching for a desired task. The use/nonuse of a task indicates if the user found what s/he was searching for.
Finished tasks	
Finished and used tasks	
Finished and unused tasks	
Metrics related to performance	
Average time for task completion	Indicate the need for improvements that minimize the time and actions for the execution of tasks.
Average number of actions for task completion	
Number of tasks concluded without errors	
Metrics for the use of help	
Frequency of the use of help	Measure the level of difficulty faced by the user. Identify if the help available provides the desired effect.
Violations made after the use of help	

The sensors used to capture the contextual data were the accelerometer (to capture the horizontal or vertical position), GPS (to capture movement), Luminosity Sensor (to capture the environment's luminosity), and the microphone (to capture noise in the environments).

It is important to stress that the infrastructure uncovers new metrics to be incorporated in the Metrics Library, which increases its adoption in different scenarios, contexts, and with the use of other sensors. For example, specific metrics could be incorporated in an application for the spatial orientation of people. Therefore, such metrics could be associated with the data provided by a mobile device's GPS, enabling the comparison of the user's interactions with information regarding positioning, speed, and route taken. In that case, the usability analysis would take into account not only how a user performs a task but also how the environment influences the user's interactions.

The subjective metrics are used to measure the emotional state of the users during their experiences with an application. The approach chosen for representing these metrics is known as the Experience Sampling Method (ESM) [5].

ESM was chosen because of the following aspects: (i) it is appropriate for use on devices with relatively small screens; (ii) it is intuitive and doesn't take much mental effort to be interpreted; and (iii) it is capable of being answered with entry modes provided by different mobile devices.

ESM measures two dimensions, the kind of emotion (positive or negative) and the intensity of the emotion. To do this, a group of pictures is displayed indicating emotional states associated with a question, as can be seen in Figure 12. The sequence of the pictures represents varying degrees of emotional intensity and can be interpreted from left to right as: very displeased, displeased, indifferent, pleased, very pleased. These questions are defined by the evaluators during the execution of the Usability Metrics Generation Tool.

Fig. 12. Example of an ESM

3.3   Tools Used in the Assessment Unit

To devise the components defined in the Assessment Unit, the following processes were performed: (i) to create and configure a FTP and database server (DB) and to make them available on the internet; (ii) to model a database capable of storing the captured information about the usability of the instrumented applications; (iii) to create tools for detecting the presence of new files on the FTP server and populate the DB; and (iv) to choose an Online Analytical Processing (OLAP) tool to analyze the data.

In order to transmit and store data on the mapping of tasks and the results of users' interactions, it is necessary to have a FTP and a DB available. For this, a micro instance of the service known as Amazon Elastic Compute Cloud (Amazon EC2) was contracted with Amazon, running on the Ubuntu operating system, version 11.10 Oneiric Server, with 613 Mbyte RAM memory and a 16 Gbytes hard drive.

To study the Data Receiver component, the FTP server ProFTPd, version 1.3.4, was installed to manage and control the transfer of files.

To devise the Database component, the DBMS MySql Community Server, version 5.1.58 was installed to store the data.

To devise the Populate Database component, a tool called Data Loader was developed. The steps executed by this tool are: (i) to detect the arrival of new files on the FTP server; (ii) to extract the data; and (iii) to load the data into the database.

To devise the Analysis component, the Pentaho Analysis Services, version 3.9.0, was chosen. It offers two possibilities for data analysis currently used in usability evaluations, OLAP and data mining tools.

4   Case Studies

This section describes the case studies performed to evaluate the functionalities and identify the potentials of the UEProject Model and the Infrastructure with the tools that give support to its implementation.

4.1   Methodology

The first step taken to carry out the experiments was the completion of an exploratory research on the internet with the objective to find applications with attractive functionalities that could be easily introduced into people's lives. Also, it was taken into consideration in the applications selection the compliance to the Android platform and the use of software modularization, allowing the application's source code to be instrumented with AOP.

Following those requirements, three applications were chosen: Mileage, ^3 (Cubed), and Shuffle[3].

The use of these applications in the case studies is based on two important aspects: (i) to show that the infrastructure can be used in usability experiments for Android applications; and (ii) to show that, although the originating process of the application has no connection with the proposed usability evaluation model, the aspects of mapping the tasks and the metrics can be easily integrated into its source code. To enable the investigations, tasks were chosen for each application that would be interesting to evaluate and that would offer more possibilities for interaction. Thus, the model can be tested with a varied group of actions.

The purpose of Mileage is to help users to control the money used on fuel and automotive maintenance services. Eight tasks were mapped in this application to complete the experiments. Some of the mapped tasks for the execution of the Mileage experiments were, for example: to register a vehicle, to add a new maintenance control, and to visualize the graph showing fuel price variation.

^3 Cubed is a music and video clip manager. In this application, six tasks were mapped. Some of the mapped tasks in the experiments were: to choose a song from a playlist, to change the appearance of the application, and to activate the equalizer.

The Shuffle application is an activity scheduler that can manage daily tasks. Ten tasks were used from this application in completion of the experiments. Some examples of mapped tasks in this application are: to insert a new activity, to download a copy (backup) of the data, and to create a new project so that new activities can be linked to it.

It is important to note that, independent of the tasks chosen for the evaluation, the user should not perceive any change in the functionality or appearance of the application. The only change implemented is the presentation of subjective questions to the user.

The applications instrumented with the traceability metrics were made available for download on the internet by users who are interested in collaborating with the experiments[3].

The experiments started in December 2011. About thirty two users downloaded the applications; however, only twenty one of them are frequent and contribute effectively to the investigations. They were categorized according to age, educational grade, field of academic study, work type and social class. The context data being collected to associate to the users' experiences are: environment luminosity, device position (vertical, horizontal and mixed) and user´s movement. In addition to these data, the screen size and resolution of the used device are identified.

The first results of the analyses indicate the possibility for different methods of analysis, such as: to verify the applications usability, to analyze the experiences provided for the users and to relate their interactions to the context of use.

To exemplify, we would like to answer three questions in this preliminary study:

1) What can be concluded regarding the users´ performance over time?
2) What kind of information the context can offer to improve the usability analysis?
3) What is the users´ satisfaction level with the applications proposed in the experiment?

4.2   Analyzing Users' Performance on Interacting with the Applications

To analyze users' performance over the period when the experiments were carried out, the average speed to execute the tasks was evaluated. Figure 13 presents the average time, in seconds, used to conclude the tasks available in the three applications.

It is possible to see that, in the first month, there is a discrepancy in the average time when set against the other months. In December, we can see that the users need more time to conclude the tasks than in the following months. This draws to the conclusion that, after the first month, the users show they are more familiar with the available resources.

---

[3] Available in ueproject.no-ip.org

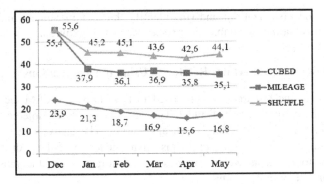

Fig. 13. Average time to execute tasks (in seconds)

4.3   Analyzing the Potential of Considering Contextual Information

It was observed in the analyzed data that the occurrence of errors in the low-income class is greater than in the other classes. To find an explanation to this result, the type of device used by those people was investigated.

It was found that the error rate was not related to the users' purchasing power, but to the low resolution of the devices used. So, as the low resolution devices are more frequently used in the low-income class, a wrong result might be found without the evaluation of a contextual factor.

In Figure 14, the relation between the purchasing power and the smartphones screen resolution is presented. It shows that the errors are more frequent when low resolution smartphones are used, regardless the purchase power.

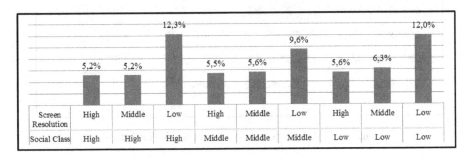

Fig. 14. Relation between the error rate and the social class and screen resolution

Another relevant factor regarding the applications' context of use is that approximately 70% of the interactions occur when the users are still, having the device in a single position and under normal environment luminosity. However, when those contextual factors change, the users make more mistakes and take longer to execute the tasks. This information suggests that the applications should, for example: (i) make the interaction impossible in positions where there is greater probability of errors, forcing the user to interact in the proper position; (ii) detect the external luminosity and try to balance the luminosity radiated by the device in order to guarantee a good visualization; and (iii) identify the user movement and make the most usual functionalities available, decreasing the visual pollution.

4.4   Analyzing Users' Feelings Related to Using the Applications

In order to cover the last question proposed in this study, the ESM technique was used, presenting the questions in Table 2. The aim was to collect subjective data from the users' feelings related to using each application. The analysis of such kind of information allows to detect problems that generate either discomfort or dissatisfaction to users, as well as to learn what attracts users the most to insert applications into their daily routine.

Table 2. Questions submitted to users

ID	Questions
1	How satisfied are you with the interface?
2	How satisfied are you with learning new functionalities?
3	How satisfied are you with using this application in your daily routine?
4	How satisfied are you with the application functionalities?
5	How will you feel when using this application again?

Figure 15 presents the percentages concerning users' answers to the questions made in the experiment for the application Cubed, according to the description and identification (ID) presented in Table 2.

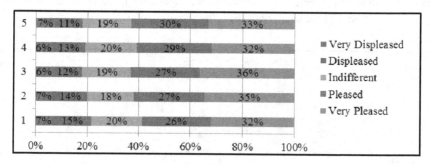

Fig. 15. ESM answers associated to the application Cubed

A fact that deserves to be highlighted is that the distribution of satisfaction level is maintained constant and increasing from very displeased to very pleased. This trend is observed in all questions submitted to users in the three applications.

Another relevant aspect is that the group of pleased and very pleased users is higher than 50% in all items evaluated. This reveals one of the reasons for the success of the experiment in maintaining the users utilizing the applications during the six months. It is essential that the applications are interesting, useful, attractive, rewarding and easy to interact with. After the findings presented, it is possible to say that the users are satisfied with the applications used in the experiments, answering, thus, the last question asked.

5   Related Works

In this section, we describe and discuss some works related to our research that uses at least one of the chosen collecting data used in our proposal to support evaluating mobile applications that is *Logging*, Devices' Sensors and Online Interviewing with users.

The systems evaluation through Logging is not a new strategy as it has been used for over two decades [3]. However, it has gained strength over the last years with the use of AOP to develop it [7][8][9] and the possibility to be applied in smartphones [4][10][11].

The data collection through Logging and sensors in smartphones is the focus of many tools [12][13][14]. These tools, in general, aim to identify the users' behavior and to associate contextual information to its use. The captured data are sent to available servers in the Web for later analysis. The tools LiveLab [11], SystemSens [12] e AnonySense [14] are examples of systems that encompass uncountable logs records, with the objective of monitoring the incoming calls, network traffic, data sharing, battery level, user location, frequency of application use, and CPU and memory use. MobileSens [13] differentiates itself from the previous tools because it uses log records to optimize some smartphones resources in real time such as, reconfiguring the system in order to minimize the battery waste when it is low and indicate more appropriate networks to be used based on the user location. Although the described tools are useful to evaluate users' behavior, they do not enable Online Interviewing with users to identify their satisfaction with the used applications.

The MyExperience [4] stands out in this sense since it uses direct interactions to obtain subjective data that refers to users' satisfaction. The study proposed by Ickin et al [15] presents a mixed methodology to evaluate the user experience, using three different resources: (i) a tool named CSS Application, to capture the log records related to the system use; (ii) ESM, to identify the satisfaction and obtain information about the user interaction context, such as location, social context and mobility level (still, walking, motorized) and (iii) DRM (Day Reconstruction Method), a questionnaire that helps identifying the relationships and results of the Quality of Experience (QoE). Although those tools allow evaluating the user satisfaction, they do not enable identifying specific usability problems, as they don't encompass particular tasks of available applications.

In this context, Paterno et al. [16] proposed a methodology and environment that allows the remote evaluation of mobile applications. The system features a Mobile Logger that collects the information from the mobile device, and a tool called MultiDevice RemUsine that processes the logged information and provides the necessary visualizations to analyze the application usability.

Another similar approach by Au et al [17] was done to test usability of handheld applications. Different aspects considered in testing the usability of handheld device applications and a proposed a list of functional requirements that automated usability testing tools should have in order to be effective were discussed. The Handheld device User Interface Analysis (HUIA) testing framework was then developed and meets most of the requirements proposed.

The EvaHelper [10] framework is another proposal for usability evaluation. Its structure is divided in three aspects: preparation of applications to be tracked, extraction of data obtained and results evaluation. Whilst its structure is similar to the one proposed in this paper, many differences can be highlighted: (i) it does not use AOP, which generates direct intrusion in the application original source code; (ii) it does not have a tool to automatically map the tasks; (iii) it does not have a tool to instrument the code automatically, without the knowledge of APIs and programming in the Android platform and, finally, (iv) it is restricted to statistical evaluations, that is, it does not make the contextual and subjective data capture possible.

6 · Conclusions

This article presented a hybrid model to capture and assess data from smartphones applications. The units of the model were structured in components that can be redefined according to evaluators' needs. Basically, the model can be described in three units: Mapping Unit, Traceability Unit, and Assessment Unit.

The proposal has as main contributions the possibility to evaluate the smartphone applications' usability by integrating, in the same experiment, metrics data, contextual data and users' feelings according to the used applications. In the literature, there is a lack of proposals that relate those three types of data and that support the performance of field experiments with users using the applications in their daily lives.

Other contributions that can be highlighted are:

- The implementation of the components that interfere in the source code of the applications using AOP, so the aspects can be inserted and removed according to evaluators' needs.
- The creation of tools that enable the use of the infrastructure and the instrumentation of applications without the need for programming.
- The provision of a database that allows continuous assessments in order to identify usability problems with a large number of users and for long periods of time.

For future research, new metrics must be developed, prioritizing common attributes of certain groups of applications. Moreover, there is an intention to incorporate to the infrastructure interactions with users that permit to identify their location and social context. Other studies will be published to present the results of the experiments carried out with the objective of contributing to new findings in the Mobile HCI area.

Acknowledgments. This research has been supported by grants from the Brazilian government agencies CAPES and CNPq. The first author thanks UNEB by removal of their academic activities to complete his doctorate.

References

1. Eustáquio Rangel de Queiroz, J., de Sousa Ferreira, D.: A Multidimensional Approach for the Evaluation of Mobile Application User Interfaces. In: Jacko, J.A. (ed.) HCII 2009, Part I. LNCS, vol. 5610, pp. 242–251. Springer, Heidelberg (2009)

2. Zhang, D., Adipat, B.: Challenges, Methodologies, and Issues in the Usability Testing of Mobile Applications. International Journal of Human-Computer Interaction 18(3), 293–308 (2005)
3. Ivory, M.Y., Hearst, M.A.: The state of the art in automating usability evaluation of user interfaces. ACM Computer Survey 33, 470–516 (2001)
4. Froehlich, J., Chen, M., Consolvo, S., Harrison, B., Landay, J.: MyExperience: A System for In Situ Tracing and Capturing of User Feedback on Mobile Phones. Mobile Systems, 57–70 (2007)
5. Meschtscherjakov, A., Weiss, A., Scherndl, T.: Utilizing Emoticons on Mobile Devices within ESM studies to Measure Emotions in the Field. In: Proc. MME in conjunction with MobileHCI 2009, pp. 3361–3366. ACM, Bonn (2009)
6. Kiczales, G., Lamping, J., Mendhekar, A., Maeda, C., Lopes, C.V., Loingtier, J.M., Irwin, J.: Aspect-oriented Programming. In: Aksit, M., Auletta, V. (eds.) ECOOP 1997. LNCS, vol. 1241, pp. 220–242. Springer, Heidelberg (1997)
7. Moldovan, G.S., Tarta, A.: Automatic Usability Evaluation using AOP. In: IEEE International Conference on Automation, Quality and Testing, Robotics, vol. 2, pp. 84–89. IEEE Computer Society, Los Alamitos (2006)
8. Tao, Y.: Toward Computer-Aided Usability Evaluation for Evolving Interactive Software. In: Proc. ECOOP – Workshop on Reflection, AOP and Meta-Data, pp. 9–16 (2007)
9. Bateman, S., Gutwin, C., Osgood, N., McCalla, G.: Interactive usability instrumentation. In: EICS 2009: 1st ACM SIGCHI Symposium on Engineering Interactive Computing Systems, pp. 45–54. ACM (2009)
10. Balagtas-Fernandez, F., Hussmann, H.: A methodology and framework to simplify usability analysis of mobile applications. In: ASE 2009: International Conference on Automated Software Engineering, pp. 520–524. IEEE Computer Society (2009)
11. Shepard, C., Rahmati, A., Tossell, C., Zhong, L., Kortum, P.: LiveLab: measuring wireless networks and smartphone users in the field. ACM SIGMETRICS Performance Evaluation Review, 15–20 (2011)
12. Falaki, H., Mahajan, R., Estrin, D.: SystemSens: a tool for monitoring usage in smartphone research deployments. In: 6th ACM Int. Work on Mobility in the Evolving Internet Architecture (2011)
13. Guo, R., Zhu, T., Wang, Y., Xu, X.: MobileSens: A Framework of Behavior Logger on Android Mobile Device. In: 6th International Conference Pervasive Computing and Applications (ICPCA), pp. 281–286 (2011)
14. Shin, M., Cornelius, C., Peebles, D., Kapadia, A., Kotz, D., Triandopoulos, N.: AnonySense: A System for Anonymous Opportunistic Sensing. Pervasive and Mobile Computing, 16–30 (2011)
15. Ickin, S., Wac, K., Fiedler, M., Janowski, L., Hong, J., Dey, A.K.: Factors Influencing Quality of Experience of Commonly Used Mobile Applications. IEEE Communications Magazine, 48–56 (2012)
16. Paterno, F., Russino, A., Santoro, C.: Remote evaluation of mobile applications. Task Models and Diagrams for User Interface Design, 155–169 (2007)
17. Au, F.T.W., Baker, S., Warren, I., Dobbie, G.: Automated Usability Testing Framework. In: Proceedings of the 9th Australasian User Interface Conference, vol. 76, Australian Computer Society, Inc. (2008)

Methods towards API Usability: A Structural Analysis of Usability Problem Categories

Thomas Grill, Ondrej Polacek, and Manfred Tscheligi

ICT&S Center, University of Salzburg
Salzburg, Austria
{firstname.secondname}@sbg.ac.at

Abstract. The usability of Application Programming Interfaces (APIs) is one of the main factors defining the success of a software based framework. Research in the area of human computer interaction (HCI) currently mainly focuses on end-user usability and only little research has been done regarding the usability of APIs. In this paper, we present a methodology on how to use and combine HCI methods with the goal to evaluate the usability of APIs. The methodology consist of three phases – a heuristic evaluation, a developer workshop and interviews. We setup a case-study according to the methodology, in which we are evaluating the usability of a service-oriented framework API. The goal was to explore different HCI methods and compare the applicability of such methods to find usability problems in an API. The case-study combined qualitative and quantitative methods in order to investigate the usability and intuitiveness of the API itself. It allowed us to identify relevant problem areas for usability related issues that could be mapped to specific types of HCI methods. Examples for this are e.g. structural problems, which are identified mainly in inspection methods, while problems regarding errors and exception handling are mainly identified during the hands-on example part of the developer workshops conducted. The resulting problem areas allow us to develop a first classification of API related usability problems that are making the relevancy of usability issues for APIs more explicit and applicable.

Keywords: API, Usability, Contextual Interaction Framework, HCI.

1 Introduction

Research in Human Computer Interaction (HCI) focuses mainly on the usability and user experience of hardware and software user interfaces. Little research has been done in methods and tools for software developers, especially when it comes to complex frameworks based on a service-oriented architecture (SOA). The developers use Application Programming Interfaces (APIs) to build rich applications with various functionalities. API is a set of reusable components such as objects, routines, or variables that provides a specific functionality. When it comes to measuring usability of an API existing methods from cognitive sciences are usually applied. Such methods are typical user tests where an end-user has to conduct a specific task or inspection methods, where experts evaluate systems based on given heuristics. Regarding the usability of APIs a number of

M. Winckler, P. Forbrig, and R. Bernhaupt (Eds.): HCSE 2012, LNCS 7623, pp. 164–180, 2012.

guidelines and heuristics exist that can be used for heuristic evaluations. Such guidelines are for example elaborated by Joshua Bloch, a software engineer at Google. In his paper "How to Design a Good API and Why it Matters" he discusses insights into requirements of a good and usable API [1]. Other guidelines are given by Scaffidi [2] where he discusses a number of challenges regarding the usability of APIs. All these guidelines have been used and applied in evaluation methods stemming from the area of human computer interaction (HCI). The existing guidelines can be mapped to specific usability attributes. For example, learnability can be linked to documentation, intuitiveness to structure, or user satisfaction to future reuse. This leads to the fact that not only heuristics but also concrete measurable evaluation criteria can be extracted. We address this in the form of a workshop that combines a tutorial or course-like setup with an evaluation approach. This evaluation approach uses methods like questionnaires, think-aloud protocol, video-taking, and interviews. This results in a combined methodology providing us with deeper insight about the usability problems of an API while investigating the applicability of our approach to a SOA-based API. The findings obtained during the study allowed us to do a categorization of the problems based on the problem area targeted by the finding. It also allowed us to map the resulting outputs to particular usability methods applied in our case study in order to highlight appropriate method for different problem areas and to show how the case study covers these areas.

2   Related Work

In the last decade a huge effort has been made to distill common usability flaws within an API. Conducting expert evaluation and user studies have led to development of several design guidelines as well as methodologies for API evaluation. The current methodologies for API evaluation can be divided into two groups according to involvement of users: user studies and expert evaluations.

Empirical studies with real users provide a deep understanding of usability flaws in an API. However, they are hardly suitable for testing large APIs with hundreds of elements because of their high costs. According to Farooq et al. [3] other limitations are difficult recruitment of the users with specific domain knowledge, time demands, and rather slow feedback. One of the first of API user studies was conducted by McLellan et al. [4]. In this study an application example (approx. 2.300 lines) containing the studied API calls was shown to the participants, who were asked to go through it and understand it. The participants were allowed to ask questions. After the test the API was redesigned based on these questions. A quantitative approach was used in the work by Robillard [5]. A questionnaire-based survey with 83 developers identified 11 categories of API learning obstacles that can be divided into five groups: *Resources, Structure, Background, Technical environment*, and *Process*.

The three studies described in the following paragraph focus on general patterns in API design. A study aiming on use of constructor parameters by Stylos et al [6] showed that developers are more effective when no constructor parameters are required. In the next study Stylos et al [7] found a large usability impact on a method placement. Ellis et al. [8] argued that the factory pattern [9] is confusing, difficult to use and should be avoided. A case study of improving an API is described by Stylos et al. [10]. They used the aforementioned general patterns as well as input from interviews with developers.

Expert evaluation methods, sometimes referred to as discount usability methods, are not as time demanding as studies with the users. In the methods an expert or evaluator analyzes the API and checks whether it is compliant with predefined set of recommendations or guidelines. The first design principles for a programming language design called "Cognitive Dimensions of Notations" was published by Green and Petre [11] in 1989. The cognitive dimensions have been successfully used for evaluating visual programming [12] as well as API design [13]. Bore and Bore [14] proposed a set of simplified API profile dimensions, namely *Specificity*, *Simplicity*, and *Clarity*. De Souza and Bentolila [15] focused only on complexity of APIs by automatic counting primitive elements exposed to the users. They also proposed a visualization of complexity of different parts of an API. Watson [16] proposed a heuristic to check consistency in naming conventions in a large API consisting of hundreds of elements.

An effective method for API usability testing is called *API Usability Peer Reviews* published by Farooq et al. [3]. They define four roles in the process: *Feature owner*, who determine the goals of API peer review, *Feature area manager*, who fill any knowledge gaps and record feedback, *Usability engineer*, who is responsible for evaluating the usability, and *Reviewers*, who are not fully familiar with the API but have some knowledge the domain. The method was compared to traditional usability test and it was found that API peer reviews are faster and less expensive, but identify lesser usability flaws and are less sensitive.

The API usability studies and personal experience with API design led to development of many API design guidelines. For example, Bloch [1] lists 39 detailed design guidelines for an API design. Scaffidi [2], on the other hand, gives 4 general challenges of API usability and discusses strategies that designers and users developed to overcome these challenges. Henning [17] gives an detailed example of poorly designed API and discusses costs of dealing with it. He also describes and discusses 8 guidelines for a good API design. Zibran [18] gives a summary of existing design guidelines and results from studies with users. In [19] Zibran et al. identify relative significance of the design guidelines by studying usability-related bug posts across five different bug repositories.

Currently the research on usability of service-oriented architecture (SOA) focuses exclusively on usability of web services. Beaton et al. [20] identify usability challenges for large SOA APIs. They also list HCI methods that can be used for evaluating SOA APIs – think-aloud protocol, expert evaluation using cognitive dimensions, and cognitive walkthrough. In Beaton et al. [21] a qualitative user study with six participants was conducted in which eight errors often made by the participants were observed. Jeong et al. [22] focused on improving documentation for an API of multiple web services. They provide 18 design guidelines for documentation of the API.

3   Methodology

Our methodological approach for evaluating API usability combines several usability evaluation methods. Each method has different strengths and weaknesses. It combines several methods in order to take full advantage of the strengths of each method. This combination provides an opportunity to get a big picture of the usability of the evaluated API. These may be not only problems and flaws in the code, but also conceptual and run-time problems as well as findings related to user experience. The methodology is the first step towards defining a structured process to achieve these goals.

3.1   Roles

Following roles are present in our methodological approach: Expert, Developer, and Evaluator.

(1) Experts are persons knowledgeable in the application domain with experience in the programming language of the evaluated API. They should not be fully familiar with the API. The experts are used in the first phase of the evaluation process – the heuristic evaluation.

(2) Developers are persons with experience in software development. They should be familiar with the programming language of the evaluated API, but they do not need to be familiar with the application domain. Developers are recruited to participate in the developer workshop (2nd phase of the evaluation process) and semi-structured interviews (3rd phase). The number of developers depends on the expected outcome of the evaluation. With low amount of developers mainly qualitative data can be obtained. With higher numbers we can gain quantitative data as well.

(3) Evaluators are persons who collect and analyze findings in each phase of the evaluation. They actively participate in the developer workshop and they also conduct the semi-structured interviews. The number of evaluators can vary between one to three depending on the number of developers and amount of work to be responsible for.

3.2   Process Overview

Figure 1 depicts the process of our evaluation approach addressing the elaboration of API distinct usability problems. Further it allows us to elaborate on an API-centric classification of usability problems as described in Section 4. The process consists of five phases: (1) planning, (2) heuristic evaluation, (3) workshop with developers, where the questions, problems, and potentials are evaluated, (4) interviews with developers and (5) the final analysis. The three different evaluation methods are conducted independently and the interviews with the developers are done right after the workshop to avoid the repetition of an introduction part to the evaluated API.

Phase 1: Planning. In the planning stage the evaluators define a number of experts and developers involved in the evaluation process and start recruiting

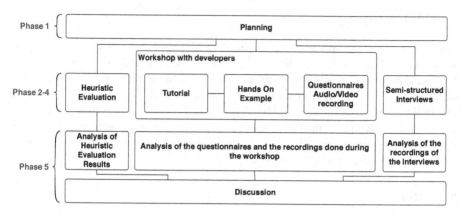

Fig. 1. Methodological Approach

them. Evaluators also decide the objectives and identify relevant parts of the API to be evaluated. They also decide logistics of the latter stages – they plan time slot for heuristic evaluation, date and place of the developer workshop and time slots for the subsequent interviews.

Phase 2: The heuristic evaluation takes place approximately 2-4 days before the user workshop is conducted as it can reveal potentially problematic parts of the API. The developer workshop should then focus on these parts to clarify the problems. *Experts* are recruited and briefed about the API to evaluate by *evaluators*. Each expert receives a list of heuristics used to find, analyze, and categorize problems identified with the API. The outcome of the heuristic evaluation consists of a list of problems identified with the API while the problems are categorized according to the heuristics defined before. After the evaluation the findings of all experts are collected and analyzed according to the occurrence, the severity, and the addressed usability problem.

Phase 3: The developer workshop consists of three parts – introduction, tutorials, and hands-on example. In the introduction, the application domain of the API is presented as well as the API itself. A simple "Hello world" example is shown in tutorials. After that the developers are asked to implement a component defined by evaluators using the API. When the scope of the API is too vast to be covered within one task, we suggest to provide different tasks for each developer in order to cover as much of the API as possible. The developers are also asked to note problems they struggle with in a prepared questionnaire. Besides the developers, evaluators are also present during the hands-on example. Their role is to observe developers, log usability problems, and provide help when they struggle with a problem for too long. Video and audio is recorded during the workshop for future analysis. Demographic questionnaire, informed consent, and non-disclosure agreement forms have to be signed by the developers at the beginning of the workshop.

Phase 4: Post-workshop interviews with developers are held right after the workshop to debrief individual experience of workshop participants. An interview is not longer than half an hour. The total length of this phase depends on the number of participants. Using multiple evaluators can accelerate this process as they can work in parallel. For example, having eight participants and two evaluators, interviews can last only two hours in total. The last interview should be taken no more than two days after the workshop as the developers may forget some important facts. An interview is recorded to allow future analysis.

Phase 5: Discussion. After collecting all materials, evaluators analyze notes, logs, questionnaires, audio, and video recordings. They identify and summarize usability problems and rank them according to severity. The output of the methodology is a list of recommendations for improving the evaluated API.

4 Case Study – The API of the Contextual Interaction Framework

The Contextual Interaction Framework (CIF) is an OSGi[1] based framework developed at the ICT&S Center, University of Salzburg . The framework was built with the goal to support the engineer during the development of contextual study setups. The characteristics of such setups are twofold. Contextual study setups are setups that use information from the environment. Such information is obtained through external sources like sensors and actuators, which provide information about the study environment, the users, and the tasks users are doing during a contextual study. The second approach is to regard to contextual studies simply by defining the environment the study shall take place. The CIF provides functionality to support rapid prototyping by providing the developer a set of functionalities tailored for the rapid prototyping of contextual study setups. The second functionality is to not only simplify the development of such study setups for programmers, but provide tools that allow usability engineers to configure and conduct simple contextual study setups using existing functionality.

Figure 2 depicts the main graphical interface of the CIF for usability engineers to setup studies and for developers to test their functionality to be developed. The CIF implements a plug-in architecture allowing the engineer to apply and extend its functionality. Such functionality encapsulated in *bundles* may be e.g. retrieving data from a sensor, logging to a database, etc. Bundles are depicted as rectangles with a title in the GUI. A bundle contains services that are capable of producing or consuming data. The services are displayed as triangles (pins) attached to the left side of the bundle (consuming data), or to the right side (producing data). The services can be linked together by wires to ensure the data exchange. The GUI provides graphical means to dynamically load, unload, start, and stop bundles and the services within bundles. In the example shown in the Figure 2, the *Data Engine* bundle is used to produce random data which is then displayed on a configurable *Dashboard* and at the same time logged to a database using the *Logger* bundle.

---

[1] http://www.osgi.org

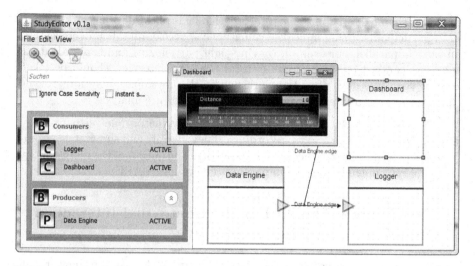

Fig. 2. Graphical user interface of the CIF in which bundles providing various functionality can be connected by creating directed wires.

The setup defined by the CIF represents a data-centric approach where the engineer defines the data-flow between the available bundles, similar to a flow-diagram used during the specification phase of a system. The advantage is that the developer can immediately try out and thus verify the specific data-flow occurring in the system.

In order to address usability problems as well as the user experience of developers with the developed application programming interface (API), we setup a study that focuses in comparison to existing work (see Section 2) on the combination of multiple evaluation methods as described in Section 3.

4.1   Study Setup

Following the methodology described in Section 3 we setup a study to obtain results stemming from the different evaluation methods. Three different types of methods have been applied. We conducted a heuristic evaluation (see Section 3 – *Phase 2*) to obtain findings identified by experts. A one-day workshop for developer (see Section 3 – *Phase 3*) has been conducted with the intention to get in-depth information about the actual usability of the API. In addition we interviewed each workshop participant individually (see Section 3 – *Phase 4*) to be able to identify qualitative data about the usability of the CIF API.

The heuristic evaluation was conducted before the workshop for developers with the goal to identify usability problems of the API of the Contextual Interaction Framework. We selected 16 heuristics based on API design guidelines identified by Zibran [18] and used them to categorize the problem areas occurring when evaluating an API. These heuristics were selected as they summarize existing guidelines available in related work. Table 1 gives a short description of each heuristic based on [18]. The matter of analysis addressed by the experts has been the framework together with the documentation of the CIF, which we made available to the experts through a browser-based interface. The heuristic evaluation was conducted with four experts that were asked to analyze the API of the CIF itself together with the accompanying documentation. The experts were selected according to their experience in software engineering and API design. The number of experts is based on the studies of Nielsen and Molich [23] where 3-5 experts find 60–75% of existing usability problems of an interface. For usability of API this was also approved by Farooq et al. [3], who found that approximately 60% of API usability problems are identified with three to five experts in an API usability expert review. A higher number of experts is resulting in more precise results (see Cockton and Woolrych [24]) and shall be addressed in future studies. The findings were collected by evaluators. The severity of findings was rated in agreement between the evaluators on a scale from one to five where five is related to highest severity.

Table 1. Selected heuristics for the CIF evaluation

Name	Description
Complexity	An API should not be too complex. Complexity and flexibility should be balanced. Use abstraction.
Naming	Names should be self-documenting and used consistently.
Caller's perspective	Make the code readable, e.g. makeTV(Color) is better than makeTV(true).
Documentation	Provide documentation and examples.
Consistency and Conventions	Design consistent APIs (order of parameters, call semantics) and obey conventions (get/set mehods).
Conceptual correctness	Help programmers to use an API properly by using correct elements.
Method parameters and return type	Do not use many parameters. Return values should indicate result of the method. Use exceptions when exceptional processing is demanded.
Parametrized constructor	Always provide default constructor and setters rather than constructor with multiple parameters.
Factory pattern	Use factory pattern only when inevitable.
Data types	Choose correct data types. Do not force users to use casting. Avoid using strings if better type exists.
Concurrency	Anticipate concurrent access in mind.
Error handling and Exceptions	Define class members as public only when necessary. Exceptions should be handled near from where it occurred. Error message should convey sufficient information.
Leftovers for client code	Make the user type as few code as possible.
Multiple ways to do one	Do not provide multiple ways to achieve one thing.
Long chain of References	Do not use long complex inheritance hierarchies.
Implementation vs. Interface	Interface dependencies should be preferred as they are more flexible.

The developer workshop had the primary goal to tutor the developers on the CIF. The workshop started with a *setup session* that had the purpose to show the developers how the CIF can be setup and explain them the particular requirements. In the course of this session, they obtained all the resources necessary to develop with the CIF and also got an introduction to the documentation of the CIF, which should help them to setup the framework. In addition they were given a demographic questionnaire that focuses on the programming experience of the developers as well as a questionnaire in the form of a categorized notebook. The categorizations have been elaborated based on the guidelines for the semi-structured interviews so that we could use the notes that the developers took during the whole workshop as a basis for adapting the interview questions based on the experiences of the particular developers.

The setup session was followed by a presentation about SOA and OSGi and an in-depth presentation providing the developers with insights about the functional parts of the CIF as well as the API that the CIF provides to be able to extend its available functionality. This was done in the form of a slideshow presentation. After the theoretical introduction the developers were given examples that show how to use the framework. Also the different available bundles have been discussed and the developers obtained an introduction to the templates provided by the framework, which act as a starting point to develop an own CIF bundle. The examples were first presented in a slideshow and then explained hands-on using the Eclipse development environment and the CIF. After this the developers were asked to start developing their own *hands-on example bundle*. They were provided with ideas of useful bundles that they could easily implement. Optionally, they also had the possibility to bring in their own ideas, but none of them did so. The developers were asked to use the documentation and templates available and to note all the problems, misunderstandings, potential bugs, and errors they identified. These notes were collected and provided us with information regarding the semi-structured interviews conducted after the workshop. In addition the workshop was recorded using audio and video which provided us with additional means of clarifying problems that occurred during the workshop.

The workshop was held at the ICT&S Center, University of Salzburg where 8 developers (all men, mean age 29, st. dev. 3.1) participated in a one-day workshop. Pre-conditions for the developers participating have been defined through required knowledge in programming Java and the Eclipse programming environment. Seven of them had a university degree, one was a university student. Five of them had at least four years of developing experience, while the experience of the rest varied from one to two years. Their Java experience varied from half a year to nine years.

Post-workshop interviews have been done right after the developer workshop on the same day and on the day after. Semi-structured interview guidelines were defined to obtain comparable qualitative results. The guidelines covered API usability issues based on Table 1 as well as usability factors of the API that have been defined based on Bloch's guidelines [1]. The factors cover the parameters of learnability, rememberability, efficiency, misconceptions, errors, perception of the API, and self-documenting structure and naming. Further parameters of the documentation in terms of completeness, understandability, and helpfulness have been addressed during the interviews. The notes that have been taken by the developers during the workshop act as a basis for the interviews as they are structured the same way as the guidelines.

4.2 Analysis

In this section we present the results of the in-depth analysis of the three different parts of the evaluation of the API of the CIF.

Heuristic Evaluation. Four experts participated in the heuristic evaluation of the API. All four experts were familiar with the application domain and they had already known some parts of the API. They inspected total of 110 classes and 30 interfaces in 29 packages. The length of one inspection varied between three to six hours.

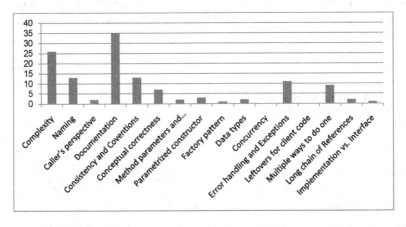

Fig. 3. Distribution of findings in heuristic evaluation

The findings were analyzed and clustered after collecting from experts. A total of 127 unique usability problems were identified by the experts with mean severity of 3.1 (1 – the least severe problem, 5 – the most severe problem) and standard deviation of 1.06. The distribution of the usability problems over heuristics is depicted in Figure 3. Most problems were in missing, incorrect, or incomplete documentation (35), unnecessary complexity (26), e.g. some classes or methods should be removed or redesigned to decrease complexity of the API. Many problems were also in obscure or wrong naming (13), and consistency and conventions (13), e.g. a setter method was missing for its getter counterpart. Heuristic evaluation explore all parts of API equally. Due to inspection-like methodology, the experts could only evaluate definition of classes, methods, interfaces etc., but were not able to analyze run-time behavior.

Developer Workshop. During the developer workshop different types of materials have been collected. The evaluators took notes, the workshop sessions have been recorded on video for post-analysis, and notes have been taken by the participants of the workshop. The collected material provided us with insights into understanding problems of the presentation and the tutorial as well as usability problems of the API and the documentation. During the whole workshop 44 usability relevant issues with the API have been identified. We first separated the findings according to the different parts of the workshop – (a) introduction, (b) presentation, (c) examples, which included a tutorial, and (d) hands-on. Figure 4(b) describes this distribution where the findings are categorized based on the defined heuristics and on the part of the workshop. During the introduction and the setup phase (Intro), where the whole system was setup based on a tutorial provided in the documentation, no API relevant usability issues could be detected. During the presentation phase, 15.91% of API usability relevant issues were detected. During the presentation and elaboration of the examples the biggest part of the usability problems was found (54.55%) while during the hands-on examples phase of the workshop, where the developers had to use the API and develop an own bundle 29.55% of the Usability problems have been identified (see Figure 4(a)).

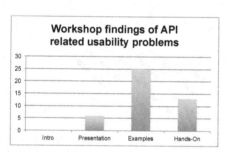

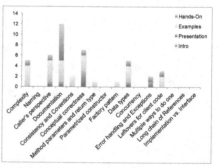

(a) Distribution of findings between the applied methods

(b) API relevant usability findings

Fig. 4. Workshop findings

The issues identified in the workshop have been split based on the categorization of the heuristics (see Table 1). Figure 4(b) shows this distribution. The most of the problems are related to the documentation issues (27,27%), to the concept in terms of conceptual correctness (15,91%), and to the caller's perspective problems (13,64%). An interesting outcome is that during the tutorial when the examples have been elaborated and tutored only 33.3% of the documentation problems were found but 58.3% of these problems could be identified during the hands-on part where developers worked directly with the API. Concluding the API is used in more depth during the real application than during the phase of

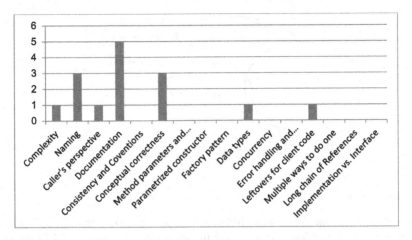

Fig. 5. Distribution of findings from interviews with developers

learning the concept. This conclusion is also supported by the fact that 60% of the identified problems regarding the complexity of the system occurred during the example phase, while only 20% of the complexity related problems emerged during the hands-on phase.

Post-workshop Interviews. The interviews with developers were conducted within the next two days after the workshop. A total of eight developers, who participated in the workshop, took part in the interviews. The interviews identified 15 unique usability problems, which developers struggled with during the workshop. Classification of these problems according to heuristics is depicted in Figure 5. The mean severity of the problems was 3.2 (sd = 1.14) on a five-point Likert scale. Again, the largest number of problems was related to documentation (5). Participants also mentioned three naming problems and three conceptual correctness problems. Interviews allowed us to gain valuable insights into the biggest problems that the developers struggled with. These problems are the most crucial to be corrected as they represent obstacles, which the developer has to overcome during the very first use. Such obstacles can then easily discourage a novice CIF developer from using our framework.

Besides usability problems, interviews revealed the subjective attitude of the developers to CIF. Three participants liked the structure of the API, four participants positively commented learnability and five rememberability. Even though most usability flaws were found in the documentation, three participants stated that the documentation is complete and very helpful. Five participants found naming of methods, classes and interfaces self documenting. The participants were also asked to comment on the idea of CIF. Five participants liked the idea, but three of them stated that it is important to have a library of bundles. In the current state, the library of bundles is rather limited, which caused two neutral attitudes. One participant did not see any added value in the CIF as he is not developing relevant applications.

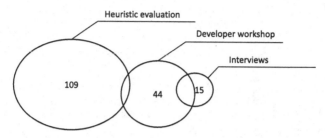

Fig. 6. Distribution of findings

4.3 Discussion

The evaluation revealed a total of 168 usability problems in our API, 157 of them were unique. 109 problems were found in heuristic evaluation, 44 in developer workshop and 15 in the interview. 9 problems were found in both, developer workshop and interviews. In the interviews these problems were addressed in more detail. Only two overlapping problems regarding missing documentation were found in the heuristic evaluation and developer workshop. The distribution of the problems is depicted in Figure 6. Surprisingly, no other overlapping problem was found.

The findings and their structure were different from each part of the methodology. Altogether, they compose a transparent picture of the whole API with focus on its most important parts. An excerpt of the findings is shown in Table 2. While findings from heuristic evaluation are formal and detailed descriptions of problems in the API, findings from the workshop focus on usability problems regarding concept and structure of the API. During the workshop we could reveal more run-time problems that are not obvious and thus cannot be found in the heuristic evaluation. Interviews not only provided deeper understanding of these problems, but also revealed their attitude towards the CIF.

The data collected during the workshop resembled usability testing. The reason why the workshop was used instead of standard usability testing was that the participants had to acquire some basic knowledge about SOA and about the idea of the CIF before taking part in the evaluation. The workshop allowed us to make a presentation of CIF and examples for all participants together in order to save time. Moreover, the presentation during the workshop initiated discussions, from which we could gain valuable insights and comments. During the workshop the developers got familiar with concept of CIF and its API and thus can be subjects for future studies without necessity of the time consuming introduction.

The severity of problems identified during the evaluation was also taken into account. The problems were rated on a five-point Likert scale where five is the most severe problem and one is only a minor problem. Table 3 shows the distribution of the degree of severity among each phase of evaluation and among the different methods applied during the workshop. In order to ensure validity and consistency of the rating, the same group of people (evaluators) assigned the severity for the findings in each phase.

Table 2. Findings example, HE = Heuristic evaluation, W = workshop, I = interviews

Finding	Phase
. . .	
class: ServiceMetaData *finding*: no default constructor, constructors have 4-8 parameters *heuristics*: parametrized constructor	HE
class: ServiceMetaData *finding*: no setter counterpart for getDate() method *heuristics*: consistency and coventions	HE
Data types produced and consumed are stored in a configuration. The configuration is created when the bundle is run for the first time. But if the types are changed after the configuration was saved, it always loads the types from the first saved configuration. The configuration has to be deleted manually and that confused four workshop participants.	W
I was not able to run my bundle for a long time, because the system allowed to instantiate only bundles with specific prefix and I was not aware of it.	I
I am not happy with names consumer, producer. From the point of view of the input device is it actually vice-versa.	I
. . .	

Table 3. Severity of API usability problems for each phase

Phase		Mean	SD
Heuristic evaluation		3.1	1.06
Workshop	Presentation	2.0	0.89
	Examples	2.8	1.30
	Hands-On	3.7	1.38
Interviews		3.2	1.14

The highest mean severity of the usability problems found is for the hands-on part of the workshop. This indicates that the severity of usability problems of an API increases the more the developers are involved in actual using the API. A more abstract engagement in the API (like in the case of the presentation and tutorial) results in the identification of less severe problems.

Results collected from all phases of the evaluation are divided into 16 fine-grained heuristics. As the heuristics do not cover especially user experience factors we developed a classification that provides another categorization of the findings based on the characteristics of the findings rather than on the applied methodology. The classification consists of the following four categories:

1. *Documentation.* This category contains all findings related to documentation – source code documentation, online documentation, tutorials, FAQs, etc. It

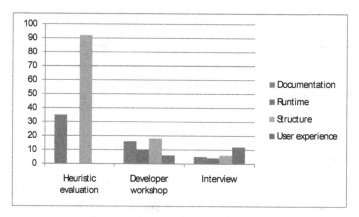

Fig. 7. Classification of the findings

is mainly covered by the heuristic "Documentation" already used in the evaluation.

2. *Runtime.* Findings that can be only revealed when working with the API during at runtime. An example of such finding can be a misuse of the API that results to a runtime exception.

3. *Structure.* Findings related to structure include low-level problems such as naming or complexity of the API, but also higher-level problems, e.g. problems related to API concept and actual perception of the API.

4. *User experience.* This category contains subjective findings related to all aspects of the experience when working with the API. This includes all usability parameters such as ease of use or efficiency, etc., as well as typical user experience attributes like attractiveness, emotions, perceived utility, perceived effeciency, etc.

The classification has been applied to the findings and the result is depicted in Figure 7. The findings from heuristic evaluation are classified either as documentation or structure problems. Neither runtime nor user experience findings were revealed in this phase as no developer was involved. This shows that heuristic evaluations are mainly applicable in order to identify problems related to the structure and also the documentation of the API. The problems identified are of formal nature and do not cover usability aspects. During the developer workshop we could identify in addition to documentation and structural findings also runtime related findings and a low number of user experience issues. During the interviews a lower number of runtime related problems, structural, or documentation issues were found. The strength of this method lies in finding user experience problems. This results in a categorization of identifiable problems regarding their characteristics.

Each applied method has its strengths and weaknesses and focuses on different areas of problems. A combination of the selected methods resulted in a more complete view about the overall usability covering not only static but also dynamic aspects appearing through the hands-on workshop. Combining such specific methods thus allows to simultaneously address related usability problems with an API in an appropriate way. Anyway, further combinations of methods and variations of the methodologies still need to be compared to identify good combinations of methods to evaluate the usability of APIs.

5   Conclusion and Future Work

To study the appropriateness of HCI methods for evaluating the usability of the API of the Contextual Interaction Framework a methodology based on a mixed methodical approach focusing on the mutual pollination of the contributing methods has been developed. Mixing the HCI methods is important as it allows us to get a big picture of problems covering all areas of API usability. We applied this method in a case-study and were able to identify the applicability of different methods for different types of results. Based on the results we could elaborate a classification that provides a mapping between usability findings and HCI methods to be applied. The identified categories reflect structural, run-time related, documentation related, and user experience related usability findings of APIs. The applied methodology generated insights based on an inspection method, a user test, and interviews. They represent a first step towards the classification of the applicability of HCI methods to identify specific usability issues in a software development process. Current limitations of our work mostly exist regarding the generalizability of the approach. In future studies, we will address this by comparing combinations of other usability methods like cognitive walkthroughs, focus groups, API reviews, etc. By doing this, we expect to obtain a more fine-grain classification of the potential methods reflecting relevant areas of usability findings in APIs. Additionally we will evaluate the applicability of user experience methodologies like questionnaires targeting user experience factors like acceptance, attitude, or emotions with respect to the usability and user experience of APIs.

Acknowledgements. The financial support by the Federal Ministry of Economy, Family and Youth and the National Foundation for Research, Technology and Development is gratefully acknowledged. The work described in this paper was supported by the Christian Doppler Laboratory for "Contextual Interfaces" and the COMET K-Project "AIR – Advanced Interface Research". Further we want to thank our colleague Michael Humer who supported us throughout the conception of the work and the user study described in this paper.

References

1. Bloch, J.: How to design a good API and why it matters. In: Companion to the 21st ACM SIGPLAN symposium on Object-Oriented Programming Systems, Languages, and Applications, pp. 506–507. ACM (2006)
2. Scaffidi, C.: Why are APIs difficult to learn and use? Crossroads 12(4), 4 (2006)

3. Farooq, U., Zirkler, D.: API peer reviews: a method for evaluating usability of application programming interfaces. In: Proc. of CSCW 2010, pp. 207–210. ACM, New York (2010)
4. McLellan, S.G., Roesler, A.W., Tempest, J.T., Spinuzzi, C.I.: Building More Usable APIs. IEEE Softw. 15(3), 78–86 (1998)
5. Robillard, M.P.: What Makes APIs Hard to Learn? Answers from Developers. IEEE Software 26(6), 27–34 (2009)
6. Stylos, J.: Informing API Design through Usability Studies of API Design Choices: A Research Abstract. In: Proc. of IEEE Symp. VL/HCC 2006, pp. 246–247 (2006)
7. Stylos, J., Myers, B.A.: The implications of method placement on API learnability. In: Proc. of ACM SIGSOFT 2008/FSE-16, pp. 105–112. ACM, New York (2008)
8. Ellis, B., Stylos, J., Myers, B.: The Factory Pattern in API Design: A Usability Evaluation. In: Proc. of ICSE 2007, pp. 302–312. IEEE Computer Society (2007)
9. Gamma, E., Helm, R., Johnson, R., Vlissides, J.: The Abstract Factory Pattern. In: Design Patterns: Elements of Reusable Object-Oriented Software. Addison-Wesley (1995)
10. Stylos, J., Graf, B., Busse, D.K., Ziegler, C., Ehret, R., Karstens, J.: A case study of API redesign for improved usability. In: Proc. of IEEE Symp. VL/HCC 2008, pp. 189–192. IEEE Computer Society, Washington, DC (2008)
11. Green, T.R.G.: Cognitive dimensions of notations. In: Proc. of the 5th Conf. of the British Computer Society, HCI Specialist Group on People and Computers V, pp. 443–460. Cambridge University Press, New York (1989)
12. Green, T.R.G., Petre, M.: Usability Analysis of Visual Programming Environments: a 'cognitive dimensions' framework. Journal of Visual languages and computing 7(2), 131–174 (1996)
13. Clarke, S.: Measuring API usability. Doctor Dobbs Journal 29(5), 1–5 (2004)
14. Bore, C., Bore, S.: Profiling software API usability for consumer electronics. In: Proc. of ICCE 2005, pp. 155–156 (2005)
15. de Souza, C., Bentolila, D.: Automatic evaluation of API usability using complexity metrics and visualizations. In: Proc. of ICSE-Companion 2009, pp. 299–302 (2009)
16. Watson, R.: Improving software API usability through text analysis: A case study. In: Proc. of IEEE Conf. IPCC 2009, pp. 1–7 (2009)
17. Henning, M.: API Design Matters. Queue 5(4), 24–36 (2007)
18. Zibran, M.: What Makes APIs Difficult to Use? IJCSNS International Journal of Computer Science and Network Security 8(4), 255 (2008)
19. Zibran, M., Eishita, F., Roy, C.: Useful, But Usable? Factors Affecting the Usability of APIs. In: Proc. of WCRE 2011, pp. 151–155 (2011)
20. Beaton, J.K., Myers, B.A., Stylos, J., Jeong, S.Y.S., Xie, Y.C.: Usability evaluation for enterprise SOA APIs. In: Proc. of SDSOA 2008, pp. 29–34. ACM, New York (2008)
21. Beaton, J., Jeong, S.Y., Xie, Y., Stylos, J., Myers, B.A.: Usability challenges for enterprise service-oriented architecture apis. In: Proc. of IEE Symp., VLHCC 2008, pp. 193–196. IEEE Computer Society, Washington, DC (2008)
22. Jeong, S.Y., Xie, Y., Beaton, J., Myers, B.A., Stylos, J., Ehret, R., Karstens, J., Efeoglu, A., Busse, D.K.: Improving Documentation for eSOA APIs through User Studies. In: Pipek, V., Rosson, M.B., de Ruyter, B., Wulf, V. (eds.) IS-EUD 2009. LNCS, vol. 5435, pp. 86–105. Springer, Heidelberg (2009)
23. Nielsen, J., Molich, R.: Heuristic evaluation of user interfaces. In: Proc. of ACM SIGCHI 1990, pp. 249–256. ACM, New York (1990)
24. Cockton, G., Woolrych, A.: Sale must end: should discount methods be cleared off HCI's shelves? Interactions 9(5), 13–18 (2002)

Putting Dementia into Context

A Selective Literature Review of Assistive Applications for Users with Dementia and Their Caregivers

Joël Vogt[1], Kris Luyten[2], Jan Van den Bergh[2],
Karin Coninx[2], and Andreas Meier[1]

[1] Department of Informatics, University of Fribourg, Boulevard de Pérolles 90,
CH-1700 Fribourg, Switzerland
{joel.vogt,andreas.meier}@unifr.ch
[2] Hasselt University - tUL - IBBT, Expertise Centre for Digital Media,
Wetenschapspark 2, B-3590 Diepenbeek, Belgium
{kris.luyten,jan.vandenbergh,karin.coninx}@uhasselt.be

Abstract. People with dementia face a decline of their cognitive functions, including memory impairment and difficulty to orient in time and space. Assistive applications can ease the effects of dementia by assuming and supporting impaired functions. Context-awareness is an accepted paradigm for assistive applications. It enables interactive systems to react appropriately to situations that occur during daily routines of people with dementia. However, there currently is no recommended framework to view symptoms of dementia in terms of context and context-awareness. The aim of this paper is to inform designers in the early design stages of assistive applications how requirements and needs of people with dementia can be represented in a context-aware application. Based on a systematic literature review, we elicit which context types are linked to the needs of people with dementia and their caregivers and how they are used in existing assistive applications in dementia care. Our focus is on applications evaluated and assessed with people with dementia. We also classify these assistive applications by the offered context-aware services. We observe that these should not be limited within the realm of the local residence; context types that are valuable in-house can, to a certain extent, also be leveraged outside a local residence. We believe the proposed framework is a tool for application builders and interface designers to accomplish an informed design of systems for people with dementia.

Keywords: Dementia, Independent living, context-awareness, assistive applications.

1 Introduction

Dementia affects about 4% of people over the age of 65 and 40% of people over 90. In Europe, at least half of the elderly population affected by dementia, have a mild form of dementia [33]. The organization Alzheimer's Disease International

M. Winckler, P. Forbrig, and R. Bernhaupt (Eds.): HCSE 2012, LNCS 7623, pp. 181–198, 2012.

estimates that the worldwide cost of dementia amounts to 1% of the global gross domestic product, or USD 604 billion [50].

Literature shows that the dementia syndrome itself does not thwart the use of digital assistive application, at least at its early stages [23,30,45]. To what extent People with Dementia (PwDs) can benefit from assistive applications greatly depends on the ability to accommodate the user's cognitive impairments and other needs [23,31,38,45]. This limits the use of standardized ICT applications [40,23]. Moreover, assistive applications should be appealing to their users and not be perceived as stigmatizing [31,45]. Hughes et al. [21] emphasize the importance to respect the dignity of PwDs. Context-aware computing allows the development of interactive systems that are aware of their users and behave accordingly [9,11,15,51]. The context-aware paradigm considers the users and the operating environment in the application design and behavior. Given the number of people with dementia and their desire for solutions to cope with dementia, building interactive systems tailored for this user group is extremely important.

1.1   Aims of the Paper

The aim of this paper is to provide a reference framework that assists the preliminary phase in the design and development of assistive applications for PwDs. Given the difficulties to evaluate this type of applications with the target audience, it is vital to maximize an informed design approach [3,38]. We approached this by analyzing services of context-aware assistive applications in dementia care and how they exploit context. We also study the type of context that these applications use to address their users' needs.

1.2   Approach

We conducted a systematic literature review of projects that developed assistive applications for PwDs. The design and development of assistive applications for PwDs is a complex and error-prone task. While traditional user-centered techniques are suitable for abled-body people, Newell et al. [34] point out that they provide little guidance as to how to work with users with special needs. Traditional user-centered design encourages members of the design team to make their design choices from the user's perspective. However people with severe cognitive impairment are too diverse and their situation cannot be reflected as an average user. In addition a user group of people with disabilities has a greater variety of characteristics of functionality which may also be conflicting [34]. We therefore focused on projects which evaluated their running applications with PwDs. We further limited the scope to applications that react to context during runtime (in contrast to design time adaption to contexts of use). Additionally, we considered only literature we could access from our university network or library.

In a first step, we searched the bibliographical databases of ACM, IEEE, ScienceDirect and PubMed. The search query specified the following criteria for the abstract or title of literature: (dementia OR alzheimer) AND (context

OR location OR activity OR ambient OR situation) AND (person OR people OR individual OR adult). ACM gave 10 results, IEEE 34, ScienceDirect 5, PubMed 1. In a second iteration, we removed candidates that did not evaluate and assess their technical solutions with PwDs. This clearly showed that very few of the research projects actually included user trials: ACM was left with 1 result [5], IEEE 0, ScienceDirect 1 [44], PubMed 1 [45]. The number of publications on dementia and context that also performed evaluations with end-users are very low and does not provide sufficient material to define a design space for creating assistive applications. However, we used these papers as a starting point and elaborated on the respective projects they originated from. In a third iteration, we therefore searched references for projects that focused on assistive applications in dementia care. This led to 3 additional Research and development projects [12,24,32].

2   The Person with Dementia as the User

This section puts a human face on dementia. It discusses the impact of dementia, in particular Alzheimer's disease (AD), on People with Dementia (PwDs) and their social context society in literature, to gain a sense of the complexity of this disease.

2.1   The Dementia Syndrome

Dementia is a syndrome of serious decline of cognitive abilities that exceed age-related decline. Common symptoms are memory problems, difficulties to perform familiar tasks, impaired judgement, language deterioration, and mood changes. Dementia is a syndrome with different etiologies, of which AD is the most common type [2,27]. Forgetfulness is generally seen as the primary symptom of dementia; however, this is not necessarily the case for every pathology. Usually, cognitive abilities irreversibly deteriorate over time and the underlying disease is incurable. There is not a single definition of dementia. However, they all do require a functional disability threshold that has to be crossed. Individuals can therefore exhibit a decline of cognitive functionalities that do meet the criteria for dementia [27]. Mandell and Green [27] describe dementia as "a syndrome of *acquired persistent* intellectual impairments characterized by deterioration in at least three of the following domains: memory, language, visuospatial skills, personality or behavior, and manipulation of acquired knowledge (including executive function)".

2.2   Alzheimer's Disease

AD is a neurodegenerative disease and the most common form of dementia [2]. Currently AD can neither be slowed down nor cured [2]. Due to the complexity of AD, some even doubt whether a cure can ever be found [36]. AD is commonly diagnosed after the age of 65, although brain damage resulting from AD can start 10 to 20 years before first symptoms appear. The cause of AD is unknown. Memory problems that exceed age-related decline are early indicators. when the damage spreads to hippocampus. As AD advances, other impairments in other cognitive domains become apparent that curtails abilities to perform everyday tasks, language difficulties, difficulties to understand visual images and spatial relationships, confusion over time and space, misplacing and losing items, mood changes and social isolation [27].

Hodges [17] characterize the clinical process of AD as stages of patterns of impairment of the cognitive abilities *memory, attention and executive abilities, language, visuospatial and perceptual* and *praxis* . The first stage, *mild cognitive impairment*, is prior to the dementia onset. The worsening of cognitive abilities is characterized by the stages *mild dementia, moderate dementia* and *severe dementia*. While early on in the clinical process deterioration of abilities vary from individual to individual, the later developments follow similar patterns. However the duration of each stage differs from person to person.

2.3   Needs of People with Dementia

Dementia is often associated with forgetfulness and confusion. Temporal and memory impairment mean that PwDs need to be reminded of future and past activities and events [13,16]. Memory impairment also manifests itself as an increasing need for information about everyday issues. Hawkey et al. [16] cite an interviewee who wanted to know the role of the participating person (in this example a physician), the location of this person and the route, departure time, and what to wear. The authors also found that some participants had difficulties to relate with time or recognize people they know.

A cause for frustration was the increasing difficulty of some participants to use familiar devices and initiating or completing even simple tasks [13,16,49]. Wherton and Monk [49] analyzed the difficulties PwDs are faced with when performing Activities of Daily Living (ADL) and how they can be assisted. They found that the difficulties were resulting from *sequencing problems, problems finding things, problems operating appliances* and *incoherence.* Sequencing problems occur when incorrect objects or actions for a given step are used. This was seen as a result of being unable to control stimulation from objects or affordances that are not relevant for that task. The second cause for this problem is the degeneration of semantic memory. The impairment makes it harder for the Person with Dementia (PwD) to distinguish similar objects types. Episodic memory problems led to forgetting steps that were already taken; hence, repeating them. Omissions of sub-goals were also reported, when the sub-goal was too similar to the overall goal. The problem finding items was seen for one as a result of episodic memory loss. The PwD would not remember which places were already searched and repeat the search. The disability to identify visible items was also attributed to either not being able to subdue task-irrelevant stimulation or semantic memory impairment. The problem with using items was seen attributable to the inability to comprehend the use of an appliance. The participants did not know when to use an appliance or found it too difficult to understand its functionality. This is seen, as a result of not being able to select between action schemas or the inability to remember the actions that need to be performed. Incoherence is seen as the problem when PwD engaged in activities that are not related to the overall goal.

Dementia aid is primarily situated within the residence of the PwDs, not on activities outdoors. Even though PwDs, at least at the early stages of their illness, appreciate outdoor activities [4]. However caregivers (CGs) fear for their love one's safety and are therefore reluctant to let their PwD leave their safe environment alone. PwDs may also be anxious about getting lost because they are uncertain about their location and finding their way home [4,13]. PwDs feel more conformable in familiar places. Brittain et al. [4] found that PwDs can use landmarks or ask other people to find their bearings. One interviewee would use photographs of older buildings to link the past memory with the current landscape. To reduce uncertainty about the PwD location, Wherton and Monk [47] suggest to reinsure both parties by mutually sharing contextual information. Through mutual awareness, "the function of the technology becomes communication instead of monitoring" [47].

Social interaction is vital for PwDs, e.g. [4,13,31,47]. However, the increased difficulty to manipulate items and problems impairment rises the bar for the PwD to interact with their social environment. Being more and more confined to their residence also affects social activities [4].

2.4   Challenges When Developing for Users with Dementia

Involving PwDs and their CGs in the design process requires empathy for the users and awareness of their abilities, needs and to their environment [1,31,38]. CGs hold considerable sway over the PwD and need to be convinced of the project's merits [3]. PwDs are in most cases older people who are affected by age related degeneration of physical abilities such as vision, hearing or tremor [16]. PwDs may be more or less aware of their conditions [16]. PwDs are also prone to emotional changes. They are easily irritated and may be insecure about their contribution or even be frustrated or anxious [28,38].

It is therefore difficult for designers who have no previous contact with PwD to grasp the complexity of such users. Yet involving PwDs is imperative to gain an understanding of their very unique needs and requirements [6,38,46]. As Stalker et al. [46] point out, if the PwD is the user, then "Reliance on carers for this information is foolhardy".

Novelty is often seen as problem for PwDs. Orpwood et al. [38] argue that "People with dementia will not be able to learn to use new devices in their home". Wherton et al. [48] offer a more nuanced perspective, suggesting that novelty itself is not the problem but rather "learning new arbitrary mappings and procedures". They found that direct implicit clues worked well to guide the PwD.

3   Context and Context-Awareness

Newell et al. [35] suggest that user interface design for people with cognitive impairment should mitigate memory impairment, avoid cognitive overload and take into account individual characteristics. While to a certain degree these requirements are desired by all users, the reduced cognitive abilities of People with Dementia (PwDs) and the emotionally very demanding situation makes these rules imperative. Context-awareness is an accepted paradigm to adapt assistive applications to known contexts of use during design time and can adapt to a dynamic environment during runtime [15,51].

This section presents the categories of context variables and context-aware behaviors for dementia care that were identified in literature. We use the definition of context and context-awareness as provided by Dey and Abowd [9]. Their definition is as follows: "Context is any information that can be used to characterize the situation of an entity. An entity is a person, place, or object that is considered relevant to the interaction between a user and an application, including the user and applications themselves. [...] A system is context-aware if it uses context to provide relevant information and/or services to the user, where relevancy depends on the users task.". This implies that context is a fairly broad concept. Their definition does however provide helpful cues to determine if a piece of information is context or not: It puts contextual information within the scope of the interaction between the user and the system and it does not limit context-aware behavior strictly to context that is obtained during runtime.

Dey and Abowd propose four primary context dimensions to describe the situation of a subject:

1. *activity:* the intrinsic properties that determine the state of an entity. E.g. feelings, tasks or status.
2. *identity:* the extrinsic properties that describe an entity independent of time and location. For example the name of a person, the phone number or personal relationships.
3. *location:* the location of an entity in a physical space.
4. *time:* the location of an entity in temporal space.

Section 3.1 extends Dey and Abowd's categorization of context for assistive applications in dementia care. We studied the research and development projects identified in Sect. 1.2 and literature on the needs and requirements of discussed in Sect. 2.3 to elicit the second level context types that are relevant to provide services and information to PwDs and their caregivers (CGs). Literature on needs and requirements drew our interest to identify context types that have not yet been used in current applications. We also studied the runtime behavior of assistive applications for PwDs in literature that use context to provide relevant services and information to the user. Section 3.2 summarizes our findings as context-aware services.

3.1 Context Types for Dementia Care

This section discusses the context types that our literature review found represent dementia related deficits for assistive applications.

Activity. The activity context type describes the intrinsic properties of an entity [9]. Dementia affects the ability of PwDs to perform activities and influences their emotions. Their abilities and emotional state influence the dialog between a Person with Dementia (PwD) and the assistive application. Activity also describes the capabilities and state of devices. The following context types were found:

- **Emotion:** Dementia influences a person's emotions and their ability to control emotions [4] and anxiety [16,4]. Rebentisch et al. [43] reckon that *frustration/fear, confusion* and *anger* were influential emotions that indicate the onset inappropriate behavior. Hoey et al. [18] consider the variables *dementia_level, awareness and responsiveness* for their activity assistant.
- **Capabilities:** Capabilities describe services or functionality of an entity. PwDs expressed the desire to know more about whom they are interacting with [16], distinguish between similar items [49] or how to use a device [16,49]. This value helps to define semantics of entities, including competencies of people, types of places, and device functionalities.
- **Action:** The action describes the goal oriented process an entity is performing [6,20,41].
- **Status:** The status describes the current state of an entity. For people, this context type can describe their availability [26]. For household appliances, the status can describe whether they are on or off [6].
- **Preferences:** Assistive applications should consider the users' personal preferences [16]. This context type specifies stable personal preferences, meaning they are not subject to frequent change. Examples include language settings, date formats, or color settings; e.g. [6].

Identity. Identity is needed to identify participants and their relationships. The *name* of an entity and *Social relationship* is of particular importance in dementia care. The social relationship context type links two or more persons. PwDs are increasingly dependent on their social context for care and social activities, e.g. [4,13,16,47]. Furthermore, PwDs may experience difficulty to recognize how they are related to some people in their social context [16,47].

Location. PwDs experience difficulty to orient themselves physical space, even in once familiar places [4,16]. They may not recognize their current location or remember how to reach a certain destination, for example their home. We identified the subtypes: *orientation, position, relative location* and *semantic location.* Orientation shows the direction in which to move from one place to another. The position determines the current location, for example for navigation assistance or monitoring. A semantic location denotes the meaning of a place. For example a "bakery" is a place that has a bread service. Hence, if the PwD's semantic location is "bakery", this person is in that place.

Time. Dementia affects episodic memory and temporal orientation [16,47]. PwDs find it increasingly difficult to recall recent events, plan activities and how to relate to time. *Precise time, time span* and *semantic time* were identified. Precise time and time span are used to set reminders, either precise or within a certain threshold. Semantic time refers to an event entity in the user's context, for example lunch time or the time to watch the evening news.

3.2   Categories of Context-Aware Services

The following services were identified in our literature review:

Reminder. A reminder system is a memory assistant to plan and structure future events and activities. The system triggers reminders when certain conditions are met (e.g. time or location is reached). A notable example of context-aware reminders is the CybreMinder [10]. In dementia care, HYCARE [14] supports setting reminders with several context types.

Activity Assistant. While reminder systems remind their users when activities are due, activity assistance tells users how to perform Activities of Daily Living (ADL). Activity assistants vary in activities they support, and the type of support they provide. The COGKNOW DayNavigator [6] displays video sequences that show how to perform a task. The user interacts with a touch screen to play a sequence. Automatic activity assistants delve in the realm of artificial intelligence. The user's context is monitored to intervene when the user is deviating from the plan to complete the task (e.g. [20,41,44]). The development of intelligent activity assistants still faces many challenges [19]. The COACH system is seen as the most sophisticated ADL assistant [19]. It guides a PwD through the hand washing process [20].

Information Provider. Information providers use context to present relevant functions or information objects to the user. The COGKNOW DayNavigator is an example for the former. It offers simplified access to in-house devices and other services. The functions available change when the PwD is outdoor.
An example for the latter are 'information appliances' [16]. These applications provide PwDs detailed information about previous, ongoing, and future activities. The MemoryLane project is exploring this area in dementia care [22].

Communication and awareness. Communication and awareness systems extend social relationships and awareness beyond time and location. Communication is either asynchronous or synchronous. For example, the COGKNOW DayNavigator has a picture-based interface to a stationary and mobile phone. The awareness function makes one entity's context visible to others. An application of awareness is dementia care is monitoring. For example the KITE system [45] shows the location of the PwD to the CG. A context-aware system for PwDs was proposed by [26]. The PwD uses a mobile phone to communicate with his social network. The system stores the type of social relationship for each contact and their availability. The personal CG can monitor the PwD's current location and schedule.

Navigation. A navigation system guides a user through physical space to a desired destination. Both the COGKNOW [32] and KITE [45] projects have a guidance function to help the PwD find their way home. A navigation system that considers location and time was proposed by [26]. Todo items are placed in the PwD's time, location and social context. The navigation system helps the PwD to find the location of a given todo list item in a timely manner.

Life-Logging. Life-Logging complements a person's memory function. It records a constant stream of information during the day as images, sounds, location and time. The information is later processed to reconstruct the user's experiences [24,22].

4   Research Projects

This paper considers the context-aware properties as an inherent part of most assistive applications for People with Dementia (PwDs) and their caregivers (CGs) to accommodate the users' needs and requirements in a dynamic environment. The motivation for this paper is to provide designers and developers with a tool to make an informed decision on the use of context and context-awareness. We

Table 1. Categories of context-aware applications in dementia care

Name	Reference	Users	Settings	Activity Assistant	Reminder	Life-Logger	Information Provider	Communication	Navigation
KITE	[45]	People with mild to moderate dementia, caregivers	outdoor					×	×
COACH	[18,20,29]	People with moderate-to-severe dementia	indoor	×				×	
COGKNOW	[6,32]	People with mild dementia, caregivers	indoor, outdoor	×	×		×	×	×
Context-Aware Wayfinder	[5]	Mental retardation, epilepsy, organic depression, Parkinsoń Disease, dementia, schizophrenia, organic brain syndrome	indoor, outdoor					×	×
CPVS	[12]	People without cognitive impairment, people with mild dementia, caregivers	indoor, outdoor		×		×		
ExPress Play	[44]	People with mild to moderate dementia	indoor	×					
MemExerciser	[24]	People with mild cognitive impairment, mild Alzheimer, moderate Alzheimer, caregivers.	indoor, outdoor			×			

Table 2. Context Types in dementia care

Projects	ACTIVITY					IDENTITY		LOCATION				TIME		
	Emotion	Capabilities	Action	Status	Preferences	Name/Identifier	Personal Relationship	Orientation	Position	Relative Location	Semantic Location	Precise	Span	Semantic Time
KITE				×		×	×	×	×			×		
COACH	×	×	×			×	×	×	×	×		×		
COGKNOW		×	×	×	×	×	×	×	×			×	×	×
Context-Aware Wayfinder						×	×	×	×			×		
CPVS				×	×	×	×					×		×
ExPress Play	×											×		
MemExerciser								×	×			×		

approach by presenting the assistive applications identified in Sect. 1.2 and discussed in more detail in Sect. 4.1 from a context and context-aware perspective. Table 1 shows who the users were, the types of context-aware services they used (see Sect. 3.2) and where the applications were deployed (i.e. indoors or outdoors). Table 2 shows which context types (see Sect. 3.1) assistive applications relied on to provide those services to their users.

4.1 Context-Aware Assistive Applications

The following projects were identified in Sect. 1.2 for our literature review:

KITE. The Keeping In Touch Everyday (KITE) [45] project developed an outdoor navigation and communication system for PwDs. The Person with Dementia (PwD) carries a mobile device. It has a call button to contact the CG and a navigation function. The navigation function presents the PwD with instructions to find their way home. Additionally, the mobile device tracks the PwD's position as well as the device and alert state. These contextual information is presented to the CG via a web interface.

COACH. COACH [18,20,29] is an activity assistant for the hand washing process. The system visually tracks the user's hand movement and process relevant items. The system bases its decisions on current observations and the user's level of dementia and emotions. Emotions are referred to as *attitude* (*dementia_level, awareness and responsiveness* [18]). Only when the PwD experiences difficulties with the task, COACH presents the user with either visual or audio prompts. If prompts are ineffective and the PwD resume the task, the CG is called. The user's comportment influences the attitude and dementia variables over time.

COGKNOW. COGKNOW [6,7,14,32] is a EU funded project to develop a comprehensive support system for people with mild dementia. COGKNOW extends the the realm of the PwD's residence. The PwD accesses services either through a stationary touchscreen interface or a mobile device. Activities are supported with a context-aware reminder system, video recorded instructions for a set of activities and simplified access to services. The reminder system triggers time-based and event-based reminders. Reminders are set by a CG [14]. Simplified access to music, radio and communication service are presented by both stationary and mobile device. Outdoors, the PwD has access to reminders and communication on the mobile device. An additional navigation function to get home is presented. Social communication is provided with a simplified interface to the phone. The PwD is presented with pictures of each CG to call. A help button is provided to directly call the main CG.

Context-Aware Wayfinder. [5] developed a navigation system for people with cognitive impairments, including dementia. The system guides their users to a destination by presenting images of the next waypoint and overlaying directions for the user's route. User and CG can call if needed. The system records the route progress and compliance. It presents this monitoring information to an authorized person.

ExPress Play. ExPress Play is an application for PwDs to engage in a creative activity through music. The system provides a touch screen and an easy to use interface. Users can select their emotion (happiness, sadness and anger) which influences the music being played and the visualization of the sound. The users interact with the application by dragging a finger across the screen. The system draws shapes depending on the speed of movement and plays different sounds [44].

CPVS. The Cell Phone Video Streaming (CVPS) system [12] is a mobile reminder for people with mild dementia. The system consists of a smart phone for the PwD and a workstation with video camera for the CG. Reminders are video clips that are presented to the PwD. The PwD's CG records and schedules the reminders for the user. The smart phone downloads videos and notifies the PwD at the given time. The PwD needs to confirm the reminder by pressing a button. Reminders' confirmation state is accessible to the CG via a web-based interface.

MemExerciser. MemExerciser [24] alleviates episodic memory impairment by recording and later replaying a PwD's passed experiences. The system consists of three parts: mobile sensors for life-logging, the CueChooser application to create a narrative of the PwD's experiences and MemExerciser to replay the narrative. A PwD carries a mobile camera with tree-axis accelerometer (Microsoft SenseCam), an audio recorder and a GPS. The camera and GPS record data in predefined time interval, the audio device records constantly. The recorded information is later preselected by the CueChooser application based on the context meta data. The CG further refines and tags the data to select good memory cues for the PwD. The PwD can partly compensate the memory impairment by "recalling" past experiences with the MemExerciser application.

5   Discussion

There is an increased focus on early detection and diagnosis of Alzheimer's disease [8,42]. A recent study commissioned by Alzheimer's Disease International [42] found that early diagnosis and intervention were beneficial to Person with Dementias (PwDs). The motivation for our research is to facilitate the design of assistive applications for people at the early stage of dementia. In this section, we reflect on what we learned about the potential of assistive applications in dementia care to prolong independent living and how People with Dementia (PwDs) and their caregivers (CGs) can be involved in the design process.

5.1   Assistive Applications to Prolong Independent Living

The purpose of our work is to help designers to map the needs and requirements of PwDs to the context dimensions *activity*, *identity*, *location* and *time* [9]. Our literature study shows, that this field is drawing a lot of interest from the research community, which is reflected by several large scale research projects. However, only few applications were tested with the actual target group. This is not surprising, given the following two reasons. First, developing and testing for PwDs is a cumbersome process. The specific disease does not allow a traditional user-centered approach that designs for average users. Designers who collaborate with PwDs face a number of challenges in their effort to understand the requirements and needs of their users [25,37,16]. They must develop systems that are tailored to individual users' context to reduce cognitive load, without putting users under pressure, who often provide only vague and sometimes conflicting information [25,37]. Second, there is no "user with dementia" archetype a designer can aim for. While PwDs share many characteristics, the advancement of the dementia syndrome is different for each person. Also the PwDs and their CGs's coping strategies will differ from case to case [39]. Designers must therefore not only consider the PwD's cognitive abilities, but also personal and social aspects. This was the main reason our survey focused on projects in which PwDs participated as users. A challenge during our survey was to determine whether a piece of data is context, as defined by Dey and Abowd [9] or not. During the study of assistive software for PwDs, the perspective of context and context-awareness provided us with a first impression of the role of context in the design process.

5.2   Design Recommendations

We summarize these findings as a set of basic design recommendations here. The recommendations are distilled from the practices presented by the projects and papers we studied for this survey. We listed good practices that occurred in one or more sources, and labeled them with a fitting title. With these design recommendations we want to provide a set of general guidelines and rules that lead to informed design for assistive applications for PwD. Since performing user evaluations with this specific user group is complex and often undesirable, having these guidelines can be of great help to create accessible assistive applications tailored according to the target group.

Represent time explicitly. PwD rely on a concrete notion of time and progress in time to alleviate the impacts of episodic memory impairment. Time is therefore an important non-functional requirement, which is present in all the services we studied. Time is often combined with other context information. E.g. a reminder for medication may also consider the location to present reminders when the PwD is in the right room. Or an activity assistant may adapt the triggering of prompts depending on the PwD's mood. An appropriate interactive system should schedule events in the interface and display reminders and other information as well as recording time stamps in live logging for later retrieval.

- This recommendation is based on [13,16,47]
- This recommendation has been applied by [5,6,20,24,44,45]

Label temporal events. Temporal impairment can be alleviated by giving a meaning to temporal events. PwDs find it increasingly difficult to make sense of time. This is referred to as semantic time in Table 2. Semantic time is inherently linked to other context dimensions. For example "lunch" is the time when a person eats at home, normally around 12:00h.

- This recommendation is based on [13,16,47]
- This recommendation has been applied by [6,12]

Make location data accessible at all times. Use location in the dialog with PwDs to mitigate topological and geographical disorientation. A typical service for the PwD is a navigation system that guides the person from its current location to a destination. Location also provides tracking capabilities to locate the PwD and trigger alerts. Semantic location is a location in combination with other context information. For example a shop or a rendezvous point, i.e. a place where two or more people are to meet at a given time. Location also manifests itself in the interface as choices of information of functionalities that are presented to the user. For example a controller removes access to the radio once the PwD leaves the house.

- This recommendation is based on [4,13,16]
- This recommendation has been applied by [5,6,12,45]

Explicitly and uniquely identify all people, concepts and objects in the user interface. To avoid confusion, label all concepts, people and objects that might be accessed through the user interface. This needs to be done in an unambiguous way to avoid confusing the PwD. E.g. when to contact someone using a contact list, people with similar names could cause confusion. In this situation extra information needs to be added to increase the discrepancy between similar items. PwD tend to misplace objects or be unsure which object to use. Activity assistants and reminders need to know which objects the PwD needs for their tasks. Identity can also be combined with subtypes of activity, such as the status of kitchen appliances.

- This recommendation is based on [13,16,47]
- This recommendation has been applied by [5,6,20,45]

Put the social network central. The first line of help comes from other people: CG, other relatives, medical professionals and friends. The interface can reassure PwD that there are people they know reachable for help by including a contact list. For example: one presentation of social relationships is an address book that lets a PwD call a contact. An alerting service uses social relationship to send notifications and escalate alerts to multiple contacts is an example for a background service. Additional information about the contacts, such as competencies or availability, can help to route notifications to contacts that are the most likely to help.

- This recommendation is based on [4,13,31,47]
- This recommendation has been applied by [5,6,12,20,45]

Show the current activity at all time. The assistive application should show what the currently planned activity is at all times. This relies on an agenda that is available with the PwD daily activities. We found "user activity" is, together with time, the most important but also the most demanding to incorporate into the system design. Preferably, the previous activity and next planned activity are included in the user interface design.

- This recommendation is based on [4,16,47,49]
- This recommendation has been applied by [6,12,20,45]

Foster Personal Identity. PwDs and their CGs are very sensitive about how they are perceived by others. Maintaining their personal identity, respect and dignity is vital for PwDs and their CGs. Assistive applications should be appealing to their users and not be perceived as stigmatizing. In addition to functional requirements, the design must therefore consider the individuals' preferences and blend into their environment.

- This recommendation is based on [4,13,16,21,31,34]
- This recommendation has been applied by [6,12,44,45]

6   Conclusion

The context and context-awareness classification and our design recommendations presented are by no means a substitute for consulting medical professional and people affected by dementia. Our aim is to provide a tool to assist a preparatory investigation for the design and development of context-aware applications for Person with Dementia (PwD). The framework informs developers and designers about possible use of context for their applications. Validation with the target group remains the best approach, but given the condition of the test users it is extremely difficult to do actual user trials. Our framework builds upon previous research and development in this domain and makes the previous experiences in building such system more accessible for developers and designers creating a new system. When use cases are defined for a project, our reference framework helps to identify the (1) dimensions of context that need to be taken into account, (2) provide a set of examples of concrete implementations for these dimensions by referring to relevant research projects and (3) helps to uncover important context dimensions that might otherwise easily missed while designing an assistive application for People with Dementia (PwDs).

Acknowledgments. Part of the research described in this article was performed in the context of the IBBT project AToM. This project is cofunded by the IBBT (Interdisciplinary institute for Technology), a research institute founded by the Flemish Government. Companies and organizations involved in the project are Televic Healthcare NV, GS1 Belgium & Luxembourg vzw, Woonen Zorgcentrum Sint-Jozef vzw, Katholieke Hogeschool Limburg, Ter Linden vzw, Pyxima NV, Bedrijfstechnische Eenheid Broeders Alexianen, with project support of IWT.

References

1. Aggarwal, N., Vass, A.A., Minardi, H.A., Ward, R., Garfield, C., Cybyk, B.: People with dementia and their relatives: personal experiences of alzheimer's and of the provision of care. J. Psychiatr. Ment Health Nurs 10(2), 187–197 (2003)
2. Association, A.: 2012 alzheimer's disease facts and figures. Alzheimers Dement 8(2), 131–168 (2012)
3. Astell, A., Alm, N., Gowans, G., Ellis, M., Dye, R., Vaughan, P.: Involving older people with dementia and their carers in designing computer based support systems: some methodological considerations. Universal Access in the Information Society 8(1), 49–58 (2009)
4. Brittain, K., Corner, L., Robinson, L., Bond, J.: Ageing in place and technologies of place: the lived experience of people with dementia in changing social, physical and technological environments. Sociology of Health & Illness 32(2), 272–287 (2010)
5. Chang, Y.J., Tsai, S.K., Wang, T.Y.: A context aware handheld wayfinding system for individuals with cognitive impairments. In: Proceedings of the 10th International ACM SIGACCESS Conference on Computers and Accessibility, Assets 2008, pp. 27–34. ACM, New York (2008)
6. Davies, R.J., Nugent, C.D., Donnelly, M.: Prototyping cognitive prosthetics for people with dementia. In: Jain, L., Wu, X., Mulvenna, M.D., Nugent, C.D. (eds.) Supporting People with Dementia Using Pervasive Health Technologies. Advanced Information and Knowledge Processing, pp. 145–163. Springer, London (2010)

7. Davies, R.J., Nugent, C.D., Donnelly, M.P., Hettinga, M., Meiland, F.J., Moelaert, F., Mulvenna, M.D., Bengtsson, J.E., Craig, D., Dröes, R.M.: A user driven approach to develop a cognitive prosthetic to address the unmet needs of people with mild dementia. Pervasive and Mobile Computing 5(3), 253–267 (2009); pervasive Health and Wellness Management

8. DeKosky, S.T., Carrillo, M.C., Phelps, C., Knopman, D., Petersen, R.C., Frank, R., Schenk, D., Masterman, D., Siemers, E.R., Cedarbaum, J.M.: Revision of the criteria for alzheimer's disease: A symposium. Alzheimer's and Dementia 7(1), e1–e12 (2011)

9. Dey, A.K., Abowd, G.: Towards a better understanding of context and context-awareness. In: CHI 2000 Workshop on the What, Who, Where, When, and How of Context-awareness, vol. 4, pp. 1–6. Citeseer (2000)

10. Dey, A.K., Abowd, G.D.: CybreMinder: A Context-Aware System for Supporting Reminders. In: Thomas, P., Gellersen, H.-W. (eds.) HUC 2000. LNCS, vol. 1927, pp. 172–186. Springer, Heidelberg (2000)

11. Dey, A.K., Mankoff, J.: Designing mediation for context-aware applications. ACM Trans. Comput.-Hum. Interact. 12, 53–80 (2005)

12. Donnelly, M.P., Nugent, C.D., McClean, S., Scotney, B., Mason, S., Passmore, P., Craig, D.: A mobile multimedia technology to aid those with alzheimer's disease. IEEE Multimedia 17(2), 42–51 (2010)

13. Dröes, R.M., Bentvelzen, S., Meiland, F., Craig, D.: Dementia-related and other factors to be taken into account when developing ict support for people with dementia–lessons from field trials. In: Jain, L., Wu, X., Mulvenna, M.D., Nugent, C.D. (eds.) Supporting People with Dementia Using Pervasive Health Technologies. Advanced Information and Knowledge Processing, pp. 113–127. Springer, London (2010)

14. Du, K., Zhang, D., Zhou, X.-S., Mokhtari, M., Hariz, M., Qin, W.: HYCARE: A Hybrid Context-Aware Reminding Framework for Elders with Mild Dementia. In: Helal, S., Mitra, S., Wong, J., Chang, C.K., Mokhtari, M. (eds.) ICOST 2008. LNCS, vol. 5120, pp. 9–17. Springer, Heidelberg (2008)

15. Gajos, K.Z., Weld, D.S., Wobbrock, J.O.: Automatically generating personalized user interfaces with supple. Artificial Intelligence 174(12-13), 910–950 (2010)

16. Hawkey, K., Inkpen, K.M., Rockwood, K., McAllister, M., Slonim, J.: Requirements gathering with alzheimer's patients and caregivers. In: Proceedings of the 7th International ACM SIGACCESS Conference on Computers and Accessibility, Assets 2005, pp. 142–149. ACM, New York (2005)

17. Hodges, J.R.: Alzheimer's centennial legacy: origins, landmarks and the current status of knowledge concerning cognitive aspects. Brain 129(Pt 11), 2811–2822 (2006)

18. Hoey, J., von Bertoldi, A., Poupart, P., Mihailidis, A.: Assisting persons with dementia during handwashing using a partially observable markov decision process. In: The 5th International Conference on Computer Vision Systems, pp. 1–10 (February 2007)

19. Hoey, J., Plötz, T., Jackson, D., Monk, A., Pham, C., Olivier, P.: Rapid specification and automated generation of prompting systems to assist people with dementia. Pervasive and Mobile Computing (2010) (in Press, Corrected Proof)

20. Hoey, J., Poupart, P., von Bertoldi, A., Craig, T., Boutilier, C., Mihailidis, A.: Automated handwashing assistance for persons with dementia using video and a partially observable markov decision process. Computer Vision and Image Understanding 114(5), 503–519 (2010); special issue on Intelligent Vision Systems

21. Hughes, J.C., Louw, S.J., Sabat, S.S.R.: Seeing whole. In: Hughes, J.C., Louw, S.J., Sabat, S.S.R. (eds.) Dementia: Mind, Meaning, and the Person, ch. 1, pp. 1–39. Oxford University Press, USA (2006)
22. Kikhia, B., Hallberg, J., Synnes, K., Sani, Z.U.H.: Context-aware life-logging for persons with mild dementia. In: Annual International Conference of the IEEE Engineering in Medicine and Biology Society, EMBC 2009, pp. 6183–6186 (2009)
23. Lauriks, S., Reinersmann, A., Van der Roest, H.G., Meiland, F., Davies, R.J., Moelaert, F., Mulvenna, M.D., Nugent, C.D., Dröes, R.M.: Review of ICT-based services for identified unmet needs in people with dementia. Ageing Research Reviews 6(3), 223–246 (2007)
24. Lee, M.L., Dey, A.K.: Lifelogging memory appliance for people with episodic memory impairment. In: Proceedings of the 10th International Conference on Ubiquitous Computing, UbiComp 2008, pp. 44–53. ACM, New York (2008)
25. Lindsay, S., Brittain, K., Jackson, D., Ladha, C., Ladha, K., Olivier, P.: Empathy, participatory design and people with dementia. In: Proceedings of the 2012 ACM Annual Conference on Human Factors in Computing Systems, pp. 521–530. ACM (2012)
26. Mahmud, N., Vogt, J., Luyten, K., Slegers, K., Van den Bergh, J., Coninx, K.: Dazed and Confused Considered Normal: An Approach to Create Interactive Systems for People with Dementia. In: Bernhaupt, R., Forbrig, P., Gulliksen, J., Lárusdóttir, M. (eds.) HCSE 2010. LNCS, vol. 6409, pp. 119–134. Springer, Heidelberg (2010)
27. Mandell, A.M., Green, R.C.: Alzheimer's Disease, pp. 1–91. Wiley-Blackwell, Oxford (2011)
28. McKeown, J., Clarke, A., Ingleton, C., Repper, J.: Actively involving people with dementia in qualitative research. J. Clin. Nurs. 19(13-14), 1935–1943 (2010)
29. Mihailidis, A., Boger, J., Craig, T., Hoey, J.: The coach prompting system to assist older adults with dementia through handwashing: An efficacy study. BMC Geriatrics 8(1), 28 (2008)
30. Mileo, A., Merico, D., Bisiani, R.: Support for context-aware monitoring in home healthcare. J. Ambient Intell. Smart Environ. 2(1), 49–66 (2010)
31. Monk, A.F.: Simple, social, ethical and beautiful: requirements for uis in the home. In: Proceedings of the Ninth Conference on Australasian user Interface, AUIC 2008, vol. 76, pp. 3–9. Australian Computer Society, Inc., Darlinghurst (2008)
32. Mulvenna, M.D., Moelaert, F., Meiland, F., Sävenstedt, S., Hettinga, M., Craig, D., Bengtsson, J.E., Dröes, R.M., Martin, S.: Designing & evaluating a cognitive prosthetic for people with mild dementia. In: Caring Technology for the Future: Proceedings of the European Conference on Cognitive Ergonomics, pp. 11–18 (2010)
33. Mulvenna, M.D., Nugent, C.D., Moelaert, F., Craig, D., Dröes, R.M., Bengtsson, J.E.: Supporting people with dementia using pervasive healthcare technologies. In: Jain, L., Wu, X., Mulvenna, M.D., Nugent, C.D. (eds.) Supporting People with Dementia Using Pervasive Health Technologies. Advanced Information and Knowledge Processing, pp. 3–14. Springer, London (2010)
34. Newell, A.F.F., Gregor, P., Morgan, M., Pullin, G., Macaulay, C.: User-sensitive inclusive design. Universal Access in the Information Society 10(3), 235–243 (2011)
35. Newell, A.F., Carmichael, A., Gregor, A., Alm, N., Waller, A.: Information technology for cognitive support. In: Sears, A., Jacko, J.A. (eds.) The Human- Computer Interaction Handbook: Fundamentals, Evolving Technologies, and Emerging Applications, 2nd edn., ch. 41, pp. 811–828. CRC Press (2007)

36. About alzheimer's disease: Treatment national institute on aging
37. Orpwood, R., Sixsmith, A., Torrington, J., Chadd, J., Gibson, G., Chalfont, G.:
    Designing technology to support quality of life of people with dementia. Technology
    and Disability 19(2), 103–112 (2007)
38. Orpwood, R., Sixsmith, A., Torrington, J., Chadd, J., Gibson, M., Chalfont, G.:
    Designing technology to support quality of life of people with dementia. Technology
    and Disability 19(2), 103–112 (2007)
39. Perry, J., O'Connor, D.: Preserving personhood (re)membering the spouse with
    dementia*. Family Relations 51(1), 55–62 (2002)
40. Peterson, C.B., Mitseva, A., Mihovska, A., Prasad, N.R., Prasad, R.: The phe-
    nomenological experience of dementia and user interface development. In: 2nd In-
    ternational Symposium on Applied Sciences in Biomedical and Communication
    Technologies, ISABEL 2009, pp. 1–5 (2009)
41. Phua, C., Foo, V.S.F., Biswas, J., Tolstikov, A., Aung, A.P.W., Maniyeri, J.,
    Huang, W., That, M.H., Xu, D., Chu, A.K.W.: 2-layer erroneous-plan recogni-
    tion for dementia patients in smart homes. In: 11th International Conference on
    e-Health Networking, Applications and Services, Healthcom 2009, pp. 21–28 (2009)
42. Prince, M.B., Bryce, R., Ferri, C.: World alzheimer report 2011: The benefits of
    early diagnosis and intervention. Alzheimer's Disease International 15, 5–65 (2011)
43. Rebenitsch, L., Owen, C.B., Ferrydiansyah, R., Bohil, C., Biocca, F.: An explo-
    ration of real-time environmental interventions for care of dementia patients in
    assistive living. In: Proceedings of the 3rd International Conference on PErva-
    sive Technologies Related to Assistive Environments, PETRA 2010, pp. 34:1–34:8.
    ACM, New York (2010)
44. Riley, P., Alm, N., Newell, A.: An interactive tool to promote musical creativity in
    people with dementia. Computers in Human Behavior 25(3), 599–608 (2009)
45. Robinson, L., Brittain, K., Lindsay, S., Jackson, D., Olivier, P.: Keeping In
    Touch Everyday (KITE) project: developing assistive technologies with people
    with dementia and their carers to promote independence. International Psychogeri-
    atrics 21(03), 494–502 (2009)
46. Stalker, K., Gilliard, J., Downs, M.G.: Eliciting user perspectives on what works.
    International Journal of Geriatric Psychiatry 14(2), 120–130 (1999)
47. Wherton, J.P., Monk, A.F.: Technological opportunities for supporting people with
    dementia who are living at home. International Journal of Human-Computer Stud-
    ies 66(8), 571–586 (2008)
48. Wherton, J.P., Monk, A.F.: Choosing the right knob. In: Proceedings of the 27th
    International Conference Extended Abstracts on Human Factors in Computing
    Systems, CHI 2009, pp. 3631–3636. ACM, New York (2009)
49. Wherton, J.P., Monk, A.F.: Problems people with dementia have with kitchen
    tasks: The challenge for pervasive computing. Interacting with Computers 22(4),
    253–266 (2010); supportive Interaction: Computer Interventions for Mental Health
50. Wimo, A., Prince, M.: World alzheimer report (2010)
51. Wobbrock, J.O., Kane, S.K., Gajos, K.Z., Harada, S., Froehlich, J.: Ability-based
    design. ACM Transactions on Accessible Computing 3(3), 1–27 (2011)

Puzzle: A Visual-Based Environment for End User Development in Touch-Based Mobile Phones

Jose Danado and Fabio Paternò

CNR-ISTI, HIIS
Via Moruzzi 1, 56124 Pisa, Italy
{danado,fabio.paterno}@isti.cnr.it

Abstract. Despite the widespread usage of mobile devices there is a lack of environments able to allow end users to create applications directly in such devices. In this paper, we present the Puzzle framework, which supports a visual environment for opportunistically creating mobile applications in touch-based mobile phones. The user interface is designed to be usable for mobile users that do not use programming languages in their daily work as well as to motivate end users to playfully experiment and create applications. In particular, we report on its user interface, framework and evaluation.

Keywords: End user development, ubiquitous computing, mobile computing, authoring tools.

1 Introduction

The number of available applications for smartphones is rapidly growing, together with the number of users interested in top-range mobile devices. In 2011 alone 472 million smartphones were sold [1]. The complexity of mobile applications is also increasing because of the many possible preferences and contexts of use [2].

In this paper, we present a framework, named Puzzle, which considers these trends and enables end users without programming experience to create applications in mobile touch-based devices. There are various reasons for this type of proposal. Professional developers lack the domain knowledge that end users cannot easily convey when transmitting requirements for a new application, and regular development cycles are too slow to meet users' fast changing requirements [3]. End-user developers outnumber professional developers, thus it is important to develop End-User Development (EUD) tools, which are easy to learn and use, and to increase their quality and relevance for the users [4]. Furthermore, the Internet, and wide spread usage of mobile devices are potential tools to create a shift from the conventional few-to-many distribution model of software to a many-to-many distribution model. In summary, Puzzle aims to allow for a smooth adaptation in fast, mobile and dynamic environments where end users can easily adapt their mobile applications to newer requirements.

M. Winckler, P. Forbrig, and R. Bernhaupt (Eds.): HCSE 2012, LNCS 7623, pp. 199–216, 2012.
© IFIP International Federation for Information Processing 2012

This paper considers two main aspects: the user interface (UI) of the environment and the framework. Regarding the UI, we aimed to design an easy to learn and use UI, which can be used in touch-based mobile devices, and copes with the limitations given by mobile use. Puzzle is based on the metaphor conveyed by jigsaw pieces to stimulate end users to combine functional building blocks. Building blocks exchange data between them to allow end users to explore possible combinations within their applications. The decision on adopting such metaphor was based on its usage on other EUD environments [5][6]. Puzzle adopts a higher level approach not just mimicking a traditional language through a graphical metaphor, but providing jigsaw pieces ready to be combined on the go, thus decreasing the learning curve and motivating users to explore and use it. Furthermore, jigsaw pieces were designed to facilitate users to combine them, and to solve errors and conflicts made during their combination. In order to allow Puzzle to be used across several mobile touch-based devices, it was implemented with established and widespread web technologies, namely HTML, CSS and Javascript.

Regarding the framework, we aim to create a framework that is flexible enough to integrate existing frameworks and technologies, and handle fast changes in the technologies used, both in the framework and the resulting applications. Mobile applications developed using Puzzle can exploit pre-existing applications or services, physical interactive devices and features of the smartphone. Starting from scratch or with available basic applications, users can define complex applications that better meet their needs.

Evaluation of the environment has included end users without programming experiences in two different stages of the Puzzle development. In particular, we evaluated the following contributions: *a)* The touch-based User Interface to support creation of applications in mobile touch-based devices, and *b)* The architecture to support creation, modification and execution in touch-based phones.

This paper is structured as follows: after discussing related work, Section 3 presents a sample application. Section 4 introduces the proposed approach for the development of mobile applications. Then, we present the environment UI, and the framework, followed by the description of the usability evaluation carried out. Lastly, we draw some conclusions and provide indications for future work.

2   Related Work

EUD environments to create context-sensitive applications for mobile devices mainly targeted desktop environments. In general, the main domains of desktop EUD environments targeting context-sensitive applications were tourism and virtual guides. Contributions range from support for a set of template applications for tourism [7] [8], domain-related content management to support guided tours [8] [7] [9], collaboration of different stakeholders [9], up to an EUD environment where the context is enriched through addition of calendar events; and EUD where the environment uses concepts such as: event-based rules, or workflow rules [10].

MIT App Inventor expresses the reasoning of building applications similar to Scratch [6], where a traditional programming style is performed by combining jigsaw pieces. In Puzzle, jigsaws are also used as a metaphor for the development of mobile applications. The contribution in Puzzle is that it hides programming constructs within the implementation of jigsaw pieces and focuses on the combination of interactive functionalities. Functionalities can then be combined through the jigsaw metaphor, which allows for reduced user's attention, lowered learning curve and motivates users to explore it. Instead of requiring the user to detail the UI and application logic, Puzzle allows users to focus on easy combination of functions that match their requirements. Furthermore, detailed customization of jigsaw pieces is possible for advanced users through access to implementation files.

Desktop EUD environments lack the advantages of enabling end users to create applications opportunistically in mobile scenarios. Recent advances in smart phones have enabled the creation of mobile EUD environments. Contributions for mobile EUD address: parameterization of the mobile terminal [11], frameworks to support mobile authoring and execution [12], mobile authoring tools [13] [12], creation of UIs through sketching or by adding interactive techniques in the touch screen [14].

Puzzle extends these contributions through combination of the jigsaw metaphor and a color help system inspired by the work of Cuccurullo et al. [13]. This proposal exploits the jigsaw metaphor to convey the notion of connecting jigsaw pieces, while the colors are used to provide intuitive cues to correctly connect the outputs of each jigsaw piece. Furthermore, the approach is general and can support different types of data for the inputs and outputs of jigsaw pieces. Puzzle also supports iteration among the interactive functionalities represented by the jigsaw pieces, access to web-services, native phone features and interactive physical objects. All the resulting applications are based on widely deployed web languages (e.g. Javascript, HTML5, CSS3) and protocols (e.g. HTTP) not requiring the addition of plugins to access native and external functions, and enabling users to customize or reuse existing powerful platforms [15].

3   A Puzzle Application

In this section, we provide an example application that can be developed with Puzzle. The application allows the user to interact with an Arduino board controlling a power outlet. Through the usage of Arduino, the application can interact with a power outlet controlling a lamp and measure its consumption for user information. First the application checks the status of the power outlet, afterwards, the user can switch the status, and finally the switch is applied to the power outlet. The Puzzle framework allows end users to develop applications able to easily control physical objects with a touch-based phone, and provides an easy framework to create or modify the application when required. In our example, the Puzzle framework can also be used to control the consumption of the power outlet through another application by reusing Puzzle jigsaw pieces.

Jigsaw pieces are used to convey interactive functions available in Puzzle. Our example requires an end user to drag three jigsaw pieces to the center of the screen and connect them, namely "check lights", "switch", and "change lights" jigsaw pieces (see Fig. 1). The first jigsaw checks if the lights are on or off, the second jigsaw switches the value, and the last jigsaw sends the value to the lights. Later, the end user could modify the application by erasing the last two jigsaw pieces and connect "check lights" with a consumption display jigsaw piece to visualize the consumption in the power outlet.

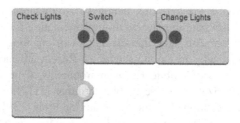

Fig. 1. Sample Puzzle Application

End users need to handle and connect jigsaw pieces as well as their connectors and types. Jigsaw pieces represent building blocks, which are able to receive outputs from other building blocks and, similarly, they output their results into other building blocks. Each building block is responsible for handling inputs and adapting them, if required, to enable adequate execution.

4   The Proposed Approach

Puzzle is a framework to support creation and execution of applications in a touch-based mobile phone. The framework is intended for users without knowledge on programming languages to playfully experiment supported functions. Puzzle provides: *a)* A jigsaw piece metaphor to convey a top-down left-to-right flow of data; *b)* Drag-and-drop interaction techniques for creation and modification of applications; *c)* A color help system to convey possible connections between jigsaw pieces; *d)* A help system in order to overcome usage doubts; *e)* Sliding and popup menus to save screen space.

The design of touch interaction in Puzzle is based on object selection, dragging and sliding. The user is able to drag jigsaw pieces into the working area, select jigsaw pieces or slide a previously hidden object. The limited screen space requires techniques to show relevant tasks and hide unused objects on the screen. For such purpose, sliding mechanisms, such as scroll bars and sliding menus are often used in its UI.

The framework generates web-based applications, and it is a web-based application as well. The motivation for this decision is based on the fact that updates can be easily performed in the framework and propagated to all clients. Furthermore, features such as CSS3 media queries, or server-side techniques can deliver CSS files based on the requested browser features in order to better adapt Puzzle to the current mobile device.

5   User Interface

The Puzzle UI is divided into 3 modules, namely main, authoring tool and execution environment, as seen respectively in Figure 2. This UI is the result of the evaluation of two previous versions, which we report in the evaluation section.

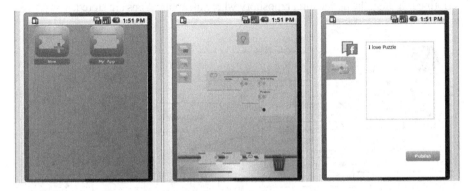

Fig. 2. a) Main b) Authoring Tool c) Execution Environment

Firstly, users are introduced to a set of applications already available in the framework (Fig. 2.a). In the Main Module, users can create a new application from scratch, or execute one of the shown applications. An icon is presented for creating an application and the remaining icons allow the execution of a related application. The icon with a plus sign and a jigsaw piece in the top left corner is used to identify the creation of an application. Next, the selection of a new application directs the user to the Authoring Tool.

In Authoring Tool, users are able to create or modify an existing application (Fig. 2.b). A Puzzle application is developed by drag-and-drop jigsaw pieces to the center, and connecting them top-down left-to-right in order to obtain the composed functionalities. One single jigsaw piece can be executed without being connected, so as to allow the end user to explore its function.

Finally, the Execution Environment enables the execution of a selected application (Fig. 2.c). In the Execution Environment, the UI presented is defined in the implementation of the jigsaw pieces in execution. Additionally, a left menu is overlaid so that users are able to go back to the Main module or edit the current application in the Authoring Tool.

5.1   Authoring Process

The authoring process in Puzzle evolves in three steps: Authoring, Properties, and Execute. Figure 3 is a workflow chart showing their temporal evolution from left to right, where rounded rectangles represent process phases, rectangles represent the actions allowed in each phase, and dotted rectangles represent stored data.

Creating an application directs the user to the authoring phase. In this phase, the user is able to add and connect the required features to the application. The available operations are: view a list of categories of jigsaw pieces, drag and connect jigsaw pieces, configure a jigsaw piece or delete it. Configure a jigsaw piece means customizing values of a jigsaw piece for a particular purpose. All the data related to jigsaw pieces are retrieved from the Building Block Repository. Afterwards, if the user is creating a new application, she is able to set its name and/or icon, and immediately pass to the last phase where the application is deployed and executed. The deployment of an application is performed through the application repository where all applications are stored.

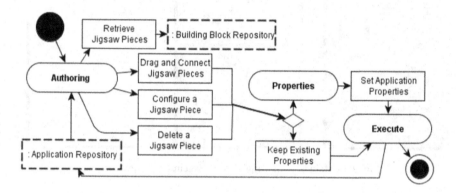

Fig. 3. Authoring Process Flowchart

5.2   Authoring Tool

The Authoring Tool has been designed taking into account the limited screen size and the interaction techniques available in mobile devices. The creation of a Puzzle application focuses on the usage of the 'jigsaw' metaphor. A jigsaw piece evokes the intuitive suggestion of assembling pieces together. Essentially, we allow users to connect building blocks and compose various arrangements through a series of top-down left-to-right couplings of pieces. Constraining connections in a left-to-right fashion provides users with the sense of a pipeline of information flow.

Each jigsaw piece has connections, named inputs or outputs. Inputs are placed in the left side of the 'jigsaw piece' and evoke the ability to receive a connection from another jigsaw piece. At the view level, inputs have an inner circular shape suggesting that they will receive a connection. At the implementation level, inputs are values received from connecting jigsaw pieces and such values are used within execution of the current jigsaw piece. Outputs are placed at the right side of the jigsaw piece and evoke the ability to connect into other jigsaw pieces. At the view level, outputs have an outer circular shape suggesting that they will send information. At the implementation level, outputs are values resulting from execution of the current jigsaw piece that can be used in connected jigsaw pieces.

In Puzzle, inputs and outputs are augmented with a color system used to indicate the possibility to connect two different jigsaw pieces only if the colors from the input and output of the jigsaw pieces match. We assumed that colors could be easier to distinguish when compared with a number of shapes to uniquely describe all matches. The function provided by a jigsaw piece is communicated to the user through a label (or icon) at the top center of a jigsaw piece (see Figure 4).

Fig. 4. Sample jigsaw pieces in Puzzle

The ability to select a jigsaw piece to use in a new application is provided to the user through a carousel, at the bottom, listing available jigsaw pieces in a category (see Figure 2.b). Puzzle has several categories of jigsaw pieces and the framework is not limited in the number of jigsaw categories as categories and jigsaw pieces can be added to the Building Block Repository (see Figure 5). Access to further categories is available through a tab icon on the left that slides a menu with the available list of categories. Currently, Puzzle has 5 categories and 10 jigsaw pieces. For example, included jigsaw pieces enable the application to: include a gallery of images from Flickr, post a message on Facebook, send a text message to a contact in the phone, list text messages, or switch lights connected to an Arduino-based board. Available jigsaw pieces were created to demonstrate the potentialities of the Puzzle framework not limiting the available functions as they can be extended.

The tabbed menu enables the user to access: the list of categories, common functions of the Authoring Tool, and execute an application (see Figure 2.b). The motivation for the usage of a tabbed menu is to allow common functions to be easily accessible while further details can be accessed and used on a sliding menu including available options related to the clicked tabbed icon. Additionally, screen space is saved for editing the application. The execute function was made available on this menu for its easy access.

The Authoring Tool also includes a help system. A help button is shown at the top of the screen if the user does not perform any interaction with the Authoring Tool for a certain amount of time. The motivation for this solution is to enable contextual tips when a user is blocked and also not disturb the user in case she has moved her attention to some other task (see Figure 2.b).

Further help on jigsaw pieces is also provided to end users. At the bottom carousel, a user can tap a jigsaw piece in order to trigger a popup menu with further information. If a jigsaw piece is at the center of the screen, a single tap on the jigsaw piece allows the user to raise a popup menu to further configure, edit or get help. The help provided is a description of the available functions of the jigsaw piece. At the bottom right corner of the screen, end users can find a trash can, which allows them to remove a jigsaw piece from an application.

In the Authoring Tool, end users are also able to view the data flow. The data flow is managed by the framework and used within jigsaw pieces tasks. The available jigsaw pieces implement tasks, such as those in the example application to change the state of a power outlet. The functions should be easily identified by a non-programming end user and easy to learn and use. A motivation for such approach is that mobile users may have a reduced attention while using Puzzle, or may not be familiar with programming control flow operations. The support of iteration among functionalities represented by various jigsaws has been added in Puzzle since it was requested by some users. For example, while controlling a light or power outlet, users may require the application to loop until they exit the application.

5.3   Execution Environment

The execution environment executes one jigsaw piece each time, and stores and retrieves input/output values as required by each jigsaw piece. As a result, the UI for an application is the sum of the rendered jigsaw pieces UIs. Currently, each jigsaw piece has its own UI, created at development time.

The execution environment is similar to a mobile browser, with the additional possibility for the applications to access native phone features without requiring the installation of plugins. During execution, users are also presented with one tab icon that once clicked allows them to go to the Authoring Tool to edit the current Puzzle application or to the Main module (see Figure 2.c).

6   Framework

Contributions of the framework are the ability to: provide access to native and remote functions using web-based technologies, store and provide complex operations ready to be combined and used in an application, and allow non-programing end users to explore and use different technologies from their mobile devices.

The motivations to use web technologies for the implementation of the Puzzle framework were the elimination of administrative tasks such as software installation and update, and the support of a network of connected users. In addition, Puzzle includes a native module to access native mobile functions, which can be accessed through HTTP requests; and a server module to allow access for interactive physical objects connected to the framework (see figure 5).

Native phone functions allow the user to integrate information and features that are usually not included in web-based applications within her application. Interaction with physical objects allows end user developers to create applications that interact with embedded sensors and actuators and also foster user exploration of the possibilities technology can provide. Puzzle allows users to use, combine and remix data from multiple sources while gathering contributions from all users. Thus, we can expect Puzzle to benefit from an "architecture of participation" to which users can contribute with applications and, possibly, building blocks.

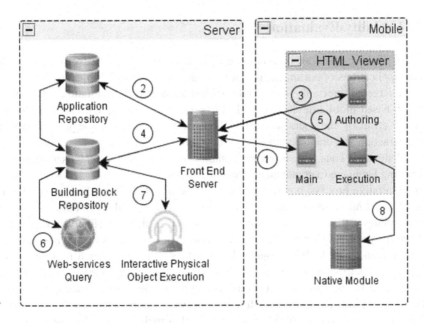

Fig. 5. Puzzle Architecture

Figure 5 describes the Puzzle architecture. The authoring tool, applications and building blocks are stored and assisted by the server managing the framework. The mobile side of the architecture contains a native application (Android) including an HTML viewer and a native module accessible through HTTP requests.

The flow of information starts in the Main module from the HTML Viewer. Once Puzzle starts, the Main module requests the list of available applications (connection 1) from the Front End Server. Such list is stored within the Application Repository and delivered to the Front End Server through an SQL request (connection 2). When an application is created from scratch, end users are directed by the Front End Server to the Authoring module (connection 3). Next, the Authoring module further requests to the Front End Server for available building blocks. Such information is stored in the Building Block Repository (connection 4). Afterwards, the Authoring module can request configuration details and further information from the Building Block Repository. When the application is created the Authoring module sends the information about the application to the Front End Server (connection 3) and stores that information in the Application Repository (connection 2).

Next, the end user is directed to the Execution module by the Front End Server while executing the previously created application (connection 5). During application execution, a building block can further request some external services, for example Flickr or Facebook (connection 6). Additionally, a building block can require interaction with physical objects, through connection 7, or request the Native module to execute native functions (connection 8).

7   Usability Evaluation

The goal of the framework is to allow end users without an IT background to create mobile applications opportunistically in touch-based devices. In order to address that goal, we targeted three sub-goals: *a)* the UI has to address the limitations of its usage on touch-based mobile devices, namely the screen size; *b)* the UI has to reduce the cognitive effort of end users without an IT background through adequate metaphors and interaction techniques; *c)* the framework has to support seamless tasks accomplishment. Thus, the framework should not require the end user to learn a programing language to create an application.

In an iterative process, creation and development of Puzzle used early prototyping to evaluate and develop design solutions and to gradually build a shared understanding of the needs of the end users as well as their possible future practices [16]. In this paper, we report on the evaluation of two previous prototypes targeting end users without an IT background, through the real usage of such prototypes (see Figure 6). In both evaluations, no tutorials or learning steps were provided to end users in order to evaluate if the UI was able to guide them through the creation of a mobile application. Furthermore, all sub-goals were addressed in both evaluations. Contributions from previous evaluations were also included in subsequent versions and newer issues of the UI were also tested. The mobile phones used within the evaluations   were Android-based devices, namely using Android 2.3.

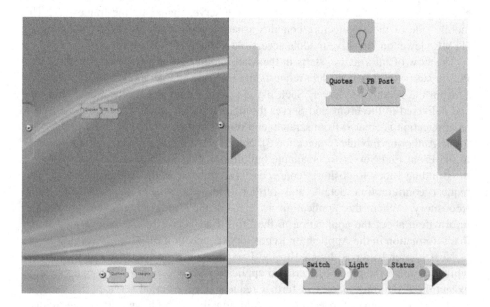

Fig. 6. a) First Prototype b) Second Prototype

The first user evaluation was performed with six mobile Internet users without an IT-related job. This evaluation focused in the ability to create mobile applications in a mobile device through the jigsaw piece metaphor, sub-goal *b)*. The group of users was also gender balanced with equal representation of both genders. Puzzle was evaluated in a relaxed home environment and the volunteers ranged from 26 up to 35 years old with an average of 31.16 years old and their jobs related to law practice, municipality administration or other municipality activities. The evaluation was conducted by one researcher involving two data collection methods: observation and questionnaire. Each volunteer was individually interviewed, where each session ranged from 40 up to 50 minutes, and the goals of the evaluation were clearly stated to volunteers.

For the second user test, a similar approach was considered. This evaluation focused on: the limitations of the UI regarding touch-based mobile devices, sub-goal *a)*; reducing the cognitive efforts of the user, sub-goal *b)*; and demonstrate that the framework could support the performance of envisioned tasks, sub-goal *c)*. Evaluations took place in an office with 7 users ranged from 31 years old up to 59 years old with an average of 44.1 years old. 5 users were females and 2 users were males. Furthermore, their jobs were not IT related, mainly in the administration of a research institute. As in the first evaluation, two data collection methods were used: observation and questionnaire. In addition, the test duration was similar and, after a general view over the framework, no further instructions were provided to test users.

7.1   Method

In both tests, the user evaluation was performed with a working prototype, so that users could realistically provide feedback on the usage of the framework. In detail, user evaluations included an introductory questionnaire, a set of tasks to accomplish, and a post-test questionnaire.

The introductory questionnaire included: *a)* Demography information, *b)* Previous end user development experiences, *c)* First evaluation of Puzzle authoring tool, and *d)* Which target users would be envisioned for such tool.

This step was performed to categorize the test users and collect data on their previous experiences. After the introductory questionnaire, users were asked to complete a set of tasks using Puzzle. The tasks included: *a)* Testing the usability of the left sliding menu to return to the list of applications (during execution), *b)* Testing the usability of the left sliding menu for editing an application and the drag and drop technique to compose an application, *c)* Configuration or deletion of a jigsaw piece while creating or reusing an application, *d)* Creation of a new application to show a map with the user's location and post it on Facebook, execute the application, and return to the list of applications. These tasks focused on sub-goal *b)*.

The test involved the basic functions available in Puzzle, namely sliding menus, drag and drop interaction techniques and the jigsaw piece metaphor for application creation and modification. Finally, a post-test questionnaire was performed. In the first user test, the questionnaire included a qualitative analysis about: *a)* Overall user evaluation of Puzzle, *b)* Evaluation on the fun, pleasure and ease of use, *c)* User's ability to create applications through that process, *d)* Best and worse characteristics on Puzzle, *e)* User's ability to use Puzzle, *f)* Type of applications that the user would enjoy to create, *g)* Interest on controlling home appliances through usage of the tool, *h)* General comments and remarks.

In the second user test, the introductory questionnaire was similar to the one on the first user test. However, the tasks to be performed included: *a)* Creation of a simple application and evaluation of the color-based connection system and help system; *b)* Creation and modification of an application combining jigsaw pieces where a message gallery was used to select a message to be sent over a phone text message or into Facebook; *c)* Creation of an application to control lights from the mobile touch-based device; *d)* Suggestions to support iteration and selection in the framework.

The information collected in the first user test regarding sub-goal *b)* was used to improve the second prototype and newer functions were included to test sub-goals *a)* and *c)*. In detail, the second user test intended to evaluate a color-based connection system and a help system to reduce the cognitive effort. The second user test also evaluated the ability to use Puzzle to create applications integrating web services, native mobile functions, and interactive physical objects. The post-test questionnaire included a quantitative and a qualitative analysis. The quantitative analysis included 18 sentences and the user was asked to evaluate each sentence within a Likert scale from 1 (Strongly Disagree) to 5 (Strongly Agree). The purpose of this set of sentences was to support the analysis of the following aspects: learnability, efficiency, effectiveness, memorability, errors and satisfaction. The qualitative analysis of the post-test questionnaire was similar to the one in the first user test.

7.2   Results

The results showed that the UI could be used with a low cognitive effort and addresses the limitations of touch-based mobile devices. In addition, the framework is also able to include, integrate, and execute the relevant tasks. Namely, the jigsaw piece metaphor, as presented, was easy to use and combine; and the framework eased integration of web-services, native phone functions and interactive physical objects. First, we present the results of the first user test followed by those of the second test. The results are presented first for the introductory questionnaire, next for the set of tasks to accomplish, and finally for the post-test questionnaire.

In the first introductory questionnaire, two users had no previous experiences regarding end user development. One user had developed simple web pages through Microsoft FrontPage. Four users had modified databases in Microsoft Access. Three users had used formulas or macros in Microsoft Excel. Finally, one user reported customization of MS-DOS batch files.

Remaining results on the first introductory questionnaire can be seen in Table 1. The first column describes the question, the second column indicates the number of users who gave the corresponding positive comments regarding the question, the third column indicates the number of users who gave the corresponding negative comments regarding the question.

After an introductory questionnaire, test users were required to accomplish a set of tasks. In the first user test, users were asked to perform four tasks. Success on completion for each task was divided in 3 categories: 0, not completed; 1, completed with difficulty or help; 2, easily completed. Observed comments were also registered.

Table 1. First introductory questionnaire results

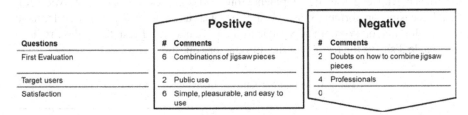

Questions	Positive		Negative	
	#	Comments	#	Comments
First Evaluation	6	Combinations of jigsaw pieces	2	Doubts on how to combine jigsaw pieces
Target users	2	Public use	4	Professionals
Satisfaction	6	Simple, pleasurable, and easy to use	0	

In the first task, the left sliding menu in execution was successfully used by five users and one required some help. Expressed concerns targeted the size of the menu. In the second task, users were easily able to drag jigsaw pieces to the center of the screen to create a mobile application. Five were able to create an application easily (2) while one required minor help (1). Suggested improvements relate to usage of different icons for creation and execution, enlarge icons and symbols, improve abbreviations, use double tap to execute an application and add help to Puzzle. In the third task, all users were able to easily identify the popup menu to configure or delete a jigsaw piece (2). The last task included combining jigsaw pieces within an application. In this task, four users were able to perform the task (2) while two required some minor help (1). Concerns in the task were related to an unclear flow of data between jigsaw pieces and the abbreviations in jigsaw pieces. It was also suggested the use of images instead of text.

Finally, a post-test questionnaire was presented to users. In the first user test only a qualitative analysis was performed. Table 2 shows the results for the first post-test questionnaire. The first column describes the question, the second column describes the number of users with positive comments regarding the question, the third column describes the number of users with negative comments regarding the question. Positive and negative expressions were added for each user. In cases where the sum of answers is more than 6, it means that there were users with both positive and negative comments regarding the question.

Table 2. Tasks performed in the first user test

Questions	Positive		Negative	
	#	Comments	#	Comments
Overall view	6	Easy and simple, useful	1	Can be improved
Satisfaction	6	Pleasurable and fun to use	2	Icon and button sizes, Add double tap to execute, improve dataflow
Creation Process	5	Intuitive and easy	1	Allow for customization, add jigsaw pieces
Best and worst	6	Useful, ability to control sensors and actuators	6	Customization, improve intuitiveness, proactive help, execution errors
Usage	5		1	Prefer existing apps
Envisioned applications	5	Smart home, social networks, work support		
Comments	2	Domain experts and professionals		

In the second user test and in the introductory questionnaire, two users had no experience with end user development, four had some experiences with Microsoft Excel focusing on formula's usage, and one was using tools for web development such as Joomla, or Wordpress. Similar to the presentation of results for the first user test, Table 3 shows the results for the introductory questionnaire.

Table 3. Second introductory questionnaire results

Questions	Positive		Negative	
	#	Comments	#	Comments
Willingness to create applications	3	Fun, leisure or improve tasks	4	Lack of motivation
Initial evaluation	7	Pleasurable and fun to use	0	
Target users	3	Public use	4	Professionals / self learners
Satisfaction	7	Simple, easy and pleasurable	0	

In the second user test, the set of tasks was changed according to the outcomes and improvements gathered from the first user test. Furthermore, completion of the tasks was also updated to a scale of 1 (Not completed) up to 5 (Easily completed). The first task included testing the color and help system during the development of an application. One user performed the action easily (5), four required minor help (4), and one required further help with language issues and finding execution (3).

The second task was the development of an application to send a text message from a message gallery and modify it to post on Facebook. One user performed the task easily (5), two required help on language issues (4), and four users required help on describing the flow of information (3). In this task, users suggested adding a trash to ease the deletion of a jigsaw piece. The third task involved development of an application to control a set of lights with Arduino. Two users completed the application easily (5), four required minor help to clarify the actions to be performed (4) and one user was not able to understand some functions and the observer helped to accomplish the task (2).

The last task included suggestions for selection of jigsaw pieces and support for iteration. Selection was preferred by making a circle around jigsaw pieces. Other approaches included taping all jigsaw pieces or perform a diagonal selection. Iteration was preferred through a special jigsaw piece connecting the initial and the final jigsaw piece. Other options included selecting jigsaw pieces for iteration and configure iteration on a popup menu.

Next, a quantitative and qualitative analysis was performed through questionnaires. The quantitative analysis evaluated learnability (questions 1-6), efficiency (7-9), effectiveness (10-12), memorability (13), errors (14-16) and satisfaction (17-18) while using Puzzle. Box plots from the user evaluation using a scale of 1 to 5 Likert scale targeting these 18 sentences are listed in figure 7. The Box plot includes the smallest observation (sample minimum), lower quartile (Q1), median (Q2), upper quartile (Q3), and largest observation (sample maximum) for each question. Bottom and upper tickers represent minimum and maximum, respectively. Bottom and upper lines for the orange boxes represent Q1 and Q2, respectively. The upper line of the blue box is the Q1. The space between limits of the orange and blue boxes helps to indicate the degree of dispersion (spread) and skewness in the data, and identify outliers. The qualitative analysis is listed and was evaluated similarly to the first user test and results are listed in table 4.

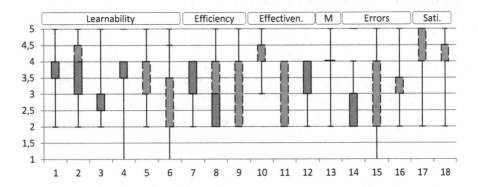

Fig. 7. Quantitative analysis results

Table 4. Tasks performed in the second user test

Questions	Positive		Negative	
	#	Comments	#	Comments
Overall view	7	Good and pleasant	0	
Satisfaction	7	Good and simple	2	Icon and button sizes, Add double tap to execute, improve dataflow
Creation Process	5	Intuitive and easy	2	Allow for customization, add jigsaw pieces
Best and worst	7	Simple UI, ability to integrate web-services, native phone features and interactive physical objects	5	Customization, improve intuitiveness, proactive help, execution errors
Usage	3	Public Use	4	Professionals and/or self learners
Envisioned applications	5	Home automation, social network integration, phone features, support for common everyday tasks		

7.3   Discussion

Puzzle evaluation validated a touch-based UI and a framework supporting end users without an IT background to create applications in the mobile device. The jigsaw piece metaphor was easily understood and applied to develop an application. The first evaluation focused on evaluating the metaphor and the results confirmed that end users were able to use it for manipulating high level functions. The UI also copes with the limitations of touch-based mobile devices, where both evaluations addressed such limitations. The size of UI components, their representation, and interaction techniques used have been evaluated to better address end users expectations. The drag-and-drop interaction technique and the bottom carousel are keys to the Puzzle UI and proved to be effective. The evaluation also demonstrated that the framework can support creation, modification and execution of applications in the mobile device.

In particular, the results regarding the UI were positive in terms of easiness to learn, efficiency, effectiveness, easiness to remember, and number of errors . Figure 8 shows the means (from the data in Fig. 7) related to the questions associated with the corresponding aspects within a Likert scale from 1 to 5.

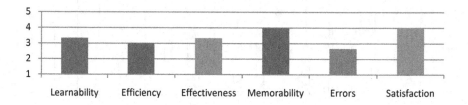

Fig. 8. Quantitative analysis average

In the first user test, a central goal in the evaluation was the assessment of using a jigsaw piece for development of applications. Even if this approach does not provide a WYSIWYG view, users were easily and immediately able to test their applications on the platform. Furthermore, the drag-and-drop interaction technique proved to be effective to add jigsaw pieces into the center of the screen and create an application. The next step was to combine jigsaw pieces and specify the data flow in an application. For that purpose, four users easily understood how to combine jigsaw pieces and how the data was flowing. However, two users pointed that the framework could easily convey a correct order to combine jigsaw pieces and correctly build the desired application.

Concerning the type of applications that users would like to develop within Puzzle, social applications and control of sensors and actuators were the main applications selected. The smart home scenario was the most mentioned, possibly integrating social networks. Users were also interested in applications that could react to previously identified contextual scenarios. As an example, enable the possibility to develop applications that turn the heating system or a hoven when the user is going home.

For the second user test, we adapted the Puzzle UI to accommodate an increase in icons and buttons size. In addition, we have restructured common UI controls for consistency between editing and execution, and simplified the UI. We also added a help system to Puzzle, so that provided hints could help users to proceed. Such hints disappear after being checked to save screen space. Finally, we added a color system to ease connection of jigsaw pieces. Concerning newer functionalities, we included newer jigsaw pieces to envision applications that took advantage of web-services, native phone features and interactive physical objects.

For such refinements, users further suggested to adjust the text size, icons and symbols, inclusion of a trash can in order to make the deletion task more intuitive, better convey the data flow in connected jigsaw pieces, and improve the color system to better indicate its purpose. In the user tests, suggestions for selection highlighted circling with the finger around objects as the preferred interaction technique. Iteration was proposed by adding a different jigsaw that would connect the begin and the end of a set of jigsaw pieces involved in the iteration.

The quantitative analysis (see Figure 6) indicates that Puzzle is easy to use and learn with improvements required for the color and help system. The metaphors used are also easily understood in terms of their meaning and usage. However, results were affected by the jigsaw snap function to connect pieces. In occasions, snapping was not working smoothly causing some problems. Puzzle is also effective as the result of functions and applications are what users expect. Indeed, functions in Puzzle are very easy to memorize as editing of an application was not causing any problems to users. The detected errors were mainly due to connecting jigsaw pieces and the snap algorithm. Improvement on the labels describing jigsaw functions is also considered.

The qualitative evaluation reinforced the positive feedback on using Puzzle and the adequacy of the metaphors and interaction techniques used. Users liked the ability to integrate different features seamlessly and further suggested improvements, namely the ability to pan, zoom and have a general view over a more complex application. The users highlighted that it would be interesting to navigate within the jigsaw pieces while developing an application with a similar interaction technique as with current map navigation.

8   Conclusions and Future Work

Puzzle targets users without programming skills willing to start developing mobile applications on their touch-based phones and further execute such applications in the touch-based mobile phone. From our results, Puzzle is addressing the initial goals and users can easily create mobile applications from scratch without a previous learning phase. Future work will include testing iteration constructs on Puzzle applications, based on the user suggestions; and adding a selection mechanism so that jigsaw pieces could be grouped and new jigsaw pieces created based on that grouped function. This would allow users to group common functions and use them in the future. Furthermore, a zoom, pan and overall view can be added to allow navigation within an application as well as allow the user to see the details of grouped jigsaw pieces. In addition, future improvements on Puzzle will include improvements in the color and help system to further support users to combine jigsaw pieces.

References

1. Gartner: Gartner Says Worldwide Smartphone Sales Soared in Fourth Quarter of 2011 With 47 Percent Growth. Press Release, Gartner, Egham, UK (2011), http://www.gartner.com/it/page.jsp?id=1924314
2. Gronli, T.-M., Hansen, J., Ghinea, G.: Android vs Windows Mobile vs Java ME: a comparative study of mobile development environments. In: Makedon, F., Maglogiannis, I., Kapidakis, S. (eds.) Proceedings of the 3rd International Conference on PErvasive Technologies Related to Assistive Environments (PETRA 2010), Article 45, 8 pages. ACM, New York (2010)

3. Lieberman, H., Paternò, F., Klann, M., Wulf, V.: End-User Development: An Emerging Paradigm. In: Lieberman, H., Paternò, F., Wulf, V. (eds.) End User Development, vol. 9, ch. 1, pp. 1–8. Springer, Dordrecht (2006)

4. Boehm, B., Abts, C., Brown, A., Chulani, S., Clark, B., Horowitz, E., Madachy, R., Reifer, D., Steece, B.: Software Cost Estimation with COCOMO II. Prentice, Upper Saddle River (2000)

5. App Inventor MIT (2012), http://info.appinventor.mit.edu/

6. Resnick, M., Maloney, J., Monroy-Hernandez, A., Rusk, N., Eastmond, E., Brennan, K., Millner, A., Rosenbaum, E., Silver, J., Silverman, B., Kafai, Y.: Scratch: programming for all. Commun. ACM 52, 60–67 (2009)

7. Ghiani, G., Paternò, F., Spano, L.D.: Cicero Designer: An Environment for End-User Development of Multi-Device Museum Guides. In: Pipek, V., Rosson, M.B., de Ruyter, B., Wulf, V. (eds.) IS-EUD 2009. LNCS, vol. 5435, pp. 265–274. Springer, Heidelberg (2009)

8. Hull, R., Clayton, B., Melamed, T.: Rapid Authoring of Mediascapes. In: Davies, N., Mynatt, E.D., Siio, I. (eds.) UbiComp 2004. LNCS, vol. 3205, pp. 125–142. Springer, Heidelberg (2004)

9. Celentano, A., Maurizio, M.: An End-User Oriented Building Pattern for Interactive Art Guides. In: Costabile, M., Dittrich, Y., Fischer, G., Piccinno, A. (eds.) IS-EUD 2011. LNCS, vol. 6654, pp. 187–202. Springer, Heidelberg (2011)

10. Realinho, V., Eduardo Dias, A., Romão, T.: Testing the Usability of a Platform for Rapid Development of Mobile Context-Aware Applications. In: Campos, P., Graham, N., Jorge, J., Nunes, N., Palanque, P., Winckler, M. (eds.) INTERACT 2011, Part III. LNCS, vol. 6948, pp. 521–536. Springer, Heidelberg (2011)

11. Tuomela, U., Kansala, I., Hakkila, J., Mantyjarvi, J.: Context-Studio? Tool for Personalizing Context-Aware Applications in Mobile Terminals. In: Proceedings of 2003 Australasian Computer Human Interaction Conference, OzCHI 2003 (Nokia Research Center), p. 292 (2003)

12. Danado, J., Davies, M., Ricca, P., Fensel, A.: An Authoring Tool for User Generated Mobile Services. In: Berre, A.J., Gómez-Pérez, A., Tutschku, K., Fensel, D. (eds.) FIS 2010. LNCS, vol. 6369, pp. 118–127. Springer, Heidelberg (2010)

13. Cuccurullo, S., Francese, R., Risi, M., Tortora, G.: MicroApps Development on Mobile Phones. In: Costabile, M., Dittrich, Y., Fischer, G., Piccinno, A. (eds.) IS-EUD 2011. LNCS, vol. 6654, pp. 289–294. Springer, Heidelberg (2011)

14. Seifert, J., Pfleging, B., Bahamóndez, E., Hermes, M., Rukzio, E., Schmidt, A.: Mobidev: a tool for creating apps on mobile phones. In: Proceedings of the 13th International Conference on Human Computer Interaction with Mobile Devices and Services (MobileHCI 2011), pp. 109–112. ACM, New York (2011)

15. Holloway, S., Julien, C.: The case for end-user programming of ubiquitous computing environments. In: Proceedings of the FSE/SDP Workshop on Future of Software Engineering Research (FoSER 2010), pp. 167–172. ACM, NY (2010)

16. Danado, J., Paternò, F.: A Prototype for EUD in Touch-based Mobile Devices. In: Proceedings of the IEEE Symposium on Visual Languages and Human-Centric Computing. IEEE, Innsbruck

Requirements Sensemaking Using Concept Maps

Shamal Faily[1], John Lyle[1], Andre Paul[2], Andrea Atzeni[3], Dieter Blomme[4],
Heiko Desruelle[4], and Krishna Bangalore[5]

[1] University of Oxford, Oxford UK OX3 0NH
firstname.lastname@cs.ox.ac.uk
[2] Fraunhofer FOKUS, 10589 Berlin, Germany
andre.paul@fokus.fraunhofer.de
[3] Dip di Automatica e Informatica, Politecnico di Torino, 10129 Torino, Italy
andrea.atzeni@polito.it
[4] Ghent University/IBBT, B-9050 Gent, Belgium
firstname.lastname@intec.ugent.be
[5] Technische Universität München, 85748 Garching, Germany
krishna.bangalore@in.tum.de

Abstract. Requirements play an important role in software engineering, but their perceived usefulness means that they often fail to be properly maintained. Traceability is often considered a means for motivating and maintaining requirements, but this is difficult without a better understanding of the requirements themselves. Sensemaking techniques help us get this understanding, but the representations necessary to support it are difficult to create, and scale poorly when dealing with medium to large scale problems. This paper describes how, with the aid of supporting software tools, concept mapping can be used to both make sense of and improve the quality of a requirements specification. We illustrate this approach by using it to update the requirements specification for the EU *webinos* project, and discuss several findings arising from our results.

1 Introduction

Techniques, tools, and artifacts may come and go, yet requirements are a consistent element in a software development project. The needs and expectations of stakeholders motivate the elicitation of requirements that software developers use as a contract for what a system should do. This makes a requirements specification the authority upon which architectural design and software implementation decisions are made.

The perceived usefulness of requirements, however, often fails to extend beyond the initial stages of system design, especially as these are often construed negatively from both a usability and developer perspective. To usability professionals, specifications of system behaviour are agnostic of usability concerns and say little about the needs of people using it. To software developers, they are seen as too abstract to effectively form the basis of an implementation; developers may feel it is easier to prototype a solution and make their own sense of the domain and what needs to be built. Because of this, maintaining system requirements is considered by many to be an unnecessary and cumbersome activity that adds comparatively little value. While this position may be reasonable in projects where all stakeholders are directly involved in the system design,

M. Winckler, P. Forbrig, and R. Bernhaupt (Eds.): HCSE 2012, LNCS 7623, pp. 217–232, 2012.
© IFIP International Federation for Information Processing 2012

for many projects this is not the case. Customers and prospective end-users may want a precise description of what a system does when explaining the system to other people, or evaluating the system for concerns such as regulatory compliance or value for money. Similarly, security engineers need models of system behaviour upon which their own analysis can be based. In such cases, prototypes that embody what they think the system should do are a poor substitute for a description of what the system is expected to do.

Requirements are seen as static artifacts which, while useful early in a project's life for motivating initial architectural design, are too unwieldy to maintain as a going concern. This perception is not helped by the fact that, as natural language text, they are often hidden away in word processors, spreadsheets, or databases. As developers become more detached from the requirements that form the basis of their work, the rationale for design changes can either become lost or become encapsulated in other design elements. Because of this, when requirements do need to be updated, the revision process can be both tedious and time-consuming. Although research by the Requirements Engineering community has been concerned with how these requirements traceability problems can be prevented, there has been comparatively little work on how these traceability challenges can be addressed once they do occur in real projects. The possible implications arising from missing, superfluous, or ambiguous requirements means that we need creative approaches for addressing these challenges. If such approaches are to be successful, we need to engage the stakeholders responsible for specifying and maintaining these requirements by helping them make better sense of what they are.

In this paper, we present an approach for using concept mapping as a sensemaking technique for requirement specifications. This improves the quality of a requirements specification while also increasing its visibility among project team members. In Section 2, we describe the motivating literature, before presenting our approach in Section 3. In Section 4 we present the results of applying our approach to update the requirements specification for the EU FP7 *webinos* project, before reflecting on these results and proposing follow-on work in Sections 5 and 6 respectively.

2 Related Work

2.1 Requirements Maintainability and Traceability

Rather than being concerned with the behaviour of the proposed system, Requirements Engineering is concerned with defining the problem being solved [1]. While it is tempting to think that, once defined, requirement specifications will be *good enough* to sustain software engineering activities, changes to the problem space, or modifications to environmental conditions affecting system design might be significant enough to challenge assumptions underpinning a requirements specification, therefore motivating the need to re-evaluate it.

As cases like the Ariane 5 failure have shown, failing to properly analyse existing requirements for their continued relevance can lead to catastrophic results [2]. Consequently, the importance of rationalising requirements has motivated the need for managing requirements traceability: the ability to describe and follow the life of a requirement, in both a forward and backwards direction [3]. When properly maintained, requirements traceability provides the rationale for requirements, provides a means for checking their satisfaction, and provides a framework for software tools. Unfortunately, while there is no shortage of requirements traceability frameworks and models, software tools for supporting them are usually restricted to requirements management tools [4]. While requirements managements tools are reasonably effective at indicating how requirements are operationalised, Winkler and von Pilgrim found that pre-requirements traceability remains poorly tool-supported. This finding confirms an argument first made by Gotel and Finkelstein [3], who claimed that pre-requirements specification traceability problems are hard to address because the dynamic nature of the sources and environment from which requirements are drawn makes categorising traces difficult.

One way for dealing with pre-requirements traceability is to employ design rationale tools to externalise the arguments underpinning requirements. For example, Burge [5] has discussed how tools like Compendium [6] provide a visual language for capturing group discussions and facilitate requirements negotiation. Similarly, Eclipse IDE plugins like Software Engineering Using RATionale system (SEURAT) can be used to capture the source of requirements, in addition to evaluating alternatives and flagging errors when alternatives violate requirements [7]. More recently, work on the open source Computer Aided Integration of Requirements and Information Security (CAIRIS) requirements management tool [8,9] demonstrated how requirement models can be motivated by usability artifacts such as scenarios and personas [10], as well as how argumentation models can be used to structure qualitative data and assumptions underpinning the characteristics of personas [11,12].

2.2 Sensemaking and Concept Mapping

While pre-requirements traceability remains a challenge, there is evidence that sensemaking — the process of searching for a representation and encoding data in that representation to answer task specific questions [13] — might assist in understanding where requirements have come from, and where they might ultimately lead. In a long-term study of software development within a company, it was found that relying on rational decisions alone to simplify assumptions increased misunderstanding of products as systems grew [14]. Consequently, the company found that rather than making what appeared to be the most rational decision, it needed to rely on sensemaking techniques to choose the most appropriate course of action. This is because trying to understand the rationale behind a particular decision may lose sight of the contextual factors at play when a decision is made. In the broader context of software engineering, collectively re-organising and synthesising information can help groups of stakeholders make sense of what this information means [15]. Sensemaking techniques have been used to supplement various aspects of usability evaluation in software design, ranging from re-designing the information architecture for a software platform [16], through to evaluating the usability of APIs [17].

In a sensemaking task of any significant complexity, external representations are important for supporting the cognitive demands made on users, but creating such a representation is itself a significant problem [13]. A popular visual representation for facilitating sensemaking by helping designers absorb knowledge is *concept mapping*. Concept maps are sensemaking tools that connect many ideas, objects, and events within a domain and, as a result, help organise and visualise knowledge [18].

Concept maps were first proposed by Novak [19] as a learning tool which allows students to build and reflect on the conceptions of a domain. For example, in a case study in organisational learning [20], individuals made sense of concepts before exposing it to the influence of others and sharing discourse. As such, the technique was able to bring people together and synthesise different views.

Although software tools such as CmapTools [21] can be used to collaboratively build concept maps, these rely on using keyboard and mice as input, potentially making concept mapping less fluid, hindering the co-creation process. Together with work by Klemmer et al. alluding to the benefits of combining the affordances of paper with electronic media [22], this has stimulated a growing interest in the use of tangible interfaces for concept mapping. For example, Tanenbaum and Antle [23] created a prototype tabletop system and software application to support the creation and revision of concept maps. This study served as a useful proof-of-concept, but it also highlighted problems such as slow object tracking, and restrictions adding new content; these suggest possible scalability problems when working with larger maps. This scalability problems were confirmed in a more recent study [24] by Oppel and Stary comparing the use of tabletop systems for concept mapping with screen based equivalents. Despite the scalability problems, the study found that the time spent on discussion was significantly higher for tabletop concept maps, and information was less likely to be filtered by 'operators' running the software tool to support the concept mapping process. It was, however, noted that participants of screen based tools tended to focus more on the process of representing the model itself. This issue of representation is important from a Requirements Engineering perspective; concept maps need to be both used and maintained as a system design evolves, and by a potentially larger range of people than those engaged in participatory concept mapping sessions.

3 Approach

Our approach uses concept mapping to both make sense of and improve the quality of a requirements specification. The approach assumes that an initial requirements specification has already been created, and that the specification is sub-divided into different functional categories. We carry out concept mapping to make sense of a system's requirements, together with the traceability associations that motivate and connect them. In carrying out this exercise, we glean a better understanding of the problem domain the system is situated in. This approach is supplemented by software tools which synthesise concept map data with other requirements artifacts to form a coherent requirements model.

By using software tools to support rather than mediate the concept mapping process, we gain the benefits of tabletop concept mapping without the suffering the scalability problems associated with tangible interfaces, or filtering problems associated with screen based concept mapping tools. The approach also has three other benefits from a broader Requirements Engineering perspective. First, the process of building the concept map also identifies and addresses duplicate or conflicting requirements. When the model is complete, the relationships between the requirements becomes apparent, as well as the most appropriate means for addressing them. Second, because this is largely a group-based exercise, an understanding of what the requirements are and how they contribute towards system design is shared by everyone involved in the process; this also helps to establish what the current scope of the system is, and to address any areas people feel should be addressed but currently are not. Third, the resulting concept map provides a basis for examining how other design artifacts fit into this conceptual model from a traceability perspective. For example, can scenarios or use cases be built into this concept map without changing the structure itself? Does the concept map align with the conceptual integrity of the planned architecture, and do the implementation level items used to drive the implementation align with this model?

This approach is applied in three stages. In the first stage, concept names are elicited from the existing requirements, and concept maps are created for each category of requirements. In the second stage, the concept maps are consolidated onto a single diagram and, as associations are made between concepts from these different sub-maps, the consolidated concept map itself evolves. In the final stage, we validate the concept map by examining how well they align and account for other requirements artifacts, and generate the resulting requirements model.

This is not the first time that concept mapping has been proposed as a technique for supporting Requirements Engineering; Kof et al. [25] have proposed concept mapping as a generating traces between requirements artifacts. However, our approach differs in two respects. First, Kof et al. are concerned with using concept mapping primarily for supporting the traceability between artifacts at different levels of abstraction, whereas our approach is primarily designed to help designers make sense of the requirements. Second, while Kof et al. uses a frequency profiling algorithm to identify concepts, our approach involves manually inspecting each requirement to infer a suitable concept characterising each requirement. This makes the process more time-consuming, but it better sensitises designers to the requirements themselves.

3.1 Category Concept Mapping

Before concept maps can be created, it is necessary to create a concept name or phrase characterising each requirement. For example, the requirement *The train control software shall control the acceleration of all the system's trains* can be characterised using the phrase *Acceleration control*. This short phrase becomes the canonical identifier for each requirement.

For each functional area associated with the specification, concept maps are then created. This involves preparing paper cut-outs of the concept names associated with each requirement, placing them on a large piece of paper and, using a pencil, drawing and annotating the relationship between each concept. This exercise is carried out in groups of between two - four for each part of the problem domain represented by the requirements category. During the exercise, the requirements specification associated with the category is available for consultation. Requirements that are redundant or out of scope are removed from the concept map, and a reason for their omission is noted. Requirements that are unclear or ambiguous are discussed within the group and, where necessary, the requirement's concept name or description is updated as appropriate.

Once each map is completed, it is transcribed to a machine readable format. For this, we use Graphviz [26]; this is a suite of graph visualisation tools, which can layout

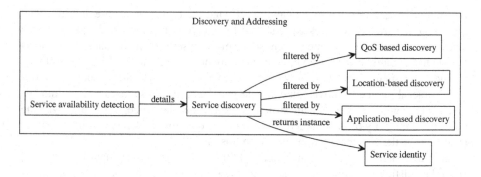

Fig. 1. Example Graphviz concept map

graphs written in a simple textual language called DOT. Figure 1 illustrates an excerpt of a Graphviz concept map.

3.2   Concept Map Consolidation

Once all the concept maps have been created, they are then consolidated onto a single concept map. Like the category concept mapping exercise, this involves drawing relationships between paper cut-outs of requirements. However, this exercise begins by re-creating each of the individual concept maps based on their respective Graphviz models. Using a similar sized group to the first stage, which includes participants involved in the development of the category concept maps, the concept maps are reviewed to clarify relationships both within and between each category. Like the category concept mapping exercise, unclear requirement descriptions are updated and, where appropriate, those deemed duplicate, redundant, or out-of-scope are removed. Similarly, like the first stage, once this exercise is complete the Graphviz versions of each category concept map are updated to incorporate any revisions and relationships between categories.

3.3   Concept Map Validation and Model Generation

Building the consolidated concept map not only shows how requirements are connected, it also helps align them with other design artifacts. This is due to the better understanding that the design team gains developing the visual model. For example, zooming out of the concept map can help retrospectively determine which scenarios the requirements were designed to support. Zooming in explores how the elicited use cases operationalise the requirements. This alignment activity also acts as an additional form of validation; by casting the concept map in a different light, existing concepts or relationships are challenged, and new requirements and traceability associations may be identified. Therefore, the final stage involves identifying design artifacts associated with each requirement concept, and updating each category DOT file to include the aligning artifact references. Our approach supports three types of aligning concepts: scenarios, use cases, and backlog items. Backlog items are items of work which are carried out when developing software as part of the Scrum method [27]. This approach does not pre-suppose Scrum is employed, and this concept can be used synonymously for any downstream design and development artifact.

If we reflect on Figure 1 then we discover that while Graphviz is useful for modelling concept maps, something more is necessary for representing requirements traceability. For example, the association between *Service discovery* and *Service identity* indicates that concepts are related to different categories, not just those associated with a given DOT file. Pasting the contents of all DOT files into a single file is feasible, but with concepts cross-referenced across different files then some duplication of associations is inevitable. It also desirable to filter these maps in some way, or visualise the consequences of the traceability alignment. Moreover, because other requirements artifacts might be maintained using different representations, there needs to be a coherent requirements models that designers can reference internally and present to others externally.

Because it supports the aligning concepts used by this approach, artifacts were converted to XML and imported into the open-source CAIRIS tool [9]. To better fit this approach, a number of modifications were made to CAIRIS. To complement its pre-existing requirements visualisations, an additional graphical view was added to CAIRIS to support the visualisation and manipulation of concept maps; this included the filtering of maps by name or functional category. In this view it is also possible to quickly assess the quality of the requirements themselves using an automated quality gateway check; the metrics are described in more detail by [28], and are based on requirements completeness, the presence of an imperative phrase, and ambiguity. These resulting metrics were visualised using cartoon Chernoff Faces [29], where each part of the face represented a different requirement quality variable. Eye-brow shape indicates the completeness of a given requirement. If no text is found in certain fields, or phrases like "TBC", "none", or "not defined" are present, the completeness score is marked down accordingly, and the eye-brows convey a negative mood. The eye shape indicates whether or not an imperative phrase exists in the requirement description. If such a phrase exists then the eyes become vertically elongated. The mouth indicates the presence of weak or fuzzy phrases, such as mostly, appropriate, normal, or adequate; the presence of these phrases turn the smile into a frown. Examples of how Chernoff Faces visualise these quality attributes are given in Figure 2. These Chernoff Faces are also coloured based on their level of pre- and post-requirements traceability.

Requirements with no evidence pre- and post- requirements traceability were coloured red. Requirements which are motivated by other requirements, based on scenarios and use cases, or refined to product backlog items were coloured blue. Requirements with both pre- *and* post- requirements traceability are coloured green. While it would be unreasonable to expect pre- and post- requirements traceability at early stages of a project, this level of traceability is important for high priority requirements. With this in mind, the labels of high-priority requirements without both pre- and post-requirements traceability are highlighted in red. This is illustrated in Figure 3 which illustrates a Chernoff Face augmented concept map based on the initial concept map in Figure 1.

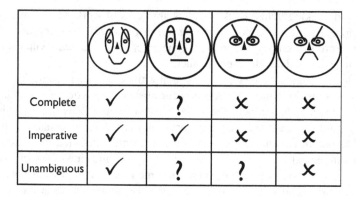

Fig. 2. Example Chernoff Faces mapping to requirement quality attributes

4 Results

We evaluated our approach by using it to update the requirements specification for the EU FP 7 *webinos* project. *webinos* is a federated software platform for running web applications consistently and securely across mobile, PC, home media, and in-car systems. More information about the project is described in [30].

This requirements specification was initially derived from a set of use cases and scenarios [31] and contained 330 requirements; these requirements were sub-divided under eight functional categories: Device and Service Functional Capability (CAP), Discovery and Addressing (DA), Identity (ID), Lifecycle (LC), Negotiation and Compatibility (NC), Policy and Security (PS), Remote Notifications and Messaging (NM), and Transfer and Management of State (TMS). These requirements were used to devise a software architecture for the *webinos* platform.

As architectural design progressed, the project team obtained a better understanding of the problem domain; this challenged many of the assumptions underpinning existing requirements artifacts. However, time constraints during the architectural design meant that the requirements could not be revisited until software development of the platform had already commenced. The platform was implemented using an iterative model based on the Scrum method [27]. Scrum teams were created for representative *webinos* platforms and the core architectural components and features developed were derived from the architectural design documentation.

The process was applied over a two month period by a team of nine part-time and one full-time team member; the part-time team members were involved in platform development activities, while the full-time team member was responsible for co-ordinating the overall approach.

4.1 Preparatory Activities

Before applying our approach, a number of preparatory activities needed to be carried to better facilitate collaboration between the team. The first step involved converting the scenarios, use cases, and requirements needed to a more accessible format given the

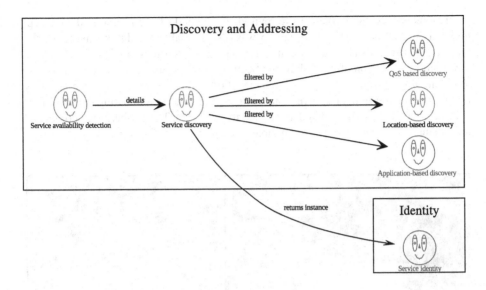

Fig. 3. Chernoff Face concepts

distributed nature of the project team. These were originally documented in Microsoft Word which proved to be too unwieldy. It was, therefore, decided to use the project wiki to maintain these. Unfortunately, because there was no easy programmatic way to access content on the wiki, a git repository [32] was used to maintain the underlying page source. Moreover, while the largely textual structure of the wiki was a fit for storing scenarios and use cases, a more structured format was felt more useful for editing requirements. Consequently, requirements for each category were stored in spreadsheet files which, like the wiki page source files, were also kept under configuration control. Scripts were written to convert both the page sources and the spreadsheets into an XML format compatible with CAIRIS.

4.2 Category Concept Mapping

Before concept names could be created to characterise each requirement, it was first necessary to improve the quality of many of the original requirements. In most cases, this involved little more than simplifying the requirements text, and breaking down large requirements descriptions into multiple requirement statements. At this stage, ten new requirements were added, but existing requirements were not removed, nor were their priorities changed. Also, in addition to the inclusion of a spreadsheet column for the concept name, an additional comments attributes was added to each requirement to indicate what original requirement each updated requirement was based on.

The team met over a two day period to begin the category concept mapping process. To acquaint the team members with the process of concept mapping, three concept maps (LC, NC, and PS) were created. As Figure 4 (left) shows, print-outs of the requirements for each category were available for participants to refer to during this exercise; these were used to refer to the requirements description and, when the group felt this text was ambiguous or inaccurate, these were revised. At the end of each session, the concept map was transcribed to DOT. A laptop was also available for directly updating the requirements spreadsheets. Each concept mapping session took approximately half a day with the exception of the Policy and Security concept mapping session which, due to the number of requirements, took one day. Following this workshop, responsibility for completing the remaining five concept maps, together with updating the DOT files and requirements, was distributed among the five partners. The partners then completed these remaining concept maps over a three week period.

Fig. 4. Concept mapping session (left) and category concept map (right)

4.3   Concept Map Consolidation

Once the remaining concept maps were developed, the team met over a further two-day period to consolidate the concept maps. The session was attended by eight of the ten team members, where each person worked on at least one of the contributing concept maps.

Like the category concept mapping exercise, this involved drawing relationships between paper cut-outs of requirements. This exercise, however, began by re-creating each of the individual concept maps. In most of the cases, this involved re-drawing the concept map based on the optimised Graphviz layout although, in two cases, partners brought their physical maps with them. Each individual concept map was placed on a table covered with butcher paper, and marginally trimmed to fit the space available. Because it contained the most requirements, the PS concept map was the most central, while other concept maps were situated around this. Also, by covering the table with paper, it became easier to draw associations between concepts. Where drawing associations were difficult to follow, then a duplicate concept label was added to the table to simplify reading of the concept map.

Rather than drawing concept mapping to a close, consolidating the maps instead caused the original concept maps to be re-examined in a new light. While participants expected to be asked to comment on the contribution their work areas made to the collective map, many did not realise that they needed to become knowledgeable in the concepts associated with the other maps. Consequently, much of the first day was spent walking through and discussing each of the five concept maps developed remotely, as well as reviewing the three concept maps created when the team last met. The first half of the second day was spent exploring how different concept maps were connected and, where necessary, updating the requirements as a better understanding was gleaned of them. The second half of the second day was spent walking through a selection of scenarios, use cases, and backlog items to check the concept map accounted for the concepts described in these artifacts. Finally, the remaining requirements were reviewed to ensure they were still within scope, their description was accurate, and they were appropriately prioritised.

Besides updating most of the requirements to improve their comprehensibility and clarity, a significant number of requirements (120) were defined as out-of-scope and removed from the specification. The most common reasons for deletion was that a requirement was either superseded or duplicated by other requirements, and what were originally understood to be platform requirements were requirements for end-user applications instead. To ensure that the reason for removing requirements was not forgotten, an *out-of-scope* spreadsheet, and moving the requirement into this sheet, together with an explanation for why the requirement was being removed.

The final consolidated map is illustrated in Figure 5.

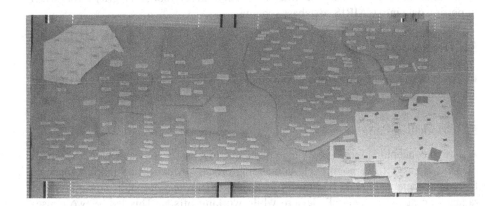

Fig. 5. Consolidated concept map

4.4   Concept Map Validation and Model Generation

Before departing the consolidation workshop, the group carried out a worked example of how the semantic zooming exercise should be carried out, and how the alignment associations between scenarios, use cases, and backlog items should be specified using DOT. Following the workshop, each partner took responsibility for carrying out this alignment activity for one or more functional categories. Because of their familiarity with the respective functional categories, the same breakdown was used as for the category concept mapping.

The participants found that aligning scenarios and use cases to requirements was straightforward because, having gleaned a better understanding of the requirements for their particular area, it was now easier to put the scenarios and use cases in context. However, the lack of post-requirements traceability meant that aligning requirements to the backlog items and implementation code was much harder. To remedy this, the lead developers were invited to review both the concept maps and the Scrum backlog list to both identify requirement concepts they believed were missing, or requirements that motivated backlog items they were working on. Working with their feedback, the participants updated the DOT concept maps for the aligning concepts based on the comments received.

Because of the wide range of artifacts and technologies, and the desire for consistency, additional work was needed to synthesise the data before importing into CAIRIS. A *build* script was created to import all of the requirements artifacts (scenarios, use cases, and requirements) that were stored in the git repository into a single requirements model in CAIRIS; the script also exported the scenarios, use cases, and requirements into both a single specification document, and a collection of wiki pages that project team members could review. When responding to comments from either the document or the wiki page, respondents were asked to update the artifacts in git rather than the wiki pages itself. To validate that people were updating the git-based artifacts, the build script was run daily to re-generate a CAIRIS model based on the contents of the git repository. When the script failed, it was often because of typographical errors in use case, scenario, or requirement identifiers; these caused referential integrity errors when importing data into CAIRIS' database schema.

5   Discussion

In this section, we discuss some of our findings and lessons we learned applying our approach.

5.1   Modelling Fatigue

Although concept mapping is easy to explain and, to a passive bystander, concept mapping *looks* easy, it is a cognitively demanding process. Moving and linking concepts forced participants to make and justify value judgements *in-situ* within a group setting, rather than at the individual's leisure while working offsite. This led to two consequences. First, there was a tendency to under-estimate the amount of time needed for concept mapping. The category concept mapping sessions took twice as long as initially planned because of the discussion generated during the sessions. Second, in a number of cases, time pressures and mental demands meant there was sometimes a tendency to designate borderline requirements as out-of-scope. These cases were most apparent in categories with large numbers of requirements. For example, the original Policy and Security category contained 115 requirements; following the update, only 58 requirements remained. In some cases, subsequent reviews meant that requirements placed out-of-scope needed to be re-introduced into the specification.

Despite the challenges, participants were still positive about their experiences applying the approach. One participant observed that although the time was under-estimated, delays were only in the region of hours, rather than the weeks and months it took to negotiate the original requirements. Participants also found that, as the concept maps became more elaborate and more requirements were incorporated into it, the complexity of the task did not increase. Moreover, participants that worked on multiple concept maps during the Catania workshop found that working on more maps helped them understand the other concept maps better, and aligning scenarios, use cases, and backlog items was considered trivial once the concept maps had been completed.

5.2 Marketing the Approach

As a vehicle for updating the *webinos* requirements specification, most participants were initially sceptical about how useful the approach would be. While the theory behind the approach were clear, many participants failed to see how moving around pieces of paper, and drawing labelled arcs between them would improve the quality of the requirements specification. Participants were, however, also sceptical about how useful the approach taken to elicit and specify the original requirements specification would be for updating them. Given the options available, the concept mapping approach was the most palatable because it directly addressed traceability problems that were facing the project at that time.

As the participants became involved in the hands-on concept mapping process itself, they found the approach both rewarding and worthwhile. In particular, working with physical objects like papers, pencils, and scissors reinforced the tangibility of requirements, something not felt when working with screen based interfaces for manipulating requirements. Nonetheless, although the biggest benefit of this approach is obtaining a better understanding of a system's requirements, to gain initial adoption it was important to focus on the immediate tangible benefits which, for this approach, is tool-supported requirements traceability. Once participants had bought in to concept mapping, they encouraged others to get involved by joining sessions, and reviewing concept maps remotely, thereby improving the visibility of the process across the project. This was a notable result because, up to that point, the requirement specification was seen as something the project contractually needed to deliver, rather than something that added value in its own right.

5.3 Human-Centered Tool Support

Although tools played only a supporting role in the process, it was invaluable for assisting what might otherwise have been tedious activities. These included printing out concept names, using spreadsheets to review requirements tables, de-duplicating traces that occurred in multiple DOT files, and generating a specification document. Consequently, rather than using software to automate the process of concept mapping, it was instead used to remove some of the drudgery associated with supporting the hands-on concept mapping sessions.

After reflecting on the sessions themselves, participants felt that, with so much information being discussed around the concept maps, software tools would have been useful for recording transcripts and annotating concepts with additional information. While someone fulfilling the role of scribe would have been useful at the formative stages of the concept mapping, participants appeared to self organise as the sessions progressed. For example, when the group decided a requirement was out-of-scope, there was usually a pause of around a minute as notes were taken to explain the rationale for de-scoping this requirements. When de-scoping took place when the concept maps were more advanced, concept maps needed to be updated to ensure links were not left hanging. By then, however, the group was confident enough to tidy up the concept map and reflect on the consequences of de-scoping the requirement while one person updated the requirements spreadsheets.

5.4 Requirements Confidence

As both the category and the consolidated concept maps took shape, participants felt confident enough to address requirements which, up to that point, had been included in the specification but had not been properly addressed in the implementation. For example, the specification made several references to *context* and the need for *webinos* to be *context-aware*. When the map was consolidated, the participants found that the better understanding of the requirements had not helped clarify how to address requirements referencing this term. As a result, the team discussed what the term should mean and, once a proper definition had been agreed, revised both the concept map and the associated requirements based on this improved understanding.

Rounding off the consolidation workshop with the requirements prioritisation exercise re-affirmed the confidence that the team had developed about the requirements. Having now seen a big picture of the requirements, the team felt better equipped to re-prioritise them based on estimated delivery schedule of *webinos*, and their importance, rather than the urgency stated by certain stakeholders.

6 Conclusion

In this paper, we presented an approach where concept mapping was used to both improve the visibility of requirements and, with the aid of tool-support, improve their quality. Moreover, our discussion suggests that, as well as improving the quality of the requirements, the approach also served as a useful pedagogical tool about the value of good requirements practice. By transposing requirements from text on a screen to a concept name on a piece of paper, and forcing debate around what particular requirements meant for the project, team members saw software requirements in a more positive light. As a foundation for future work, this paper makes two additional contributions.

First, we have demonstrated that sensemaking and organising learning techniques can provide practical support to participative Requirements Engineering activities. In particular, we found that concept mapping gave team members the confidence to make value judgements. We accept, however, when tired and under pressure, such judgements might be made too easily. For this reason, future work considering the group dynamics of concept mapping for supporting software engineering activities would be valuable.

Second, we have shown that lightweight software tools, where applied appropriately, can augment the concept mapping process without getting in its way. Our discussion suggests that desired tool-support shares many of the characteristics of Computer Aided Qualitative Data Analysis (CAQDAS) such as Atlas.ti [33]. While the ability to quickly search for concepts and other data was available once the data had been imported into CAIRIS, it wasn't during the concept mapping process itself. While recent work has looked at how CAQDAS tools might interface with requirements management tools when developing personas [12], our results suggest that understanding how tool interaction might be useful for supporting other design techniques warrants further investigation.

Acknowledgements. The research described in this paper was funded by the EU FP7 *webinos* project (FP7-ICT-2009-05 Objective 1.2).

References

1. Cheng, B.H.C., Atlee, J.M.: Research directions in requirements engineering. In: Future of Software Engineering 2007, pp. 285–303. IEEE Computer Society (2007)
2. Nuseibeh, B.: Ariane 5: Who dunnit? IEEE Softw. 14, 15–16 (1997)
3. Gotel, O., Finkelstein, C.: An analysis of the requirements traceability problem. In: Proceedings of the First International Conference on Requirements Engineering, pp. 94–101 (April 1994)
4. Winkler, S., von Pilgrim, J.: A survey of traceability in requirements engineering and model-driven development. Software and Systems Modeling, 1–37 (2009)
5. Burge, J.E., Carroll, J.M., McCall, R., Mistrik, I.: Rationale-Based Software Engineering. Springer (2008)
6. The Open University: Compendium web site (2012), compendium.open.ac.uk
7. Burge, J.E., Brown, D.C.: Seurat: integrated rationale management. In: Proceedings of the 30th International Conference on Software Engineering, ICSE 2008, pp. 835–838. ACM (2008)
8. Faily, S., Fléchais, I.: Towards tool-support for Usable Secure Requirements Engineering with CAIRIS. International Journal of Secure Software Engineering 1(3), 56–70 (2010)
9. Faily, S.: CAIRIS web site (June 2012), http://github.com/failys/CAIRIS
10. Faily, S., Fléchais, I.: A Meta-Model for Usable Secure Requirements Engineering. In: Proceedings of the 6th International Workshop on Software Engineering for Secure Systems, pp. 126–135. IEEE Computer Society (2010)
11. Faily, S., Fléchais, I.: The Secret Lives of Assumptions: Developing and Refining Assumption Personas for Secure System Design. In: Forbrig, P. (ed.) HCSE 2010. LNCS, vol. 6409, pp. 111–118. Springer, Heidelberg (2010)
12. Faily, S., Fléchais, I.: Persona cases: a technique for grounding personas. In: Proceedings of the 29th International Conference on Human Factors in Computing Systems, pp. 2267–2270. ACM (2011)
13. Russell, D.M., Stefik, M.J., Pirolli, P., Card, S.K.: The cost structure of sensemaking. In: Proceedings of the INTERACT 1993 and CHI 1993 Conference on Human Factors in Computing Systems, CHI 1993, pp. 269–276. ACM, New York (1993)
14. Jantunen, S., Gause, D., Wessman, R.: Making sense of product requirements. In: 2010 18th IEEE International on Requirements Engineering Conference (RE), pp. 89–92 (2010)
15. Russell, D.M., Jeffries, R., Irani, L.: Sensemaking for the rest of us. In: CHI 2008 Sensemaking Workshop (2008)
16. Dubberly, H.: Using concept maps in product development. In: Kolko, J. (ed.) Exposing the Magic of Design: A Practitioner's Guide to the Methods & Theory of Synthesis, pp. 109–124. Oxford University Press (2011)
17. Clarke, S.: How usable are your apis? In: Oram, A., Wilson, G. (eds.) Making Software: What Really Works, and Why We Believe It, pp. 545–565. O'Reilly (2011)
18. Martin, B., Hanington, B.: Universal Methods of Design: 100 Ways to Research Complex Problems, Develop Innovative Ideas, and Design Effective Solutions. Rockport (2012)
19. Novak, J.D., Gowin, D.B.: Learning How To Learn. Cambridge University Press (1984)

20. Sutherland, S., Katz, S.: Concept mapping methodology: A catalyst for organizational learning. Evaluation and Program Planning 28, 257–269 (2005)
21. IHMC: CmapTools web site (2012), http://cmap.ihmc.us
22. Klemmer, S.R., Newman, M.W., Farrell, R., Bilezikjian, M., Landay, J.A.: The designers' outpost: a tangible interface for collaborative web site. In: Proceedings of the 14th Annual ACM Symposium on User Interface Software and Technology, UIST 2001, pp. 1–10. ACM, New York (2001)
23. Tanenbaum, K., Antle, A.N.: A tangible approach to concept mapping. In: AIP Conference Proceedings, vol. 1127, pp. 121–132 (2009)
24. Oppl, S., Stary, C.: Effects of a Tabletop Interface on the Co-construction of Concept Maps. In: Campos, P., Graham, N., Jorge, J., Nunes, N., Palanque, P., Winckler, M. (eds.) INTERACT 2011, Part III. LNCS, vol. 6948, pp. 443–460. Springer, Heidelberg (2011)
25. Kof, L., Gacitua, R., Rouncefield, M., Sawyer, P.: Concept mapping as a means of requirements tracing. In: 2010 Third International Workshop on Managing Requirements Knowledge (MARK), pp. 22–31 (2010)
26. AT&T: Graphviz web site (June 2012), http://www.graphviz.org
27. Schwaber, K.: Agile Project Management with Scrum. Microsoft Press, Redmond (2004)
28. Wilson, W.M., Rosenberg, L.H., Hyatt, L.E.: Automated quality analysis of natural language requirement specifications. In: Proceedings of Fourteenth Annual Pacific Northwest Software Quality Conference, pp. 140–151 (1996),
http://www.pnsqc.org/proceedings/pnsqc1996.pdf
29. Chernoff, H.: The Use of Faces to Represent Points in K-Dimensional Space Graphically. Journal of the American Statistical Association, 361–368 (1973)
30. Fuhrhop, C., Lyle, J., Faily, S.: The webinos project. In: Proceedings of the 21st International Conference Companion on World Wide Web, WWW 2012 Companion, pp. 259–262. ACM, New York (2012)
31. Webinos Consortium: webinos project deliverable D2.1: Use Cases and Scenarios (January 2011), http://webinos.org/content/
webinos-Scenarios_and_Use_Cases_v1.pdf
32. Software Freedom Conservancy: git web site (May 2012), git-scm.com
33. Muhr, T.: User's Manual for ATLAS.ti 5.0. ATLAS.ti Scientific Software Development GmbH, Berlin (2004)

Towards Conflict Management in User Interface Composition Driven by Business Needs

Anne-Marie Déry-Pinna, Audrey Occello, and Michel Riveill

Laboratoire I3S (Université de Nice - Sophia Antipolis - CNRS)
Bâtiment Polytech'Sophia – SI 930 route des Colles – B.P. 145
F-06903 Sophia Antipolis Cedex, France
{pinna,occello,riveill}@polytech.unice.fr

Abstract. This paper presents a composition engine that handles User interface (UI) in the context of application composition. The aim is to detect and manage conflicts that may arise when composing UI driven by business needs. The originality of this composition engine is to reason at an Abstract level which simplifies the composition algorithm and makes it reusable and oblivious to technology. The composition engine is the core of the Alias framework that reduces the re-engineering efforts needed to obtain the UI of an application built by composition of smaller ones following the "programming in the large" paradigm.

Keywords: User Interface composition, functional composition, composition conflicts.

1   Introduction

The "programming in the large" approach aims at constructing applications by composition of smaller ones. The presentation level is not considered in the paradigms that enable programming in the large such as Service Oriented Architectures (SOA) [1] or Component Based Software Engineering (CBSE) [2, 3]. In this context, developers usually need to apply a complete development cycle (from requirement analysis, task model, to tests through design and programming) to build the UI from scratch; they cannot reuse former UIs that come with the applications to be composed, pieces of them or even analysis elements.

Our goal is to reduce the re-engineering efforts needed to obtain the UI of an application built by composition. Application types are wide; we do not pretend to handle any kind of them. In fact we consider SOA applications built by composition of services. Even if the resulting application corresponding to a new service can be itself composed with other ones, this recursive composition process is not infinite. Hence, the granularity of the units to be composed is not coarse. This means that the corresponding UIs that we handle focus on rendering the use of service operations.

We propose a composition engine that exploits information about the functional composition (the business needs and then desired usages) to deduce which part of UIs should be reused and which interaction links with the functionalities should be

M. Winckler, P. Forbrig, and R. Bernhaupt (Eds.): HCSE 2012, LNCS 7623, pp. 233–250, 2012.

maintained. This deduction is based on an abstract representation which focuses on the UI composition needs in order to propose an algorithm reusable on several platforms. UIs, FCs and functional compositions are then expressed in a pivotal formalism [4].

The abstract representation used by the composition engine is based on an architectural decoupling derived from the separation of concerns principle. We assume that each application is made of two distinct parts: the functional core (FC), and an attached UI. This assumption is not very restrictive in the sense that many architectures prone for the separation of the UI from the FC like in the Arch model [5], in the PAC model [6] and in the MVC model [7] for example. The composition engine deduces UI composition based on functional composition provided that the functional composition (using orchestrations in SOA) is performed by the developers in response to end-user business needs after a requirement analysis: functional compositions may be seen as an implicit and partial incarnation of the desired usages expressed from the business point of view.

The composition engine output allows for the generation of a first sketch of the UI to the designer using transformation rules. This sketch reuses parts of former UIs, preserves the consistency between the functional level and the UI level respecting the composition needs and the previous interaction links between UIs and FCs in the composed applications. Then, the designer may concentrate on ergonomics. For this, the composition engine builds automatically an operational UI sketch for an application A as a function of: 1) the way FCs of smaller applications are composed to form A (functional composition); and 2) the interactions between each FC to be composed and their respective UIs. In this paper, we focus on the composition engine rules, on the UI composition conflicts that may arise, and on conflict management.

The remainder of this paper is organized as follows. Section 2 presents related word around composition. Section 3 describes a case study to illustrate the interest of using information about functional composition to drive the UI composition choices. Section 4 gives an outlook of the context of use of the composition engine: the Alias framework's process and the underlying models. Section 5 focuses on the composition engine and on composition conflict management. Section 6 evaluates the composition engine proposal. Last section concludes.

2   Related Work

We classify work around compositions according to the parts of applications they cover. We mentioned the functional core (FC) part and the UI part in the introduction. We add a third concern: Tasks are used in the HCI research field for user centered design and development in order to express end-user requirements. Task formalization allows designers, ergonomists end developers to agree and respect the user needs. Consequently it is important to consider works on Task composition as well as on FC or UI compositions. This classification highlights three categories of related work:

- Works only considering *functional composition* [8, 9, 10, 11] which results imply to build a new UI from scratch to use the composed application.
- Works only considering *UI composition*, either for defining specific toolkit for adaptive UI [12], either based on abstract definition of UIs [13, 14] or either adopting end-user programming [15] which results are UIs not linked to application functionalities (a non runnable application). Work around Mashups such as iGoogle and Netvibes enables end-user to create their own application. To achieve the composition, one can only juxtapose different applications in the same workspace leading to independent UIs.
- Works considering *several parts of applications* [16, 17, 18, 19, 20]. The interesting element in these approaches is that most of them exploit Task information either directly from Task analysis models either indirectly to propose a composition approach of entire applications.

Works of the two first categories are limited to truncated applications where a lot of additional development is needed. Our approach belongs to the third category of works that aim at composing entire applications to deliver runnable applications.

Yahoo!Pipes provides a Mashups environment to draw a workflow that aggregates information from multiple sources. However, users do not have any control on the UI produced by the workflow description. In [16], a planning problem describing user needs is transformed into a task representation, which is then transformed into a UI. A weak point of this approach is the independency of functional elements which are not composed. In [17, 18, 19, 20], composition only proposes to aggregate UIs without elements merging. [17, 18, 19] require a specific development for the UIs. [19, 20] do not use all the possibilities offered by the functional composition.

In contrast, our approach determines UI elements required in the composite application including the possibility to merge them. We do not have to realize a specific development to use our approach but only to follow a good separation of concerns.

Our originality is to establish a connection between the "FC domain" and the "UI domain" by deducing the UI composition from the functional composition and by conserving former associations between UI and FC. This connection preserves the consistency between the two main parts of an application. The reuse of former UIs assures a transfer of UI design analysis. Our proposition takes into account the fact that tasks are unfortunately not embedded in applications now but some of them are hidden in functional compositions which express business needs. Then a part of the desired usage is partially recoverable. For example, users' tasks chaining is injected as sequentiality or parallelism in the expression of the functional composition.

3   Building Application through Composition: The Human Resource System Case Study

In the rest of this paper, we focus on a Human Resource system case study. We consider two services: the first one provides access to Social Insurance account (e.g.

French "carte vitale") and the other one provides access to a corporate directory (e.g. IBM blue pages). Users interact with these services through corresponding UIs.

For a user to interact with a new service built from these services, one must extract useful features from the existing services, to compose them using orchestrations and also to compose the relevant parts of the corresponding UIs consistently.

In the remainder of this section, we illustrate the interest of using information about functional composition to drive the UI composition choices using these services and two orchestration samples to show UI composition possibilities.

3.1   Service Descriptions

Let *S1* be a service to access social insurance information. It exposes a *getByCard* operation with a *card identifier* input and with a *last name*, a *first name*, a *birthday*, a full social insurance *number*, a *medical referee* (the doctor that ensures a custom medical supervision), a *family status*, a *handicap* rate and an *address* outputs. Figure 1a outlines *UI1* the UI attached to the *S1* service.

Let *S2* be a service to access business information about an employee. It exposes a *getBusinessInfo* with a *full name* (last name plus first name) input and with a *full name*, a *position*, an *email* address, *office* numbers, *buildings* and *addresses* outputs. Figure 1b outlines *UI2* the UI attached to the *S2* service.

(a) *UI1* attached to *S1*   (b) *UI2* attached to *S2*

Fig. 1. Possible representation of UI

3.2   Composition Cases

Let suppose now that the firm's Department of Human Resources needs some business and personal information about employees to manage sick leave for illness.

A first approach may be to use the two services simultaneously as in the mash up manner with the goal to group business and insurance information for a given person.

The UIs are displayed side by side but there is no information exchange between the two services. This kind of composition may engender a set of UI problems: The name is shown twice, addresses are dispatched in the two UIs and so on.

Another way to proceed is to compose the two services using orchestration mechanisms and reuse partially the former UIs to interact with the new service.

Let *Composition1* be the orchestration of *S1* and *S2* in sequence such that the data input of *S2* operation (the *full name*) is provided by the concatenation of the *first name* and *last name* outputs of S1 operation. *S3,* the new service resulting from this orchestration, exposes a *getEmployeeHRInfo* operation with a *card identifier* input (the data used to invoke *S1* in the orchestration). The outputs of *S3* operation are: the *first name*, the *last name*, the personal *address*, the professional *offices*, *buildings* and *addresses* the insurance *number*, the *medical referee*. This is not the union of *S1* and *S2* operation outputs because information such as the *handicap rate* are not needed by the HR Department and should not be disclosed for privacy considerations anyway. Let *UI3* be the UI attached to *S3* that reuses parts of *UI1* and *UI2* (Fig. 2).

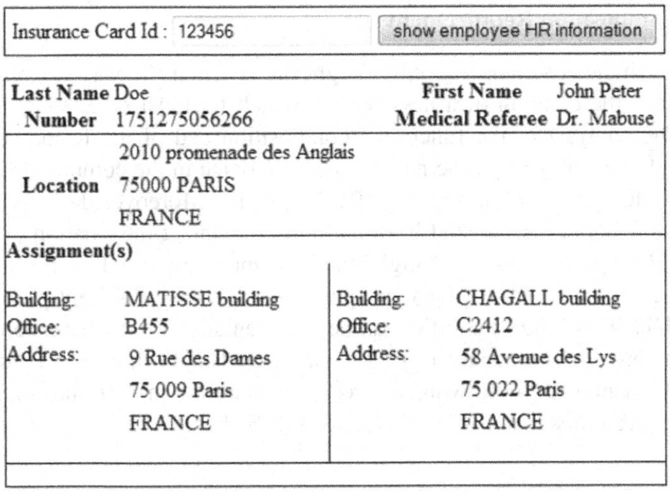

Fig. 2. A possible UI attached to S3

Let *Composition2* be a variation of *Composition1* where the personal *address* output from *S1* and the professional *addresses* output from *S2* are merged as they concern contact information in both cases. Then, *S4*, the service corresponding to this new composition, exposes an operation that holds a parameter less than the *S3* operation because of the merged outputs.

Figure 3 illustrates possible UIs that may be built from previous UIs reflecting the use of *S4*. In Figure 3a, addresses are stacked vertically and identified with a "location" label. In Figure 3b, addresses are laid out as a mosaic and identified with a "address" label.

(a) Addresses are represented like in *UI1*   (b) Addresses are represented like in *UI2*

Fig. 3. Possible UIs for *S4*

3.3   UI Composition Requirements

These two examples of composition highlight the fact that the way of composing *S1* and *S2* implies the creation of a new service which UI must be adapted to the new behavior. The analysis of the functional composition and of the former UIs should detect redundant display (e.g.: the name appearing twice in the composed UI) and not to display useless information (e.g. the family status). Moreover the new UI should ensure layout grouping for related information (e.g. contact information both present in *S1* and *S2* respective UIs). *S4* highlights a complexity in UI composition when the functional composition involves grouping data that have different presentation in the former UIs. This kind of conflict can be representative of incoherence in the way the user centered design analysis of the services has been done. How will the addresses be displayed? Following the recommendations in *UI1* like in Fig. 3a or following the recommendations in *UI2* like in Fig. 3b?

4   Context of Use of the Alias Composition Engine

This section gives an outlook of the context in which is used the proposed composition engine. We describe the composition process in which the engine is integrated, the underlying models on which the engine rely and an intuitive presentation of the proposed composition mechanisms.

The Alias process starts from a set of separate services with associated UIs and from a composition of these services. An automatic learning phase creates (1) abstract models of the relationships between UIs and FCs and between FCs. Then, the composition engine (2) analyzes all models with its set of composition rules and proposes (3a) potential conflicts or (3b) a possible UI for the service composition. The process ends with (4) the generation of code for the new UI and for the links to the FC part. Figure 4 sums up the process steps. Steps 1 and 4 are platform dependent

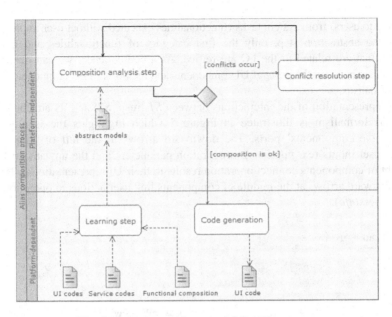

Fig. 4. Main composition steps of the Alias process

as we need to produce transformation rule for each technological space to be handled. Steps 2 and 3 are platform independent as the Alias composition engine is technological agnostic.

In Alias, each application is modeled as an assembly of a UI component and a FC component and compositions are expressed in a similar way to component assemblies such as in UML2.0 component diagram [21]. Describing formally the underlying models is not in the scope of this paper but they can be found in [4]. UI and FC parts of an application are represented as components with ports and compositions as bindings between components. However the granularity of the port is finer here: at the data or operation level not at the programming interface level. UI input ports correspond to user inputs (collected through widgets such as textfields, lists, checkboxes, ...) and UI output ports correspond to system output (rendered through widgets such as labels, images, tables, ...). FC intput ports correspond to operation input parameters and FC output ports correspond to operation output parameters. Trigger ports correspond to user actions in UI (fired through widgets such as buttons, menu items, ...) and to operation calls in FC.

This abstract representation of applications is obtained by automatic transformations (see section 6). From this abstract representation, the composition engine produces a suggested UI (the first sketch of the composed UI). The suggested UI is then transformed into code making the application operational.

The bindings between a UI component and a FC component are very important for the UI composition computation as they help in identifying which functionality is related to which UI elements and vice versa. Searching for such bindings during the abstraction step makes it possible to differentiate functionalities related to user tasks (functionalities that are called as a result from a user interactions and/or functionalities which results are presented to users) from system tasks (functionalities executed without user implication). During the abstraction step, only the first category of functionalities and only UI elements that are related to the FC are reified. As a consequence, we can observe an isomorphism between the ports of UI components and the ports of FC components in the Alias formalism.

The representation of the interactions between *S1* (resp. *S2*) and its attached UI in the Alias formalism is illustrated in Figure 5 which highlights the isomorphism between the components' ports. The downward arrows at the left of components connect user inputs (ex. *fullname*) to operation parameters and the upward arrows at the right of components connect operation results to their UI representation (*address*). The downward arrows at the middle of components link user actions to operation calls (*getBusinessInfo*).

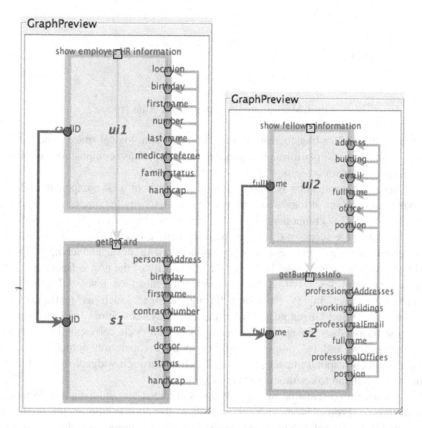

Fig. 5. Representation of S1/UI1 and S2/UI2 in Alias

In Alias, each functional composition is also modeled as an assembly of components. The bindings between FC components are very important for the UI composition computation as they help in identifying which functionalities and data are kept in the functional composition.

The representation of *Composition1* (the first orchestration of *S1* and *S2* services) in the Alias formalism is illustrated in the Figure 6. The *S3* component represented at the bottom of the figure is composed of the two former components: *S1* and *S2*.

The composition engine of Alias deduces which UI elements to reuse and which of them trigger conflicts by correlating information about: 1) functionalities and data that should be kept thanks to FC bindings and 2) their corresponding elements at the UI level thanks to UI to FC and FC to UI bindings. Potential conflicts may occur when two parts of former UIs are bound to the same operation of the new FC. Figure 6 shows the application corresponding to *Composition1*: UI3 is bound to *S3*.

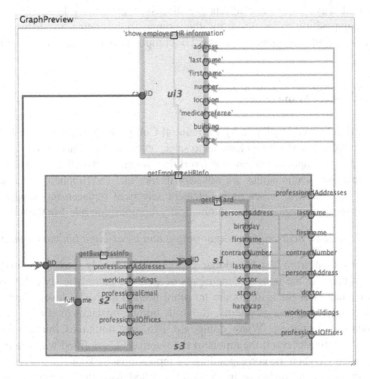

Fig. 6. Representation of S3 and its corresponding UI in Alias

The Alias framework has been implemented in Java for the abstraction and concretization steps (steps 1 and 4) and the composition engine has been implemented in Prolog (steps 2 and 3). The transformations involved in steps 1 and 4 have been written for Flex and SWING for the UI part, WSDL for the service part, and BPEL for the orchestration definition.

5   Alias Composition Engine

This section describes the composition engine which deduces a first sketch of the UI preserving the interaction consistency between the new UI and the new FC. The composition engine makes it possible to:

- **Identify** which UI elements of the former UIs to keep. In our example (see Figure 2), the *handicap* rate output is not exposed outside the "functional box" in the Figure 6. Then it is not represented in the UI component (*UI3*). The *medical referee* output is published (made available outside of the "functional box"). Then it is kept and represented in UI component (*UI3*).
- **Analyze** the data flows and reproduce them at the UI level.
- **Point out** the potential conflict points for UI composition.
- **Solve** the detected conflicts either automatically or interactively.

The different ways to solve conflicts are discussed informally in section 5.1. The different composition rules used by the composition engine to deduce the UI composition, to identify and solve the UI composition conflicts are described in section 5.2.

5.1   UI Conflict Management

a. UI Selection Solved implicitly by Functional Composition Choices. The functional composition indicates which UI elements to select automatically when: (1) an output of a FC is bound to the input of another one (workflow impact at the UI level) and (2) some outputs, inputs or functionalities are not kept in the final FC (implicit selection of UI elements). The following cases of UI element selection/ replacement /suppression is managed by the composition engine automatically (composition rule 1 in the section 5.2).

Case of UI selection deduced from input-output and input-input functional bindings

Using information from the functional compositions avoids reusing redundant UI elements. When FCs are bound, some inputs of a FC are automatically collected from outputs of other FCs. Such inputs are no more needed at the UI level. Then similar information may disappear implicitly. It avoids human mistakes or confusion caused by redundant information. When composed FCs are bound to internal FCs, the situation is slightly different: the inputs of the internal FC are filled with the inputs of the composed FC. Then the corresponding UI inputs must be kept.

In the example, the *fullname* input of S2 is filled with the concatenation of the *firstname* and *lastname* outputs of *S1* then the input of *S2* is no more exposed by *S3* and *S4*. In consequence, the *fullname* is no more present in the new UI. The *contract number* input of *S1* is exposed by *S3* because it is needed by the *getEmployeeHRInfo* operation (the operation that calls the *getByCard* operation of *S1* in the orchestration). In consequence, the insurance *number* is kept in the new UI.

Case of UI selection/replacement deduced from the elements exposed in the functional composition (composite)

Using information from the functional compositions avoids reusing useless UI elements. When an input is not selected in the new behavior, the user should not have to give its useless value via the UI anymore. When a result is no more calculated in the new behavior, its visualization becomes obsolete. When functionalities are no more needed or when they shift from interactive tasks to system tasks (because of bindings), the composed FC does not exposed it anymore. Then, the UI elements corresponding to functionality triggers disappear as the user will not activate these functionalities anymore. On the other side, the internal functionalities not exposed but bound to a functionality of the composed FC are managed separately. Their corresponding UI element is replaced by that of the functionality of the composed FC.

In the example, UI elements like the *family status* are no more present in the new UI as *S3/S4* does not expose the corresponding outputs. Moreover, as the *getBusinessInfo* operation becomes a system task (*all* its inputs are automatically filled), the "show fellow's information" button is not kept in the new UI. Finally, the "show insurance information" button is replaced by a "show employee HR information" button in the new UI as the *getEmployeeHRInfo* operation of *S3/S4* calls the *getByCard* operation of *S1*.

b. Conflicts Solved explicitly by the Composition Engine. The composition engine cannot proceed to automatic UI element selection when several UI inputs (resp. outputs) are bound to a unique input (resp. output) of the composed FC (composition rules 2 and 3 in section 5.2). In such cases, the composition engine detects potential conflict points (composition rule 4 in section 5.2) and alerts the developers (Fig. 7). In the example, *Composition2* raises a conflict since there are two possibilities for displaying merged addresses.

Fig. 7. Conflict detection in *UI4*

To proposed conflicts management methods are either to: 1) keep all UI elements, 2) keep one of the possible elements, or 3) create a new UI element. The framework may let the developers choose the conflict management method as shown in Figure 8. For example, the developer may decide between several former UI design in order to inform the engine about the best choice for usage.

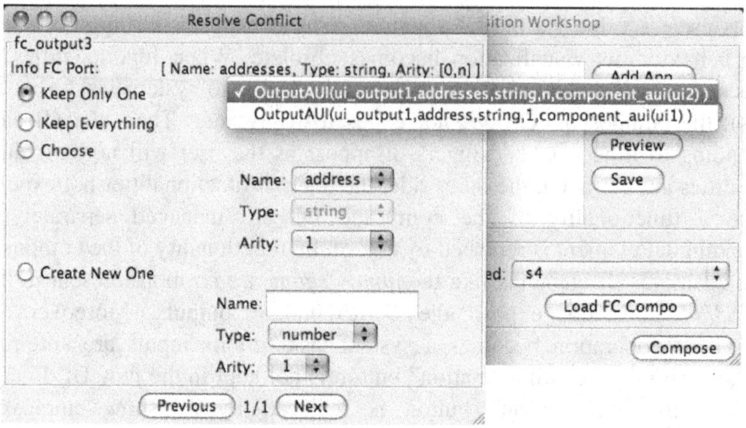

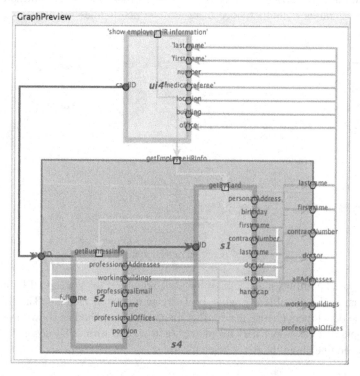

Fig. 8. Alias framework menu to choose the conflict resolution method (shown for *UI4* here)

In the example (*Composition2*), the representation of merged addresses may be (i) like in *UI1* or (ii) like in *UI2* or (iii) a new element may be created. This first possibility is illustrated in Figure 9 (the *location* element from *UI1* is kept whereas the *address* element from *UI2* is not).

Fig. 9. A possible UI for S4 proposed by Alias as a function of the UI conflict resolution

5.2   Composition Rules

The composition engine is based on a set of rules identifying the elements to keep from former UIs and detecting conflicts between UI elements.

Composition rule 1 - Potential Reused UI element detection

This rule determines the set of UI elements which are not used in the new UI and thus the set of UI elements that may be reused in the new UI. This rule signals to the developers which UI elements are not kept by the functional composition. Then they may change the functional composition if they think that the removal of some UI elements highlights a consequence of a bad interpretation of the user requirements in term of functionalities.

Composition rule 2 - Potential conflicting UI output detection

This rule determines the set of UI outputs which are potential conflict points for the new UI (bound to the same output of the new FC).

Composition rule 3 - Potential conflicting UI input detection

This rule determines the set UI inputs which are potential conflict points for the new UI (bound to the same input of the new FC).

Composition rule 4 - Conflict resolution

Several strategies could be adopted: 1) the engine may solve conflicts *automatically* using assumptions either provided by the developers or default choices; 2) the engine may also operate *interactively* asking the developers to remove the conflicts using an extra UI (the UI of the framework dedicated to conflict management).

Resolution algorithm or automatic solving. This algorithm takes in parameter the *predominant* UI and returns the set of kept UI elements. The predominant UI choice indicates which representation to advantage in case of ambiguities. This information may be given by the developers at the beginning of the process after an analysis of the hidden design choices made on the former UIs. The default value (the first UI declared in Alias) can be used to obtain a first sketch rapidly otherwise.

The conflict resolution algorithm uses information about UI elements: the kind of representation (multiple or single). A multiple representation serves to visualize a set of values (set of radio buttons, list box ...), a single representation serves to visualize a unique value (text field, label ...). The conflict resolution algorithm also uses different UI composition operators to solve the conflicts: *selection, union* or *union without redundancy.* The underlying ergonomic rule is to minimize UI redundancy in order to avoid confusion in usage. The algorithm selects the best UI composition operator to apply depending on the kind of representation of the UI elements that are in conflict:

1. If there is only one "multiple" representation, then that representation is chosen to present the merged data
2. If there are several "multiple" representation, then the "multiple" representation of the predominant UI is chosen to present the merged data.

3. If all the representations are "single", then all the UI elements are kept. In this last case, the engine informs the developers of the semantic similarities between the kept UI elements. Such information helps the developers to select which UI elements to group when performing the layout of the new UI. It may also points out an inconsistency between the functional composition and user requirements that may imply revising the functional composition design.

Algorithm for interactive solving. Conflict resolution can be guided by the developers who can choose the composition operator they want to apply and the UI representation(s) they want to keep or the creation of a new UI element and its representation (this last choice is not possible in automatic mode) as shown in Figure 8.

Composition rule 5 - UI usability warning

At this step, the labels associated with the elements of the new UI are compared. If labels with same names are associated with different UI elements, a warning is sent to the developers. The framework gives the possibility to the developers to rename some of them if they want.

Application to the case study

In the second example of composition (*Composition2*), the composition engine deduces that the *fullname* input of *UI2* will not be reused in *UI3* as well as the *family status*, the *handicap* rate and the *birthday* outputs of *UI1* and the *email* and *position* outputs of *UI2* (composition rule 1). At this step, the developers can verify if the functional composition is well suited. If they feel that a UI element is missing and seems to lack to the usage (the worker *position* for example), they can decide to adjust the functional composition so as to keep it in the new UI.

The composition engine also deduces that there is a conflict point concerning the *location* output of *UI1* and the *address* output of *UI2* (composition rule 2) and that there are no conflict points on UI input elements (composition rule 3).

To solve the detected conflict in interactive mode, the developers must choose between the *location* output representation (single) of *UI1* and *address* output representation (multiple) and the operator to apply. They can also decide to create a new element and choose a new representation. In Figure 3a, they decide to keep the representation of *UI1* and to apply the union operator. In Figure 3b, they decide to keep the representation of *UI2* and to apply the selection operator.

To solve the detected conflict in automatic mode, the engine compares the representations of the UI elements that are in conflict and choose the best one. To understand the different solving methods, let consider three cases:

1. If the *professional addresses* are visualized in a list box ("multiple" representation) in *UI2* and the *personal address* in a text field ("single" representation) in *UI1*, then the engine chooses the UI element from *UI2* (the one with a multiple representation) containing the union of data from the *professional addresses* output of *S2* and from the *personal address* output of *S1*.
2. If the *professional addresses* and the *personal address* are both visualized in a list box ("multiple" representation) then the predominant UI representation is kept (*UI1* here).

3. If the *professional addresses* and the *personal address* are both visualized in labels ("single" representation) then the engine chooses to keep the two representations. The engine also informs the developers of the semantic similarities of the UI elements. The developers will then be able to place the UI elements side by side to group contact information.

In this example, no usability warning is detected by the engine because each UI element is associated with a unique label (there is no label having same names).

6   Evaluation of the Alias Approach

The Alias composition engine has been evaluated from different points of view: (i) modeling pertinence and coverage, (ii) composition engine coherence and (iii) user interaction with tool assessment. For evaluation purpose, several case studies have been implemented including the published ones: the mail/notepad scenario [22], the tour operator [23] and the human resource system (presented in this paper).

Modeling pertinence and coverage: In [23], we have shown how Alias exploits Model Driven Engineering (MDE) [24] transformations to fill the gap between the composition engine that is technological agnostic and the real world by: a) abstracting applications into the Alias formalism automatically (step 1 of the Alias process), and b) concretizing the sketch of the new UI deduced by the composition engine automatically as well as the interaction links with the FC part of the composed application (step 4 of the Alias process). The case studies have been useful to check the advantages of modeling architectural constraint as well as the possibility to abstract intrinsically different graphical toolkits such as Java SWING (desktop toolkit) and Flex (web toolkit).

Composition engine coherence: The composition rules described in this paper respect the formal properties listed in [25]. We checked the rules coherence by feeding the Prolog engine with a bunch of facts and by analyzing and comparing the inferred results with the expected ones. This work has consolidated the pivotal formalism and has been useful to check that the engine conflict detection covers a satisfying set of conflicts associated with the potential functional compositions.

User interaction with tool assessment: The framework prototype has been designed and continuously evaluated using the 9 heuristics of Nielsen and Molich [26]. Only the last heuristic "Help and documentation" is not covered as the tool is only at a stage of research prototype. Using such method is a first step toward assessment of user interaction with tool but it is not sufficient as end-users do not take part of the process in formative evaluation methods such as this one. Then, we are using a summative user-centered evaluation method called cooperative method [27] to collect application developers' feedbacks and to assess the usability of the framework and of the composition engine UI with real users. We are currently establishing evaluation protocols. Our goal is to evaluate the ability of users (developers) to perform tasks such as: understanding conflict detection, selecting the best conflict resolution regarding a composition goal, etc. The protocols are also designed to allow us to compare what the developers expect as the UI composition result (they provide it as a diagram) and what they obtain by using the Alias framework which also provides diagrams (Figures 5, 6 and 9 are extracts of such diagrams). This cooperative evaluation is still in progress.

7   Conclusion

Alias is an approach for composing SOA applications including their user interfaces (UIs). The originality of Alias composition engine comes from the fact that UI composition is deduced from the way functional parts of applications are composed. This paper has shown: 1) how the Alias composition engine builds a first sketch of the UI by reusing and composing elements from former UIs and by maintaining the interaction links between the UI level and the functional level and 2) how it manages composition conflicts.

The goal is not to provide a UI directly usable by end-user in an ergonomic sense but to shorten UI development cycles by providing a consistent and automatic way to reuse former UIs while preserving the interaction links with their corresponding application functional part. To finalize the application, developers have to improve ergonomic aspects of the UI.

Apart from creating a UI sketch, the Alias composition engine offers additional usages. It can be used to simulate both UI composition and functional composition results prior to real developments. The composition engine feedbacks (missing UI elements, conflict points ...) are clues making it possible to verify that the functional composition is such that developers expect it to be.

The experiments convince us about the pertinence of the Alias composition engine for the reuse of web application UIs developed with Flex and of desktop application UIs developed with SWING. Our short-term perspectives are to check the possibility to abstract intrinsically different SOA implementations. With the growing use of Restful services, we believe that providing abstraction transformations (step 1) for such SOA implementation is needed as well as for web service ones. Despite the fact that REST does not fit well with the message-oriented paradigm of the Web service, we claim that this has no impact on our modeling since the latter fits well with workflow as well as data flow compositional logic.

Finally, the underlying open issue is to manage divergent composition choices: between user interaction needs such as proposed in [16, 17] and functional requirements as we propose. One approach brings the user point of view and usability properties whereas the other one offers technical requirements on functionality implementation details (typing rules, semantics, etc.). Another challenge is to cope with compositions held at different time (runtime or design time) in a coherent way.

Acknowledgments. We thank the DGE M-Pub 08 2 93 0702 project for his funding.

References

1. Papazoglou, M.P., Van Den Heuvel, W.J.: Service oriented design and development methodology. Int. J. Web Eng. Technol. 2(4), 412–442 (2006)
2. Szyperski, C.: Component Software - Beyond Object-Oriented Programming. Addison-Wesley (1999)
3. Heineman, G., Councilln, W. (eds.): Component-Based Software Engineering, Putting the Pieces Together. Addison-Westley (2001) ISBN : 0-201-70485-4
4. Occello, A., Joffroy, C., Pinna-Déry, A.-M., Renevier-Gonin, P., Riveill, M.: Metamodeling user interfaces and services for composition considerations. In: SEDE 2010, pp. 33–38. ISCA (2010)
5. Bass, L.J., Coutaz, J.: A Metamodel for the Runtime Architecture of an Interactive System. UIMS Tool Developers Workshop. SIGCHI Bull. 24(1), 32–37 (1992)
6. Coutaz, J.: PAC: An object oriented model for implementing user interfaces. SIGCHI Bull. 19(2), 37–41 (1987)
7. Reenskaug, T.M.H.: MVC xerox parc. (1979),
   http://heim.ifi.uio.no/~trygver/themes/mvc/mvcindex.html
8. Marino, J., Rowley, M.: Understanding SCA (Service Component Architecture), June 30, 360 pages. Addison-Wesley Professional (2009)
9. Objectweb Consortium: The Fractal Component Model (2008),
   http://fractal.objectweb.org/
10. Khalaf, R., Mukhi, N., Weerawarana, S.: Service-oriented composition in bpel4ws. In: WWW 2003, Alternate Track Papers and Posters, Budapest, Hungary (2003)
11. Mosser, S., Blay-Fornarino, M., Riveill, M.: Service Oriented Architecture Definition Using Composition of Business-Driven Fragments (workshop). In: MODSE 2009, pp. 1–10. Denver, USA (2009)
12. Grundy, J.C., Hosking, J.G.: Developing Adaptable User Interfaces for Component-based Systems. Interacting with Computers 14(2), 175–194 (2002)
13. Dery, A.M., Fierstone, J.: Component Model and Programming: a First Step to Manage Human Computer Interaction Adaptation. In: Chittaro, L. (ed.) Mobile HCI 2003. LNCS, vol. 2795, pp. 456–460. Springer, Heidelberg (2003)
14. Lepreux, S., Hariri, A., Rouillard, J., Tabary, J., Tarby, D., Kolski, C.: Towards Multimodal User Interfaces Composition Based on UsiXML and MBD Principles. In: Jacko, J.A. (ed.) HCI 2007. LNCS, vol. 4552, pp. 134–143. Springer, Heidelberg (2007)
15. Fujima, J., Lunzer, A., Hornbæk, K., Tanaka, Y.: Clip, Connect, Clone: Combining Application Elements to Build Custom Interfaces for Information Access. In: UIST 2004, Santa Fe, NM, pp. 175–184 (2004)
16. Gabillon, Y., Petit, M., Calvary, G., Fiorino, H.: Automated planning for userinterface composition. In: Proc. of the 2nd Int. Wksp. on Semantic Models for Adaptive InteractiveSystems: SEMAIS 2011. Springer HCI series, 5 pages (2011)
17. Feldmann, M., Hubsch, G., Springer, T., Schill, A.: Improving Task-driven Software Development Approaches for Creating Service-Based Interactive Applications by Using Annotated Web Services. In: Fifth International Conference on Next Generation Web Services Practices, pp. 94–97 (2009)
18. Nestler, T., Feldmann, M., Preußner, A., Schill, A.: Service Composition at the Presentation Layer using Web Service Annotations. In: Proceedings of the First International Workshop on Lightweight Integration on the Web at ICWE 2009 (2009)
19. Tsai, W.T., Huang, Q., Elston, J., Chen, Y.: Service-oriented user interface modeling and composition. In: ICEBE 2008, pp. 21–28. IEEE Press, New York (2008)

20. Ginzburg, J., Rossi, G., Urbieta, M., Distante, D.: Transparent Interface Composition in Web Applications. In: Baresi, L., Fraternali, P., Houben, G.-J. (eds.) ICWE 2007. LNCS, vol. 4607, pp. 152–166. Springer, Heidelberg (2007)
21. Object Managemant Group: Unified Modeling Language Specification 2. OMG. Document formal/2009-02-02 (2009)
22. Pinna-Dery, A.-M., Joffroy, C., Renevier, P., Riveill, R., Vergoni, C.: ALIAS: A Set of Abstract Languages for User Interface Assembly. In: IASTED SEA 2008, pp. 77–82. ACTA Press (2008)
23. Occello, A., Joffroy, C., Dery-Pinna, A.-M.: Experiments in Model Driven Composition of User Interfaces. In: Eliassen, F., Kapitza, R. (eds.) DAIS 2010. LNCS, vol. 6115, pp. 98–111. Springer, Heidelberg (2010)
24. Schmidt, D.C.: Model-Driven Engineering. IEEE Computer 39(2), 25–32 (2006)
25. Joffroy, C., Caramel, B., Dery-Pinna, A.-M., Riveill, M.: When the functional composition drives the user interfaces composition: process and formalization. In: EICS 2011. ACM (2011)
26. Nielsen, J., Molich, R.: Heuristic evaluation of user interfaces. In: Proc. ACM CHI 1990 Conf., Seattle, WA, April 1-5, pp. 249–256 (1990)
27. Monk, A., Wright, P., Haber, J., Davenport, L.: Improving your human-computer interface: A practical technique. Prentice Hall International (UK) Ltd. (1993)

A Model for Assessing Organizational Learning in Software Development Organizations

Oumout Chouseinoglou[1] and Semih Bilgen[2]

[1] Statistics and Computer Science Department, Başkent University,
06810, Ankara, Turkey
umuth@baskent.edu.tr
[2] Electrical and Electronics Engineering Department, Middle East Technical University,
06531, Ankara, Turkey
semih-bilgen@metu.edu.tr

Abstract. In order to keep up with the continuously increasing competition and to obtain competitive advantage, software developer organizations (SDO) need to possess the characteristics of Learning Software Organizations (LSO). Maturity is directly related to both learning and knowledge management (KM). However, the major software process improvement (SPI) approaches do not explicitly address how learning capabilities of a SDO can be assessed or what knowledge needs to be managed and how, when, where, or by and for whom. This paper introduces a model for evaluating the organizational learning characteristics of a SDO. We report the results of applying the model in a university course on software development.

Keywords: Learning software organization, software process improvement, SQ4R.

1   Introduction

None of the well-known models currently in use for evaluating the level of quality in software products and the maturity of development processes (ISO15504, CMMI) explicitly focuses on organizational learning; that is the process of learning by individuals and groups in a software organization through the development process, even though CMMI provides an infrastructure for organizational learning and systematic improvement [1].

Learning is the necessary prerequisite of knowledge as well as maturity. The basis for increasing the level of maturity is the ability for organizational learning. Knowledge is one of the most important assets of an organization. The importance of knowledge as an asset increases for organizations that use knowledge-intensive processes. In order to keep up with the continuously increasing competition and to obtain competitive advantage, Software Development Organizations (SDO) need to *obtain* the correct knowledge, *use* it efficiently and *pass* it to future projects. These three constitute the major process areas of knowledge management (KM). A SDO that manages the processes of obtaining, using and passing knowledge, and learns while

M. Winckler, P. Forbrig, and R. Bernhaupt (Eds.): HCSE 2012, LNCS 7623, pp. 251–258, 2012.

developing software, is a Learning Software Organization (LSO). As software process improvement (SPI) is a knowledge-intensive task, many SDOs have recognized the importance of administrating knowledge effectively, productively and creatively at both the individual and organizational levels [2]. Organizations with greater learning-related scale, knowledge, and diversity are more likely to initiate and sustain the assimilation of complex technologies such as SPI [3].

Below, we introduce a model that will allow SDOs to assess their knowledge management activities in all process areas, identify those that need improvement and monitor their continuous improvement.

The rest of the paper is organized as follows: First, we briefly review the basic literature on KM and LSO. Section 3 presents our model for representing and assessing organizational learning in SDOs. A case study is presented in Section 4 and its results are discussed in Section 5 providing a validation of the model based on expert opinions. The last section concludes the paper.

2   Learning Software Organizations

Learning organizations are defined in [4] as organizations where people continually expand their capacity to *create* the results they truly desire, where *new and expansive* patterns of thinking are nurtured, where *collective aspiration* is set free, and where people are *continually* learning how to learn together and in [5] as a group of people who systematically extend their capacities so as to accomplish *organizational goals*. Therefore the learning process should be tailored, designed and applied accordingly to serve the overall goals of the organization, resulting in "organizational learning".

Focusing specifically on SDOs [5], and similarly [6], define an LSO as an organization that learns within the domain of *software development, evolution* and *application* where the objects of learning can consist of models, knowledge and lessons learned related to the different processes, products, tools, techniques and methods applied during the different stages of the software development process.

Regarding the significance of KM in software engineering, it is stated in [7] KM acknowledges the importance of *individuals* having access to the correct information and knowledge when they need to complete a task or make a decision and works toward SPI by explicitly and systematically addressing the management of organizational knowledge. The main shortcoming of the major SPI approaches such as the CMMI is that they do not explicitly state what knowledge needs to be managed and how, when, where, or by and for whom. Therefore, KM needs to address this limitation of the existing SPI approaches in order to support the establishment of a LSO.

[8] and [9] review the KM literature, showing that only a few studies are related to SPI, and that there is a need for different KM insights within the domain of software engineering. Various authors ([11,12,13]) group the processes proposed in each model under four stages; namely the stages of creation, storage, dissemination and utilization with the supplementary phase of measurement. [10] and [14] define the

knowledge evolution cycle which consists of five phases of organizational knowledge[1], linked to each other in a cyclic fashion.

Investigating the proposed KM models and schemes, two important conclusions may be drawn: firstly, that KM is not a monolithic process but instead it consists of several different processes that need to be addressed and measured separately and secondly that the KM process is of a continuous nature.

3   The Proposed Model

Based on the literature survey on LSO and KM, which is provided in detail in [15], we propose a model for the assessment of organizational learning in SDOs. The main aims of this model are a) to provide a framework for comparison between SDOs with respect to their organizational learning capabilities, b) to allow SDOs to identify their deficiencies and shortcomings, and c) to provide a starting point for SPI and to measure the realized improvement. The model consists of 3 major process areas that map to the three major objectives of a LSO and are connected to each other in a continuous fashion to depict the continuity of the learning activity, which can be assessed with respect to 12 core processes that are an elaboration of the 3 major process areas. In contrast to surveyed KM models in [11], the proposed model focuses on the human factor and not on knowledge stored in tools and knowledge bases, acknowledging the importance of humans and groups in the organizational learning process [16]. With that viewpoint, the model tries to capture and assess the organizational learning realized in human agents and teams but also on human developed artifacts, such as documents, practices and processes. The basic structure of the model is shown in Fig. 1.

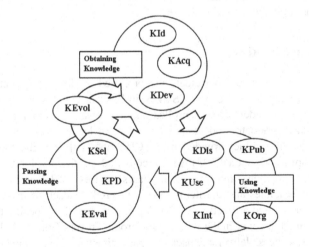

Fig. 1. The proposed model with 3 major process areas and 12 core processes

---

[1] Namely originate/create knowledge, capture/acquire knowledge, transform/organize knowledge, deploy/access knowledge and apply knowledge [14].

In [15], we describe, in detail, the following 12 core processes constituting the 3 major process areas of LSOs.

- **Obtaining Knowledge**
  - Knowledge Identification (Discovery or Capturing) - *KId*
  - Knowledge Acquisition (Buying) - *KAcq*
  - Knowledge Development (Creation or Construction) - *KDev*
- **Using Knowledge**
  - Knowledge Organization - *KOrg*
  - Knowledge Dissemination (Sharing or Distribution) - *KDis*
  - Knowledge Publication - *KPub*
  - Knowledge Usage (Application or Utilization) - *KUse*
  - Knowledge Integration (Routines) - *KInt*
- **Passing Knowledge**
  - Knowledge Preservation (Retention or Archiving and Deleting) - *KPD*
  - Knowledge Evaluation (Valuation) - *KEval*
  - Knowledge Selling - *KSel*
  - Knowledge Evolution - *KEvol*

In order to assess a SDO within the proposed model, appropriate indicators are necessary. The importance of measuring the KM process is discussed in [17] and a list of measurement models in literature related to a KM process is provided in detail in [11]. In order to identify and define the appropriate measurements for the proposed model we used the Goal/Question/Metric (GQM) approach [18]. The full description of the undertaken GQM approach and its resulting metrics are given in [15]. Generic measures of the model are listed in Table 1.

4   The Case Study

A case study was conducted to validate the proposed model in the context of a one semester software engineering course, İST478, in Başkent University. 15 undergraduate and 4 graduate level students were enrolled and 4 software development groups were formed, with each graduate student assigned as team leader. The course followed a customization of the outline provided by CSCI577ab[2] [19] applying the Incremental Commitment Spiral Model (ICSM) which consisted of the Exploration, Valuation, Foundations, Development, and Transition phases (phases 1,2,3,4 and 5 respectively). The deliverable deadlines and the items to be delivered for each of these phases were predefined. The tasks and artifacts to be developed were based on specific templates and they were described in detail in the ICSM – Electronic Process Guide[3]. A detailed list of deliverable phases, dates, deliverable packages and artifacts is provided in [15].

---

[2] Software Engineering I – Fall 2011, http://greenbay.usc.edu/csci577/fall2011/index.php
[3] http://greenbay.usc.edu/IICMSw/index.htm

Table 1. The proposed model and the relative generic measures

Major Process Area	Core Process	Generic Measure	Short Name
Obtaining Knowledge	Knowledge Identification	Internal Trainings	KId1
		Tasks Completed Internally	KId2
		Documents Completed Internally	KId3
	Knowledge Acquisition	External Trainings	KAcq1
		Utilized External Communication	KAcq2
		Trained Topics	KAcq3
		Utilized External Documents	KAcq4
	Knowledge Development	Creative Idea Development	KDev1
		Creative Idea Evaluation	KDev2
Using Knowledge	Knowledge Organization	Horizontal document linking	KOrg1
		Vertical document linking	KOrg2
	Knowledge Dissemination	Information messages from management	KDis1
		Amount of meetings	KDis2
		Length of meetings	KDis3
		Meeting Discussion Efficiency	KDis4
	Knowledge Publication	Internally Distributed Guidelines	KPub1
		Externally Distributed Guidelines	KPub2
		Academic Publications	KPub3
	Knowledge Usage	Creative Idea Application	KUse1
		Deliverable Quality	KUse2
		Meeting Functional Efficiency	KUse3
	Knowledge Integration	Task Differentiation within phases	KInt1
		Deliverable Differentiation within phases	KInt2
		Deliverable Correction	KInt3
Passing Knowledge	Knowledge Preservation and Deleting	Knowledge evaluation and assessment	KPD1
		Task differentiation from guidelines	KPD2
		Deliverable differentiation from templates	KPD3
	Knowledge Evaluation	Valuated Items	KEval1
	Knowledge Selling	Shared Documents	KSel1
		Shared Tasks	KSel2
		Trainings Given	KSel3
	Knowledge Evolution	Guideline Evolution between Projects	KEvol1
		Task Evolution between Projects	KEvol2
		Deliverable Evolution between Projects	KEvol3

To determine whether the proposed model assesses the difference of organizational learning between different groups, two of the groups were assigned a differentiated development method, SQ4R (Survey, Question, Read, Recite, Review, and wRite) [20], based on critical thinking, to enhance their learning experience. The SQ4R approach was undertaken by two randomly assigned groups (namely Group 2 and 3) in all five phases of the software development lifecycle of İST478 course. The details on how the SQ4R approach was utilized are given in [15].

The core processes in Table 1 were investigated with respect to their applicability to the course structure. The non-applicable core processes were not assessed. Moreover, the generic measures proposed were refined with respect to course characteristics, the artifacts produced and the deliverables developed by the project groups, and were transformed into actual metrics. The evaluation period of the measures has been identified as the predefined five development phases. The detailed list and explanation of each generic and applied metric, the calculation formula and the interpretation of each result are presented in [15].

5   Results of the Case Study

The learning ability of the groups based on the measures was calculated and assessed at the end of each phase by individual questionnaires [15] and the meeting minutes. Exit interviews were conducted with each group to resolve any inconsistencies or anomalies in the questionnaires.

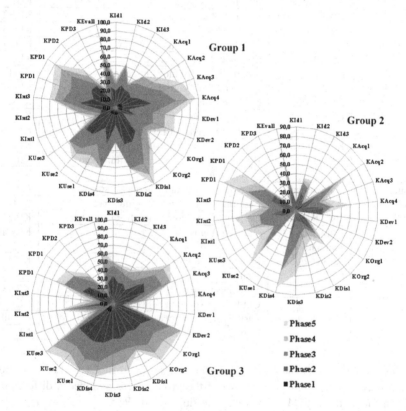

Fig. 2. The Organizational Learning footprint of the groups in the case study

The students undertook 7 in-class examinations to measure the amount of preserved knowledge within the group (KPD1), and the submitted documents were graded to assess the product quality of the deliverables (KUse2), but also to identify the document defects and the defect removal ratio (KInt3). All measures were normalized appropriately [15]. Fig. 2 displays the organizational learning progress of each group with respect to the measured key process areas.

Among the groups, only Group 1 had not undertaken the SQ4R approach. From the footprints it can be seen that Group 1 scores low in knowledge identification, organization, integration and preservation. On the other hand Group 2 scores low almost in all key processes, except knowledge acquisition and integration. Group 3 also scores low in knowledge identification and integration. As the majority of the students in these groups lack any professional software engineering development practice experience or relative knowledge, we were expecting low scores in knowledge identification and development, but higher in knowledge acquisition. The results of Group 2 can be justified by a communication problem between group members. On the other hand Group 1 has scored high due to the high cohesion between its members. The high scores of Group 3 have resulted from the SQ4R approach that allowed the members to build a commitment towards the software development process.

As it can be seen from the footprints, with the use of appropriate and correct metrics, the organization can easily identify its weak learning process areas and thus develop a strategy to provide a solution for these weaknesses. Although the metrics were coined to meet the specific requirements of an in-class software development group, they can be easily modified to match the needs of any SDO.

The exit interview with team leaders led to the conclusion that learning ability assessment enabled by this model can be fully used in SPI.

6   Conclusions

We have introduced a model that allows SDOs to measure and assess their learning capabilities, identify their strengths and weaknesses in terms of learning and to proceed with building a competitive advantage by becoming a LSO. Based on the case study results and the expert opinions it is evident that the proposed model is a step towards this goal. Although the findings show that it can be applied in the organizational context, further implementations of the SQ4R approach in the business environment are currently under way to provide better insights of its value for software development activity.

As stated in [21] the validity of the model and of the embedded formulations must be strengthened through numerous case studies. As an extension of this study, it is of crucial importance to continue with the integration of the identified core processes with existing software maturity models.

References

1. Glazer, H., Dalton, J., Anderson, D., Konrad, M., Shrum, S.: CMMI or Agile: Why Not Embrace Both! Software Engineering Institute of Carnegie Mellon University (2008), http://www.sei.cmu.edu/publications/documents/08.reports/08t n003.html

2. Santos, G., Montoni, M., Figueiredo, S., Rocha, A.R.: SPI-KM - Lessons Learned from Applying a Software Process Improvement Strategy Supported by Knowledge Management. In: Münch, J., Abrahamsson, P. (eds.) PROFES 2007. LNCS, vol. 4589, pp. 81–95. Springer, Heidelberg (2007)
3. Fichman, R., Kemerer, C.: The Assimilation of Software Process Innovations: An Organizational Learning Perspective. Management Science 43, 1345–1363 (1997)
4. Senge, P.M.: The Fifth Discipline: The Art and Practice of the Learning Organization. Doubleday/Currency, New York (1990)
5. Ruhe, G.: Learning Software Organisations. In: Chang, S. (ed.) Handbook of Software Engineering and Knowledge Engineering, vol. 1, pp. 663–678. World Scientific Publishing (2001)
6. Henninger, S., Lappala, K., Raghavendran, A.: An Organizational Learning Approach to Domain Analysis. In: 17th International Conference on Software Engineering, pp. 95–104. ACM Press, New York (1995)
7. Rus, I., Lindvall, M.: Knowledge Management in Software Engineering. IEEE Software 19(3), 26–38 (2002)
8. Bjørnson, F., Dingsøyr, T.: Knowledge Management in Software Engineering: A Systematic Review of Studied Concepts, Findings and Research Methods Used. Information and Software Technology 50(11), 1055–1068 (2008)
9. Sharma, N., Singh, K., Goyal, D.: Can Managing Knowledge and Experience Improve Software Process? - Insights From the Literature. Research Cell: An International Journal of Engineering Sciences 4, 324–333 (2011)
10. Maier, R.: Knowledge Management Systems: Information and Communication Technologies for Knowledge Management. Springer, New York (2004)
11. Oliveira, M., Goldoni, V.: Metrics for Knowledge Management Process. In: IAMOT 2006 15th International Conference on Management of Technology, Beijing (2006)
12. Lee, K.C., Lee, S., Kang, I.W.: KMPI: Measuring Knowledge Management Performance. Information and Management 42(3), 469–482 (2005)
13. Bose, R.: Knowledge Management Metrics. Industrial Management & Data Systems 104(6), 457–468 (2004)
14. Agresti, W.: Knowledge Management. Advances in Computers 53(1), 171–283 (2000)
15. Chouseinoglou, O., Bilgen, S.: A Model for Assessing Organizational Learning in Software Organizations and a Case Study. Technical Report. METU/II-TR-2012-01, Department of Information Systems. Middle East Technical University (2012), http://www.baskent.edu.tr/~umuth/METU-II-TR-2012-01.pdf
16. Haas, M.R., Hansen, M.T.: Different Knowledge, Different Benefits: Toward a Productivity Perspective on Knowledge Sharing in Organizations. Strategic Management Journal 28, 1133–1153 (2007)
17. Ahmed, P.K., Lim, K.K., Zairi, M.: Measurement Practice for Knowledge Management. Journal of Workspace Learning: Employee Counseling Today 11(8), 304–311 (1999)
18. van Solingen, R., Berghout, E.: The Goal/Question/Metric Method: A Practical Guide for Quality Improvement of Software Development. McGraw-Hill Publishing, London (1999)
19. Boehm, B., Lane, J.: Using the Incremental Commitment Model to Integrate Systems Acquisition, Systems Engineering, and Software Engineering. Cross Talk, 4–9 (2007)
20. Thomas, E.L., Robinson, H.A.: Improving Reading in Every Classroom: A Source Book for Teachers. Allyn & Bacon, Boston (1982)
21. Runeson, P., Höst, M.: Guidelines for Conducting and Reporting Case Study Research in Software Engineering. Empirical Software Engineering 14, 131–164 (2009)

A Personality Based Design Approach Using Subgroup Discovery

Kay Behrenbruch[1], Martin Atzmüller[2], Christoph Evers[3],
Ludger Schmidt[1], Gerd Stumme[2], and Kurt Geihs[3]

[1] University of Kassel, Human-Machine Systems Engineering, Mönchebergstr. 7
[2] University of Kassel, Knowledge and Data-Engineering, Wilhelmshöher Allee 73
[3] University of Kassel, Distributed Systems, Wilhelmshöher Allee 73
34125 Kassel, Germany
{K.Behrenbruch,L.Schmidt,Evers,Geihs}@uni-kassel.de,
{Atzmueller,Stumme}@cs.uni-kassel.de

Abstract. To facilitate user-centered software engineering, developers need an easy to grasp understanding of the user. The use of personas helps to keep specific user needs in mind during the design process. Technology acceptance is of particular interest for the design of innovative applications previously unknown to potential users. Therefore, our research focuses on defining a typology of relevant user characteristics with respect to technology acceptance and transferring those findings to the description of personas. The presented work focuses on the statistical relationship between technology acceptance and personality. We apply sub-group discovery as a statistical tool. Based on the statistically derived subgroups and patterns we define the mentioned personas to help developers to understand different forms of technology acceptance. By integrating the specifically defined personas into existing methods in the field of software engineering the feasibility of the presented approach is demonstrated.

Keywords: Technology Acceptance, Personality, Software Engineering, User-centered Design, Subgroup Discovery.

1   Introduction

Research in the field of Human-Computer-Interaction (HCI) generates models concerning technology acceptance. Those models provide determinants of technology acceptance and explain the causal relation between these determinants. This knowledge from HCI-research is potentially helpful for software-development, but stays isolated from day-to-day praxis of software engineering - mainly because the information is pegged into abstract und theoretical frameworks. In this paper we bridge the gap between theory and praxis by transferring our empirical findings to the textual description of personas [5] that combine personality traits with the determinants of technology acceptance. We use the approved structure of theoretical frameworks as a guideline to implement our findings in the description of personas. A

M. Winckler, P. Forbrig, and R. Bernhaupt (Eds.): HCSE 2012, LNCS 7623, pp. 259–266, 2012.

persona is a representation of the goals and behavior of a hypothesized group of users. Personas are described in a narrative text that includes behavior patterns, goals, skills, attitudes, and environment. Fictive but characterizing personal details are added to make the persona a realistic character [16]. We propose ways to methodologically integrate the personas in software engineering, namely the agile method SCRUM.

To design personas we use data mining techniques, i.e. sub-group discovery and analysis within the framework of the Technology Acceptance Model (TAM) [6]. The data basis for the statistics is the evaluation of a prototype of an innovative application called Meet-U with the potential target group of the application. The evaluation is based on a questionnaire that contains items to acquire the determinants of TAM and the personality traits taken from the Five Factor Model (FFM) of personality psychology [12]. FFM encompasses five personality traits: extraversion, agreeableness, conscientiousness, openness to new experience, and emotional stability. Subgroup discovery is conducted with the aim to define subgroups with high impact on technology acceptance. Groups are defined by the characteristics of personality traits in correspondence with Perceived Usefulness (PU), Perceived Ease of Use (PEOU), and Intention to Use (IU) taken from TAM. The focus lies on the potential accepters and rejecters of the application. By this, valuable insight concerning those who will be most likely and most unlikely to accept their design is derived. A specific configuration of personality traits in combination with PU and PEOU reveals the types of potential users with respect to technology acceptance. With this knowledge, software-developers are able to search specifically for solutions that will convince skeptics to accept the application while keeping in mind the interests of likely accepters. The following section explains the theoretical background of the presented approach in detail.

2   Theoretical Background

In recent years the effect of personality on technology acceptance has been demonstrated by various authors. Especially, the use of social networks has been a major focus of research activity [2,11,13]. Another field of attention has been personality in acceptance of mobile commerce [1,22]. Many aspects of personality were considered in HCI-research such as innovativeness [1,14], need for recognition and sociability [11], computer anxiety [15], computer self-efficiency [7,15], resistance to change [14,15], and interest in the application domain [18]. The most important characterization of personality is FFM [2,7,11,13,14,18,22].

In many cases structural models were generated. Those models determine causal architectures that combine general personality traits with usage and/or intention to use. A direct causal link from personality to usage/intention is an exception to the rule [1]. In most models the influence of personality on usage/intention is mediated by PU and PEOU as determinants of TAM [7,15,18,22]. TAM was chosen as the theoretical framework of this study because it is the most influential and generally accepted-model in information science concerning acceptance [17,20]. Within TAM the Intention to Use (IU) the technology is influenced by two beliefs of the potential user concerning usage: PU and PEOU. In this paper, we combine TAM with the - in the context of technology acceptance - frequently used Five Factor Model (FFM) of personality psychology. FFM is a well-accepted instrument to grasp general personality [12]. We use the Theory of Reasoned Action (TRA) [8] to integrate FFM with TAM. TRA explains behavior in general and was used as a matrix in the development of TAM [6]. TRA states that personality traits are external variables and affect the beliefs that are important to the behavior in question [8]. Regarding the use of information technology we assume that the five personality traits of FFM have a direct influence on the beliefs PU and PEOU and that the influence of personality on behavior is moderated by PU and PEOU (see Fig. 1).

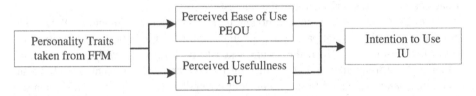

Fig. 1. Integration of the Technology Acceptance Model (TAM) with the Five Factor Model (FFM) in compliance with the Theory of Reasoned Action (TRA)

Authors [7,18] report a significant influence of personality traits directly on PEOU and PU. Authors [18] identify a significant correlation between PU, PEOU and IU with extraversion and agreeableness. Moreover, a significant correlation of PU and PEOU with openness to new experience was reported. In addition a significant correlation for PEOU and emotional stability is indicated [18]. All listed correlation coefficients are lower than 0.21. The significant correlations of emotional stability, openness and agreeableness with PU [7] do not succeed this value either. In fact, none of the articles cited in this chapter found strong correlations (>0.5) of personality factors to constructs used in models for technology acceptance. Even moderate correlations (>0.3) are very rare. Against this background several structural models were constructed that combine different constructs to explain behavior. Structural models display complex networks of relationships that are no more than interesting to practitioners. They lack a direct link to development praxis and stay abstract and theoretical in their nature. In the following section we present a concretization to those models that bears in mind the needs of software-developers. We suppose that correlation coefficients or structural models alone are not handy and convincing enough to find their way into practice. The presented approach, based on the definition of personas [16], connects research results with common design methods in the field of software engineering and user-centered design.

3   Empirical Study and Statistics

We conducted an evaluation of a prototype that supports mobile social networks, group interaction and mobility, called Meet-U [4]. Meet-U is a mobile application for Android devices that is still under development and is designed for the group of 20- to 35-year-olds. Meet-U supports its users in organizing meetings with friends at events. Events can be public or private happenings like concerts or parties. The application helps to plan the event, navigate the user to the event, and supports the user at the event itself. Meet-U proposes events to the users that fit their individual interests as well as their personal calendars. The application suggests means of transport and informs about possible delays, e.g. when using public transport. At the event, information concerning the location, the program, and tickets can be retrieved from automatically integrated services. If desired by the user Meet-U is able to suggest new friends based on the user's settings and interests.

We evaluated Meet-U with the potential user group (157 students, 68 female, 89 male, age 19-37). Participants were given basic information about the prototype in form of a presentation. Next, they were asked to perform tasks with the prototype: compiling a profile, finding and confirming friends, creating an event, searching an event, and being navigated to the event. Subsequently, they filled in a questionnaire. The questionnaire contains items concerning PU, PEOU, and BI taken from [19] as well as the five personality traits of FFM taken from [9]. The questionnaire uses a nine-point Likert-Scale reaching from "strongly agree" to "strongly disagree".

The data from the nine-point Likert-Scale was used to build three categories: high, medium, low. Boundaries of the three categories were defined for each construct individually. Therefore we identified first quartile and third quartile for each construct. By this we were able to define equally distributed categories for each construct. We compared our data for FFM with standard values [9] to assure that there are no particularities in our sample that will cause the relative classification with quartiles to be unrealistic for standard values.

The data abstraction (mapping nine levels to three nominal categories) was conducted for applying subgroup discovery and analysis on the pre-processed data. We applied semi-automatic subgroup discovery for the characterization of "acceptance groups" according to the given data. In general, subgroup discovery [21] aims at identifying interesting patterns with respect to a given target property of interest (e.g., "Accepter"). The method is especially suited for identifying local patterns in the data that only hold for specific subsets. It can automatically uncover hidden relations captured in small subgroups, for which variables are only significantly correlated in these subgroups. We can discover, for example, the subgroup defined by "conscientiousness=low AND PU=high" for the target concept "Accepter" in Table 1. The quality of the subgroup is determined by the lift factor, which measures the target share in the subgroup relative to the target share in the whole data. Thus, a lift of 2 indicates an improvement of the target in the subgroup by 100%. Additionally, we tested the significance using a four-field chi-square test. We applied the open-source VIKAMINE [3] software for discovering interesting subgroups: The automatic component provided several hypotheses, which could then be semi-automatically refined, evaluated and validated.

4   Results: Subgroups and Personas

The results of the subgroup discovery are displayed in Table 1. We selected the four subgroups with highest relevance for technology acceptance. Relevance was defined by the lift factor (>2) and the subgroup size (>10% of the sample). Two subgroups are indicated as accepters and two as rejecters. Subgroup size, lift factors, and significances are displayed for each subgroup. Each subgroup combines personality factors with TAM beliefs. All defined subgroups are significant at least on a level of 0.05.

Table 1. Subgroups concerning technology acceptance and personality

Subgroup	Subgroup Size	Lift Factor	Significance
Accepter 1	17	2.0	p<=0.01
Accepter 2	16	2.2	p<=0.001
Rejecter 1	16	2.0	p<=0.05
Rejecter 2	16	2.4	p<=0.001

Subsequently the statistical findings of Table 1 were implemented in four personas. Table 2 shows a selection of phrases that can be used to transfer high and low manifestations of the big five personality traits to the description of personas.

Table 2. Phrases to describe Persona with extreme occurrence of Personality Factors

Personality Factors	Positive occurrence	Negative occurrence
Openness to experience	appreciation of art, inventive, creative, curious, sensitive to beauty, aware of feelings	not cautious, plain, straightforward, not subtle, bad imagination, uninspired
Conscientiousness	organized, efficient, show self-discipline, act dutifully, always prepared, exact	easy-going, careless, unobserving, act unconcerned, shirk something
Extraversion	energetic, show positive emotions, full of energy, enthusiastic, action-oriented	solitary, be reserved, seem quiet, keep in the background, withdrawn, distant
Agreeableness	friendly, compassionate, cooperative, friendly, helpful, generous, optimistic	antagonistic towards others, self-interested, unfriendly, uncooperative, abusive
Emotional stability	calm, even-tempered, secure, confident, not easily upset, no persistent negative feelings	sensitive, nervous, unpleasant feeling, anxious, depressive, vulnerable, worried

The personas are meant to guide designers in the process of user-centred design. Sex of the personas was determined freely because no significant relation of sex with technology acceptance was found.

Accepter 1: Conscientiousness Low and PU High

Michael is 24 years old. He is still living at his parent´s home. He studies economics and takes his time. At the moment he should learn for a written exam but he lost the records and decided to take the exam next year. He tested the new pro-totype. Michael likes that Meet-U helps him to organize things. Often he forgets about dates, misses the train, or forgets to call people when he is late. He hopes Meet-U will help him without much effort from his side.

Accepter 2: Emotional Stability High and PEOU High

Cindy is a 19-year-old who just moved into town and started her studies at the university. She takes courses in psychology but is not quite sure if she will stick to this field of study. She liked high-school a lot but the change and the new situation are also nice. At the moment she is satisfied with exploring campus and university, and making new friends. She participated at the test of Meet-U and plans to download the newest version now. She just finished learning for the first exams and thinks the application will help her to have a good time with interesting events now.

Rejecter 1: Emotional Stability Low and PEOU Low

Martha is 31 years old and is afraid that she will not be able to pass her last exams to finish her studies in social work. Her mother says she does not mind her taking more time but Martha feels guilty not to be able to make her own living at her age. She participated in the evaluation of Meet-U. When she was told about the features of Meet-U she hoped that Meet-U might help her to meet people despite her shyness. But when she had to perform the tasks with Meet-U she was irritated. To her the application seems much more complicated than the others say.

Rejecter 2: Agreeableness Low and PU Low

Frank is 24 years old and studies chemistry. His girlfriend just moved into his flat and he likes her to be around. She makes him feel good – and also she is much better at cleaning the house than he ever has been. Frank is at home and tells his girlfriend about the evaluation of Meet-U he participated in: "Why should I organize thinks for those who are not able to get along by themselves. I know that I want to go out with you and which places I like. Why should I give all my personal data to Meet-U when there is no use to it."

5   Methodological Integration

Personas are a part of user-centered design [5,16]. Often they are used in scenarios that help to describe and explain the context of use. This kind of scenario is part of the process of analyzing the context of use and defining user-requirements. We suggest applying the personas also in the process of implementation of software. The agile software engineering method SCRUM incorporates user stories. Those stories are actually a list of requirements, normally in the form of: "As a <user type> I want to <do some action> so that <desired result>". We propose substantiating the <user type> to a persona. There should be a set of personas well-known to the whole development team. The personas give the team a vivid impression of people, who should use their system. The personas should act as a symbol for or connection to knowledge about the potential users of the system. With respect to technology acceptance and the definition of personas in this paper, the development team will be able to keep in mind the issue of acceptance by being confronted with the personas. In the case of Meet-U question like this arise: "I don't think we should make this dialogue too complex. Martha will be afraid and will give up." It is in the responsibility of the product owner (a role in SCRUM) to decide which persona is the right one for which user-story. In the present case the product owner should be familiar with the issue of technology acceptance.

In addition to that, SCRUM is designed to provide executable software throughout the whole design-process. This feature opens up possibilities to meet the following needs to foster technology acceptance in the development process of innovative applications. We are arguing to intensify the iteration of evaluation in the case of the development with regard to uncertain technology acceptance. Therefore we propose to evaluate partially functional prototypes parallel to programming software. Each sprint of SCRUM provides this kind of prototypes as executable software. Evaluation parallel to programming needs to be fast and flexible. This is why we suppose to let the partially functional prototypes be evaluated by usability experts instead of real users. Experts use inspection methods to check for usability problems and are able to provide results much faster. To incorporate the user's view on technology acceptance the evaluating experts should also be familiar with the personas used in SCRUM. The feedback of the evaluation results to the developers is ensured by the participation of the usability experts in the sprint planning meeting that is done on a regular bases in SCRUM.

6   Outlook

This paper presents an approach to transfer research findings from HCI-research on technology acceptance and personality to development-practice. We present ongoing research of an empirical study in the context of methodological reflections. At the present stage it is not possible to provide an approved set of personas. Within the VENUS project (http://www.uni-kassel.de/eecs/iteg/venus/) data is currently gathered for technology acceptance and personality traits in two other development projects. The objective is to generalize the statistical findings for Meet-U with respect to different application properties and to other user groups. At the same time we apply the presented methodological integration in three different development-projects and are gaining new insights to further improve it for practical application. The integration of personas to user-centered design and software engineering proved to be a target-aimed approach. The evaluation of partially functional prototypes parallel to the implementation of software is a vital part of the ongoing work and was applied successfully. A major topic of future research will be to approve the effectiveness of the presented approach related to agile software engineering.

Acknowledgments. We thank Hesse's Ministry of Higher Education, Research, and the Arts for funding VENUS as part of the research funding program "LOEWE – Landes-Offensive zur Entwicklung Wissenschaftlich-ökonomischer Exzellenz".

References

1. Aldás-Manzano, J., Ruiz-Mafé, C., Sanz-Blas, S.: Exploring individual personality factors as drivers of M-shopping acceptance. Industrial Management & Data Systems 109(6), 739–757 (2006)

2. Amichai-Hamburger, Y., Vinitzky, G.: Social network use and personality. Computers in Human Behavior 26(6), 1289–1295 (2010)
3. Atzmueller, M., Puppe, F.: Semi-Automatic Visual Subgroup Mining using VIKAMINE. Journal of Universal Computer Science (JUCS), Special Issue on Visual Data Mining 11(11), 1752–1765 (2005)
4. Comes, D., Evers, C., Geihs, K., Saur, D., Witsch, A., Zapf, M.: Adaptive Applications are Smart Applications. In: Proceedings of International Workshop on Smart Mobile Applications, San Francisco (2011)
5. Cooper, A.: The Inmates Are Running the Asylum: Why High-tech Products Drive Us Crazy and How to Restore the Sanity. Sams, Indianapolis (2004)
6. Davis, F.D., Bagozzi, R.P., Warshaw, P.R.: User Acceptance of Computer Technology: A Comparison of Two Theoretical Models. Management Science 35(8), 982–1003 (1989)
7. Devaraj, S., Easley, R.F., Crant, J.M.: Research Note–How Does Personality Matter? Relating the Five-Factor Model to Technology Acceptance and Use. Information Systems Research 19(1), 93–105 (2008)
8. Fishbein, M., Ajzen, I.: Belief, Attitude, Intention and Behaviour: An Introduction to Theory and Research. Addison-Wesley (1975)
9. Gosling, S.D., Rentfrow, P.J., Swann, W.B.: A very brief measure of the Big-Five personality domains. Journal of Research in Personality 37(6), 504–528 (2003)
10. He, Q., Wu, D., Khosla, P.: The quest for personal control over mobile location privacy. IEEE Communications Magazine 42(5), 130–136 (2004)
11. Hughes, D.J., Rowea, M., Batey, M., Lee, A.: A tale of two sites: Twitter vs. Face-book and the personality predictors of social media usage. Computers in Human Behavior 28(2), 561–569 (2012)
12. McAdams, D.P.: Five Factor Model in Personality. Journal of Personality 60(2), 329–361 (1992)
13. Moore, K., McElroy, J.C.: The influence of personality on Facebook usage, wall postings, and regret. Computers in Human Behavior 28(1), 267–274 (2011)
14. Nov, O., Ye, C.: Personality and Technology Acceptance: Personal Innovativeness in IT, Openness and Resistance to Change. In: Proceedings of the 41st Annual Hawaii International Conference on System Sciences, HICSS 2008, p. 448 (2008)
15. Nov, O., Ye, C.: Users' Personality and Perceived Ease of Use of Digital Libraries: The Case for Resistance to Change. Journal of the American Society for Information Science and Technology 59(5), 845–851 (2008)
16. Pruitt, J., Adlin, T.: The persona lifecycle: Keeping people in mind throughout product design. Elsevier, Amsterdam (2006)
17. Schepers, J., Wetzels, M.: A meta-analysis of the technology acceptance model: Investigating subjective norm and moderation effects. Information & Management 44(1), 90–103 (2007)
18. Svendsen, G.B., Gunnvald, B., Johnsen, K., Almås-Sørensen, L., Vittersø, J.: Personality and technology acceptance: the influence of personality factors on the core constructs of the Technology Acceptance Model. Behaviour & Information Technology, 1–12 (2011)
19. Venkatesh, V., Gordon, B., Davis, F.: User Acceptance of Information Technology: Toward a Unified View. Management Information Systems 27(3), 425–478 (2010)
20. Venkatesh, V., Davis, F.D.: A Theoretical Extension of the Technology Acceptance Model: Four Longitudinal Field Studies. Management Science 46(2), 186–204 (2000)
21. Wrobel, S.: An Algorithm for Multi-Relational Discovery of Subgroups. In: Proc. 1st European Symposium on Principles of Data Mining and Knowledge Discovery, pp. 78–87 (2007)
22. Zhou, T., Lu, Y.: The Effects of Personality Traits on User Acceptance of Mobile Commerce. International Journal of Human-Computer Interaction 27(6), 545–561 (2011)

Assessing Use Complexity of Software:
A Tool for Documentation Designers

Brigit van Loggem

Open Universiteit, Valkenburgerweg 177,
6419 AT Heerlen, The Netherlands
brigit.vanloggem@ou.nl

Abstract. One way to support end users of software is to provide documentation materials such as user manuals and online Help. As not all software is equally difficult to master, documentation designers need to determine the quality and quantity of the information to be included in the user documentation. A first step towards this end would be to assess the complexity of the software from the user's point of view. This paper suggests one approach to such an assessment, based on the idea of use complexity as a multi-dimensional construct. A consideration of width, depth and height of use complexity can help designers determine documentation requirements.

Keywords: user documentation, use complexity, documentation design.

1   Introduction

Among the practitioners who work to support users of software are the designers of user documentation. Since manuals and Help systems contain information that is recorded and stored before the software is used in naturalistic environments, documentation designers cannot observe the software being applied to real-life tasks. Matching the quantity and quality of the information to the user's needs, without being able to assess those needs directly, constitutes a major challenge when designing user documentation. Documentation designers need to couple their own in-depth knowledge of the software to be documented with a methodical approach; so that even if they can carry out only abstract analyses, these yield valid starting points for design.

This paper briefly outlines one such approach, in which a series of abstract analyses is carried out to assess software complexity from the user's point of view. This is referred to as *use complexity*: that part of task complexity that originates from the software rather than from other elements in the task environment, including the user. Unlike design complexity, which is the degree to which a program exhibits emergent behavior [1], use complexity is a measure of the learning requirements (and therefore the documentation requirements) for a particular software system.

As user documentation aims to support users in applying software to real-life tasks, its design must be task-oriented rather than system-oriented [2]. To do so, it must contain more than straightforward procedural instructions on how to interact with the system, and cover the whole of the "User Virtual Machine" or UVM; which is defined

M. Winckler, P. Forbrig, and R. Bernhaupt (Eds.): HCSE 2012, LNCS 7623, pp. 267–274, 2012.

as "not only everything that a user can perceive or experience (as far as it has a meaning), but also aspects of internal structure and processes as far as the user should be aware of them" [3]. The visible part of the UVM is what these authors refer to as the "perceptual interface" and what is more commonly referred to as the user interface; but the UVM as a whole is a much larger conceptual machine that exists in the user's mind. A software system is a self-contained "world" with its own objects (think of the Clipboard in many operating systems; of templates, style sheets and fields in a word processing environment; or of layers in an image editor). These software-specific objects, with their mutual dependencies and the rules governing their behavior, are as much part of the UVM as is the interaction layer through which they are accessed. A user needs a thorough understanding of the UVM to gain complete mastery of a particular software tool, and apply it successfully to every task it can possibly be applied to. Such understanding is fostered through meta-communication in the shape of documentation or training [4].

Use complexity describes the UVM, providing a measure of what the UVM consists of rather than how a user interacts with it. As such it is not directly or inversely related to usability, which focuses on the user interaction component of the UVM as indicated in the ISO 9241-11 standard by the definition of usability as *the extent to which a product can be used by specified users to achieve specified goals with effectiveness, efficiency, and satisfaction in a specified context of use.* Usability is prescriptive, in that high usability is desirable; whereas use complexity is descriptive, in that high use complexity is not necessarily undesirable. Use complexity is a necessary consequence of versatility [5, 6] and a complex system may, but need not, have high usability just as a simple system may, but need not, have low usability.

2   Dimensions of Use Complexity

Complexity is a multi-dimensional construct [7, 8]. The quality and quantity of the learning required to achieve full mastery of a particular software tool can be analyzed from a number of different viewpoints. It is then possible to take the idea of dimensions literally and visualize the results of the separate analyses, leading to an image of use complexity offering pointers for the design of documentation.

2.1   Width: Novelty

The first dimension of use complexity to look at is involved with quantity of things to be learned. Learning is required when the software brings novelty to the task environment. Novelty comes in the form of hitherto unknown concepts, with their associated rules and interdependencies, that are exposed to the user and with which he may choose to interact. Where the user is exposed to many novel concepts that he can choose to interact with, and many choices are "wrong" in that they will not lead to an optimum end result, there is much to learn before full mastery is reached. Where at the opposite end of the spectrum there is no novelty to choose, or every choice is equal to every other choice, there is hardly any requirement for learning at all.

This quantitative dimension, related to the number of meaningful choices open to the user that originate from novelty in the software world, can be pictured as the "width" of the use complexity. *The width of the use complexity is proportionate to the number of hitherto unknown concepts (with their associated rules and interdependencies), brought to the task environment by the software, that are exposed to the user and with which he may choose to interact so that his choice makes a difference.*

Several theoreticians have independently presented a hierarchical description of interactive systems. Moran [9], for example, distinguished four levels, or layers, at which a computer tool can be described, one of which (the interaction layer) describes physical interactions with the computer hardware such as: "key presses and other primitive device manipulations". In the context of standard computer use, at least for fully-grown users who are not physically restricted and who possess basic computer skills, the interaction layer can a priori be assumed to be fully mastered. This leaves three layers at which to describe software:

- The *task layer* is that aspect of a software tool that describes the possible end results of the user's interaction with the software.
- The *semantic layer* is that aspect of a software tool that describes the intermediate steps that the user may carry out to realize a certain result.
- The *syntactic layer* is that aspect of a software tool that describes a user's choice of commands with which he directs the software's behavior.

The use complexity is not necessarily equally wide at the syntactic, the semantic and the task layers. At the task layer the user chooses to work towards a certain end result. At the semantic layer he chooses the next step to realize the result. At the syntactic layer, finally, he chooses which screen area to click or touch, which key or keys to press, which sequence of characters to enter, or which command to vocalize.

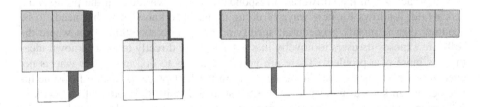

Fig. 1. Width of use complexity sketched for Notepad (left), WordPad (center) and Word2007 (right)

When analyzing the layers one by one it is important to take all novel opportunities for choice into account, as there is no way of knowing which are important and which are not. Since the higher layers build upon the lower ones, even misunderstandings at the syntactic layer can lead to grief. Concepts such as pressing the Enter key on the keyboard resulting in a paragraph being created, or a space character not being nothing can, when not thoroughly understood, make laying out even the simplest text document very difficult. Conversely, novel concepts at the higher layers may provide meaning to the lower ones. For example, the presence of the concept of "wildcards" at the semantic level may lead to unexpected results for an uninitiated user attempting to search his text for the occurrence of an asterisk.

In Figure 1 the width of the use complexity is roughly sketched, using a relative scale of 1 ("very little") to 10 ("very much"), for three different text processing applications that have all been marketed by Microsoft®. The base corresponds to the syntactic layer, then comes the semantic layer, and the top represents width of the use complexity at the task layer.

Notepad is judged to have very little novelty to interact with at the syntactic layer: its interface is uncluttered and most of the options open to interaction are well known. At the semantic layer a bit more novelty is found, for example in Notepad's dealing with word wrapping and the use of variables in its page setup; while at the task layer its uses are acknowledged as a tool for holding and converting electronic text that was never intended to be printed. WordPad on the other hand holds a little more complexity at the syntactic layer, mostly due to its formatting capabilities, but less at the task layer as it is mainly geared towards producing a document that is to be printed as laid out on the screen. For Word2007 much more novelty is found at all three layers, more so as we move up towards the task layer.

2.2   Depth: Mapping

The difficulty brought to an activity by a software tool can be seen as stemming from an experienced gap between the software world and the non-software world. To close the gap, the novel concepts that are open to interaction must be reconciled with meaningful ideas in the pre-existing task world [10, 11]. This is relatively easy when there exists a correspondence between the novel software concepts on one side of the gap and known concepts in the outside world on the other side. Yet software can bring to an activity not only new ways to do things, but also new things to do.

Where novelty in the software corresponds to pre-known ideas in the pre-existing task world, it allows for new ways of doing things. The knowledge that needs to be acquired then is mostly procedural: specifying how to do something. Yet where the software exposes its users to novelty that does not map directly onto pre-known ideas there is more of a problem. There are now new things to do, and a user who is not even sure what it is that he should be doing in the first place, is unable to frame his interactions in such a manner as to use the software to its full potential. To achieve full mastery, the user will need to acquire more than just procedural knowledge.

This distinction constitutes a qualitative dimension of use complexity that can be visualized as its "depth". The less tightly that the novelty brought to the task by the software is coupled to pre-known concepts, the deeper the use complexity. *The depth of the use complexity is proportionate to the degree of mapping between the novelty brought to the task by the software and pre-known concepts.*

The degree of mapping between software novelty and pre-known concepts can most readily be determined by considering the outcome of the user's interaction with the software. When the outcome of the interaction lies within the software only, there is no direct mapping. This is the case, for example, at the task layer of software for creating websites and at the semantic layer of text editing software that allows for regular expressions in searching and replacing. In other cases, the outcome of the interaction lies partly outside and partly inside the software. The software then holds a model of something in the physical world or in the user's mind, and it is the model that is modified. The mapping is then much more straightforward. Think, for example, of a kitchen planner such as offered by many home furnishing stores, whose task layer is involved with constructing a model of your new kitchen; or a calculator program where at the semantic layer the memory functions M+, M- and MR mimic a scratchpad holding intermediate results.

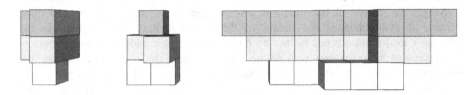

Fig. 2. Depth of use complexity added to the analysis for Notepad (left), WordPad (center) and Word2007 (right)

Figure 2 shows the sketches from the previous figure enhanced with depth to indicate novelty for which there is no straightforward correspondence with the pre-known world. Approximately half of Notepad's novelty at the semantic and task layers is considered not to correspond to pre-known concepts; whereas WordPad is judged to expose the user to non-mapping novelty only at the semantic layer, and a significant proportion of Word2007's novelty at all layers has meaning within the software world only.

2.3   Height: Impact

Turning our attention now to the use that is made of software, we find in Activity Theory a different three-tiered hierarchy; one which is fluid rather than fixed, user-centered rather than tool-centered. Central to the theory is the idea that all human activity is mediated by tools and context and that these fundamentally change the activity. Activity Theory covers many different aspects and offers a rich framework for the development of theory and practice alike [see 12, 13]. For the purpose of assessing use complexity of software, however, further details of the activity-theoretical framework can be largely ignored, taking from it only the following decomposition of human activity:

- An *activity* is a sequence of actions, undertaken one after the other in order to achieve an object, which provides the overall intention to do the work.
- An *action* is a sequence of operations, undertaken one after the other in order to achieve a goal within the wider framework of the activity's overall intention.
- An *operation* is a routinely carried-out observable behavior.

The task layer in any given software tool does not necessarily correspond to the activity, nor the semantic layer to actions or the syntactic layer to operations. Task layer, semantic layer and syntactic layer are tool-centered and objective. To determine what they consist of, it is sufficient to consider only the software. Activities, actions and operations on the other hand are human-centered and subjective. They change over time and from one performer to another and to determine what they are, it is sufficient to consider only the user. Aligning the two hierarchies, the human-centered and the tool-centered, exposes the relative roles of the two partners in a man-machine system.

These are not always the same [14]. The software component does not necessarily affect all the levels in an activity: situations are easily imaginable in which only part of the activity is computer-mediated. Software that affects the activity only insofar as it changes the nature of operations is less complex than that which touches upon actions, or even changes the nature of the activities that are possible. As the software's mediation reaches further up into the activity, it adds more uncertainty to constructs that were not very well defined to begin with: the goals of actions and the intention of the activity. This third dimension can be visualized as the "height" of the use complexity, enhancing the impact of the width and depth. *The height of the use complexity is proportionate to the degree to which the software can affect an activity (in the activity-theoretical sense of the word).*

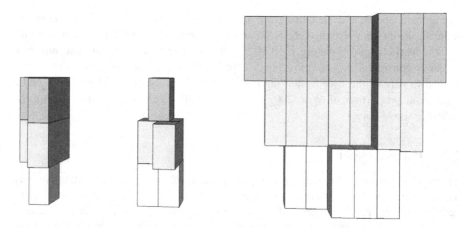

Fig. 3. Height of use complexity added to the analysis for Notepad (left), WordPad (center) and Word2007 (right)

To determine the height of the use complexity, first ask whether the outcome of the task layer could ever be imagined to constitute a valid object, providing the intention to sit down to work. If so, the software reaches up into the level of the activity; if not, its application constitutes no more than the goal of an action and it reaches no further than into the level of the separate actions. This is reflected in the visualization by "pulling up" the use complexity to the level of the actions (left and center in Figure 3) or all the way to the overall activity (right).

The outcomes of Notepad's and WordPad's task layers are relatively modest, and in this example they are not seen to provide more than the goal for an action such as writing a short note or making a shopping list. The outcome of Word2007's task layer on the other hand could well be imagined to be an object in itself, such as the complete production and layout of a camera-ready manuscript or the programming of a word processing environment for third parties to use.

3   Conclusions

Use complexity is a promising concept to structure and direct documentation design efforts. However, much more work is required before it can be fruitfully deployed in sound engineering practice and is scalable for different types of software. A stepwise course of action must be developed for documentation developers to assess use complexity in a methodical manner, and measurable indicators must be established for all three dimensions. How to determine when a concept in the software world contributes to width and possibly depth of the use complexity, and by how much? How to decide whether the task level of the software reaches up into the intention for an activity or merely constitutes the goal of an action? To allow for learning the approach and to limit inter-rater variance, stringent definitions and ordinal scales on all three dimensions must be developed, unambiguously illustrated with standardized examples.

Therefore, further research is very much needed (and indeed planned), preferably in close cooperation with the direct stakeholders: the designers of user documentation.

These are uncharted waters. The field of documentation design tends to focus on the effects of specific interventions rather than underlying mechanisms or methodological approaches to the design process [2]. Task analysis in HCI (human-computer interaction) is usually carried out before a new system or version is developed, while CSCW (computer-supported cooperative work) considers tasks and working practices emerging from new technology for groups of people working together, rather than individuals. Usability, as we have seen, refers to only part of the User Virtual Machine and there is no consensus as to its metrics or even its constituent parts [15]. Dix et al, for example, see usability as having three constituents: learnability or the ease with which new users can begin effective interaction and achieve maximal performance, flexibility or the multiplicity of ways the user and system exchange information, and robustness or the level of support provided to the user in determining successful achievement and assessment of goals. Each of these constituents is in this framework seen as a function of underlying aspects, resulting in predictability, synthesizability, familiarity, generalizability, and consistency; dialog initiative, multi-threading, task migratability, substitutivity and customizability; and observability, recoverability, responsiveness and task conformance as factors to usability [16]. Comprehensive as this overview seems, it bears little likeness to the definition in the ISO 9241-11 standard. Indeed, other authors (for a more in-depth discussion, see [15]) present different indicators for the same concept of usability. And although some of the many aspects mentioned (e.g. familiarity) reduce use complexity, others (e.g. flexibility) may actually lead to increased use complexity. Use complexity is thus a concept that, appropriately operationalized to become a practical tool rather than a theoretical construct, can provide practitioners in documentation design with much-needed guidance.

Acknowledgment. I am indebted to Gerrit C. van der Veer and three anonymous reviewers for their insightful comments on the first draft of this paper. They pointed me to relevant literature, and helped me distinguish the concept of use complexity from its practical applicability and from other, related concepts.

References

1. Aiguier, M., Le Gall, P., Mabrouki, M.: A Formal Definition of Complex Software. In: Proceedings of the 2008 The Third International Conference on Software Engineering Advances, pp. 415–420. IEEE Computer Society (2008)
2. Schriver, K.: Dynamics in document design. John Wiley & Sons, New York (1997)
3. van der Veer, G.C., van Vliet, H.: The Human-Computer Interface is the System: A Plea for a Poor Man's HCI Component in Software Engineering Curricula. In: Ramsey, D., Bourque, P., Dupuis, R. (eds.) Proceedings of the 14th Conference on Software Engineering Education and Training, pp. 276–286. IEEE Computer Society (2001)
4. van der Veer, G.C., Tauber, M.J., Waern, Y., van Muylwijk, B.: On the interaction between system and user characteristics. Behaviour & Information Technology 4, 289–308 (1985)
5. Norman, D.A.: The Invisible Computer. The MIT Press, Cambridge (1999)
6. Norman, D.A.: Living with Complexity. The MIT Press, Cambridge (2010)
7. Nadolski, R.J., Kirschner, P.A., van Merriënboer, J.G., Wöretshofer, J.: Development of an Instrument for Measuring the Complexity of Learning Tasks. Educational Research and Evaluation 11, 1–27 (2005)
8. Kim, S., Soergel, D.: Selecting and measuring task characteristics as independent variables. Proceedings of the American Society for Information Science and Technology 42, n/a–n/a (2005)
9. Moran, T.P.: The Command Language Grammar: a representation for the user interface of interactive computer systems. International Journal of Man-Machine Studies 15, 3–50 (1981)
10. Payne, S.J., Squibb, H.R., Howes, A.: The Nature of Device Models: The Yoked State Space Hypothesis and Some Experiments With Text Editors. Human-Computer Interaction 5, 415–444 (1990)
11. Payne, S.J.: On Mental Models and Cognitive Artefacts. In: Rogers, Y., Rutherford, A., Bibby, P.A. (eds.) Models in the Mind: Theory, Perspective and Application. Academic Press, London (1992)
12. Bødker, S.: Through the Interface – A Human Activity Approach to User Interface Design. Lawrence Erlbaum Associates, Hillsdale (1991)
13. Nardi, B.A. (ed.): Context and Consciousness: Activity Theory and Human-Computer Interaction. The MIT Press, Cambridge (1996)
14. Mirel, B.: "Applied Constructivism" for User Documentation. Journal of Business and Technical Communication 12, 7–49 (1998)
15. van Welie, M., van der Veer, G.C., Eliëns, A.: Breaking down Usability. In: Interact 1999, Edinburgh, Scotland, vol. 99, pp. 613–620 (1999)
16. Dix, A., Finlay, J., Abowd, G.D., Beale, R.: Human-Computer Interaction. Pearson (Prentice-Hall), Harlow (2004)

Collecting Users Profiles for Web Applications

Amin Rasooli[1,2], Peter Forbrig[1], and Fattaneh Tagivareh[2]

[1] University of Rostock, Computer Science Department, Albert-Einstein-Str. 21,
18051 Rostock, Germany
{amin.rasooli,peter.forbrig}@uni-rostock.de
[2] School of Electrical and Computer Engineering, University of Tehran, Tehran, Iran
{rasooly,ftaghiyar}@ut.ac.ir

Abstract. Currently providers are trying to personalize their websites according to user profiles. With respect to the wide variety and great volume of websites, providers look for a design that is more attractive than that of competitors. They look for a unique solution. In this uniqueness, any point such as design, user-friendliness, and content offered to the customer plays a key role in its success. The main objective of this study is to provide profiles of different kinds of users. Later on, this information can be used to design appropriate websites. This kind of information can be explored from social networks. We obtained a dataset of 500 users and we have clustered this dataset to 12 clusters, and then applied Collaborative Filtering on user data to improve the results. The paper will present the corresponding results and provide an interesting overview of different profiles of users in different parts of the world.

Keywords: User Profiles, Web Application, Personalization, Web Design.

1 Introduction

Most of the time, standard solutions provided by web design techniques have limited personalization ability. Owners would like to have their website usable, aesthetic and attractive according to their personal feeling. Any point such as design and user friendliness, content, services offered to the customer and etc. can play a significant role to make a website succeeds. The first impression the user gets of a website is through its appearance. She/he may like the website at his/her first view and finally be loyal to it while churn probability will be minimized. Many modern techniques have been presented in data personalization in order to collect behavioral information of the users; for example: suspension time in user interface, ratio of the observed links to the total number of links and user interaction on any accessible data [1], [2]. These new inputs can be employed to understand the hidden interests of users in order to choose the best personalized data for them. We started by introducing the goals of our work and now we present our experiment in Section 2. Finally, we will summarize the main contributions of our work in Section 3. Because of lack of space we focus on our experiment. A discussion of related work can be found in [3].

M. Winckler, P. Forbrig, and R. Bernhaupt (Eds.): HCSE 2012, LNCS 7623, pp. 275–282, 2012.

2   Experiment

Based on the analysis of popular web sites different designs were collected. These designs have been clustered in 30 different types. These types were presented to users of social networks and their votes were collected according to the following rules.

Three choices were displayed to a user. After a user selected his/her favorite design a new page provided more choices.

The system had announced to the users that the first choice they observe is not necessarily an optimized one and they have to declare their vote without looking at the presented order. 58% of the users have voted to the first choice, 26% to the second one and remaining 16% to the third choice. The software contains a learning system in such a way that it updates the design rating considering the positive vote and the user's cluster. Therefore, when the user gives his/her positive vote to a design, the ratio of votes given to a specific design toward the total votes was added to its rating. This value divided by remaining designs in a group will also be subtracted from the total number of designs. Similarly, designs will tend to be optimized which will result in a powerful learning system.

The total number of the participants was 481 with 840 valid votes for the existing design templates, while 664 additional votes were added to first level votes taking into account the details.

3   Results

3.1   Color Preferences

Colors with darker tones such as blue and brown were more attractive to men, while designs having a color spectra such as pink, purple, red and yellow, in comparison with other colors, were a prevalent trend among women's choices. Designs with the desired tone for men were 48% of total designs, 67% of which were voted as the first choice and the remaining 33% were voted as second choices. Designs with the desired tone for women were 30% of total designs, 82% of which were selected as the first choice while the other 18% were voted as secondary choices. The sampling set was

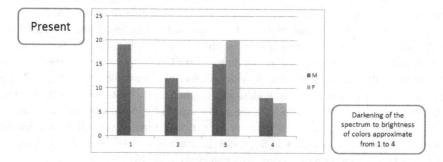

Fig. 1. Sex towards color

composed of 268 male and 192 female participants. Designs were also tagged such that they were sorted in four groups from the darkest to the lightest tone. It was observed that women show more interest in lighter colors, whereas men show more interest in darker colors. In Fig. 1, the horizontal axis of the diagram shows the average dark to light approximate tone scaled from 1 to 4 and the vertical axis of the diagram indicates the redundancy of each group.

Since most of the participants who have taken part are from Iran and some European countries, the results in the Middle East and 1st level European countries (more prosperous) have provided the most accurate results. Fig. 2 compares chosen countries and favorite kinds of colors of the participants.

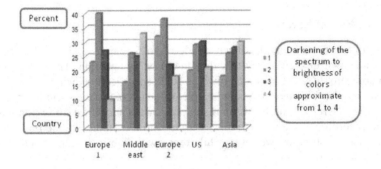

Fig. 2. Color toward User's Location

As shown in Fig. 2, lighter color designs have attained higher ratings in Asia and the Middle East compared to other tones; meanwhile European countries have experienced a rather reversed regime. Asian countries, especially those in Middle East, have chosen light colors. In Fig. 2, the horizontal axis of the diagram shows the average dark to light approximate tone scaled from 1 to 4 while the vertical axis of the diagram indicates the percent of designs chosen by individuals in each group.

3.2   Time Spent in Website with Relation to User's Education

According to Fig. 3 those who have a higher education spend more time on a website. Many participants with a higher education have spent 40-45 sec time using the website. In this diagram, the horizontal axis shows the education level while each color is indicative of the average time spent on the website. The vertical axis shows the percent of designs chosen by individuals in each group. The average time spent on web pages as reported by the literature was higher than the time we inferred based on our research.

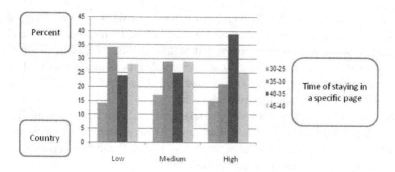

Fig. 3. Spent time in website towards user's education

3.3   The Role of Location

Location of the participants has been divided into 5 regions and the characteristics have been shown in such a way that they could be comparable. These diagrams are used to compare different locations towards some specifications which have revealed successful results. This diagram is indicative of the average time spent by individuals on websites. Thereby, time has been displayed and location of each region has been specified according to the average time. People who live in the Middle East and USA spent the shortest time on websites, while those who live in EU and South America spent the longest time on web pages.

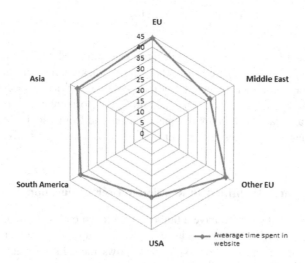

Fig. 4. Location towards average time spent in websites

Fig. 5 illustrates the number of links in web pages since the average number of links towards each region has been specified on the diagram. The number of links affects user's concentration and accuracy of his/her choice. Whenever the number of links is greater, it would be more difficult for the user to choose his/her favorite link.

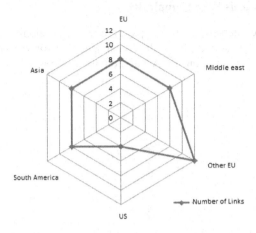

Fig. 5. Location towards number of links

There could be a solution by combining links with help information. People, who live in 2nd level European countries, are more interested in greater number of links.

Considering the interest of people from various regions in the world in higher or darker tone colors, Fig. 6 reveals the relation between the color variety and the location of the participants. In this diagram, the amount of color variety has been determined for each region. People from North America show less interest in high variety of colors.

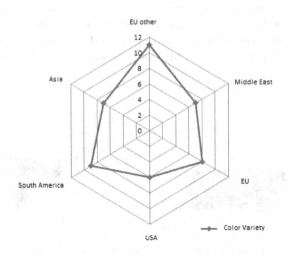

Fig. 6. Location towards color variety

3.4   Location towards Page Complexity

Fig. 7 focuses on the interest in complex pages in various regions. In this diagram, the average tagged amount of complexity has been specified for each region. Advanced European countries in addition to Asian countries show great interest in more complex pages.

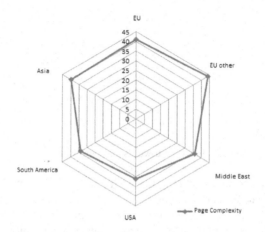

Fig. 7. Location towards page complexity

3.5   Age towards Number of Links

In this diagram, the horizontal axis has 4 values: 1 for the age group presented on the X axis, 2 and 3 for the age group of presented on the Y axis (between 18 and 31 years old which has been divided into two sets), and 4 for the age group of presented on the Z. Loads of the diagram are the number of links and the vertical axis represents the redundancy.

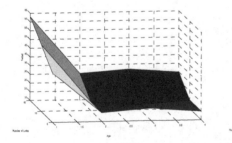
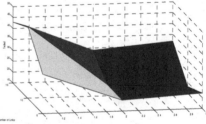

Fig. 8. Age towards number of links   **Fig. 9.** Education towards number of links

As can be observed, users of lower ages have chosen the greatest number of links. The trend in this diagram is similar to the previous one and it is possible to interpret relations between age and education. One of the horizontal axes is education in which value "1" denotes lower education levels and value "4" denotes higher education ones; while the other one is the number of links. The vertical axis represents the redundancy. It can be seen that lower education has been accompanied by the greatest number of links.

4   Summary

The paper presented some aspects that were analyzed based on experiments with users that have been attracted from social networks. Thze results can be summarized in the following way.

Users with lower education level together with users of lower income are interested to be placed the overview columns at the right. It can therefore be concluded that they have been more related to the Persian websites whose exploring experience was limited to simple issues in Iran governmental websites e.g. websites of gas card, post, Housings and etc. which usually have their column at right. One conclusion made from these observations was that exploring experience of a user has direct impacts on his/her favorite styles.

People who have education level less than bachelor, prefer less than 8 links. Users having an education level lower than master show the least attention to page components. They are also interested in greater number of links.

Users who have low income level like to visit a website with light colored and busy header pictures. On the other hand, users with high income level are keen to visit websites with warm colored and nature header pictures. Individuals whose average time spent on various web pages is more than normal, are interested in third type of websites which do not have columns or busy design.

Users older than 31 years choose the header picture from busy ones. They also use the darkest colors to design the website and prefer plenty of pictures in it. With respect to the limitations such as participation of users in all ranges under study, some of the specifications have adequate resources while others lack such resources. For example, majority of the sampling population are Iranian students who will affect education level and financial situation as well as other specifications

One other drawback experienced was related to the difficulty to bring people of other countries to agreement. The least number of participants were from Africa and Australia while the number of participants from America was not enough as well. It seems that the income criteria have not been answered properly. The major limitation of the research was in social networks in which users hardly trust newly released applications due to incidence of virus worms. Therefore, it will be rather difficult to satisfy those users.

Achievements of this research can be further employed in the design of dynamic websites which requires much time and cost; to conform page patterns regarding the tags from page classification in which the users have shown interest and to develop results obtained from observing users' behavior toward other practical areas.

Considering greater number of characteristics with more details in addition to more users can certainly impose a positive effect on the model and tagging the designs, meanwhile it will make results more accurate. Furthermore, if user's exploring behavior is recorded in longer period of time, the results will be of higher accuracy. A number of parameters have been considered here for the voting system and page ranking. For example, receiving feedback from the user affects its class cluster designs in such a way that adds a coefficient for the positive votes and subtracts it for the negative ones. Modification of these coefficients can lead to higher performance. Coefficient mentioned for distinction of specifications for each part of the website can also be altered. Changing the normalizing parameters can have positive effects on the results.

Some characteristics which have been collected from questionnaires may lack enough accuracy. Besides, some people may not allow their demographic information to be published through social networks due to security issues.

Applying techniques to make them agree to do so, (for example through trust let techniques) can have significantly influence the accuracy of data.

References

1. Mobasher, B., Cooley, R., Srivastava, J.: Automatic personalization based on Web usage mining. Communications of the ACM 43(8), 142–151 (2000)
2. Schiaffino, S., Amandi, A.: User–interface agent interaction: personalization issues. International Journal of Human-Computer Studies 60(1), 129–148 (2004)
3. Rasooli, A., Taghiyareh, F., Forbrig, P.: Categorize Web Sites Based on Design Issues. In: Jacko, J.A. (ed.) HCII 2011, Part IV. LNCS, vol. 6764, pp. 510–519. Springer, Heidelberg (2011)
4. Wei, K., Huang, J., et al.: A survey of E-commerce recommender systems. Service Systems and Service Management. In: 2007 International Conference on Service Systems and Service Management, pp. 1–5 (2007)
5. Casteleyn, S., De Troyer, O., Brockmans, S.: Design Time Support for Adaptive Behaviour in Web Sites. In: Proceedings of the 18th ACM Symposium on Applied Computing, pp. 1222–1228. ACM (2003) ISBN 1-58113-624-2
6. Leonidis, A., Antona, M., Stephanidis, C.: Rapid Prototyping of Adaptable User Interfaces. International Journal of Human Computer Interaction (2011)
7. Stephanidis, C.: The concept of Unified User Interfaces. In: Stephanidis, C. (ed.) User Interfaces for All - Concepts, Methods, and Tools, pp. 371–388. Lawrence Erlbaum Associates, Mahwah (2001) ISBN 0-8058-2967-9
8. Stephanidis, C., Paramythis, A., Sfyrakis, M., Savidis, A.: A Case Study in Unified User Interface Development: The AVANTI Web Browser. In: Stephanidis, C. (ed.) User Interfaces for All - Concepts, Methods, and Tools, pp. 525–568. Lawrence Erlbaum Associates, Mahwah (2001)
9. Stephanidis, C., Paramythis, A., Zarikas, V., Savidis, A.: The PALIO Framework for Adaptive Information Services. In: Seffah, A., Javahery, H. (eds.) Multiple User Interfaces: Cross-Platform Applications and Context-Aware (2004)
10. Antona, M., Savidis, A., Stephanidis, C.: A Process–Oriented Interactive Design Environment for Automatic User Interface Adaptation. International Journal of Human Computer Interaction 20(2), 79–116 (2006)
11. Petit-Rozé, C., Grislin-Le Strugeon, E.: MAPIS, a multi-agent system for information personalization. Information and Software Technology 48(2), 107–120 (2006) ISSN 0950-5849
12. Kazienko, P., Adamski, M.: AdROSA—Adaptive personalization of web advertising. Information Sciences 177(11), 2269–2295 (2007)
13. Seo, J., Lee, K.: Development of Website Design Personalization Service Using Design Recommender System (2003), http://citeseerx.ist.psu.edu/viewdoc/summary?doi=10.1.1.108.3769 (access time: October 2010)

Creativity Patterns Guide: Support for the Application of Creativity Techniques in Requirements Engineering

Elton R. Vieira[1], Carina Alves[1], and Letícia Duboc[2]

[1] Informatics Center, Federal University of Pernambuco
[2] Computer Department, State University of Rio de Janeiro
{ervs,cfa}@cin.ufpe.br, leticia@ime.uerj.br

Abstract. Creativity techniques are tools for stimulating creative thinking. The importance of creativity fostering techniques in software development has been recognized and investigated by researchers for over a decade, yet the greater software engineering (SE) community makes little use of the myriads of techniques available. In order to encourage a wider adoption and to support the use of creativity techniques in software development, we have reviewed a large number of creativity techniques and have created a Creativity Patterns Guide. This paper describes the part of the guide tailored for the requirements engineering phase. The guide has been evaluated in real-world projects.

Keywords: Creativity Techniques, Requirements Engineering, Design Patterns.

1   Introduction

Software development is a problem-solving activity, from software inception to testing. Many of these can be solved creatively. Creativity is particularly important in the requirements engineering (RE) phase. The obvious case is market-driven products, which must contain innovative features for attracting customers [1]. Furthermore, the requirements analyst is often faced with problems involving different disciplines, multiple stakeholders, a highly dynamic context, uncertainties and trade-offs. Understanding and solving such complex problems also requires creativity [2]. Research suggests that problems can be solved creatively through the use of techniques that stimulate idea generation [3, 4]. Some techniques have been studied in the RE context and shown to be powerful tools for elaborating requirements [2, 7]. Despite of benefits and the myriads of techniques available [9], the software engineering community still makes a limited use of creativity techniques [8].

The contribution of this work is two-folded. We have reviewed a large number of creativity techniques, selecting the ones that we believe to be suitable for stimulating creativity in software development. We have also adapted and organized them with a structure, language and examples that are familiar to software developers. This paper presents the Creativity Patterns Guide, a catalogue of creativity techniques for supporting idea generation during software development. In order to facilitate its adoption by software engineers, creativity techniques are presented following the familiar concept of Design Patterns [16]. The reminder of the paper is organized as

M. Winckler, P. Forbrig, and R. Bernhaupt (Eds.): HCSE 2012, LNCS 7623, pp. 283–290, 2012.

follows. Section 2 discusses related work. Section 3 describes the steps to develop the Creativity Patterns Guide. Section 4 presents the results of empirical studies analyzed using the Goal-Question-Metric (GQM) technique [21]. Finally, Section 6 summaries the main contributions and briefly discusses future work.

2   Background

Even though there is no consensus on a definition of "creativity", researchers seem to agree that the term is related to the identification and resolution of problems [11]. It is also accepted that creativity is not necessarily a natural-born talent, but something that can be encouraged, supported and trained [10]. Creativity techniques are tools that can stimulate creative thinking and idea generation [3] from a rich variety of activities [4]. The literature presents a large number of such techniques [5, 6, 9].

In the software industry, the development of innovative market-driven products and services has intensified the discussion about creativity [1]. Software development is a problem-solving activity, from start to end, and could therefore benefit from techniques that help problems to be solved creatively. Yet, little space is dedicated for practices or the study of techniques that stimulate creativity in the software development process [15]. A notable exception is the field of requirements engineering, in which a few research groups have been studying creativity for over a decade [16]. Even though creativity is recognized as an important aspect of software development, and requirements engineering in particular, only a handful of techniques have been studied and the wider software engineering community still pays little attention to such techniques [8]. With this goal in mind, we have built the Creativity Patterns Guide, following the structure of design patterns.

Gamma et al. [17] created patterns that described common problems in software design, generic solutions to these problems and the consequences of using them. They follow the same structure, which eases the understanding and application of the pattern [17]. Design patterns are not mutually exclusive; in fact they are rarely used separately and are best combined [18]. They can also be categorized by the activity they support. Design patterns have been widely used by software developers [18]. Like design patterns, creativity techniques are best applied in combination [19]. They also can be classified along a number of categories that will help to pick and choose the best technique for a particular context. Following the idea of design patterns, we have created a catalogue where creativity techniques are explained, categorized and exemplified in the context of software engineering.

3   The Creativity Patterns Guide

One of the main challenges for the adoption of creativity techniques is to identify which techniques to use on a particular context [9]. Both creativity techniques and the phases of the software development have particular characteristics. Our guide categorizes creativity techniques and maps them to the software development phases, so that engineers can pick the most appropriate ones. In this paper, we report on the part of the catalogue concerning the *requirements engineering (RE)* phase; techniques for this phase were selected as follows:

Step 1 involved an ad-hoc search of digital libraries to identify articles and books discussing the topic "creativity" [5, 6, 9, 10], which led to a list of 254 techniques.

Step 2 analyzed the objectives and operations of each technique, and the ones considered redundant or too similar were removed, reducing the list to 98 techniques.

Step 3 evaluated the techniques with respect to its suitability to the RE phase. First we selected techniques that could be adapted to the software context, that is, techniques designed to specific areas, such as arts or marketing were removed. Second, we have classified them according to four criteria proposed in the creativity literature and then examined the RE literature to map this criteria to RE activities.

The four criteria for classifying the techniques were: (i) The control criteria, defined by Grube and Schmid [14] describes whether the technique requires physical artifacts or not, and whether it is applicable to a group or an individual. (ii) The operation criteria classify the techniques according to the four model types defined by Boden [13]: exploration, combination, transformation and evaluation [9]. (iii) The approach criteria, also defined by Schmid e Grube [9], groups techniques according to their basic activity: free association, different viewpoints, questions list, structuring, area expert and random entry [14]. (iv) Finally, the direction criteria determine whether the style of the technique is convergent or divergent [13].

RE comprises the activities of: identification of stakeholders, recognition of different viewpoints, problem understanding, scope definition, and elaboration, negotiation, documentation and validation of requirements [20]. In order to map these activities to the above criteria, we reviewed the literature, looking for observations and studies that suggested particular mappings. For example, Pressman [20] observes that requirements may be elicited by means of group meetings or individual interviews [8], which suggests the suitability of techniques classified as "individual" or "group. Kirton observes that requirements analysis demands convergent thinking to validate requirements [12], indicating that a technique classified as "convergent" might be suitable for the requirements validation activity. As a result of this mapping, 41 creativity techniques were judged suitable for the RE phase. The list of techniques and their mapping can not be shown for space constraints. While we sought to ground our mapping on well-established research, we recognize that this mapping is subject to our interpretation of the works reviewed. Further validation will assess its appropriateness.

The **Creativity Patterns Guide** was developed to encourage and support the use of creativity techniques in the context of software development. For such, we have taken the following measures: (i) adopted the familiar structure of design patterns, (ii) illustrated the techniques with software-related scenarios, (iii) adapted the language to software engineers, and (iv) used an attractive layout with decentralized columns, symbols and highlighted concepts. As show in Figure 1, each technique is described by a short and expressive (1) **name**, its (2) **intent**, an (3) **example** in the software context, an (4) **idea direction** (convergent or divergent), its (5) **applicability** (through scenarios), its (6) **participants** characteristics (individual, group, resource), (7) **more information**, a (8) **symbol** representing the software development phase, and the (9) **time** it requires.

INTENT

Reverse Brainstorming helps to solve issues through ideas combinations and reversal techniques. The challenges are put in opposite direction to the intentions of solving them, in order to identify potential projects issues.

EXAMPLE

Reverse Brainstorming is a good technique for creative solving, and can lead to robust solutions.

How It Works:

1.   Cleary identify problem or challenge, and write it down.

2.   Turn over the problem or challenge with the question like "How could I possibly cause a loss of information from the database?" or "How could I get the database to stay inaccessible?"

3.   Brainstorm in inverse problem to generate ideas from then. Allow a freely flow of ideas. Do not reject any idea at this stage.

4.   Once you've accomplished all the brainstorm for solving the inverse problem, now reverse these ideas in solution to the original problem or challenge.

5.   To evaluate these ideas solutions.

IDEA DIRECTION

Convergent and/or Divergent

APPLICABILITY

Requirements Definition Phase

Requirements Definition: Putting the challenge in opposite direction, force the techniques users to identify recurring problems and find creative answer.   At stage of identifying requirements, the technique can help participants to see problems, solutions and functions outside the scope of their previous knowledge, however, relevant to the project.

PARTICIPANTS

Can be used in groups or alone, do not need physical tools.

MORE INFORMATION

Operation: exploration, combination.

Approach: question list.

Fig. 1. Elements of Creativity Patterns Guide

4   Empirical Study

An empirical study was conducted in two software development projects to analyze the impact of using the Creativity Patterns Guide during the Requirements Engineering phase: **Project A** involved the development of Advergame. The team comprised 6 professionals: one project manager, one requirements analyst one senior developer, two junior developers and one designer. The project lasted two months. **Project B** consisted on the development of Educational Networking applications. The team had 8 professionals: one project manager, one designer, one specialist in social networks one senior developer and four junior developers. This team has expertise in web development, Human-Computer Interaction, testing, social media and educational software development. The project has been developed for the last 3 years and it is still in execution. The study was conducted in the installations of each company. One of the authors acted as facilitator.

The main objective of the empirical study was evaluating the overall benefits of our proposal. The Goal Question Metric approach [21] was adopted to structure the study. The GQM is a technique that helps to define metrics for particular goals. It starts with a goal, define questions for assessing goals and create metrics that allows for questions to be answered. The main goals, questions and metrics are described in Table 1. Goal 1 evaluates the overall acceptance of the guide, while Goal 2 evaluates number of ideas and requirements that are considered relevant to the final product. This is a similar criteria used to evaluate other methods for stimulating creativity in RE, such as [7, 9, 10, 15].

Table 1. Goals, Questions and Metrics of the GQM Technique

Goals	Questions	Metrics
(G1)) Assess the acceptance of the Creativity Patterns Guide by development teams as a suitable tool to stimulate creativity.	(G1Q1) Participants considered the guide ease to use?	Opinions regarding the usability of the guide. Suggestions to improve the guide.
	(G1Q2) Participants would use the guide in other projects?	Opinion regarding their interest to adopt the guide in future projects.
	(G1Q3) The structure of the guide based on design patterns facilitates its use?	Comments regarding the influence of design patterns to explain creativity techniques. Data regarding previous knowledge and experience of participants in design patterns.
(G2) Assess the usefulness of the Guide to help development teams generating ideas and requirements.	(G2Q1) How many idea alternatives were generated?	Number of ideas generated during the study.
	(G2Q2) The idea alternatives generated may be adopted to develop the final product?	Participant opinion on the relevance of generated ideas. Number of ideas that can be included as real requirements.

Each team received a fragment of the guide, containing techniques that were used during a creativity workshop. Initially, the facilitator explained the guide and gave the techniques presented in the Guide as depicted in Figure 1. Project A used the Method 635 and Reverse Brainstorming creativity techniques. While Project B used the techniques Method 635, Reverse Brainstorming, Free Association and Provocation. The techniques were selected because they were considered fast to apply, yet possessing great creative potential. The ideas generated were written in whiteboards to be discussed by all team members. The study with Project A had one workshop session that lasted 2 hours, and the Project B study had one session that lasted 4 hours. After the workshops, we conducted a short focus group to discuss their impressions of the Guide. In addition, we also collected data by applying a semi-structured interview. Eight participants were interviewed, two from Project A and six from Project B. Each interview lasted less of 30 minutes. There were three basic questions about the Guide (related to G1) and two questions about the quality of ideas (related to G2).

4.1   Results

The results of the study are classified to answer the questions stated in the GQM technique as presented in the previous section:

(G1Q1) – Participants provided positive impressions after using the Guide. They stated that techniques are well explained and easier to apply in the context of software development. All participants affirmed they understood the techniques and concepts presented in the Guide, even those who had never used creativity techniques. The visual design and contextualization of creativity techniques for software development scenarios were considered important features. In terms of criticism, participants posed that the Guide still needs to improve the description of tasks and some examples for using techniques. Participants also proposed the following suggestions: separate the techniques in blocks, specifying which SE phase that block is intended; specifying the amount of time required to apply each technique. These suggestions were incorporated in the guide as presented in the paper.

(G1Q2) – All team members of both projects confirmed they would use the guide to stimulate creative thinking in other projects. Even though, these impressions are considered a rather subjective measure, we believe that these preliminary positive feedbacks indicate the guide is a promising approach to integrate creativity activities with other traditional phases of SE. Participants also stated the guide was fun the use and could be a relaxation moment to escape from the constant pressure of projects.

(G1Q3) – The adaptation of creativity techniques to the context of RE, and the use of concepts already known in design patterns, directly influenced the rapid assimilation of the Guide by participants. These characteristics received a unanimous positive response. The creativity activities conducted by the participants of the study were guided only by the examples present in the technique description. The majority of participants had previous contact with design patterns, this familiarity led to a direct understanding of elements present in the Creativity Patterns Guide.

(G2Q1) – The total of ideas generated was 121. In Project A, participants generated 37 different ideas; while in Project B, participants proposed 94 ideas. It is worth noting that not all idea alternatives were incorporated as requirements. Another aspect to analyze is the substantial difference between the number of ideas generated by both teams. This may be due to the fact that study with Project B lasted 4 hours.

(G2Q2) – The number of ideas generated was considered high by the teams. In Project A, more than 70% of ideas had direct influence in the requirements for the advergame. In Project B, we could not assess the real adoption of ideas generated because the project was not fully implemented by the time of writing this paper. Regarding participants opinion on the relevance of generated ideas, they observed that some ideas were useful triggers to develop more innovative features. These opinions were used to measure the quality of ideas.

As the subjects selected few techniques, the usefulness of the guide for stimulating creativity could only be assessed for the selected techniques. In order to assess the full guide, more experiments are needed. It is also important to note that this study did not aim to evaluate the completeness of the guide or whether the structure of the guide has helped subjects to select the best techniques for the problem in hand. Nevertheless the volunteers were asked about the suitability and ease of use of the guide for understanding and selecting techniques. The results in terms of number of ideas and their impact in the final product showed that the chosen techniques were appropriate to stimulating creativity.

5   Conclusions and Future Work

This paper presented the Creativity Patterns Guide, an artifact to stimulate the adoption of creativity techniques in software engineering. The guide adopts the familiar concepts of Design Patterns to explain the use of creativity techniques in the context of software development. To construct the guide we gathered relevant knowledge on creativity techniques available in literature, mapped this knowledge using four classification criteria and structured this knowledge in a catalogue as elements of patterns. Our aim to develop the Creativity Patterns Guide was to provide a practical and ease to use tool to enhance creative thinking of development teams. In particular, a key contribution of our approach is to encapsulate a relevant knowledge body in creativity using appropriate vocabulary and providing several examples understandable for software engineers.

In order to conduct an initial evaluation of the guide, we employed the GQM technique to structure the goals of the study and help collecting empirical data to answer the proposed questions. As key results, we observed that the analogies with design patterns were considered a very positive manner to structure creativity knowledge. These features enabled the easy learning and application of presented creativity techniques. Even participants who had never used creativity techniques confirmed the simplicity of the guide. It is important to observe that the adoption of design pattern does not aim to propose a formal pattern to adopt creativity. In fact, the patterns act more as a guidance to use existing creativity techniques. It serves as a basic reference for software engineers to adopt creative thinking more easily in their daily activities. In addition, given that creativity is a very subjective and intuitive task, it is not possible to assess if participants selected a correct or wrong technique. Further research is needed to assess the overall suitability of the guide. We obtained very positive responses regarding the acceptance of the guide. However, in order to obtain representative and reliable data we need to conduct more formal studies. Finally, we aim to perform experiments comparing the number and quality of ideas generated by two teams, one using the guide and the other team applying creativity techniques published in other sources.

References

1. Alves, C., Ramalho, G., Damasceno, A.: Challenges in Requirements Engineering for Mobile Games Development: The Meantime Case Study. In: Requirements Engineering Conference (2007)

2. Solís, C., Ali, N.: Distributed Requirements Elicitation Using a Spatial Hypertext Wiki. In: IEEE International Conference on Global Software Engineering (2010)
3. Forster, F., Brocco, M.: Understanding Creativity-Technique Based Problem Solving Processes. In: Lovrek, I., Howlett, R.J., Jain, L.C. (eds.) KES 2008, Part II. LNCS (LNAI), vol. 5178, pp. 806–813. Springer, Heidelberg (2008)
4. Norman, D.A.: Emotional Design: Why do We Love (Or Hate) Everyday Things. Basic Books (2004)
5. Mycoted (2012), http://www.mycoted.com/
6. Mind Tools (2012), http://www.mindtools.com/
7. Maiden, N., Jones, S.: Provoking Creative Design: Making it Scale. British Computer Society (2008)
8. Maiden, N., Jones, S., Karlsen, K., Neill, R., Milne, A.: Requirements Engineering as Creative Problem Solving: A Research Agenda for Idea Finding. In: 18th IEEE International Requirements Engineering Conference (RE), Sydney (2010)
9. Grube, P., Schmid, K.: Selecting Creativity Techniques for Innovative Requirements Engineering. In: 3rd International Workshop on Multimedia and Enjoyable Requirements Engineering (2008)
10. Michalko, M.: Thinkertoys. A handbook of creative-thinking techniques, 2nd edn. TenSpeed Press, Berkley (2006)
11. Mich, L., Franch, M., Berry, D.M.: Classifying Web-Application Requirement Ideas Generated Using Creativity Fostering Techniques According to a Quality Model for Web Applications. In: Proceedings of the 12th International Workshop on Requirements Engineering: Foundation for Software Quality, Luxembourg (2006)
12. Kirton, M.J.: Adaptors and innovators: Styles of creativity and problem solving. Routledge, London (1989)
13. Boden, M.A.: Computer models of creativity. AI Magazine 30(3), 23–34 (2009)
14. Grube, P., Schmid, K.: State of Art in Tools for Creativity. idSpace Project. University of the Netherlands (2008)
15. Glass, R.L.: Software Creativity 2.0. Developer *Books (2006); Mich, L., Anesi, C., Berry, D.M.: Requirements Engineering and Creativity: An Innovative Approach Based on a Model of the Pragmatics of Communication. In: Proceedings REFSQQ Workshop (2004)
16. Lemos, J., Alves, C., Duboc, L., Rodrigues, G.: A Systematic Mapping Study on Creativity in Requirements Engineering. In: ACM Symposium of Applied Computing (2012)
17. Gamma, E., Helm, R., Johnson, R., Vlissides, J.: Design Patterns: Elements of Reusable Object-Oriented Software. Addison-Wesley, Reading (1995)
18. Braz, S.: A Qualitative Assessment of Modularity in CaesarJ components based on Implementations of Design Patterns. M.Sc. thesis, Universidade Nova de Lisboa (2009)
19. Buschmann, F., Meunier, R., Rohnert, H., Sommerlad, P., Stal, E.: Pattern-Oriented Software Architecture: A System of Patterns, vol. I. John Wiley & Sons, England (1996)
20. Pressman, R.: Software Engineering, 6th edn. Mcgraw Hill (2006)
21. Basili, V., Caldeira, G., Rombach, H.D.: The Goal Question Metric Approach. In: Marciniak, J. (ed.) Encyclopedia of Software Engineering. John Wiley & Sons, USA (1994)

Exploring Local Cultural Perspectives in User Interface Development in an Indian Offshoring Context: A View from the UK

Malte Ressin[1], Cecilia Oyugi[1], José Abdelnour-Nocera[1], David Lee[2], and Dharam Panesar[1]

[1] University of West London, Centre for Usability and Internationalisation
W5 5RF London, United Kingdom
{malte.ressin,cecilia.oyugi,jose.abdelnour-nocera,
dharam.panesar}@uwl.ac.uk
[2] VocaLink
EC2V 7BB London, United Kingdom
david.lee@vocalink.com

Abstract. In this paper, we present the results of an exploratory case study on the impact of culture on software development in an offshoring context in India. Our research aims to understand the role of culture in outsourced software development. We interviewed human-computer interface professionals such as frontend developers, user interface designers and usability specialists working for a software development outsourcing vendor in India. The interviews were analysed for occurrence of common themes. Thereafter the cultural models of Hofstede and Hall were used to make sense of these emerging themes.. Our results indicate that cultural influence occurs and has an overarching influence in software development. Three proposals are made in response to the cultural issues highlighted.

Keywords: offshoring, outsourcing, culture, software development.

1 Introduction

Offshoring has been an attractive option for some western countries mainly due to the lower costs involved. PricewaterhouseCoopers carried out a research establishing that 79% of the companies in western countries indicated that lower transactional costs were their main reason for offshoring [1]. Other important reasons that have driven the developed nations to offshore include the shortage of skilled workers and the continued improvement of the global transport and communication network. Initially, the IT industry started by offshoring services that are low cost, such as IT help desk call centres. However, development in offshoring has seen the IT sector expand to offshore complex high-end skills and knowledge work activities such as software development. It is predicted that this type of activity will continue to grow. For instance, NASSCOM predict Indian IT business process outsourcing revenues of USD225 billion by 2020 [2]. Since cost is a central consideration while making a decision to offshoring, it is possible that other issues such as cultural differences

M. Winckler, P. Forbrig, and R. Bernhaupt (Eds.): HCSE 2012, LNCS 7623, pp. 291–298, 2012.
© IFIP International Federation for Information Processing 2012

between the offshoring client and the offshoring vendor are easily overlooked. Cultural differences have the potential to affect not only the software development process but also the product itself (for example in the cases where localisation is involved).

The study of how culture relates to ICT development is a growing discipline in the Human Computer Interaction (HCI) community. However, most of the current work in this area has been on how culture affects the user interaction with the end product (e.g. [3], [4] and [5]).   The focus of this paper is the importance of cultural implications for offshoring which have not been extensively researched. This report is a follow-up of a larger research where an on-line questionnaire was implemented to investigate the effects of culture on the quality of software in an offshoring context [6]. The web based survey attracted 436 responses representing 44 declared nationalities. The regional / country groups represented were West (UK, US and Australia), Eastern Europe (Hungary, Moldova and Romania) and Asia (India, Bangladesh and China). The data analysis of the online questionnaire suggested that there is a significant difference in attitudes occurring between the western clients and the offshoring vendors. Consequently, this can lead to misunderstandings between the two players which can in turn manifest in terms of poorly developed software.

2   Cultural Considerations within Offshoring

Culture is a difficult and elusive concept to define partly because of the pluralistic interest that it has gained from various academic disciplines with each of them having its own focus [7]. As a result of the varied understandings of the concept of culture, authors such as Honold propose that researchers should select the definition of culture that best suits their context [8]. Therefore, the definition that will best suit the scope of this research is the one based on shared value patterns across individuals and within groups. Specifically, Hofstede's definition of culture will be adopted during this investigation: "Culture is the collective programming of the mind which distinguishes the members of one group or category of people from another" ([9], p. 9). This computer programming parallel implies that all people have comparable brains and refers to culture as the 'software of the mind'. This means that the patterns of thinking, feeling and acting are as a result of culture which acts like 'mental programs'. Further, these 'mental programs' become part of people's lives during their interactions with the environment when growing up.

In order to better understand customs and practices in a target culture, researchers have used the concept of cultural models. These models are based on the assumption that cultural differences are a result of social learning through interaction with the environment which has taken place for long periods of time. Two of these models, Hofstede's [9] and Hall's [10], will be considered in this study.

Hofstede [9] proposes that culture varies along relationships with people (individualism vs. collectivism), the extent to which a culture embraces social inequality (power distance), the extent to which members of a culture tend to stay away from uncertain situations (uncertainty avoidance), the degree to which people prefer values of success and competition over modesty and concern for others (masculinity vs. femininity), and finally their relationship to time horizon (long term vs. short term orientation).

In his cultural model, Hall [10] proposes that a culture is either high or low context, is monochronic or polychronic in its orientation to time, decodes and acts on messages slowly or quickly and has differences in its sense of space dimensions.

The cultural dimensions proposed by Hofstede have been extended and applied in offshoring for example by [11]. However, the extent to which these theoretical cultural dimensions continue to be relevant and extendable has been questioned (e.g. [12], [13], [14] and [15]). Nonetheless, Hofstede has aptly responded to some of this criticism and his work remains highly influential in the area of cross-cultural research [16]. This paper will therefore use the theoretical underpinning of the cultural models of Hofstede [9] and Hall [10] to understand how cultural differences can and do impinge on global software development.

3   Methodology

To gather data for the study, we got an opportunity to conduct interviews with employees of an Indian offshoring software development company. As contact to our host companies prior to our field work was informal, we decided to use semi-structured interviews for our data gathering to account for the unknown range of access we would have on location. We therefore developed a solid interview script which would allow us to explore the subject area (cultural influences on the development process in offshoring projects), yet retain flexibility in branching out into the specialist areas of knowledge of our unknown interview partners.

The interview script was developed iteratively, taking as a starting point the survey questions from [6]. The interviews started off by asking the interviewees about their exact role, work experience and education. They then continued with questions about the interviewee's perceptions of quality in software, both absolutely and in relation to schedule and budget constraints, as well as in relation to client's and the host company's interests. Further topics discussed in the interviews included requirements gathering, specifications and documentation, the working relationship to clients and the employed development methodologies.

In some questions, we asked interviewees for their opinions and judgement. For example, question 14 was:

> *Consider the three targets Schedule, Budget and Quality. Which one is the most important for you personally? In your opinion, which one does your employer (the offshoring vendor) value most? Which one do your clients value most?*

We also allowed interviewees to simply relate to previous experiences. For example, questions 5 and 6 were:

Tell me about the most successful outsourcing project that you were part of. How did you know it was successful? What do you think were the reasons for its success?

Tell me about an outsourcing project you were part of that did not go well. What were the major problems? What do you think caused the problems? How could the problems have been corrected or avoided? If that didn't happen, why do you think it didn't happen?

Last but not least, we gave interviewees the opportunity to hypothesize. For example, question 16 was:

If you could change anything in the way your software is developed, what would that be and why?

Depending on the answers, additional questions were inserted at the interviewer's discretion to deepen or clarify a point, etc.

Our host company has more than 10.000 employees working on outsourcing services across the whole range of software development services. Development is mostly done in several locations in India, but subsidiaries in several overseas countries exist. Fifteen interviews were conducted over six work days at two of our host company's sites in Mumbai and Pune. They took between 35 and 55 minutes (average 43:16). Interviewees worked on user interface development for website and software development offshoring projects in the roles of frontend developer (5), user experience specialist (8) , and project manager (2).

In addition, one additional interview with a user experience specialist and a group session with ca. 30 HCI professionals at another offshoring company in Pune. This second company also offers offshoring for software development projects with development centres in several locations in India and additional offices overseas.

4   Data Analysis and Results

To analyse the data, the researcher who collected the data from India and one other independent researcher listened to the audio recordings of the interviews independently. The goal of this exercise was for each researcher to independently hand-pick important themes from the interviews and then compare the recurring themes between the two researchers. This structure was used to mitigate for individual bias and increase reliability. Therefore, the interviews were examined for common or contradictory themes indicated in the answers of the interviewees. Behaviour and implications as interpreted by us were also considered. The discovered themes were compared with cultural models of Hofstede and Hall, and pre-existing categories derived from previous cultural research were also underpinning the higher-level analysis. To mitigate for individual bias and increase reliability, analysis was conducted independently and in a parallel fashion by two of the authors. After comparing notes, the authors used their agreed results to create a number of conjectures how cultural differences manifest themselves in offshoring development.

Following is a highlight of the most important but expected cultural dependencies from the interview analysis. For example, interviewees regularly deferred questions on their own views or opinions to the authority of their superiors and loyalty to their company. In another example, many interviewees went out of their way to avoid statements which could be interpreted as criticizing others. When asked about it, they elaborated that criticism on the work of others were demeaning and therefore ethically questionable.

Most interviewees had BSc or MSc degrees in a software engineering discipline and had changed into HCI or a usability-related job role at a later date. Often, this change had been motivated by personal interest. However, almost no interviewee had received formal education in the HCI field. As far as their knowledge around HCI and usability was concerned, they were essentially self-taught. This is hardly surprising since HCI as a discipline is comparatively young and at the time many of today's professionals were studying, the number of HCI-related studies on offer was more limited than today.

During our interviews, the criteria comprising quality in software products was strongly influenced by the role of the interviewee. Those in an engineering role, e.g. frontend developer, considered quality in code-related terms like absence of bugs or fast execution speed/short application reaction time. Interviewees in a role related to classical usability, e.g. usability specialist, considered quality in terms of user-related terms like intuitive use and easy learnability. This is not particularly surprising: admittedly, an individual's role and its associated aims influence the perception of quality, and respective criteria must be informed by one's own discipline. Otherwise, a confounding impact on project and work aims would follow. However, the strong apparent dependence on role is surprising insofar as, as previously discussed, most interviewees have a code-related background and can be expected to have a certain knowledge in associated technical quality criteria. In that light, we would have expected code-related quality criteria to feature in each interviewee's answer to at least some extent. It is also noteworthy that at least to some extent, quality goals seem to be handled on an individual basis and no project- or company-overarching mantra or guideline was mentioned.

The actual development methodologies used at the host company in the user interface development were difficult to determine. Interviewees' statements did not always align in that regard. Some interviewees identified the development methodologies as linear or even categorized it specifically as Waterfall model. Other interviewees on the same project or even the same team described the development methodologies as agile. Unfortunately, as we did not consult additional documentation, we cannot be sure what methodology is or was actually in use in the respective projects.

A number of interviewees mentioned that they found Western clients easier to deal with than Indian clients because of the explicit nature of the work assignment. Interviewees stated that Western clients usually have a very clear idea what they want and communicate their expectations, often in relation to their budget. Indian clients on the other hand, on top of usually having stricter budget limitations, seem to keep project scopes more flexible and negotiate it together with the vendor, often in conjunction with project costs.

5   Discussion

We found clear indications supporting Hofstede's views on authoritative hierarchy, and reluctance to criticize in collectivist cultures. In addition to that, we came up with a number of conjectures relating our observations with Hall's cultural dimensions, in particular High Context vs. Low Context, and India being a high-context culture:

- Quality criteria are not necessarily elaborated explicitly. Instead, it is left in the interpretation of each individual on the project.
- Work processes are not explicitly specified or described. Individuals instead find their role and their work processes through interpretation.
- Qualification is considered less dependent on formal education, and is instead seen in personal interest and effort.
- Implicitness, possibly in combination with local negotiation customs, conflicts with the explicitness in software development, in particular writing code.

Summarized and re-phrased, the general relative nature of high-context cultures means that virtually everything can be subject to vagueness and/or post-hoc interpretation. This does not stop in software development.

There is evidence to certain collectivist traits as well. Further, at a lower level of practice, there seems to be evidence that IT professionals are converging culturally in certain attitudes to quality and management [17].

Consequently we propose three points of action as a result of this exploratory investigation. First, the issue of quality of software needs to explicitly be defined at the start of the project especially from the western client's perspective. Second, the methodologies used during the software development process as well as code documentation need to clearly be addressed at the start of the project. Third, in-house training could be encouraged to standardize the software development process because of the lack of formal qualification among the software vendors.

6   Conclusion

We believe that these conjectures provide an interesting insight into the offshoring vendor context. Unfortunately, we have to acknowledge limitations to the scope of our study. The number of individuals interviewed, as well as the fact that almost all of them worked for the same company and exhibited similar career paths, impacts the applicability on the larger group of HCI professionals.

In future research, our data and results might be put in comparison, for example by comparing HCI professionals from India to HCI professionals from other countries, particularly those with low-context cultures. Quantitative data gathering and statistical analysis should be employed to test those conjectures which can be operationalised, e.g. the correlation between quality criteria and role despite constant education/background. Future qualitative data could include formal project documentation where available. Focus groups could discuss items which were ambiguous in the interviews, for example regarding the contradicting statements about development methodologies.

There is a certain amount of criticism in the researcher community to the general concept of trying to "measure" culture along dimensions [18], or to apply such classifications to software development [19]. We believe that a comparison with Hofstede is legitimate, though, since both his and our participants are technologists.

Offshoring will remain an important aspect of software development. The dependency between client and vendor cultures continue to be in the spotlight, especially considering that it is not inconceivable any more that the direction outsourcing has been taking in the past, from West to East, might eventually reverse.

References

1. PriceWaterhouseCoopers: Offshoring Set to Double in the Financial Services Sector by 2008 (2005), http://www.pwc.com/in/en/press-releases/offshoring-financial-services.jhtml (accessed May 28, 2012)
2. NASSCOM: IT-BPO Sector in India: Strategic Review 2010, Executive Summary (2010)
3. Yeo, A.: Global Software Development Lifecycle: An Exploratory Study. In: Jacko, J., Sears, A., Beaudouin-Lafon, M., Jacob, R. (eds.) CHI 2001: Conference on Human Factors in Computing Systems, p. 104. ACM Press (2001)
4. Vatrapu, R., Pérez-Quiñones, M.: Culture and Usability Evaluation: The Effects of Culture in Structured Interviews. Journal of Usability Studies 1(4), 156–170 (2006)
5. Oyugi, C., Dunckley, L., Smith, A.: Evaluation methods and cultural differences: studies across three continents. In: Proceedings of the 5th Nordic Conference on Human-Computer Interaction: Building Bridges, Lund, Sweden. ACM International Conference Proceeding Series, vol. 358, pp. 318–325 (2008)
6. Lee, D.: An investigation into the relationship between quality, national culture and cost in offshore software development. PhD thesis, University of West London (2008)
7. Williams, R.: Keywords: A Vocabulary of Culture and Society. Oxford University Press, New York (1983)
8. Honold, P.: Culture and Context: An Empirical Study for the development of a Framework for the Elicitation of Cultural Influence in Product Usage. International Journal of Human-Computer Interaction 12(3&4), 327–345 (2000)
9. Hofstede, G.: Culture's consequences: Comparing values, behaviors, institutions, and organizations across nations, 2nd edn. (2001)
10. Hall, E.T.: Beyond Culture. Doubleday, Garden City (1976)
11. Carmel, E., Tjia, P.: Offshoring information technology: sourcing and outsourcing to a global workforce. Cambridge University Press, Cambridge (2005)
12. McSweeney, B.: Hofstede's Model of National Cultural Differences and their Consequences: A triumph of faith – A failure of analysis. Human Relations 55(1), 89–118 (2002)

13. Baskerville, R.F.: Hofstede Never Studied Culture. Accounting, Organizations and Society 28, 1–14 (2003)
14. Ratner, C., Hui, L.: Theoretical and Methodological Problems in Cross-Cultural Psychology. Journal for the Theory of Social Behavior 33, 67–94 (2003)
15. Kruger, T., Roodt, G.: Hofstede's VSM-94 Revisited: Is it reliable and valid? SA Journal of Industrial Psychology 29(1), 75–85 (2003)
16. Hofstede, G.: Dimensions Do Not Exist – A Reply to Brendan McSweeney. Human Relations 55(11) (2002)
17. Lee, D., Smith, A., Mortimer, M.: Cultural differences affecting quality and productivity in Western/Asian offshore software development. In: Proceedings of India HCI 2011 (2011)
18. Hall, P.: The Cross-Cultural Web. In: Day, D.L., Dunckley, L.M. (eds.) Designing for Global Markets 3 (IWIPS 2001), pp. 109–113 (2001)
19. Abufardeh, S., Magel, K.: The Impact of Global Software Cultural and Linguistic Aspects on Global Sofware Development Process (GSD): Issues and Challenges. In: Proceedings of the 4th International Conference on New Trends in Information Science and Service Science, pp. 133–138 (2010)

Improving Support for Visual Task Modelling

Fabio Paternò, Carmen Santoro, and Lucio Davide Spano

CNR-ISTI, Via G. Moruzzi 1,
56124 Pisa, Italy
{fabio.paterno,carmen.santoro,lucio.davide.spano}@isti.cnr.it

Abstract. ConcurTaskTrees (CTT) and its supporting environment (CTTE) have been widely used for a significant period of time. However, users have expressed various concerns regarding their usability. In this paper, we present the modifications made so as to provide more effective support. In particular, the environment has been enhanced in order to make it more suitable for designing real-world applications, including improved support for task model editing and early prototype generation. We also report on two evaluation tests that provided useful feedback in order to decide how to improve the environment.

Keywords: Task models, Visual Tool Support, CTT.

1   Introduction

Task models provide structured representations of how activities should be carried out in order to reach users' goals. They can be seen as a "lingua franca" between the various stakeholders in the development of interactive systems (users, designers and developers, to mention just a few). On the one hand, they are high-level descriptions that are comprehensible even to people without a programming background. On the other hand, they provide precise requirements for user interface software development as well. Over the years various notations for task modelling have been proposed together with the tools to support their development and analysis. However, often these approaches have been used mainly by the groups who developed them, and the associated tools were perceived as not mature enough. In this regard ConcurTaskTrees (CTT) [7] and the associated ConcurTaskTrees Environment (CTTE) [6] are an interesting exception. The environment made it possible to graphically represent, edit, export, interactively simulate, and check the consistency of task models represented in CTT.

The community using, extending, and applying CTT has steadily increased over the years, and various research contributions have involved CTT: some were aimed at extensions in order to increase its capabilities, while others applied it to new application domains. For the sake of brevity we mention only a small number of them. A more extended list is available at http://hiis.isti.cnr.it/tools/CTTE/CTT_publications/publications.html.

An example of a new application domain for task modelling is discussed in [1], where CTT is applied to serious games for training nurses. An example of a CTT extension is [4], which provides ideas to improve the scalability of the notation. The

M. Winckler, P. Forbrig, and R. Bernhaupt (Eds.): HCSE 2012, LNCS 7623, pp. 299–306, 2012.

COMM notation [2], instead, is aimed at extending the CTT notation in order to improve support for designing multi-user and multimodal systems. In [3], the consideration of contextual aspects in task modelling has led to the development of another extension to CTT. In CTT the context is mainly considered from the multi-device point of view, with the possibility to specify which tasks are supported by specific platforms. Other task modelling notations have considered contextual aspects to some extent in their approaches (e.g. [5]). The notation is currently being considered for standardization, and an initial version of a standard for task models based on CTT has been published by W3C[1]. It overcomes limitations of previous standards [5].

In this paper, we report on the environment evolution, which was based on some usability evaluations, and discuss the changes that have been made, in particular to the associated visual tool.

2   Key Concepts of the CTT Notation

We first introduce a few key concepts of the CTT notation in order to better understand the concepts discussed in the paper. Further details on CTT can be found in [17]. CTT is a notation for describing task models. CTT tasks have a tree-based representation for their hierarchical structure: the children of a given task represent a more detailed description of their parent task. Tasks at the same level are connected through temporal operators. Each task belongs to one *category*: i)*user* for internal cognitive activity, ii)*application* for only-system performance, iii)*interaction* for tasks involving both user actions with associated system feedback, iv)*abstraction* for tasks that have sub-tasks belonging to different categories. The task *type* allows designers to classify tasks depending on their semantics. Each category has its own set of task types. A task can be associated with one or multiple domain objects that it manipulates. Each task can also have some properties: platform(s) (those suitable for its performance), informal description, and so forth. It is also possible to have a temporal operators among tasks, and even unary operators (iteration and optionality).

An important issue in designing task model notations is to find the right trade-off between expressiveness and complexity. One extension to improve the expressiveness of CTT has been the introduction of pre and post conditions, specified according to an appropriate syntax. Indeed, the execution of a task is often subject to the availability of a given resource or depends on the value of a certain variable. In order to express these dependencies, the CTT language already contained a precondition attribute in the task definition. However, the field was just a simple string, and the designer was not bound to any formalism in order to express the conditions, which were often specified in natural language. Despite its flexibility and the ability to describe these conditions in a human-readable way, its lack of formalism is not suitable for an automatic tool support. For instance, one of the most appreciated features of CTTE is the opportunity to simulate the execution of a task model so as to identify modelling errors or to show the support for a given scenario. Informal specifications of the preconditions would not allow coherent simulation because of possible ambiguities.

---

[1] http://www.w3.org/TR/task-models/

Although other ways of modelling conditions and constraints already exist (see e.g. OCL, a formal high-level language used to describe properties on UML models) we preferred to define a simple and flexible solution in order to find a trade-off between the capability of expressing conditions and the ease with which these conditions can be handled. In CTT a pre or post condition (which can be associated to a task) is a Boolean expression that is obtained by applying logical operators to constants and/or objects values. Their hierarchical structure allows the representation of complex Boolean conditions.

3   Evaluation

In this section we report on two evaluation tests that were conducted in different contexts in order to better assess the effectiveness of the tool. One involved undergraduate students and the other a group of designers recruited from an industrial project.

The students participating in the first evaluation had no particular UI development experience. However, before the test, they were given a quick introduction to the key concepts of UI modelling, and CTT/CTTE in particular. The goal of this test was to assess whether students were able to quickly become sufficiently proficient with the notation/tool to be able to model an interactive system of low-medium complexity. The test took place during a lecture and the users were observed by one of the authors.

The second evaluation involved developers/designers working in companies, who therefore had very different characteristics, time constraints and motivations compared to the students. They had, on average, more experience in UI development/programming but, differently from the students, they had not attended any specific training on UI models (apart from the basic knowledge gained in the project). Their motivation was understandably lower, as they were willing to spend only a short amount of time learning the features of the notation/tool. Moreover, the evaluation with the second group of users was conducted remotely so, it was not possible to observe the users. Information was provided in a written format and communication was mainly made by email.

3.1   University Course Test

The goal of this test was to understand whether people without experience in task modelling could create CTT task models with minimal training/assistance.

Participants. 20 undergraduate students in Humanities Computing took part (11 females). They had low familiarity with models but they were trained before the test.

Test Material and Procedure. The students first attended a 90 minute lesson on requirements, scenarios, task analysis and modelling during which CTT and its tool support were introduced. Then, they were allowed 90 minutes to carry out the tasks required by the test. In the case where the exercise was not completed within the time, they could submit the built task model later via email. During the 90 minutes in the lab, one of the authors observed the class as they worked, and provided help, if requested, by explaining aspects related to the notation as well as the tool.

Test Tasks. Students had to develop the task model of an existing or future interactive computer-based system. The model was to have at least 3 levels of task decomposition, and include at least 15 tasks. In addition, it had to be correct according to the language (there is an automatic feature in the tool to check this property). The task type was to be indicated at least for the interaction and system tasks.

Results. All 20 students were able to complete the exercise and provide meaningful and correct task models. The correctness was assessed both syntactically, through the tool, and semantically (we manually checked the meaningfulness of the models). Despite having the same background, students' performance was very different, ranging from one who finished in 60 minutes to one who submitted it after a couple of weeks. Six students finished the exercise in the 90 minute session, and the others terminated it at home and sent the results by email.

The class exercise was also a good opportunity to observe some usability issues. One problem was adding the temporal relations into a CTT model. In the tested CTTE version users had to select the left sibling task and then select the operator to be included on the right hand of the selected task using a vertical bar. However, the observer noticed that some students tried to graphically select the two tasks by boxing them with the cursor and then attempted to insert the operator between them (by selecting it from the related bar). We realized that the students' behaviour was more intuitive then the selection process implemented at that time in the tool, so we decided to add this feature to the tool.

One aspect that disoriented some students was a tool feature which automatically changed the category of a parent task depending on the category of subtasks that were dynamically added. This feature had been introduced to ensure that the CTT specifications are correct according to the language. However, this proactive tool behaviour was perceived as slightly intrusive/unexpected by some users, who as a result might not have completely understood the rules for defining the task categories. Thus, we decided to disable this automatic support, and introduce it only on request by the user. The students also expressed the desire for some kind of rough preview of the resulting user interface. Accordingly, we introduced this feature, as explained in the following sections.

3.2   Industrial Project Test

The introduction of the preconditions was also stimulated during an industrial project, in which a multi-device (desktop and mobile) application for monitoring health was developed. Through this application users receive messages/reminders/notifications regarding their health, monitor how active they have been in the past, and how consistently they are taking medicines. Some preconditions were included in the task model and modelled by using the mechanism previously described. We performed a test to see whether developers/designers were able to understand/modify these model-based descriptions.

Participants. Volunteers were recruited through the project network (an email message was sent to the project mailing list). In the end, the test involved 8 people (3 female) from Italy, The Netherlands, Finland, and Belgium (average age: 35.7, with a range of 27-59). Six users held a degree, 2 were postgraduates. 5 users worked in research and 3 in an ICT company. User's knowledge of UI development was just a little above average (M= 3.13; SD= 0.83) on a scale from 1 to 5, where 1 is the most negative score (very bad), and 5 the most positive one (very good). Users' familiarity with models was very low (the majority had never created models before).

Test Material and Procedure. The test was conducted remotely: users performed it in their own environment and using their own equipment. Participants were emailed a document with some background information about task modelling and a task list to carry out. They were given a pre-built CTT task model, and instructions to download the CTTE tool. After completing the tasks, the testers   filled in a questionnaire, divided into: i)a section collecting some user background information (gender, age, education, familiarity in developing applications through the use of models); ii)a section focusing on CTT/CTTE use, where users commented on the task model; iii) a section in which users provided further feedback. To fill in the questionnaire, the participants used the same 1-5 semantic scale as before. The modified material (the CTT task model and the filled questionnaire) was then returned to the evaluators.

Test Tasks. The tasks were selected so that users would explore and analyse both the language (CTT) and the corresponding tool (CTTE). The task model considered for the test was a simplified version of the model for a healthcare application (desktop platform), which also contained some preconditions already modelled in it. For the test, users had to import the task model within the CTTE tool and to analyse it. Then they performed the following two tasks: i) add the possibility for users to monitor glucose level to the model; ii) add the possibility that the system sends a notification to the user whenever the glucose level goes beyond a certain threshold.

Results. Regarding the effectiveness of the tool, all the users -apart from one- managed to provide syntactically correct task models. Just one user built a task model with one missing temporal relationship. We also assessed the semantic correctness of the task models produced. The following aspects were checked: i) whether the added tasks were correctly included within the provided task model (e.g. in the right place); ii) the appropriateness of the temporal relationships included; iii) whether the category for the included tasks was meaningful; iv) whether users provided a proper refinement of the higher level tasks that have to be included in the task model. On the one hand, users performed the highest number of errors while setting the task category (3 users wrongly used task category). On the other hand, users made the fewest errors while positioning the tasks within the task model (only 2 users made this mistake in one of the tasks) and while refining the specification of the two high-level tasks to be added in the task model (only 2 users did not provide a complete description of the required tasks). 3 users successfully completed all test tasks and provided an error-free task model. 4 users correctly completed the first task, 4 users did the same with the second task.

Participants also had to rate the comprehensibility of CTT (M = 3.13; SD= 1). Only one worst score was given (1= "very unclear"), commenting that he did not think of user interactions in terms of task trees. 3 participants found the underlying CTT logic quite clear and the tool easy to use (and they gave 4 marks to this aspect) thanks to the graphical representation used. This was true even in the case where participants had little expertise. However, one tester was confused by the way the CTTE tool handles the "interaction" and "user" task categories. The remaining 4 people rated this aspect with a 3 ("neutral" rating). Among them, one expressed annoyance with the fact that the automatic check changed the category of tasks to ensure the consistency of the specification (this was also mirrored in the highest number of errors on selecting the proper task category). Another user commented that CTT language might be hard to use without a learning phase and that its approach is better for developing "standard" UIs rather than UIs with customized controls. Another one found it unclear how to modify the model as requested in the test. The last user found using CTTE not intuitive per se, but quite easy to understand after reading the instructions.

4   Improved Tool Support

The new version of CTTE, which is also publicly available, addresses some usability issues detected in the user tests. In this section we summarise the main changes carried out.

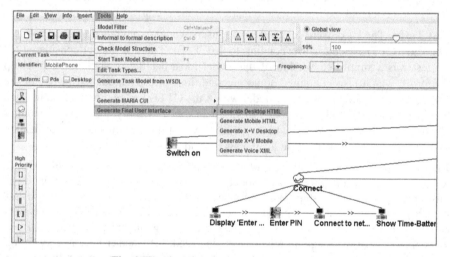

Fig. 1. The Activation of various tools in CTTE

In order to derive implementations more easily from task models, we added to CTTE the possibility of automatically generating user interfaces starting from the current task model. This came out from the test with the students: some of them explicitly asked for a tool which provided a preview of the UI automatically derived from the task model. While in the evaluated CTTE version this was not possible, in the new version of the tool, designers can obtain UIs at different abstraction levels. In particular, they can choose (see Figure 1) at what abstraction level (abstract, concrete, implementation) they want to see the corresponding user interface. In the case of concrete descriptions, they can choose on the basis of the target platform (desktop, mobile, vocal, multimodal combining graphical and vocal modalities). The abstract and concrete descriptions are represented by the MARIA language [9]. The implementation languages currently possible are HTML, VoiceXML, X+V, but there are plans to further extend the range. Clearly, what is automatically generated is just a skeleton of the UI, which therefore needs some further editing in order to improve its presentation design. For example, the labels generated are those automatically derived from task and object names and may need some refinements, as well as the choice of the colours, and the size/position of the various graphical elements. However, such early prototypes provide concrete indications of the UI corresponding to the current task model, and can speed up the process of designing usable UIs.

As Figure 1 shows, there are various functionalities that can be activated in CTTE. A recent addition was the automatic generation of CTT models from WSDL descriptions, which is useful where service-based applications are considered.

Another revision, suggested by the user tests, was to add the possibility of editing task names directly on the tree-based graphical representation of the model. In a previous version the tool supported the possibility of editing the name of a task either by activating the window showing all the task properties, or by editing it in a textfield provided in the CTTE main window. Thus, we enabled them to change the task name by just double-clicking on the task name beside the task icon.

As said before, another modification we performed in the tool (which emerged from both the tests) was to remove the automatic check on the task category during the model editing. This check was then left only for those tool features which truly required it (e.g. before activating automatic generation of UIs) or when users explicitly want to check the correctness of the task model. Indeed, while such checks are important when we want to automatically generate UIs starting from the developed task models, in other cases their application may not be required (i.e. during brainstorming about the design of the task model). This was a compromise between the correctness of the task model and the usability of the tool, which led to improved flexibility and better user control (which is in turn typically connected with higher user's satisfaction in the use of the tool).

Another improvement made in the tool (resulting from the test with students) was the possibility to set the (same) temporal operator for more than two tasks. We enabled users to associate one operator to multiple tasks through just a single action, by selecting a set of sibling tasks. This change was introduced to enhance efficiency (by avoiding users making multiple, repetitive actions).

In addition, we introduced the possibility to create and edit task preconditions. The user defines the preconditions by creating a hierarchical representation of the corresponding rule. The user selects the rule group to edit and then selects the Boolean operator to connect the sub-rules or sub-rule groups. In order to edit a rule, the user defines the first and the second operand by selecting either a task object (displayed in a drop-down list) or a constant value (that can be inserted through a text box). Another addition was the possibility to specify postconditions that should be verified after the task performance.

5   Conclusions, Future Work, and Acknowledgments

A number of important and more general lessons for model-based tools have stemmed from this experience. Firstly, it is always better to offer a trade-off between the need to present complete information to users and the manageability of this information. Therefore, the idea is to provide a subset of limited information (which should be the most important and frequently used) and then provide further details on request.

Moreover, it is advisable to avoid automatic support which can be considered disruptive: correction of the specification is useful when triggered by a user's request, whereas a continuous automatic check can be perceived as intrusive and confusing. The visual tool should be able to support immediate selection and modification of parts of the specification that are logically connected, such as tasks that share the same temporal operator. In addition, it is important to provide some idea of the appearance of the user interface resulting from the model developed.

In conclusion, CTT and its tool represent an interesting case study in the area of visual modelling because of their wide use for various purposes (teaching, industrial applications, research). Here we report on a representative set of issues that have been detected, and discuss how they have been addressed. However, we are aware that various improvements are still possible in various directions. For example, the combined use of graphical and vocal interaction can have interesting applications for facilitating the development of task models, also considering the evolution of vocal technologies in recent years. The wide adoption of touch-based smartphones also stimulates interest in supporting this platform for activities such as editing task models. We also plan further empirical evaluation as well as inspection-based evaluation experiments that exploit methods such as cognitive dimensions.

This work has been partly supported by the SMARCOS Project, http://www.smarcos-project.eu/.

References

1. Cabas Vidani, A., Chittaro, L.: Using a Task Modeling Formalism in the Design of Serious Games for Emergency Medical Procedures. In: VS-GAMES 2009, pp. 95–102 (2009)
2. Jourde, F., Laurillau, Y., Nigay, L.: COMM notation for specifying collaborative and multimodal interactive systems. In: EICS 2010, pp. 125–134 (2010)
3. Luyten, K., Van den Bergh, J., Vandervelpena, C., Coninx, K.: Designing distributed user interfaces for ambient intelligent environments using models and simulations. Computers & Graphics 30(5), 702–713 (2006)
4. Martinie, C., Palanque, P., Winckler, M.: Structuring and Composition Mechanisms to Address Scalability Issues in Task Models. In: Campos, P., Graham, N., Jorge, J., Nunes, N., Palanque, P., Winckler, M. (eds.) INTERACT 2011, Part III. LNCS, vol. 6948, pp. 589–609. Springer, Heidelberg (2011)
5. Meixner, G., Seissler, M., Breiner, K.: Model-Driven Useware Engineering. In: Hussmann, H., Meixner, G., Zuehlke, D. (eds.) MDD of Advanced User Interfaces. SCI, vol. 340, pp. 1–26. Springer, Heidelberg (2011)
6. Mori, G., Paternò, F., Santoro, C.: CTTE: support for developing and analyzing task models for interactive system design. IEEE Transactions on Software Engineering, 797–813 (2002)
7. Paternò, F.: Model-Based Design and Evaluation of Interactive Application. Springer (1999) ISBN 1-85233-155-0
8. Paternò, F.: Tools for Task Modelling: Where we are, Where we are headed. In: Proceedings TAMODIA 2002, pp. 10–17. INFOREC, Bucharest (2002) ISBN 973-8360-01-3
9. Paternò, F., Santoro, C., Spano, L.D.: MARIA: A Universal Language for Service-Oriented Applications in Ubiquitous Environments. ACM Transactions on Computer-Human Interaction 16(4), 1–30 (2009)
10. Rich, C.: Building Task-Based User Interfaces With ANSI/CEA-2018. IEEE Computer 42(9) (August 2009)

Integrating Usability Evaluation
into Model-Driven Video Game Development

Adrian Fernandez, Emilio Insfran, Silvia Abrahão,
José Ángel Carsí, and Emanuel Montero

ISSI Research Group, Department of Information Systems and Computation
Universitat Politècnica de València
Camí de Vera s/n, 46022, Valencia, Spain
{afernandez,einsfran,sabrahao,pcarsi,emontero}@dsic.upv.es

Abstract. The increasing complexity of video game development highlights the need of design and evaluation methods for enhancing quality and reducing time and cost. In this context, Model-Driven Development approaches seem to be very promising since a video game can be obtained by transforming platform-independent models into platform-specific models that can be in turn transformed into code. Although this approach is started to being used for video game development, there is a need for usability evaluation methods specifically tailored to this type of development process. In this paper, we present a usability inspection method that can be used along all the stages of the model-driven video game development. The method relies on a Usability Model that is aligned with the ISO/IEC 25010 (SQuaRE) standard and decomposes usability into measurable attributes and metrics specific for the video game domain.

Keywords: Video Game, Usability Inspection, Model-Driven Development.

1 Introduction

The video game development industry is a strong economic sector that deals with the development of highly interactive software, i.e., video games, for a wide variety of technology platforms such as PCs, consoles, Web browsers, and mobile devices. The interaction between the game and the players is a critical factor in the success of a video game. Usability and playability are considered to be the most important quality factors of video games [13]. *Usability* is defined as the degree to which the video game can be understood, learned, used and is attractive to the user, when used under specified conditions [10]. *Playability* is defined as a collection of criteria with which to evaluate a product's gameplay or interaction [11]. Playability is often evaluated by using early prototypes and iterative cycles of playtesting during the entire video game development cycle. However, the evaluation of usability in current video game development practices is often deferred to late stages in the game development cycle, thus signifying that usability problems from early stages may be propagated to late stages of the development, and consequently making their detection and correction a very expensive task.

A model-driven video game development approach could provide a suitable context for rapid iteration early in the development cycle. Platform-independent (or

M. Winckler, P. Forbig, and R. Bernhaupt (Eds.): HCSE 2012, LNCS 7623, pp. 307–314, 2012.

platform-specific) models (i.e., PIM or PSM) can be evaluated during the early stages of video game development to identify and correct some of the usability problems prior to the generation of the source code of the final video game application. We are aware that not all the usability problems can be detected based on the evaluation of models since they are limited by their own expressiveness and, most important, they may not predict the user behavior and preferences. However, as suggested by previous studies [4], the use of inspection methods for detecting usability problems in product design (models in our context) can be complemented with other evaluations performed with end-users before releasing a video game to the public.

The contribution of this paper is a usability inspection method that can be integrated in early stages of model-driven video game development. This method relies on a Video Game Usability Model which decomposes the usability characteristic proposed in the ISO/IEC 25010 (SQuaRE) standard [10] with new usability attributes for the video game domain. These attributes are quantified through their association with generic measures that can be operationalized by establishing a mapping between their generic definition and the specific modeling primitives of the software artifacts to be evaluated.

This paper is organized as follows. Section 2 discusses usability evaluation techniques for video game development. Section 3 discusses our strategy for integrating usability into model-driven video game development. Section 4 describes the Video Game Usability Model while Section 5 proposes a strategy to apply this model for performing early usability evaluations in model-driven video game development. Finally, Section 6 presents our conclusions and further work.

2   Related Work

The state of the art for game development in Software Engineering has been recently summarized in a systematic literature review [3]. The results of this review show a significant lack of studies in the key dimensions of video game quality: playability and usability. However, some efforts have been made to integrate current usability evaluation methods into the game development industry and game research, and a brief review of current game usability techniques has been provided in [13].

Some usability evaluation methods (usually referred as empirical methods) are based on capturing and analyzing usage data from real players. Some representative examples are *think-aloud* methods and *focus group* [9]. In *think-aloud* methods, the player sits down to play the video game and narrates his experiences while a user experience evaluator sits nearby listening and taking notes. In *focus group* methods, game designers gather a small group of potential game players together to discuss their opinions of the design of the interface, along with the game mechanics and story.

Other kind of usability evaluation methods (usually referred as inspection or analytical methods) are performed by expert evaluators or game designers and are based on reviewing the usability aspects of software artifacts (which are commonly game user interfaces) with regard to their conformance with a set of guidelines. The most representative example is *heuristic evaluation*, which is a common inspection method for evaluating the usability of video game interfaces in both early and functional game prototypes. Examples of heuristic evaluation methods were presented in the work of Federoff [7] and Pinelle et al. [15], in which a set of guidelines for creating a good game were defined, based on the experience of a game development case study, and PC game reviews, respectively.

In this paper, we focus on inspection methods since they do not involve the players' participation and can be employed during the early stages of the game development process. Specifically, our method extends previous approaches by providing specific video game usability attributes and measures that can be quantified by means of model-transformations. The objective is to reduce the subjectivity of existing methods that are mainly based on plain checklists of desired features with no specific guidelines on how they can be applied. Model-driven development provides a suitable context for early usability evaluations since traceability between high-level artifacts (models) and source code is maintained throughout the development process [1]. Finally, approaches based on usability models have been successfully employed as inspection methods in other domains, such as model-driven software development [2] and model-driven Web development [8]. However, as far as we know, no usability model has been proposed for model-driven video game development.

3   Usability in Model-Driven Video Game Development

The usability of a video game application obtained as a result of a transformation process can be assessed at several stages of a model-driven development process. We propose the use of a Video Game Usability Model which contains a set of usability attributes and measures that can be applied by the video game designer in the following phases of a MDA-based development process: **i)** in the PIM, to assess different models that specify the video game application independently of platform details (e.g., screen flow diagrams, screen mock-ups, screen navigation diagrams); **ii)** in the PSM, to assess the concrete design models related to a specific platform; and **iii)** in the code model, to assess the generated video game application (see Fig. 1).

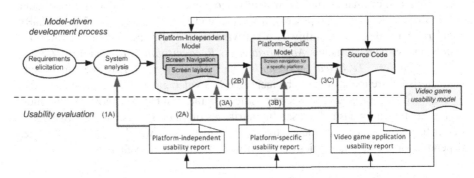

Fig. 1. Integrating a Video Game Usability Model into model-driven development processes

It should be noted that the process is driven by the PIM, which is automatically transformed into a PSM, and this PSM into source code. Therefore, the evaluations performed at the PIM produce a *platform-independent usability report* that provides a list of usability problems with recommendations to improve the system analysis stage (Fig. 1 (1A)). Changes in the PIM are reflected in the CM by means of model transformations and explicit traceability between models. This prevents usability problems to appear in the generated video game application (CM).

The video game designer should select the set of relevant usability attributes and measures from the Video Game Usability Model. There are some usability attributes (e.g., degree of attractiveness) that can only be evaluated on a specific platform and taking into account the specific components of the video game UI (PSM) or the components that build the final application (CM). Evaluations performed at the PSM produce a *platform-specific usability report*. If the PSM does not allow obtaining an application with the required level of usability, the report will suggest changes to correct the following: the PIM (Fig. 1 (2A)), the transformation rules that transform the PIM into PSM (Fig. 1 (2B), and/or the PSM itself (Fig. 1 (3B)). Nevertheless, the evaluations at the PIM or PSM level should be done in an iterative way until these models allow generating a video game application with the required level of usability.

Finally, evaluations performed at the CM level produce a *final application usability report*. Rather than suggest changes to improve the final application (CM), as is usual in other approaches, this report will suggest changes to correct the PIM (Fig. 1 (3A)), the transformation rules (Fig. 1 (3C)), and/or the PSM (Fig. 1 (3B)).

4   Defining the Video Game Usability Model

The term usability has several definitions. In this work, we use the ISO/IEC 25010 (SQuaRE) standard [10] as the basis for defining our Video Game Usability Model. In this standard, three different quality models are proposed: the Software Quality Model, the Data Quality Model and the Quality in Use Model.

The goal of our Video Game Usability Model is to extend the Software Quality Model proposed in SQuaRE, specifically the usability characteristic, for specifying, measuring, and evaluating the usability of video games that are produced throughout a model-driven development process from the end-users perspective. The SQuaRE standard states that the usability of a software product can be decomposed into the following sub-characteristics: *Appropriateness Recognisability*, *Learnability*, *Ease of Use*, *Helpfulness*, *Technical Accessibility* and *Attractiveness*. However, these sub-characteristics are too abstract to be measured in a video game development context.

We therefore propose the decomposition of these sub-characteristics into more representative and measurable usability attributes of video games, and the association of each one of these attributes to specific measures, which can be calculated depending on the characteristics of the software artifact to be evaluated.

4.1   Usability Attributes for Video Game Usability

The decomposition of the aforementioned sub-characteristics into usability attributes is presented as follows, and is summarized in the second column of Table 1. These attributes have been defined by considering and adapting ergonomic criteria for user interfaces [5] as well as knowledge from other domains such as Web development [8], and the underlying usability principles from the existing body of literature in the video game domain [12, 14].

Appropriateness Recognisability contains all the attributes of the video game that ease the understanding of the game. This sub-characteristic is decomposed into the following attributes: *Visibility*, which focuses on visual recognisability, and legibility by measuring the ease of perception of the game's graphic information; *Interface Simplicity* and *Control Simplicity*, which evaluate the complexity of the graphical user interface and the game controls, respectively; and *Consistency*, which focuses on the degree of similitude and coherence between the elements of the video game.

Learnability contains the attributes of the video game that allow players to learn how to play the game. This sub-characteristic is decomposed into the following attributes: *Feedback support*, which focuses on the game capability to provide information about the current state of the game and its players; and *Tutorial Support*, which verifies whether the game offers a tutorial to teach the players how to play it.

Ease of Use contains all the attributes of the video game that facilitate players' control and operation, both inside and outside gameplay. This sub-characteristic is decomposed into the following attributes: *Control Consistency*, which refers to the degree of semantic similitude of the players' actions with regard to the game controls; *Internal Navigational Simplicity*, which refers to how to navigate between the menu options of a single screen; and *External Navigational Simplicity*, which concerns how to navigate between game screens.

Helpfulness contains the attributes of the video game that provide help when the players need it. This sub-characteristic is decomposed into the following attributes: *Hint Support*, which refers to the game's capability to provide useful hints with which to guide the players; and *Goal Support*, which refers to the video game's capability to provide clear goals for the players to pursue.

Technical Accessibility contains all the attributes that allow physically impaired users to play the video game. This sub-characteristic is decomposed into the following attributes: *Subtitle Support*, which refers to the game's capability to provide adequate subtitles for hearing impaired players; and *Magnifier Support*, which concerns the game's capability to provide adequate sized subtitles for visually impaired players.

Attractiveness contains the attributes that make a video game more appealing to the players. This sub-characteristic is decomposed into the following attributes: *Customization*, which refers to how players can alter the game's graphical user interface and controls to fit their preferences; and *Wait Reduction*, which refers to the degree of inactive waiting the players are forced to undergo.

Table 1. Decomposition of the SQuaRE into measurable attributes and generic measures

Sub-characteristics	Attributes	Measures
Appropriateness Recognisability	Visibility	Percentage of Screen Usage
	Interface Simplicity	Total Number of GUI Elements
	Control Simplicity	Total Number of Control Mappings
	Consistency	Ratio of Similitude Between Screens
Learnability	Feedback	Total Number of GUI Elements Displaying State Changes
		Ratio of GUI Elements Highlighting State Changes
		Ratio of Meaningful Messages
	Tutorial Support	Tutorial Interactivity
		Tutorial Coverage

Table 1. (*continued*)

Sub-characteristics	Attributes	Measures
Ease of Use	Control Consistency	Ratio of Similitude Between Colliding Game Actions
	Internal Navigational Simplicity	Internal Menu Navigation Depth
		Internal Menu Navigation Breadth
	External Navigational Simplicity	Shortest Path To Gameplay
		Shortest Path To Exit
		Shortest Return Path To Gameplay
Helpfulness	Hint Support	Availability of Hints
		Hint Understandability
	Goal Support	Goal Visibility
		Goal Understandability
Technical Accessibility	Subtitle Support	Availability of Subtitles
		Subtitle Support for Hearing Impaired Players
		Subtitle Style Differentiation
	Magnifier Support	Subtitle Resize Support
Attractiveness	Customization	Control Remapping
		Interface Customization
	Wait Reduction	Inactive Wait
		Skip Capability of Non-Interactive Content

It is worth to mention that we cannot guarantee that our usability model covers all the possible usability attributes for the video game domain. Our model is an attempt to operationalize subjective heuristics, usability guidelines and recommendations into usability attributes that can be quantified by means of measures. We focused on a set of usability attributes identified by the domain experts.

4.2   Generic Measures for Video Game Usability

Once the measurable usability attributes have been identified, generic measures are then associated with these attributes in order to quantify them. The measures are generic in order to ensure that they can be operationalized in different software artifacts (from different abstraction levels) from different model-driven video game development methods. For the sake of simplicity, only one of the proposed measures from the Video Game Usability Model is presented in Table 2. All the generic measures are summarized in the third column of Table 1.

Table 2. An example of measure from the Video Game Usability Model

Measure	Shortest Return Path To Gameplay (SRPTG)
Attribute	Ease of Use / External Navigational Simplicity
Description	Minimum number of screens that players have to navigate in order to restart the game when the game is over
Formula	Minimum number of steps between the game over screen and the gameplay screen
Scale	Integer greater than or equal to 0
Interpretation	A value of 0 signifies that the game has no menu screens, and players can directly restart when the game is over. Higher values indicate that the players have to navigate many screens before restarting the game.

5   Applying the Video Game Usability Model

In order to apply the Video Game Usability Model to a specific model-driven video game development, we follow a usability evaluation strategy. A typical video game development process consists in the following activities: requirements specification, game design, implementation, and playtesting, along with the usability evaluation. The usability evaluation is conducted by applying the following steps:

1. The Establishment of Evaluation Requirements. The *purpose of the evaluation* as well as all the factors that will condition the evaluation of the game are determined in this phase. *Evaluation profiles* are chosen in order to specify which model-driven game development method is employed, which type of video game is developed, what the target technological platform is, and at which target players the game is aimed. Given a specific model-driven game development method, *software artifacts (models)* and *usability attributes* from the Video Game Usability Model are selected to perform early usability evaluations. The measures associated with the selected attributes are operationalized.

2. Early Usability Evaluation. In this phase, each selected video game software artifact (model) is evaluated according to a set of measures. Each measure provides a numeric value within a specific threshold that indicates whether there is or not a usability problem in the video game. A usability report is consequently generated.

3. Usability Evaluation In-Use. Even when early usability evaluation is performed on video game software artifacts (models), the game should also be further evaluated from the end-users (players) perspective in a specific context of use. This usability-centered playtesting is well documented in the game community [9]. Since this paper focuses on early usability evaluation in model-driven development, usability evaluation in-use is not within the scope of this work.

After usability evaluations, game designers should perform changes to the models in order to solve the usability problems. Early usability problems detected in the game design can be corrected in each model of the corresponding development stage (e.g., PIM, PSM) prior to the code generation.

6   Conclusions

This paper presented a usability inspection method that can be used in early stages of model-driven video game development. The method relies on a usability model that has been developed specifically for the video game domain. This model is aligned with the SQuaRE standard and allows the evaluation of the usability of video games developed according to a model-driven development process.

The inherent features of model-driven development provide a suitable context in which to perform usability evaluations since usability problems that may appear in the final application can be detected and corrected at the model level. Model-driven development also allows automating common usability evaluation tasks that have traditionally been performed by hand. The proposed usability inspection method can also be integrated into any model-driven video game development processes by establishing the relationships between the generic measures from the usability model and the modeling primitives of the different software artifacts of the selected development process.

Nevertheless, we are aware that a further comparison with the users' perception on the usability of a video game obtained by applying a model-driven development process is needed. For this reason, we are currently performing an empirical study to compare the predicted usability of two video games measured using a set of measures from the Usability Model with the perceived usability of these video games measured using a modified System Usability Scale (SUS) [6].

Future works include the empirical validation of the proposed measures with the participation of game software developers, and the empirical validation of the usability model's use in a real industrial model-driven game development project.

Acknowledgments. This research work is funded by the MULTIPLE project (MICINN TIN2009-13838), the FPU program (AP2007-03731) from the MEC-Spain.

References

1. Abrahão, S., Iborra, E., Vanderdonckt, J.: Usability Evaluation of User Interfaces Generated with a Model-Driven Architecture Tool. In: Maturing Usability: Quality in Software, Interaction and Value, pp. 3–32. Springer (2007)
2. Abrahão, S., Insfran, E.: Early Usability Evaluation in Model-Driven Architecture Environments. In: 6th IEEE International Conference on Quality Software (QSIC 2006), pp. 287–294. IEEE Computer Society, Beijing (2006)
3. Ampatzoglou, A., Stamelos, I.: Software engineering research for computer games: A systematic review. Information and Software Technology 52(9), 888–901 (2010) ISSN 0950-5849, doi:10.1016/j.infsof.2010.05.004
4. Andre, T.S., Hartson, H.R., Williges, R.C.: Determining the effectiveness of the usability problem inspector: a theory-based model and tool for finding usability problems. Human Factors 45(3), 455–482 (2003)
5. Bastien, J.M., Scapin, D.L.: Ergonomic Criteria for the Evaluation of Human-Computer Interfaces, version 2.1 (1993)
6. Brooke, J.: SUS - A quick and dirty usability scale. In: Jordan, P.W., et al. (eds.) Usability Evaluation in Industry, pp. 189–194. Taylor & Francis, London (1996)
7. Federoff, M.: Heuristics and Usability Guidelines for the Creation and Evaluation of Fun in Video Games. Indiana University Master of Science Thesis (2002)
8. Fernandez, A., Insfran, E., Abrahão, S.: Integrating a Usability Model into Model-Driven Web Development Processes. In: Vossen, G., Long, D.D.E., Yu, J.X. (eds.) WISE 2009. LNCS, vol. 5802, pp. 497–510. Springer, Heidelberg (2009)
9. Greenwood-Ericksen, A., Preisz, E., Stafford, S.: Usability Breakthroughs: Four Techniques To Improve Your Game. In: Gamasutra (2010), http://www.gamasutra.com/view/feature/6130/usability_breakthroughs_four_.php
10. ISO/IEC 25010: Systems and software engineering, Systems and software Quality Requirements and Evaluation (SQuaRE), System and software quality models (2011)
11. Järvinen, A., Heliö, S. Mäyrä, F.: Communication and Community in Digital Entertainment Services. Prestudy Research Report, Hypermedia Laboratory, University of Tampere, Tampere (2002), http://tampub.uta.fi/tup/951-44-5432-4.pdf
12. Microsoft: Best Practices for Indie Games 3.1, http://create.msdn.com/en-US/education/catalog/article/bestpractices_31
13. Nacke, L.: From Playability to a Hierarchical Game Usability Model. In: FuturePlay at Game Developers Conference, Canada, Vancouver (2009)
14. Nokia: Top Ten Usability Guidelines for Mobile Games. In: Design and User Experience Library v2.0, http://library.forum.nokia.com/topic/Design_and_User_Experience_Library/top10_usability.pdf
15. Pinelle, D., Wong, N., Stach, T.: Heuristic Evaluation for Games: Usability Principles for Video Game Design. In: Proceedings of the Special Interest Group in Computer Human Interaction (SIGCHI 2008), pp. 1453–1462. Association for Computing Machinery (2008)

Lessons Learned from Evaluating the Usability of Mobile Spreadsheet Applications

Derek Flood, Rachel Harrison, and Claudia Iacob

Oxford Brookes University
Gipsy Lane, Oxford, United Kingdom
`{derek.flood,rachel.harrison,iacob}@brookes.ac.uk`

Abstract. It is estimated that 90% of all the analysts in business perform calculations on spreadsheets. Due to advances in technology, spreadsheet applications can now be used on mobile devices and several such applications are available for platforms such as Android and iOS. Research on spreadsheets revolves around several themes, but little work has been done in evaluating the usability of such applications (desktop or mobile). This paper presents lessons learned and usability guidelines derived from laboratory usability testing of mobile spreadsheet applications. Twelve participants were given a task to be solved using a mobile spreadsheet application and based on the video recordings of their interactions with the application patterns of recurring actions and sequences of actions were derived. Navigation, selection, feedback, and transparency of features were some of the main themes in the results of the testing, pointing to a set of guidelines which are also generalizable across other types of mobile applications.

Keywords: Mobile applications, usability guidelines.

1   Introduction

Spreadsheets are widely used for tasks such as inventory administration, educational applications, scientific modeling, financial systems, etc. [1]. It is estimated that 90% of all analysts in business perform calculations on spreadsheets [2], the financial business being the domain where spreadsheets are most used. Due to advances in technology spreadsheet applications may be used on mobile devices, several such applications being available for platforms such as Androids or iOS. A recent study has shown that 79% of the participants (all recruited through the European Spreadsheet Risk Interest Group) required access to a spreadsheet while away from a desktop computer, mostly in the following contexts: a) daily commute, b) demonstrating data to clients, c) inbound email onto a mobile device, d) discussing urgent changes with coworkers [3]. However, the majority of the participants used mobile spreadsheet applications less than once a month, mostly because of the usability challenges such applications bring.

Research on spreadsheets has focused on various aspects, including expanding spreadsheet language through direct manipulation and gestures [4], communicating unit error messages in spreadsheets [5], type inferences for spreadsheets [6],

M. Winckler, P. Forbrig, and R. Bernhaupt (Eds.): HCSE 2012, LNCS 7623, pp. 315–322, 2012.

graph-based visualizations [7], testing [8], and web based spreadsheet-mediated collaboration [9]. However, little work has been done in identifying the usability issues revolving around spreadsheet applications (mobile or desktop-based) and ways to go about resolving them. To address this gap, this paper describes the results of a series of human-centered laboratory usability tests performed on mobile spreadsheet applications, pointing to some of the lessons learned and guidelines applicable to the mobile context design.

2   Related Work

Zhang and Adipat highlighted a number of issues that affect the usability of mobile applications, such as the mobile context, small screen size and different display resolutions, limited processing capability and power and tedious data entry methods [10]. Efforts have been made to look into some of these issues, focusing mostly on mobile web browsing [11, 12, 13] and mobile guides [14]. Schmield et al. describe the results of a multidimensional study which investigates usage scenarios as well as the usability of mobile tailored websites, answering questions such as: what kinds of websites are most often accessed using a mobile phone and who are the users etc. [12]. The findings show (for example) that the typical mobile phone user is male, between 20 and 29, and of the mobile tailored sites investigated, 55% fell in the category 'Information services', while 20% were social networking sites.

A discussion on the optimal information hierarchy for mobile use and the usability effects for reduced screen size is presented in [11]. Slow reading speed, poor comprehension and poor information retrieval performance are just a few of the usability effects reduced screen size brings [15]. Ways of dealing with such issues include adapting the way information is structured in hierarchies [11]. A comparative study of four hierarchies on three different devices found that users preferred narrower hierarchies on all the devices. In [16], a comparative study of zoomable UIs (with and without overviews) used in the context of mobile maps, diagrams, and web pages shows that for zoomable UI overviews the "effectiveness in search tasks is highly dependent on the type of information overviews can provide and on the structure of the considered space". For example, applications involving maps with dynamic content could benefit from zoomable UIs with overviews. The results of a usability study in which users' mobile web browsing experience was evaluated in comparison to desktop web browsing have also been described [13]. All the participants managed to complete all the tasks given to them on the desktop, but only one participant achieved this on the mobile device. Moreover, 80% of the time was dedicated to completing the tasks on the mobile device. Also subjects found it more difficult to correct their mistakes when using the mobile device. Overall, even if the subjects found the changes of the usual page structure on the mobile device easy to understand and learn, they experienced difficulties while interacting with it and this affected their satisfaction.

3   Evaluating the Usability of Mobile Spreadsheets

For evaluating the usability of mobile spreadsheet applications, laboratory usability tests were run with 12 participants, whose actions were video recorded, coded, and further analyzed. The participants were given the task of editing nine cells and locating seven pieces of information located on a given spreadsheet using an iPhone device (which had the Spreadsheet app installed, the most currently used and representative spreadsheet mobile app). Out of the 12 participants, 75% of the participants rated their level of experience with spreadsheets as being intermediate. Only 1 participant (8.33%) rated their level of experience as being novice. As far as experience with the iPhone was concerned, 60% of participants rated themselves as either intermediate or expert. With the exception of one participant, the remaining participants all had experience on other smart phone devices. In terms of age, the majority of participants (42%) were between the age of 21 and 30. During the laboratory tests, the actions of the participants were video recorded while using the mobile spreadsheet application. These recordings were coded for analysis by associating each action with one of the codes depicted in Figure 1. The most often performed action while using the mobile spreadsheet application was scrolling from left to right. This may be explained by two points: 1) Zooming out was performed infrequently (less than 2% of the video fragments being assigned this code) which led to the need to navigate within a spreadsheet using scrolling and 2) There was very little feedback from the application on the participants' actions, so the participants were at times uncertain as to which part of the spreadsheet they were viewing and how this part was related to the rest of the spreadsheet. Navigation was common also between screens, the participants switching from one spreadsheet to another quite frequently.

Figure 1 highlights the high percentage of actions coded with "*sameCellSelect*" (i.e. the user clicks on the same cell they clicked on during the previous action) and "*wrongCellSelect*" (i.e. the user clicks on a different cell than the one they intended to click on). The discussion would also include "*multipleCellSelect*" (i.e. the user clicks on multiple cells at once by mistake) even if the percentage for this is much lower. What often happened was that the participants would aim to select one cell, but they were either selecting another cell close to the one desired or they were not getting any feedback on the action so they tried to select the same cell again to ensure the cell was selected. The percentage of actions coded with "*newCellSelect*" (i.e. the user clicks on the right cell at a first attempt) was just a little bit higher than "*sameCellSelect*". Particularly important, "*actionFeedback*" would mark the times when the participants perceived and were supported by feedback from the application on their interactions with it (e.g. trying to close one spreadsheet, they would be asked for confirmation). However, such occurrences were rare, the distribution of such actions being the lowest. Even so, the participants (with few exceptions) did not give up the task or parts of it.

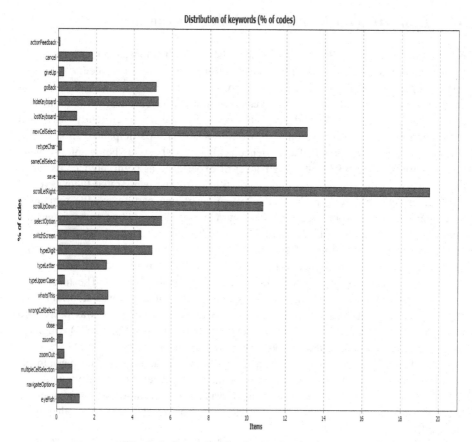

Fig. 1. Action codes distribution for the lab tests

"*Whatsthis*" was used to code actions during which the participants were puzzled by the answer of the application to their actions. Apart for this, the system provided very little feedback, and lacked support for issues such as: a) was the action successful (e.g. Is the background color set?), b) what are the consequences of an action, especially if it was made by mistake (e.g. Selecting the wrong cell), c) where is the cursor located, etc. There was very little use of features such as fisheye, zoom in and zoom out.

In addition to analyzing the frequency of each individual action, we also analyzed the common sequences of actions (Figure 2). Some recurring sequences of actions participants performed bring to light potential issues with the application itself. The act of *Saving* changes indicates that the participant successfully made the desired modifications. In more than a half of the cases, this led to navigating the spreadsheet further on. Navigation was mostly performed through scrolling, zooming actions being performed rarely. In 37.9% of the cases, scrolling from left to right led to more scrolling. This is partially explained by the fact that most of the time a scroll to the left would immediately be followed by a scroll to the right and vice versa. Similarly, scrolling up and down led to more scrolling. Also, not surprisingly, switching to another screen mostly led to navigating within the screen through scrolling actions.

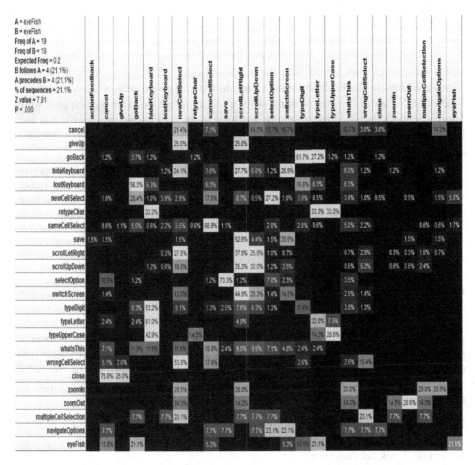

Fig. 2. Sequence code distribution for the lab tests

"*SameCellSelect*" led to the same action in 66.9% of the cases, showing that selecting the same cell over and over again was common. Due to lack of feedback from the application, the participants would select the same cell several times in a row. The maximum repetition of this action was 9 times. Right after selecting a wrong cell (different from the one desired), the participants would select the one desired in more than half of the cases. However, 17.9% percent of the cases point to the situation where the same cell (the wrong one) was selected. Selecting an option (e.g. selecting the background color for a cell) led to saving the modifications in 73.3% of the cases. However, at times, selecting an option would lead to reselecting that particular option. This was partially because the application would provide no feedback leading to confusion on the completion of the action. As an answer to that, the participants would at times try to repeat the action in order to check or validate that the action had been performed. 75% of the cases when the participants intended to close the application were followed by a cancelation of the action. This was particularly interesting since in most cases it was not clear to the participants that the close button would close the whole application and not just the open spreadsheet. Only when asked whether they want to save the work (as result of closing), did it become clear that the close button closes the application entirely. In the majority of cases, the participants would hide the keyboard right after typing some characters because otherwise the keyboard would impede the navigation within the spreadsheet. Preceding *"whatsthis"* coded actions were: a) zooming actions (the participants were uncertain of what caused the zooming and how to go back to the previous state) and b) canceling an action (without any feedback the participants sometimes became confused).

To determine the level of satisfaction participants had, they were asked to complete a SUS questionnaire, the average overall SUS score for the spreadsheet app being 50.42%. In addition to the low score, when asked if they would use the mobile spreadsheet application again, only half of the participants said that they would.

4   Lessons Learned, Guidelines, and Discussion

Based on direct observation and on the results drawn from the study, this section describes a set of 4 guidelines and lessons learned.

1. Make navigation features obvious. The laboratory tests showed that features such as fisheye, or zooming in and/or out were rarely used, leading to poor navigation and overall awareness. Most of the participants were not even aware of the existence of these features. Such features should be clearly signaled such that the user is aware of the full potential of the application.

2. Provide feedback. Feedback supports users in understanding their actions and the impact of their actions in relation to the application. During the study, five types of needed feedback became evident.

a) **Validation feedback.** Once the user performs an action on the application, it is helpful for them to understand whether that was a correct action with respect to the interaction context they are in. For example, selecting a spreadsheet cell should be accompanied by feedback on whether the cell was the right cell or not.

b) **Location feedback.** Due to the small size of mobile devices, it is easy for users to get disoriented with respect to the cursor's location on the screen or to the position of the part they are visualizing in the overall document For such disorientation to be avoided, it is important for the user to be provided with feedback on the location of what they are currently viewing in the overall picture.

c) **Neighborhood feedback.** Participants needed to navigate through the document for extensive periods of time also to become aware of the data contained by the cells surrounding those visible on the screen. Feedback on such information would reduce the users' navigation overload.

d) **Selection feedback.** One of the main issues observed during the study was that the participants were not always sure that the cell they were trying to select was indeed selected. In answer to that, they kept selecting the same cell repeatedly. In part, this problem could be solved by providing feedback once a cell is selected by highlighting its margins or bringing the cell to the front. Similar techniques could be used for applications which use other types of selections.

e) **Keyboard feedback.** The location of the keyboard was not always clear to the participants. At times, they struggled to understand how to hide the keyboard or, on the contrary, how to make it accessible. The application should support the user by providing feedback on the current state of the keyboard at all times.

3. Hints as to the consequences of each action. Users might be unaware of the consequences of some actions and realize only after the action has been performed what it led to. Even worse, in some cases users might not perceive the answer of the application to their action or fail to understand it. Hints on what each action led to would help users. As a concrete example, the color changing of a cell in the spreadsheet application could be modeled as a wizard where all the steps are specified a priori and the user is aware of what the next step is.

4. Provide evident milestones. At times during the study, participants faced difficulties in trying to cancel an action by clicking mistakenly on the button closing the application. It was not always clear how to save, cancel or quit the application and this affected their interaction with the application. Such features should be made evident and distinct, so that at any time during his/her interaction with the application the user is aware of how such features work and how they are different.

5   Conclusions

In this paper, we looked at the results obtained through a pilot study addressing the usability evaluation of mobile spreadsheet applications. We learned that several types of feedback are particularly important when interacting with a mobile application, some of them being feedback on the state and location of the keyboard, feedback on the location of the cursor and on the currently viewed part of the overall document. Also, navigation features should be made evident since only experienced users made any use of zooming or fisheye features. Functions such as saving the work done, closing the application, or canceling an action should be clear and the difference should be made clear to the users. Our results will indicate to mobile spreadsheet application designers some of the difficulties and challenges users face while using such applications.

References

1. Hermans, F., Pinzger, M., van Deursen, A.: Supporting professional spreadsheet users by generating leveled dataflow diagrams. In: Proceedings of ICSE 2011, pp. 451–460 (2011)
2. Winston, W.L.: Executive education opportunities. OR/MS Today 28(4) (2001)
3. Flood, D., Harrison, R., McDaid, K.: Spreadsheets on the move: An evaluation of mobile spreadsheets. In: The European Spreadsheet Risk Interest Group Annual Conference (2011)

4. Burnett, M.M., Gottfried, H.: Graphical definitions: expanding spreadsheet languages through direct manipulation and gestures. ACM Trans. Com-Hum. Interact. 5(1), 1–33 (1998)

5. Abraham, R., Erwig, M.: How to communicate unit error messages in spreadsheets. In: Proceedings of the First Workshop on End-user Software Engineering, pp. 1–5 (2005)

6. Abraham, R., Erwig, M.: Inferring templates from spreadsheets. In: Proceedings of ICSE 2006, pp. 182–191 (2006)

7. Kankuzi, B., Ayalew, Y.: An end-user oriented graph-based visualization for spreadsheets. In: Proceedings of the 4th International Workshop on End-user Software Engineering, pp. 86–90 (2008)

8. Rothermel, G., Burnett, M., Li, L., Dupuis, C., Sheretov, A.: A methodology for testing spreadsheets. ACM Trans. Softw. Eng. Methodol. 10(1), 110–147 (2001)

9. Ginige, A., Paolino, L., Sebillo, M., Shrodkar, R., Vitiello, G.: User requirements for a web based spreadsheet-mediated collaboration. In: Proceedings of AVI 2010, pp. 133–136 (2010)

10. Zhang, D., Adipat, B.: Challenges, Methodologies, and Issues in the Usability Testing of Mobile Applications. International Journal of Hum-Comp. Interaction 18(3), 293–308 (2005)

11. Geven, A., Sefelin, R., Tscheligi, M.: Depth and breadth away from the desktop: the optimal information hierarchy for mobile use. In: Proceedings of MobileHCI 2006, pp. 157–164 (2006)

12. Schmiedl, G., Seidl, M., Temper, K.: Mobile phone web browsing: a study on usage and usability of the mobile web. In: Proceedings of MobileHCI 2009 (2009)

13. Shrestha, S.: Mobile web browsing: usability study. In: Proceedings of Mobility 2007, pp. 187–194 (2007)

14. Kjeldskov, J., Graham, C., Pedell, S., Vetere, F., Howard, S., Balbo, S., Davies, J.: Evaluating the usability of a mobile guide: the influence of location, participants and resources. Behaviour and Information Technology 24(1), 51–65 (2005)

15. Jones, M., Marsden, G., Mohd-Nasir, N., Boone, K., Buchanan, G.: Improving Web Interaction on Small Displays. In: Proc. WWW-8, pp. 1129–1137 (1999)

16. Burigat, S., Chittaro, L., Parlato, E.: Map, diagram, and web page navigation on mobile devices: the effectiveness of zoomable user interfaces with overviews. In: Proceedings of MobileHCI 2008, pp. 147–156 (2008)

ProtoTask, New Task Model Simulator

Lachaume Thomas, Girard Patrick, Guittet Laurent, and Fousse Allan

LIAS / ISAE-ENSMA, University of Poitiers
86961 Futuroscope Chasseneuil Cedex, France
{Thomas.Lachaume,Patrick.Girard,Laurent.Guittet,
Allan.Fousse}@ensma.fr

Abstract. One major objective of task modeling is to improve communication between design stakeholders. Current task model simulators, which require their users to understand task model notations, and provide for inappropriate information, are not really suitable for this topic. We designed ProtoTask, which allows the user to experiment task models by the way of building scenarios, without understanding task model notations. This tool presents new mechanisms that aim at facilitating the understanding of task models for all users.

Keywords: Task Model, Simulation, Human-Computer Interaction, User Experience.

1   Introduction

The interest for task modeling techniques and tools is increasing in the Human Computer Interaction (HCI) community, thanks to their solid theoretical foundations, which allow, for example, the building of automatic transformation approaches. Some task model characteristics allow the models to be executed through tools named simulators. These tools simulate the activity described by the task models according to their semantics, and provide scenarios of execution.

A new area for these tools consists in exploring how they can help in facilitating exchanges between users and designers that aim at expressing the user needs. Nevertheless, simulators usually share the same design, and require task-modeling knowledge to be used and understood by final users [1]; indeed, in these tools, one has to look at the task tree to understand the simulation. This tree has edges with semantic notation. We present here a new tool, ProtoTask, which has been designed specifically to address this new area. It does not need to look at and understand the task model notation, and focuses on information and tasks that specifically address task model validation by end-users.

After a short presentation of the task-modeling field, we present an analysis of existing simulation tools, before detailing and contrasting the ProtoTask approach, which is illustrated on an example.

M. Winckler, P. Forbrig, and R. Bernhaupt (Eds.): HCSE 2012, LNCS 7623, pp. 323–330, 2012.
© IFIP International Federation for Information Processing 2012

2   Task Models and Simulation

Task models are based on the goal/sub-goal decomposition of Norman's theory [2]. Mostly, with task tree, they provide hierarchical representations for the modeling of activity. As any trees, task models have leaves and nodes. Leaves are called elementary tasks, which represent the concrete tasks that can be made during the activity. On the opposite, nodes stand for compound tasks, which are decomposed in two or more subtasks, and are not really included in the activity. They are structuring tasks, which represent the goal/sub-goal decomposition. Depending on the different models, tasks get some attributes such as goal, priority, type, and frequency.

Even if tasks have static attributes for a better understanding, activity is dynamic and includes a lot of indeterminate situations. This dynamics is expressed by scheduling and optional operators, and preconditions[3]. Scheduling operators depend on the model. CTT[4], and HAMSTERS[5] use LOTOS operators. K-MAD[6] and AMBOSS[7] use different operators, which are equivalent to a subset of the CTT's operators. Operators can be expressed between tasks at a same level of decomposition (CTTE) or linked to task decomposition, and common to all sub-tasks (AMBOSS, HAMSTERS, K-MAD, VTMB[8]). Expressiveness of task models can be enhanced by expressions, which manipulate objects.

One of the aims of task models is to improve communication between design stakeholders, end users, HCI experts, and software developers[9]. As for every notation, this point requires all participants to figure out the dynamic behavior of the model, which is the most important topic. In order to help in this task, simulation tools have been designed. They allow concrete examples of scenarios to be run on the model, giving a good understanding of the behavior of the model. Simulators are close to debuggers; they offer a step-by-step execution, and allow users to confirm, deny or simply discuss about the scenario. They are usually part of task design environments, such as CTTE, K-MADe, AMBOSS, HAMSTERS, or VTMB.

The major drawback of simulation tools is that they are designed as tools for task specialists. All the information provided to users is related to the task model. It is necessary for simulator users to lean on the task model itself, and it is not possible to understand the context of the simulated tasks without looking at the task model. Moreover, richer the model, more complex is the layout of the simulator. This is good for designers, who master the notation, and are able to deal with all the shown information. This is not good for end-users who need to learn the task tree notation to understand the simulation and to deal with inappropriate information. A previous study shown that this prerequisite is an obstacle to using task model simulators as a medium of communication between end-users and HCI specialists[1].

Our approach consists in exploring the idea that end users do not need to really understand the task model notation to validate the task analysis. The goal of such a validation can be summarized by two points: (1) the user must be able to run the scenario he/she has in mind, and (2) for each step of the scenario, all different options are legal. For that purpose, we created a tool, ProtoTask, specially designed to promote exchanges between users and designers, which allows building scenarios without showing the task tree. ProtoTask is built on top of, but not linked to, the K-MAD notation.

3   Simulation Tools Analysis

In this section, we describe the usage of simulators, by giving a concrete example. Even if the K-MADe simulator is closer to our solution, we chose to mainly illustrate the simulators by CTTE, the environment for the CTT notation, for two reasons: (1) the K-MADe simulator is the most complex simulator that can be found in task modeling tools, and (2) CTTE is the most widely used tool. Nevertheless, we examine different tools, and try to generalize our study to all approaches.

3.1   A Short Description of the CTTE Simulator

The main goal of simulators is to allow the execution of the model, i.e. running one task after another at the right time, according to the model temporal semantics. The most important visible area within the CTTE simulator is the task tree (cf. zone 1 Figure 1). Once the simulation is launched, the user can see, surrounded by green squares, the *enabled task sets*[3], i.e. the tasks that can be done at present time according to the model semantics. Enabled tasks can only be leaves, i.e. only the most accurate description of the model, and the user must look at the tree to understand the context (e.g. the node task and the operator) and how it is a part of the decomposition. The user can use the enabled tasks (zone 2 Figure 1) panel to search for the task to be run (a click on the enabled task centers the tree on the task in the display).

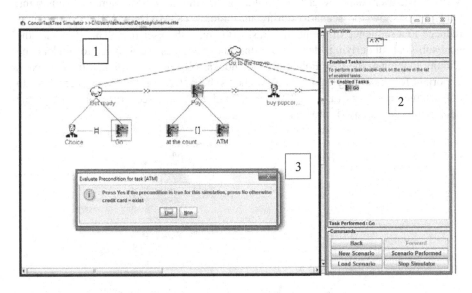

Fig. 1. CTTE simulation tool

In this simulator, the user can easily access the type and the identifier of the task displayed in the tree, but other attributes like description or frequency are not accessible. The operators between tasks are visible too; nevertheless, remembering and understanding these operators needs some apprenticeship time. The precondition system is based on task objects. Conditions are comparisons (equals, differs, contains, ends, starts) between objects or between objects and values are fixed before the simulation. During the simulation, preconditions are displayed in pop-up windows (zone 3 figure 1), which ask the user for the precondition value. The user can answer *yes* or *no*; if the condition is true, the task is added to the enabled tasks sets, if not the task cannot be chosen. The user cannot change his/her choice without starting a new simulation or loading a previous scenario. If the parent task is repetitive for example the question is asked again.

3.2   Simulator Analysis

Using simulators as a basis of discussion between end users and task analysts is hard, because of several simulator design choices that have bad consequences. This section results from preliminary studies we made to experiment the usage of simulators.

Firstly, simulators do not provide for appropriate task information during simulation. Tasks are only known by their name in the model, which stands for a short description. Some simulators hide much information (CTTE) or provide too much information (K-MADe), which makes end-users lost. We assume that some information from tasks, such as a more detailed description of the task, is very important for end-users during validation.

Secondly, scenarios are not directly visible in the simulator, such as for CTTE or VTMB. The user cannot refer to them during the simulation to be sure he/she is right. Other tools show the scenario during its building (K-MADe, AMBOSS), but it is reduced to a sequence of elementary tasks (the ones the user run). This list hides the goal/sub-goal underlying decomposition, and becomes very hard to understand without looking at the tree. Following Go and Carroll[10], we think that the context is important for scenarios. Figure 2 below shows the difference between a scenario with only elementary tasks (as in CTTE or K-MADe), and a scenario that displays the task/subtask hierarchy (ProtoTask).

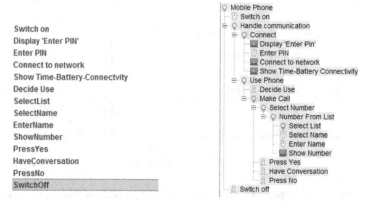

Fig. 2. A simple scenario (left), and the same structured scenario (right)

Thirdly, carrying out a simulation with all simulators requires the user to look at the tree. While it is not a problem for task modelers, other stakeholders need explanations or need learning about notations. More important, the communication is being focused on the task model notation, instead of staying focused on the task model itself, the only thing stakeholders are really interested in.

Lastly, the support for condition execution is not appropriate to end-users. In CTTE, they can give at one time a value (*yes* or *no*) for the condition, which is used during the simulation. If the user needs to use it again (because it is part of a repetitive task, for example), he/she cannot have a remind of its previous value. In K-MADe, expressions lean completely on objects, which leads to very complex manipulations.

4   ProtoTask

In order to switch the primary focus on communication about the activity itself, we designed ProtoTask, a new simulator for task models. Its interface does not display the task tree and allows building scenarios step by step, with a top-down approach (i.e. nodes need to be started and finished). We chose to hide much information such as frequency and duration, because our first experiences show that, in most cases, they are not relevant in the early stage of the software life cycle. On the opposite, we emphasized the full description of the task, which is clearly visible, and concentrated on information that is important for end-users.

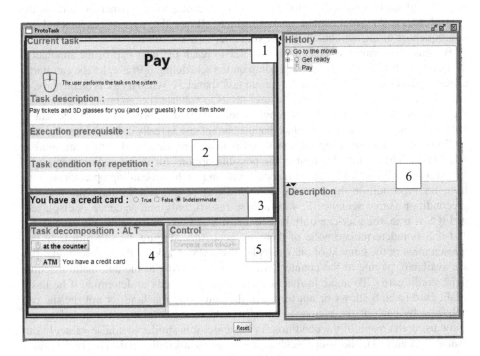

Fig. 3. ProtoTask

The main panel (zone 1 figure 3) represents the current task. The panel is divided into four areas: the task description (zone 2), the condition area (zone 3), the task decomposition area (zone 4), and the control area (zone 5). A second panel (zone 6) shows the scenario being built, under the name of "History".

In Figure 3, the example task model is centered on "going to see a movie". The "History" part shows a tree, with no scheduling operators. It represents the current scenario. Nevertheless, the structure of the tree enhances the parent/child relationship. It displays only started tasks. One can see the main task, "Go to the movie" (in progress), a "Get ready" task, which has been completed (the + symbol at the left indicates that this task is compound), and the current opened task, "Pay". By providing a correct and a hierarchical sequence of tasks, this history can be used as a scenario for designers, but this history is also important for the user to remind the context. By default, only the path of the last task is expanded.

The first panel is completely devoted to the current task. The description area, below the name of the task, refers to the extended description of the task, which allows a good understanding of what the task does. This description can be changed directly in ProtoTask, and saved in the model. Below, the precondition of the current task is displayed, and then, the iteration expression if it exists.

A black border delimits the condition area, which contains both the iteration of the current task (not in the figure), and the precondition of the subtasks that can be started. Conditions are sentences or groups of sentences including OR, AND, and NOT operators. For each task, in the context of the current scenario, the user must state whether a condition is true, false, or indeterminate (default value). Depending on the state of each sentence, buttons in the task decomposition panel (4) and in the control panel (5) are enabled or not, which allows the user to understand the consequences of his/her choices for the reminder of the scenario.

Buttons from panels 4 and 5 allow the user to reach the next step of the simulation. According to his/her choice, and depending on the scheduling operator, he/she can start a subtask (panel 4), finish or repeat the current task (panel 5). When a task is elementary, or when it has no mandatory subtask, the user needs to validate (i.e. no error) and complete the task. No other simulation tool provides this function. It appears very important to confirm, in the end-user mind, the fact that the current task is really correct and completed.

Condition sentences keep their state if the task is repeated and if they are used in other tasks. Their value determines the possible options for the user. For example, if two sub-tasks, T1 and T2, can be launch according to the scheduling operator, and T1 have for precondition the sentence S, with a true result, and T2 have the opposite precondition (same sentence S, with a false result), only one sentence is displayed, and if S is true, the user can only launch T1, if S is false, he/she can only launch T2, and if S is indeterminate none of them are accessible. Figure 4 and 5 illustrate this management in the context of our example. The current task is "Pay". Two modalities are available: paying at the counter (with cash), or paying at the automatic machine (with credit card). To make his/her scenario, the user needs to determine if he has a credit card (which allows or not to pay at the automatic machine) or not (he/she can only pay by cash at the counter). Indeterminate is the default value, and does not allow using the result of the condition; in this case, it is similar to a false value. In our example (figure 4), the user decided he/she owns a credit card. The two options (paying at the counter or by card) are always available, which is correct.

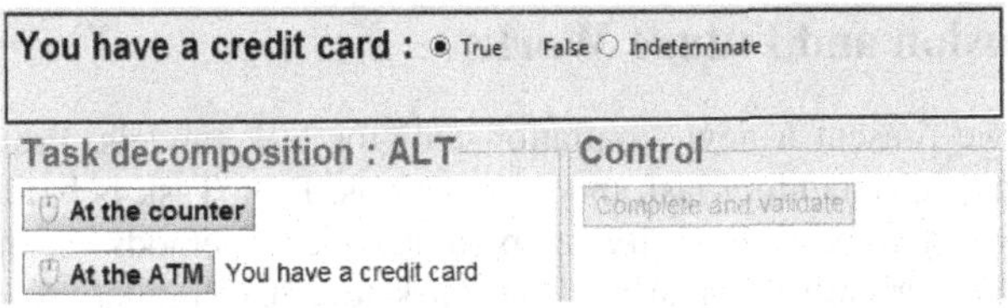

You have a credit card : ● True   False ○ Indeterminate

Task decomposition : ALT	Control
○ **At the counter**	Complete and validate
○ **At the ATM** You have a credit card	

Fig. 4. The context or the "Pay" task, when the user owns a credit card

In fact, the user decided to pay at the counter, choosing the "at the counter" subtask. This is an elementary task, which must be completed and validated explicitly. The next point is illustrated by figure 5: the current task is "Pay" again (it is not explicitly completed). Because its decomposition is "ALT" (a choice, one sub-task among all) the two subtasks are disabled. The "at the counter" has been struck, so, all subtasks are now disabled. The user must complete and validate the task, or decide that the model is wrong, because something else should be done, for example.

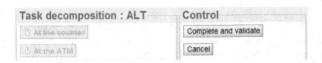

Fig. 5. Explicitly finishing the "Pay" task

When the user clicks on the "Complete and validate" button, the "Pay" task is completed and ProtoTask comes back to the "Go to the movie" task to pursue it with respect to the task model.

ProtoTask differs from other simulation tools into several important aspects.

- Firstly, we chose to highlight the task description. This description is informal and allows writing lot of information such as reference documents, procedures, stories, etc. It can be edited jointly with the end-user during the simulation.
- Secondly, users construct and see their scenario when they perform the simulation, in a structured (tree) way, conforming to the task/subtask decomposition of the model. This feedback helps the user to ensure he/she is right, and can help him/her when he/she is lost, after a discussion or a break for example.
- Thirdly, users do not need to look at and learn about the task tree notation. As early results have shown [11], the user can understand the context better by using a top-down approach and he/she can use the history when he/she is lost.
- Lastly, condition systems are new too, the sentence format allowing to be focused on the task and not on the algorithm; the task modeler can, for example, refer to a document where all conditions are written ("Conditions in document HC53 are verified").

5   Conclusion and Future Works

In this paper, we present a new simulation tool for task models, ProtoTask, which does not require understanding task model notations. ProtoTask is built on top of the K-MAD method, but can be easily adapted to other methods, such as CTT for example. We are currently comparing ProtoTask to other simulation approaches for understanding and validating task models. First result with computer designers [12] showed that for understanding a new model, ProtoTask gets best results than simulators such as CTTE or K-MADe. We need to enhance this study with end-users.

ProtoTask can be improved in several ways. At present time, all features of task models have not been included and we have to study their interest for final users. Multi-actor and parallelism need to be studied cautiously.

K-MADe uses objects for expressing conditions[13]. Instead, Prototask abstracts the conditions. We need to study how we can insert full conditions for later stage of the life cycle, and how the understanding and the validation are impacted.

References

1. Caffiau, S., Guittet, L., Scapin, D.L., Sanou, L.: Utiliser les outils de simulation des modèles de tâches pour la validation des besoins utilisateur: une revue des problèmes. In: ERGO'IA, pp. 257–258. ESTIA, Biarritz (2008)
2. Norman, D.A., Draper, S.W.: User Centered System Design. Lawrence Erlbaum Associates (1986)
3. Paternò, F.: Model-Based Design and Evaluation of Interactive Applications. Springer (2000)
4. CTTE, http://giove.cnuce.cnr.it/ctte.html
5. Hamsters, http://www.irit.fr/recherches/ICS/softwares/hamsters/index.html
6. K-MADe, http://lisi-forge.ensma.fr/forge/projects/kmad
7. Giese, M., Mistrzyk, T., Pfau, A., Szwillus, G., von Detten, M.: AMBOSS: A Task Modeling Approach for Safety-Critical Systems. In: Forbrig, P., Paternò, F. (eds.) HCSE/TAMODIA 2008. LNCS, vol. 5247, pp. 98–109. Springer, Heidelberg (2008)
8. Biere, M., Bomsdorf, B., Szwillus, G.: The Visual Task Model Builder. In: Vanderdonkt, J., Puerta, A. (eds.) Third Conference on Computer-Aided Design of User Interfaces (CADUI 1999), pp. 245–256. Kluwer Academic Publishers, Louvain-la-neuve (1999)
9. Diaper, D.: Understanding Task Analysis for Human-Computer Interaction. In: Diaper, D., Stanton, N.A. (eds.) The Handbook of Task Analysis for Human-Computer Interaction, pp. 5–48. Lawrence Erlbaum Associates, Inc., Mahwah (2004)
10. Go, K., Carroll, J.M.: Scenario-Based Task Analysis. In: Diaper, D., Stanton, N.A. (eds.) The Handbook of Task Analysis for Human-Computer Interaction, pp. 117–134. Lawrence Erlbaum Associates (2004)
11. Lachaume, T., Girard, P., Guittet, L., Fousse, A.: Prototypage basé sur les modèles de tâches: une étude pilote. In: IHM 2011, pp. 2–5. Sophia-Antipolis, France (2011)
12. Lachaume, T., Caffiau, S., Girard, P., Fousse, A., Guittet, L.: Comparaison de différentes approches de simulation dans les modèles de tâches. In: ERGO-IHM 2012. ACM Press (in press, 2012)
13. Caffiau, S., Scapin, D.L., Girard, P., Baron, M., Jambon, F.: Increasing the expressive power of task analysis: systematic comparison and empirical assessment of tool-supported task models. Interacting with Computers 22, 569–593 (2010)

The Usage of Usability Techniques in Scrum Projects

Yuan Jia[1], Marta Kristin Larusdottir[2], and Åsa Cajander[3]

[1] Indiana University, Indiana Avenue 719 Indianapolis, United States
jiayuan@umail.iu.edu
[2] Reykjavik University, Menntavegur 1, 101 Reykjavik, Iceland
marta@ru.is
[3] Uppsala University, Lägerhyddsvägen 2 Uppsala, Sweden
asa.cajander@it.uu.se

Abstract. Over the past decades, usability techniques have been introduced into software development practices. At the same time many software development teams have started to use the agile development process – Scrum – to plan and organize their software projects. The focus of this study is to explore how usability techniques are integrated during software development in Scrum projects. The most commonly used usability technique in Scrum projects is workshops, followed by lo-fi prototyping, interviews and meetings with users, all used by more than half of the participants. The technique that is most frequently used is lo-fi prototyping used by more than half of the participants two to four times a month. All these usability techniques are informal, meaning that these techniques can be used quickly without much preparation. Formal usability evaluation with users is a highly ranked technique by the participants but not commonly used by them.

Keywords: Usability techniques, User centred design, user involvement, usability, agile software development, Scrum.

1 Introduction

Scrum, as one of the agile software development processes, has been gaining popularity in software development over the last few years to plan and organize software development projects [5]. In Scrum the projects are split up in two to four weeks long periods called sprints, each ending up with a potential shippable product that the end users should be able to use right after delivery. In Scrum self organizing and well compounded software development teams are heavily emphasized, typically with six to eight interdisciplinary team members [7]. The main characteristics of the process are simplicity and speed [1] which possibly is one of the reasons for its popularity in industry. One of the benefits of using agile development processes was claimed to be that customers' needs are taken more into account than when developing software using more traditional processes [7]. Traditional Scrum has been criticized for not involving real users in their software process and for not adequately addressing their usability needs [8]. One of the main conclusions in an extensive literature study on the integration of the usability needs into agile processes is that the

M. Winckler, P. Forbrig, and R. Bernhaupt (Eds.): HCSE 2012, LNCS 7623, pp. 331–341, 2012.

end user needs have not yet been sufficiently included in the agile development processes [9].

At the same time as Scrum became popular in industry, the term usability emerged during the mid 1980s, and was accepted in the 1990s by the software industry. This was partly as a response to the new challenges that web-based software - to be used by a large number of diverse users - put on IT (Information Technology) professionals. However, the body of knowledge of usability is large and includes various perspectives from usability engineering to more context-oriented approaches and these have not yet been accepted fully by industry [3].

For the past decade, usability techniques used in various areas in the industry have been studied by researchers. For example, Venturi & Troost [10] studied how User-Centered Design (UCD), one of the main approaches in the usability field, was integrated in software development. Larusdottir et al. [5] studied the effect of using a particular development process in industry on the use of user involvement techniques. In that study, about half of the participants were using their own process to plan their work and about one third were using Scrum as their development process. When asked about, if usability is important the participants using the Scrum process were the most negative ones. The most popular user involvement method was meetings with users used by almost all the participants. The use of user involvement methods varied quite extensively according to which process is used for software development. The results from these studies motivated us to examine the use of usability techniques in projects using one particular process, namely the Scrum process.

This paper describes and discusses the results of a survey study on how usability techniques are being used in software projects using the Scrum process to plan and organize the work. The focus of the study is to explore what usability techniques are used, if the usage of one technique is correlated with the usage of the other techniques, how often the techniques are used and how useful they are for IT professionals. The motivation for the study is to gain understanding of what IT professionals need to be able to integrate usability activities more extensively while using the Scrum process in software development.

2   Background

Several studies have been conducted on how usability techniques are integrated into software development. It has been explored in some of the studies what software development processes are used, but often it is not analyzed how or if the software process affects how usability techniques were used. In this chapter an overview is given of some of the current literature on how usability techniques have been integrated in software development in industry.

Bygstad, Ghinea, and Brevik [3] surveyed professionals working at Norwegian IT companies to investigate the relationship between software development methodologies and usability activities. In their findings, there was a gap between intention and reality. The IT professionals expressed interests and concerns about the usability of their products, but they were less willing to spend resources on it in industrial projects with time and cost constraints. The results of their survey also revealed that the IT professionals perceived usability activities and software development methods to be integrated, which the authors believed is a positive sign.

Bark et al. [2] conducted a survey on the usage and usefulness of HCI methods during different development phases. They examined whether the type of the software projects had any effects on HCI practitioners' perception of the usefulness of the methods. The results show that there was fairly little correlation between the frequency of using a particular technique and how useful it was perceived by the HCI practitioners. One conclusion in the study is that HCI practitioners tend to have a personal and overall evaluation of the different techniques rather than evaluating the actual usefulness of the methods in their daily work when developing particular software.

An international web-based survey by Monahan et al. [6] reported the state of using several field study techniques and how effective they were considered to be by usability practitioners in education and industry. The results show that more than half of the respondents rated observations as an extremely effective method and about 40% of the respondents rated user testing as extremely effective. The most influential factor for choosing a method for participants working in the software industry was time constrains.

Venturi, Troost and Jokela [11] investigated the adoption of user centred design (UCD) in software industry. The results of the study show that the most frequently used method was user interviews. Additionally, hi-fi and low-fi prototyping methods were frequently used. Overall, the most frequently used evaluation methods are qualitative, allowing rapid feedback to the design activities using expert and heuristic evaluation or "quick and dirty" usability test methods. The results also show that UCD methods are typically used during the early phases of the product life cycle.

A survey study on the usage of 25 usability techniques was conducted in Sweden by Gulliksen et al. [4]. The results show that the usability techniques that received the highest rating by the usability professionals were those that were informal, involved users and were concerned with design issues. Techniques such as expert-based evaluations and benchmarking that do not involve users, received the lowest ratings by the usability professionals. There was a general agreement among the participants that it is important to integrate usability techniques into the software development process they were using. Some participants mentioned difficulties during the integration, especially those that were using RUP (Rational Unified Process) as their development process.

3   Research Method

The research method in this study was a questionnaire-based survey. The questionnaire was distributed to IT professionals who were experienced in using Scrum as their software development process and were using usability techniques in their software development.

In the survey we asked IT professionals about their usage of different usability techniques and how useful they rated the techniques. We define usability techniques as the various techniques and methods used in software development to enhance the usability of an IT system.

3.1 Survey Conduction

The survey was constructed in QuestionPro, which is an online survey tool (http://www.questionpro.com/). The survey included 41 multiple-choice questions and 5 open questions. The questions were developed according to a literature review and interviews with two IT professionals experienced in using Scrum.

The list of 13 usability techniques was a result from a literature review based on Gulliksen et al. [4], Venturi et al. [11] and Larusdottir et al. [5]. However, not all techniques from these studies were chosen since we did not want the list to be too long and risk a low response rate. We chose 5 data gathering techniques: interviews, workshops, questionnaires, meetings with users and field studies, three techniques often used for analysis: usability goals, scenarios and personas, two types of design techniques: lo-fi prototyping and digital prototyping and three techniques for evaluation: formal usability evaluations with users, informal evaluations with users and one expert evaluation technique, the heuristic evaluation. With this selection we wanted to cover a wide range of usability techniques used in software development practice today. The respondents were asked if they had used any other techniques. Two participants responded to that question naming one technique each.

The questions in the questionnaire were grouped into four sections: (1) Information on the companies/organizations and experience of the respondents, (2) the Scrum process in one particular project, (3) the usability techniques that have been used in the particular Scrum project and (4) open questions on usability activities.

Two pilot tests were conducted in order to enhance the quality of the survey. The participants were experts in HCI working in the software industry and using Scrum as their development process. To estimate the approximate time for taking the survey, the first pilot test was timed without any interruption. An interview was conducted after the test. Think-aloud method was used in the second pilot test to detect problems while answering the survey.

3.2 Survey Distribution

The survey link was distributed in three different ways. First, the survey link was sent to an email list of software development companies in the Stockholm and Uppsala area. The email list was provided by the Uppsala Tax Office and Lokaldelen, which is a website offering information on companies in Sweden (http://www.lokaldelen.se/). The second way of sending the survey was through directly contacting the target respondents. In order to get more responses, the survey link was also posted on an online discussion group called Scrum Alliance, (http://groups.google.com/group/scrumalliance) which is an international forum for IT professionals using Scrum.

During a period of 40 days, from 25th April 2011 to 4th June 2011, totally 49 respondents responded to the survey and 35 of the participants completed all the questions.

3.3   Respondents

Respondents came from 7 countries around the world. The vast majority, 78% of the respondents came from Sweden, the rest of them came from China (8%), USA (6%), France (2%), Greece (2%), Lithuania (2%) and South Africa (2%).

About 70% of the respondents had a university degree either a Master or a Bachelor degree. Fourteen out of 49 respondents were certified Scrum Masters, which is a particular role while using the Scrum process. The result shows that about 30% of the respondents had programming as their main job role and 20% responded that usability engineering was their main job role. Around 20% of respondents had a management role in their projects. Others worked for example on code design (10%), on requirement gathering (10%) and on UI design (8%). None of the participants indicated that software testing or evaluation was their main job task.

About one third of the respondents were employed at companies or organizations having up to 50 employees, one third of the respondents at companies/organizations having 50-249 employees and one third of respondents in companies/organizations that had more than 250 employees. Over 40% of the IT professionals worked on projects for the Internet or the e-commerce area, around 20% worked in the IT industry in general, about 20% were working in particular domains like in the health and medical sector, telecommunication sector or in the financial sector. Respondents also reported some other business types that were not listed in the question.

In the second part of the survey the respondents were asked to select one particular project to give information on. Seventy present of respondents had been working on multiple projects simultaneously for the last 3 months. When asked about the type of the project that they had selected, about 40% responded that the particular project was web related. About 25% of the professionals were developing software products for sale, around 15% were developing software systems for clients and about 15% were developing internal software systems. The remaining respondents mentioned developing other types of systems, including embedded software systems and hardware systems.

4   Results

This chapter presents the results on what usability techniques are used by IT professionals, how often they use the techniques, how the IT professionals rate the usefulness of the usability techniques and how the usage of one usability technique is correlated with the usage of other usability techniques.

4.1   Usability Techniques Used in Scrum Projects

Before asking about the usability techniques, all techniques were listed and explained to make a common understanding of the steps taken while using the techniques and what the names of the techniques actually meant. In Table 1 the usability techniques are listed according to how many respondents had used them. The results in Table 1 show that workshops are the most commonly used usability technique in Scrum projects followed by lo-fi prototyping, interviews and meetings with users. Heuristic evaluation was used by only 11% of the participants and questionnaires were used by about 20% of the participants. Evaluations with users are not that common, about one fourth of the participants had conducted informal evaluation with users and about one third of the participants had conducted formal usability evaluation with users.

Table 1. The Usage of Usability Techniques

Usability techniques	Used	Total	Percentage
Workshops	30	41	73%
Lo-fi prototyping	20	36	56%
Interviews	25	46	54%
Meetings with users	21	40	53%
Scenarios	17	36	47%
Digital prototyping	17	36	47%
Personas	15	35	43%
Field studies	17	40	46%
Usability goals	15	38	40%
Formal usability evaluation with users	11	36	31%
Informal usability evaluation with users	8	35	23%
Questionnaires	9	42	21%
Heuristic evaluation	4	35	11%

4.2   The Frequency of Using Usability Techniques

The respondents were asked about the frequency of using the usability techniques during one Scrum project. The results from that question are shown in Table 2.

Table 2. The Frequency of Using the Usability Techniques

Usability techniques	Once a week or more	2 -3 times a month	7 – 12 times a year	2 – 6 times a year	Once a year or less	N*
Interviews	9%	13%	22%	44%	13%	25
Questionnaires	0%	0%	0%	25%	75%	9
Workshops	7%	7%	25%	50%	11%	30
Meetings with users	15%	10%	30%	35%	15%	21
Field studies	0%	0%	7%	53%	40%	17
Usability goals	21%	7%	29%	29%	14%	15
Scenarios	24%	24%	18%	24%	12%	17
Personas	6%	19%	13%	25%	38%	15
Digital prototyping	24%	12%	6%	35%	24%	17
Lo-fi prototyping	40%	20%	15%	20%	5%	20
Formal usability evaluation**	0%	0%	18%	82%	0%	11
Informal usability evaluation**	25%	25%	13%	50%	13%	8
Heuristic evaluation	0%	25%	0%	50%	25%	4

* N represents the number of respondents who had used the technique in their projects.
** With users participating.

The technique that is most frequently used is lo-fi prototyping, used once a week by about 40% of the respondents. About half of the participants use scenarios two to four times a month. About 75% of respondents who had used questionnaires said that they used that technique only once a year or less frequently. About 40% of the respondents used personas once a year or less than that. The remaining techniques were used two to six times a year.

4.3   The Ratings of the Usability Techniques

The ratings of how useful the respondents find the usability techniques are presented in Table 3. The participants were asked to rate the techniques on a five-point scale from very good to very bad.

Table 3. The Rating of the Usability Techniques

Usability techniques	Very good	Fairly good	Neither good or bad	Fairly bad	Very bad	N*
Interviews	28%	60%	8%	4%	0%	25
Questionnaires	0%	33%	56%	11%	0%	9
Workshops	38%	62%	0%	0%	0%	30
Meetings with users	38%	57%	5%	0%	0%	21
Field studies	59%	29%	12%	0%	0%	17
Usability goals	53%	20%	27%	0%	0%	15
Scenarios	35%	59%	0%	6%	0%	17
Personas	40%	40%	13%	7%	0%	15
Digital prototyping	59%	30%	12%	0%	0%	17
Lo-fi prototyping	50%	25%	20%	5%	0%	20
Formal usability evaluation**	73%	18%	9%	0%	0%	11
Informal usability evaluation**	25%	75%	0%	0%	0%	8
Heuristic evaluation	25%	50%	0%	25%	0%	4

*   N represents the number of respondents who had used the technique in their projects.
** With users participating.

The result reveals that about 75% of the respondents thought that formal usability evaluation with users was very good and about 60% rated field studies and digital prototyping as very good. Around half of the respondents said usability goals, lo-fi prototyping worked very well. No participant rated questionnaires as a very good technique.

If the ratings "Very good" and "Fairly good" are combined, the top five rated usability techniques used by IT practitioners are: 1) workshops 2) informal usability evaluation with users 3) meetings with users 4) scenarios and 5) formal usability evaluation with users.

4.4   Correlation of the Usage of Usability Techniques

Some significant and interesting correlations were found among the usage of usability techniques in Scrum projects. Results in Table 4 shows that there were totally six usability techniques, which had significant correlations with field studies. These techniques are interviews, workshops, meetings with users, personas, lo-fi prototyping and heuristic evaluation. Interviews are significantly correlated with meetings with users. Questionnaires are significantly correlated with digital prototyping, formal usability evaluation with users and informal usability evaluation with users. Workshops are significantly correlated with personas. Usability goals are significantly correlated with scenarios. Digital prototyping is significantly correlated with heuristic evaluation. Lo-fi prototyping is significantly correlated with personas and formal usability evaluation with users.

Table 4. Correlation of the Usage of Usability Techniques

	Interviews	Questionnaires	Workshops	Meetings with user	Field study	Usability goals	Scenarios	Personas	Digital prototyping	Lo-fi prototyping	Formal usability evaluation	Informal usability evaluation	Heuristic evaluation
Interviews				+	*								
Questionnaires									+		*	+	
Workshops					+			*					
Meetings with users	+				+								
Field studies	*		+	+				+		+			*
Usability goals							+						
Scenarios						+							
Personas			*	+						+			
Digital prototyping		+											+
Lo-fi prototyping					+			+			+		
Formal usability evaluation		*								+			
Informal usability evaluation		+											
Heuristic evaluation					*			+					

+ Represents that the correlation is significant at the 0.05 level.

* Represents that the correlation is significant at the 0.01 level.

Some of these techniques are related in character like meetings with users and interviews could be conducted in a similar way. Furthermore, interviews are often conducted in the field, so the correlation between field studies and interviews could be expected. On the contrary, the correlation between field studies and heuristic evaluation is rather surprising. The fact that there is a correlation between using the techniques does not mean that these techniques are necessarily used at the same time, but that an IT professional is more likely to conduct heuristic evaluation if that person conducts field studies. Furthermore, a correlation between formal usability evaluation with users and digital prototypes could be expected, but formal evaluations are correlated only with lo-fi prototypes. Questionnaires seem to be used in correlation with evaluation with users, both during formal and informal evaluation. Usability goals seem to be stated in correlation with writing scenarios.

5   Discussion

The survey asked the respondents to rate both the usefulness and how often they use the 13 usability techniques. The results show that the top five rated usability techniques used by practitioners are: 1) workshops 2) informal usability evaluation with users 3) meetings with users 4) scenarios and 5) formal usability evaluation with users. This result is partly consistent with the practitioners' perception of the effectiveness of usability techniques in software development projects presented by Gulliksen et al. [4]. The top five rated techniques in that study were: 1) the think-aloud method 2) lo-fi prototyping 3) interviews 4) field studies and 5) scenarios.

Our results show that the top five frequently used usability techniques by IT professionals are: 1) workshops 2) lo-fi prototyping 3) interviews 4) meeting with users and 5) scenarios. This result is also partly consistent with the study from Venturi et al. [11]. Their top five frequently used usability techniques are: 1) user interviews 2) heuristic evaluation 3) qualitative usability evaluations 4) hi-fi prototyping and 5) lo-fi prototyping.

When comparing our results on the top five rated and frequently used usability techniques with those of other studies, it is difficult to draw conclusions regarding the differences. First, the study presented in this paper provided an exact description for each usability technique in the survey, which was not done in the other studies. It may not be viable to compare two ranks of usability techniques when the researchers and the respondents may have had different understanding of what it includes to use a particular usability technique. Secondly, the usability techniques used in the different studies were not the same. For example, workshops are rated as the top usability technique in this study, but workshops are not included in the study by Gulliksen et al. [4]. Moreover, all the usability techniques mentioned in this study were used in software project using the software development process Scrum, but the other two papers are about software development in general.

However, despite these differences some interesting things are worth noticing when comparing the results from the studies. The results from this study show that heuristic evaluation is not often used but the techniques get reasonable ranking in this study and the results from Venturi et al. [11] show that heuristic evaluation was one of the top five frequently used techniques. One possible explanation to this difference is that heuristic evaluation may not fit well in the Scrum process. Another possible reason is that the usage of heuristic evaluation as an evaluation method has been decreasing in software development in general, and that the survey results from this study, which was conducted in 2011, indicate a general trend.

The usefulness rated by the participants and the frequency of using the techniques are not correlated. For example, about 75% of the respondents consider the technique formal usability evaluation with users very good, but only about 30% used it in their projects. One possible explanation for this inconsistency is that the most important characteristic of Scrum is speed. The duration of one Scrum sprint usually last two to four weeks, but sometimes practitioners need longer time to use a particular usability technique. It usually takes practitioners long time to prepare formal usability testing, recruit participants and conduct the tests, for example.

The techniques digital prototyping and field studies were also rated highly and used two to six times a month. Still, these techniques were only used by one third of the respondents. The technique lo-fi prototyping is more frequently used than the technique digital prototyping. Still the usefulness of digital prototypes was higher ranked than the usefulness of lo-fi prototyping. One of the main advantages of lo-fi prototyping is its quickness and accessibility to any team member in the development process. One explanation could be the focus on speed during Scrum projects.

As shown in the results of the correlation among usability techniques, field studies are significantly correlated with interviews, workshops, meetings with users, personas, lo-fi prototyping and heuristic evaluation. Field studies can help collecting and preparing interview questions and the technique interviews also can provide some valuable information for the process of the field studies. The correlation between field studies and heuristic evaluation is more surprising, because these types of evaluations are rarely conducted in the field. Furthermore, the knowledge that is needed to use the two techniques is not that related. Another technique – formal usability evaluation with users – has strong correlation with the technique questionnaires. One reasonable explanation is that questionnaires can be used to prepare the test tasks or as a post-test survey for the formal usability evaluation with users. Formal evaluation has also a correlation with lo-fi prototypes, which is positive, because it has been suggested in the HCI literature for many years that evaluations should start as soon as possible during the software development.

6   Conclusions

This study investigates the integration of usability techniques in software projects using the Scrum process in industry. The findings from the study indicate that the technique workshops are the most commonly used usability technique in Scrum projects, followed by: lo-fi prototyping, interviews, meetings with users and scenarios. Besides, the top five highest rated usability techniques according to usefulness for the IT professionals are: 1) workshops 2) informal usability evaluation with users 3) meetings with users 4) scenarios and 5) formal usability evaluation with users. A novel contribution of this study is that there were significant correlations of the usage among different usability techniques in Scrum projects. If IT professionals use workshops they are more likely to use personas is an example of these correlations.

Acknowledgements. We would like to thank all the participants in the study that took their time in answering the questionnaire. Additionally, we would like to thank the PhD student Simon Tschirner and the former PhD students Niklas Hardenborg and Stefan Blomkvist in Human Computer Interaction in Uppsala University for taking part in piloting the questionnaire. Furthermore, we would like to thank the research and teaching assistant Tao Yang at School of Informatics in Indiana University in U.S. for his valuable comments when reviewing the paper.

References

1. Abrahamsson, P., Warsta, J., Siponen, M.T., Ronkainen, J.: New Directions on Agile Methods: a Comparative Analysis. In: Proceedings of the 25th International Conference on Software Engineering. IEEE Computer Society, Los Alamitos (2003)
2. Bark, I., Følstad, A., Gulliksen, J., McEwan, T., Benyon, D.: Use and usefulness of HCI methods: Results from an exploratory study among nordic HCI practitioners. In: People and Computers XIX - The Bigger Picture, pp. 201–217. Springer, London (2006)
3. Bygstad, B., Ghinea, G., Brevik, E.: Software development methods and usability: Perspectives from a survey in the software industry in Norway. Interacting with Computers 20(3), 375–385 (2008)
4. Gulliksen, J., Boivie, I., Persson, J., Hektor, A., Herulf, L.: Making a Difference: A Survey of The Usability Profession in Sweden. In: Proceedings of NordiCHI 2004, Tampere, Finland, pp. 207–215 (2004)
5. Larusdottir, M.K., Haraldsdottir, O., Mikkelsen, B.: User involvement in Icelandic software industry. In: Proceedings of the I-Used 2009 Workshop at INTERACT 2009, Uppsala, Sweden, pp. 51–52 (2009)
6. Monahan, K., Lahteenmaki, M., Mcdonald, S., Cockton, G.: An Investigation into the use of Field Methods in the Design and Evaluation of Interactive Systems. In: Proceedings of the 22nd British HCI Group Annual Conference, People and Computers, pp. 99–108 (2008)
7. Schwaber, K.: Scrum development process. In: OOPSLA 1995 Workshop on Business Object Design and Implementation (1995)
8. Singh, M.: U-SCRUM: An Agile Methodology for Promoting Usability. In: Proceedings of the AGILE 2008 Conference, Toronto, Canada, pp. 555–560 (2008)
9. Sohaib, O., Khan, K.: Integrating usability engineering and agile software development: A literature review. In: Proceedings of the ICCDA 2010 - International Conference on Computer Design and Applications, Qinhuangdao, Heibei, China (2010)
10. Venturi, G., Troost, J.: Survey on the UCD integration in the industry. In: Proceedings of the NordiCHI 2004 Conference, Tampere, Finland, pp. 449–452 (2004)
11. Venturi, T., Troost, J., Jokela, T.: People, organizations, and processes: An Inquiry into The Adoption of User-Centered Design in Industry. International Journal of Human-Computer Interaction 21(2), 219–238 (2006)

Usability Reporting with UsabML

Johannes Feiner[1] and Keith Andrews[2]

[1] FH JOANNEUM, Internet Technology,
Werk-VI-Straße 46, 8605 Kapfenberg, Austria
Johannes.Feiner@fh-joanneum.at
http://www.fh-joanneum.at/itm
[2] Graz University of Technology, Inffeldgasse 16c, 8010 Graz, Austria
kandrews@iicm.edu
http://www.iicm.tugraz.at/keith

Abstract. Usability practitioners conduct formative evaluations, such as heuristic evaluations and thinking aloud tests, to identify potential problems in a user interface as part of the iterative design cycle. The findings of a formative evaluation (in essence, a list of potential problems) are usually compiled into written reports and typically delivered as a PDF or Word document. A written report is convenient for reading, but makes it difficult to reuse the findings electronically. The usability markup language (UsabML) defines a structured reporting format for the results of usability evaluations. In agile software development the direct handover of usability findings to software engineers can speed up development cycles and improve software quality.

Usability managers can now enter the findings of formative evaluations into a new, web-based system called Usability Reporting Manager (URM). Findings can be exported in UsabML format, which in turn can easily be imported by software engineers into an issue-tracking system connected to a source code repository. UsabML can also be transformed into other formats such as HTML and PDF via stylesheets (XSL).

Keywords: formative evaluation, usability findings, exchange, XML, reporting format.

1 Introduction

Formative usability studies form an integral part of iterative software design and development. Heuristic evaluations or thinking aloud tests, for example, can help identify problems in a user interface. Usability practitioners typically compile the findings and deliver them as a written report, say in PDF format. This paper discusses the UsabML format and its applications to usability reporting, particularly with regard to reuse of usability data during software development.

The are many examples of written report styles for formative tests, for example Molich et al. [1] and the NIST IUSR Formative Project [2]. There is even an ISO standard [3] for written reports of summative tests (formal experiments). However, results on paper or in written reports are hard to reuse (see Figure 1).

M. Winckler, P. Forbrig, and R. Bernhaupt (Eds.): HCSE 2012, LNCS 7623, pp. 342–351, 2012.
© IFIP International Federation for Information Processing 2012

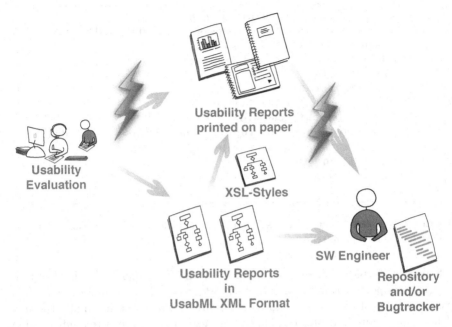

Fig. 1. Life-cycle of evaluation reports: The information exported via UsabML can be processed by other systems. For example, software engineers can import findings into a bug-tracking system.

It is difficult to import the findings into other systems, such as bug-tracking systems used by software engineers. In the age of agile development, fast feedback cycles are essential. The ability to automatically import usability findings into the issue-tracking systems associated with software code repositories would be extremely valuable.

The definition of the UsabML usability reporting exchange format is an important step towards formalising the reporting of usability results and will greatly simplify the handover of such findings to software development teams.

2   The UsabML Markup Language

For exchange of data, the extensible markup language (XML) is convenient, because XML can be readily parsed with standard tools and is extensible to further functionality without breaking existing code. Formulating UsabML in XML guarantees not only well-formed XML documents, but allows documents to be validated against the XSD schema provided. A tree hierarchy of tags defines the sections, subsections, and details for the various parts of typical usability evaluation reports. Tags hold their main information as XML text nodes. Tag attributes are used only for computer generated information or meta-information, such as unique identifiers, references to other tags, and sort-order.

```
 1  ?xml version=" 1.0 " encoding="UTF-8" ?>
 2  <xs:schema xmlns:xs=" http://www.w3.org/2001/XMLSchema"
        attributeFormDefault=" qualified ">
 3    <xs:element name=" project ">
 4      <xs:complexType>
 5        <xs:sequence>
 6          <xs:element name=" title " />
 7          <xs:element name=" description " />
 8          <xs:sequence id=" reports " maxOccurs=" unbounded ">
 9            <xs:element ref=" report " />
10          </xs:sequence>
11        </xs:sequence>
12        . . .
```

Listing 1.1. Top elements of the schema definition file hold information about the project and one or more reports

Separate UsabML schemas are defined for the two different kinds of reports currently supported: thinking aloud (TA) test and heuristic evaluation (HE). The overall outline of UsabML is shown in Figure 2, where the internal structures of heuristic evaluation and thinking aloud test reports are listed side-by-side, so differences within the schemas become evident. Within a schema, only very few sections are marked as **required** to give users of the UsabML standard more freedom to omit parts they do not require. The detailed schemas can be found online at the project web site [4]. Roughly speaking, the structure shown in Listing 1.1 is enforced by each schema. In particular:

- The root xml tag **project** (see Listing 1.1) holds general information (title, description) about a software project and one or more usability reports.
- The **report** xml tag specifies the kind of evaluation (for example "TA" or "HE"), further meta-information ("generated" timestamp), and the main report contents. This includes first the **title**, date/time of the report, **author**(s), **description** and **summary**, a general **introduction** and a description of the **methodology**. Some of these tags may hold pre-formatted text, which is used later as introductory text in the generated PDF or HTML reports.

For a HE report, the **heuristics, evaluators** their **environment** come next, followed by the **heuristicissues**:

- A **heuristic** section provides a fixed list of (about ten) heuristics. Many practitioners use those suggested by Jakob Nielsen [5]. More specialised sets of heuristics are sometimes used when evaluting specific kinds of interface, such as mobile devices or information dashboards.
- The **heuristicissues** section stores the positive and negative findings of the HE evaluators. Detailed information about findings including their **severity** and steps to **reproduce** them can be entered.

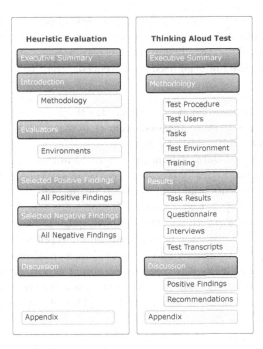

Fig. 2. The internal structure of heuristic evaluation and thinking aloud test reports

For a TA report, the `users`, `testenvironment`, `tasks` and `questionnaire` sections follow the introductory part. The findings are available in detail in the sections named `taskresults` and `questionnaireresults`:

- The `users` section holds several TA test `persons` with their profile (`gender`, `education`, `itexperience` and so forth). Information about test users is connected to the `video` clip(s) of their thinking aloud test.
- An `environment` section allows the specification of the environment used for the TA test, including the location and any hardware (computers, monitors, cameras) and software (screen capture) used.
- The section `tasks` denotes the tasks prepared in advance by the test team for the test users. A task requires a `title`, `description`, and `prerequisites` as well as `possilbesolutionpath`, `endingcriteria`, and `scheduledduration`.
- Details of the element `taskresult` are `start`, `end`, `actualduration`, and percent of `completion`.
- A `questionnaire` represents a list of `questions` and information about any rating scale (Very easy – Very hard) used. The answers to the questions are normalised values (say, points from 0 to 6 for a 7-point rating scale) stored for each answer per user.
- For each user, an `interview` and a `testtranscript` may optionally be provided.

The final part of a report are the `discussion` section, which contains an interpretation of the evaluation results, and an `appendix`:

- The `discussion` section holds information about findings, including a list of recommendations. For a TA as well as for a HE report, there is the possibility to store details like `video` clips and `codereferences`.
- In the `appendix` the material used is referenced. URLs to online resources are given.

Several tags, for example `heuristicissues`, `findings`, or `transcript-logs`, are designed to hold one or more (`codereference`) items, indicating a source code location (say, a potential origin of a bug).

With all this detailed data at hand, it is easy to automatically generate both comprehensive and aesthetically pleasing reports, in say HTML or PDF formats. Note, that not all elements hold numeric information such as numbers and dates, many hold descriptive free text passages. Reports are generated by applying a stylesheet (XSL) transformation to the UsabML data. Different XSL stylesheets might be provided to generate highly customised reports for different target groups. For example, managers might generate just a short report with executive summary and a main overview. Programmers might export prioritised bug lists. Other stylesheets allow the generation of comma-separated values (CSV) files of selected data for later statistical analysis. Stylesheets to generate HTML are available at the project web site [4].

3   Usability Reporting Manager

To create a report in UsabML, evaluation managers could hand-edit XML directly. A more comfortable alternative is to use web-based software called the Usability Reporting Manager (URM). URM provides a web interface to enter, manage and export data in UsabML and is shown in Figure 3. Optionally, the exported reports can be styled with stylesheets for rendering in browsers as HTML.

The main web page is shown in Figure 4a and the details for entering information about recommendations can be seen in Figure 4b. The equivalent information rendered in HTML can be seen in Figure 4c. Further formats can be created simply by adding further style sheets (XSL files).

The URM software is open source and can be downloaded from the GIT repository [6]. More detailed specifications and documentation is available from the project web site [7].

4   Reuse and Exchange of Usability Findings

UsabML is great for reuse and exchange, because it is standardised XML and can be processed accordingly. It is easy to parse the files and data points can be extracted automatically at any given time. It is possible, for example, to imagine tools to compare evaluation results from different studies, like a `diff` on two data sets in respect of number of findings or severity of findings. This would allow

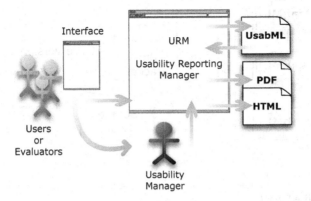

Fig. 3. URM enables evaluation managers to enter reporting data via a web interface

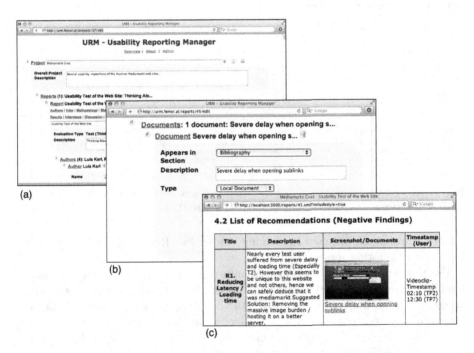

Fig. 4. (a) URM allows management of reports in a single, interactive AJAX and HTML5 enabled page. (b) Multimedia information, for example recommendations with screenshots and videos, can be entered. (c) The browser renders XML with selected XSL for pretty printing.

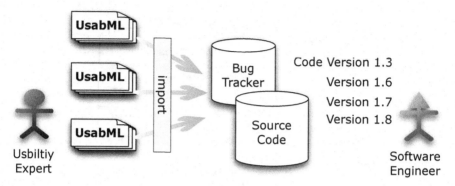

Fig. 5. Handover of evaluation results between different domains becomes possible by using standardised XML

Ticket #659 (new enhancement)

Modify ↓

Reducing Latency / Loading Time			Opened **44 seconds ago**
Reported by:	johannes.feiner@...	Owned by:	TA 1
Priority:	major	Milestone:	milestone1
Component:	component1	Version:	1.0
Keywords:	Interface, Usability	Cc:	
Release Notes:			
API Changes:			

Description

Nearly every test user suffered from severe delay and loading time (Especially T2). However this Reply
seems to be unique to this website and not others, hence we can safely deduce that it was mediamarkt
Suggested Solution: Removing the massive image burden / hosting it on a better server.

Fig. 6. Automated import into bug tracking systems becomes possible with scripts using web services to create new tickets out of UsabML

a more automated approach to running studies like Rolf Molich's Comparative Usability Evaluation series [8].

UsabML supports the exchange of information between different domains. Usability testers can hand over their findings to software engineers, who then integrate the findings automatically into their bug tracking system. That is a huge improvement over reports on paper, where bugs must be extracted and entered into bug tracking systems manually. We are currently working on import tools (see Figure 5) for well-known open source bug tracking systems such as Trac, Bugzilla, and Mantis. Automated import can be accomplished by converter scripts which parse UsabML and submit new issues via XML-RPC (Trac, Bugzilla), ReST (Bugzilla), or a SOAP web service (Mantis) as appropriate. The finding (problem report) shown in Figure 4c is converted into a corresponding Trac ticket in Figure 6.

5   Related Work

The importance of usability evaluation in general was promoted by Nielsen [9]. The use of usability evaluation to increase the quality of software is discussed in many papers such as Komiyama or Law [10,11]. Many books [12,13,14,15] advocate the use of usability methods. Howarth et al [16] discuss the need for tool support, especially for novice usability practitioners.

A collection of the most common usability evaluation methods is described in detail in Andrews [17]. For formative usability evaluation, the two classical methods are heuristic evaluation (HE) and thinking aloud (TA) testing. Both are supported by UsabML to manage and generate reports. A standard written report structure for reporting the results of summative evaluations (formal experiments) was developed by NIST as the Common Industry Format (CIF) [18] and is now an ISO standard [3]. A similar effort to standardise written reports of formative evaluations was started under the name IUSR Formative Project [2], but has yet to produce a draft standard (Theofanos [19]).

The Extended Structured Problem Report Format (ESPRF) for capturing problem reports during a usability inspection (heuristic evaluation) was introduced by Cockton et al. [20]. However, each ESPRF covers the reporting of a single problem rather than an entire structured report, and furthermore is limited to the case of heuristic evaluation.

The general idea of a markup language for usability findings to promote their electronic reuse was proposed in previous work by Feiner, Andrews and Krajnc [21].

As shown with the Usability Reporting Manager URM, evaluation managers can automate parts of their workflows using software tools. Loitzl [22] presents a web based software tool for data collection and reporting when performing heuristic evaluations.

UsabML generated out of URM focuses on formative evaluation and differs therefore from Wilson et al. [23] and Spacco et al. [24] who view issues more or less as standard software bugs.

Wilson et al. compare the approach of storing usability issues directly in the standard bug tracking system with the technique of creating a dedicated usability issues database. With URM we provide a standalone usability issues database with the possibility to export into bug databases, hence both approaches are supported.

Spacco implemented the idea of comparing issues from one software version to another by creating extensions for code analysis tools. In contrast, the UsabML format prepares for comparison between versions of usability evaluation data in a tool agnostic way, requiring XML comparison feature only.

6   Concluding Remarks

UsabML defines a new standard file format for formalised usability reporting. The XML format allows easy reuse of formative evaluation reports. It provides advantages for structuring a report and for transforming usability reports into different formats. Furthermore, it has the built-in possibility to store cross-references from usability findings to corresponding source code locations (these cross-references must be established manually by project managers). UsabML has the potential to bridge part of the gap between usability specialists and software developers and improve overall software quality.

With the URM web application, UsabML can be created on a server by entering data through the web. The information is stored in a central database and can be modified or appended any time. On demand, one or several reports in different formats can be generated. So, in future, a cycle of creation and reuse is feasible. The electronic handover (see Figure 5) of usability findings to software engineers is now becoming possible.

Although UsabML as described currently only supports the generation of HE and TA reports, it can of course in future be extended analogously to cover other forms of formative evaluation, such as cognitive walkthrough.

UsabML and URM will be evaluated in the near future during an upcoming project with industry partners. A case study will demonstrate the potential advantages of reusing usability data for development of real world software applications.

The UsabML specification, schema files, and example reports are available at the project web site [4].

References

1. Molich, R., Chattratichart, J., Hinkle, V., Jensen, J.J., Kirakowski, J., Sauro, J., Sharon, T., Traynor, B.: Rent a Car in Just 0, 60, 240 or 1,217 Seconds? — Comparative Usability Measurement, CUE-8. Journal of Usability Studies 6(1), 8–24 (2010), http://www.upassoc.org/upa_publications/jus/2010november/JUS_Molich_November_2010.pdf
2. NIST: Common Industry Format (CIF) IUSR Formative Project. National Institute of Standards and Technology (2010), http://zing.ncsl.nist.gov/iusr/formative/
3. ISO: SO/IEC 25062:2006 Software Engineering – Software Product Quality Requirements and Evaluation (SQuaRE) – Common Industry Format (CIF) for Usability Test Reports. International Organization for Standardization (2006), http://www.iso.org/iso/iso_catalogue/catalogue_tc/catalogue_detail.htm?csnumber=43046
4. Feiner, J., Andrews, K.: UsabML: The Usability Markup Language (2010), http://usabml.fh-joanneum.at
5. Nielsen, J.: Ten Usability Heuristics (1994), http://www.useit.com/papers/heuristic/heuristic_list.html
6. Feiner, J., Andrews, K.: github - Usability Reporting Manager (2012), https://github.com/internettechnik/urm
7. Feiner, J., Andrews, K.: URM - Usability Reporting Manager (2012), http://itm.fh-joanneum.at/usabml/urm
8. Molich, R.: CUE - Comparative Usability Evaluation (2012), http://www.dialogdesign.dk/CUE.html

9. Nielsen, J.: Usability Engineering. Morgan Kaufmann (1993) ISBN 0125184069
10. Komiyama, T.: Usability Evaluation Based on International Standards for Software Quality Evaluation. Technical Report 2, NEC (2008),
    http://www.nec.co.jp/techrep/en/journal/g08/n02/080207.pdf
11. Law, E.L.C., Hvannberg, E., Cockton, G.: Maturing Usability: Quality in Software, Interaction and Value. Springer (2007) ISBN 1846289408
12. Barnum, C.M.: Usability Testing Essentials: Ready, Set...test. Morgan Kaufmann (2010), ISBN 012375092X,
    http://booksite.mkp.com/barnum/testingessentials/
13. Krug, S.: Don't Make Me Think!: A Common Sense Approach to Web Usability, 2nd edn. New Riders (2005) ISBN 0321344758,
    http://www.sensible.com/dmmt.html
14. Rubin, J.B., Chisnell, D.: Handbook of Usability Testing: How to Plan, Design, and Conduct Effective Tests, 2nd edn. John Wiley & Sons (2008) ISBN 0470185481
15. Stone, D.L., Jarrett, C., Woodroffe, M., Minocha, S.: User Interface Design And Evaluation. Morgan Kaufmann (2005) ISBN 0120884364
16. Howarth, J., Smith-Jackson, T., Hartson, R.: Supporting Novice Usability Practitioners With Usability Engineering Tools. Int. J. Hum.-Comput. Stud. 67(6), 533–549 (2009), doi:10.1016/j.ijhcs.2009.02.003
17. Andrews, K.: Evaluation Comes in Many Guises. In: CHI 2008 Workshop on BEyond Time and Errors: Novel evaLuation Methods for Information Visualization, BELIV 2008 (2008),
    http://www.dis.uniroma1.it/beliv08/pospap/andrews.pdf
18. NIST: Common Industry Format for Usability Test Reports. National Institute of Standards and Technology (1999),
    http://zing.ncsl.nist.gov/iusr/documents/cifv1.1b.html
19. Theofanos, M., Quesenbery, W.: Towards the Design of Effective Formative Test Reports. Journal of Usability Studies 1(1), 28–45 (2005),
    http://www.usabilityprofessionals.org/upa_publications/
    jus/2005_november/formative.pdf
20. Cockton, G., Woolrych, A., Hindmarch, M.: Reconditioned Merchandise: Extended Structured Report Formats in Usability Inspection. Extended Abstracts on Human Factors in Computing Systems (CHI 2004), pp. 1433–1436. ACM (2004), ISBN 1581137036, doi:10.1145/985921.986083
21. Feiner, J., Andrews, K., Krajnc, E.: UsabML - The Usability Report Markup Language. In: Proc. 2nd ACM SIGCHI Symposium on Engineering Interactive Computing Systems (EICS 2010), pp. 297–302. ACM (2010) ISBN 1450300839, doi:10.1145/1822018.1822065
22. Loitzl, M.: The Heuristic Evaluation Manager (HEM). Master's Thesis, Institute for Information Systems and Computer Media (IICM), Graz University of Technology (2006), http://www.iicm.tugraz.at/thesis/mloitzl.pdf
23. Wilson, C.E., Coyne, K.P.: The Whiteboard: Tracking Usability Issues: To Bug Or Not To Bug? Interactions 8(3), 15–19 (2001), doi:10.1145/369825.369828
24. Spacco, J., Hovemeyer, D., Pugh, W.: Tracking Defect Warnings Across Versions. In: Proc. International Workshop on Mining Software Repositories (MSR 2006), pp. 133–136. ACM (2006) ISBN 1595933972, doi:10.1145/1137983.1138014

Visualizing Sensor Data: Towards an Experiment and Validation Platform

Claudia C. Gutiérrez Rodriguez and Anne-Marie Déry-Pinna

I3S – CNRS - University of Nice - Sophia Antipolis
930 route des colles – BP 145, 06902 Sophia Antipolis, France
{cgutierr,pinna}@i3s.unice.fr

Abstract. In the last decade, technological improvement on sensors increasingly motivates the use of sensor data in numerous application domains such as environmental, health, transportation, etc. Progressively, with the advances on user terminals, there is a strong trend towards interactive sensor data visualization. As viewing raw sensor data stored in multiple databases does not specially fulfill user requirements, data visualization raises challenges about supporting users to easily use and handle sensor data. In this paper, we address this particular subject with an extensible visualization and interaction platform. Within this platform, we provide developers the facility to experiment and validate multiple visualizations for sensor data, specially based sensor data properties and users' requirements. We illustrate our platform with a medical study case focused on ECG data visualization.

Keywords: Information Visualization, HCI, Sensor Data, Medical Applications, Experimentation platform.

1   Introduction

Nowadays, data visualization is increasingly resorted considering the tremendous benefits by creating, exploring and interacting with large collections of data. Visualization currently supports several tasks such as medical diagnosis [1,2], training simulations [3] or architectural reconstructions [4], as well as monitoring streams of data coming from sensors employed on several application domains like transportation or environmental [5].

Even if different visualization techniques and forms (i.e. charts, maps…) have been proposed to support both, use and interaction over large amounts of data [6], visualization of sensor data fulfilling users' requirements is not a simple task. It implies several challenges and requires different elements, such as: a good comprehension of data itself (e.g. properties and structure), a deep understanding of basic HCI and the principles that underline them, together with a proper interpretation of the potential usages of these data by experts.

In this paper, we address these challenges with a platform oriented to experiment and validate multiple visualizations for sensor data. The main goal of this platform is to provide users (i.e. developers and experts) with a tool capable to assist them in the definition and design of possible sensor data visualizations and interactions for

M. Winckler, P. Forbrig, and R. Bernhaupt (Eds.): HCSE 2012, LNCS 7623, pp. 352–359, 2012.

particular usage contexts. With this platform, users are able to evaluate the accuracy of possible visualizations, identify new functionalities or specializations being useful to adapt and increasing the usage capabilities.

This paper is organized as follows: Section 2 discuss approaches on visualization techniques for sensor data. Section 3 introduces the specificities of our extensible platform. In Section 4, we explain how the platform is used for extensibility in a medical case study managing data coming from an Electrocardiogram (ECG). Finally, Section 5 presents our conclusions and future work.

2   Overview

Visualization is an important mechanism when working with large amounts of data as sensor data. It makes more comfortable for users to interact within, as for select or filter data of interest, data can be understood faster and easier [3,6]. However, visualizing sensor data is not a trivial task. Multiple views of sensor data can be extracted according to several aspects such as context of use, users' requirements, data properties, etc., and thus several questions arise such as: *How sensor data can be reasonable visualized?*

In the last few years, more and more interactive tools have been proposed to support users (i.e. domain experts) exploring and presenting data that might be stored, analyzed or simulated [7,8]. The information analysis on such interactive tools is supported by user interfaces based on visualization and interaction techniques, visual design, human perception and cognition understanding [9]. According to [10], the challenges of this kind of tools are to visualize in a way that balances complexity with conciseness and accuracy with essence. They must avoid providing confuse pictures of information or inadvertently or deliberately miscommunicate users.

Recent prototypes and guidelines look forward new opportunities on information visualization by providing task (i.e. Zoom) and visualization taxonomies (i.e. 1-, 2-, 3- dimensional data, temporal...) [11], modeling visualization elements, considering hardware and software to visual design (i.e. Smartphone, PC, tablets...) [12] or even regarding user himself as a primary key on visualization development.

Several research works are also focused on sensor data analysis through visualization techniques [5,11]. This work leads to several proposals matching tasks and sensor's type in order to provide a possible visualization or providing clues for guidelines between sensor type and visualization taxonomy. Such kinds of visualizations are unfortunately stand-alone applications and have no facilities for interacting with multiple cases of study. They provide graphical environments for specific sensor data representation like combining text with visual indicators (i.e. tables, icons...), real-time charts (i.e. temperature, speed...), maps (i.e. location) and perform only some specific operations over sensor data like Zoom.

Analyzing requirements on emergent applications exploiting sensor data lead us to conclude that visualization in this context must goes beyond a simple illustration of text or matching relations between visualization elements. More and more, integrate different means of interaction and visualization is required to support users in their tasks (i.e. diagnosis, monitoring, supervision…). We distinguish two main requirements accordingly: (i) provide visualizations adapted to specific data type and application context and (ii) provide adapted functionalities that support further data visualization extensibilities by means of users' experience and needs.

Regarding these requirements, we propose in the next section an extensible platform oriented to experiment and validate sensor data visualization. In such a platform several generic visualizations are proposed and its design enables users to identify and implement the most adequate visualizations for a specific usage context. In fact, a definitive list of visualizations cannot be provided and thus we decide to focus on the extensibility and adequacy of the platform. .

3   Towards an Experiment and Validation Platform

Designing a platform to experiment and validate sensor data visualizations enables, among other, to analyze the consistency and relevancy of potential visualizations related to users' needs and their usage context. To this end, we introduce in the following paragraphs, an extensible platform oriented to assist experts visualizing and interacting sensor data.

3.1   General Overview and Architecture

Through this platform, developers attended by domain experts, may identify and implement the most appropriate visualizations to support users into tasks such as monitoring, medical diagnostic, tracking, etc. Our platform is thus designed to facilitate: (i) adding new types of sensors (data formats, data transfer protocols…) (ii) extracting useful data to be displayed (iii) enabling data correlation from different sensors (iv) associating appropriate visualizations to data type and (v) adding new visualizations and interactions.

The platform is built on 3-tier architecture. A *database* (DB) dedicated to store data to be displayed, a *server* where basic functionalities for managing data are deployed and a *client* which is the interactive part of the architecture allowing users to test visualizations and feedback developers about their particular needs on data representation. For this paper, we especially focus on the visualization aspect of the architecture describing the main functionalities to experiment and validate possible sensor data visualizations and interactions.

3.2   Developers and Domain Experts: Providing Adapted Functionalities

In order to provide an extensible experiment and validation tool, we offer in this platform several visualization and interaction functionalities both at the server and client side. Our approach proposes extendable visualization libraries and data model enabling to extend the capacities of the platform and also provides a set of functionalities enabling experts to experiment and feedback developers.

On the server side, implemented functionalities are organized on two main axes: *Data* and *Visualization management*. Data management enables to manage data records of several data types. Developers and experts are then allowed to import data of different types, extract them, associated to specific visualizations (i.e. ordered by adequacy: map and chart for gps data records) and making them persistent. Together, visualization management assists developers adding, creating and deleting visualizations. Developers can create a new visualization which extends of the existing ones providing their specificities through associated metadata. For example, we can specify if visualization can be used for particular cases like synchronization, real-time display, selection or composition. Further, such visualization is then available for new data records association. Actually, this association is given by the developers; however we aim to automate this process by defining adapted semantic rules.

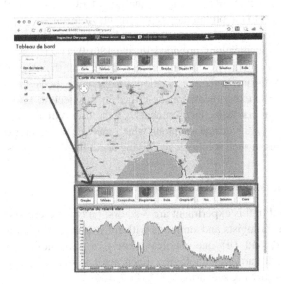

Fig. 1. Dashboard: visualizing two data records

On the client side, we propose a visualization tool which act as a mediator between developers and experts. It can be described by three main features: *Dashboard*, *Data management* and *User profile*. The dashboard implements functionalities to associate data types to specific visualizations, list and select data records, interact with the suggested visualizations (all adapted to sensor data representation depending on the type of data record and the associated list of visualizations) and displaying one or several data records visualizations. Together, traditionally functionalities adapted to dynamic sensor data are also provided, such as: *Zoom* (selecting a piece of a graph) or *Markers* (displaying reference points with color and description). Data management allows importing extract and gathering data coming from one or several sensors. Users can manage such records and create, add, delete or modify them and then test visualizations and interact with it in order to better understand and explain their requirements. Our platform proposes to manage user profile by controlling user access with an *id* and a *password*.

The prototype of this extensible platform is based on Web applications technology (Figure 1). Such a technology opens new possibilities of implementation such as Web Services, REST protocol, HTML5, etc. Also, it offers a better collaboration and information sharing, as well as a bridge to target mobile devices such as Smartphones and Tablets.

4   Experimentation and Platform Validation: Visualizing ECG Data

In order to validate the feasibility of our platform, we experiment into an application oriented to support medical experts in the analysis of ECG data. To this end, we have adapted our platform to the preliminary requirements of the usage context and interacted with the experts to evaluate its extensibility and adequacy. This evaluation process is very close to the specifications provided by the ISO 9241-210[1] standard for Human-centered Design for Interactive Systems, which defines all the aspects related to user's experience and its impact on the presentation, functionality, behavior and capabilities of the system. Thus, the experimentation described in this section takes into account the context of use (i.e. users, tasks, environments...), the user requirements (through all the development process), the design solutions which meet these requirements and the user-centered evaluations of such solutions, modifying according to the users' feedback.

4.1   Users: Implant and Medical Experts

The users involved in this experiment are 3 actors: (i) two experts on cardiac implants which provide cardiologists and surgeons with infrastructures to monitor the behavior of such implants, and (ii) one medical expert, a cardiologist, which provide a diagnostic and treat cardiac pathologies. Each actor is supposed to test our platform according to the following scenario.

4.2   Scenario: Ongoing Experimentation and Validation Process

In our scenario, the expert requires to analyze a data stream coming from an ECG both in *real-time* and *a posteriori*. In order to adequate our solution to users' requirements, we experiment our platform by following three main phases described hereafter.

Phase 1: User requirements analysis when presenting the platform and the possible visualizations and interactions to the experts.

Feedback: Based on the provided functionalities, experts give a direct feedback to the developers and asked for the possibility to load ECG data type (i.e. xml-hl7), to visualize such data on the typical visualizations recommended by the cardiologist (i.e.

---

[1] http://www.iso.org/iso/catalogue_detail.htm?csnumber=52075

cardiac derivations, peaks,...) and to create visualizations dynamically according to traditional ECG results (i.e. EVI compositions...)

Results: The developer validates the possibility to manage new data types, as for example *.hl7. Also, a specific composition for ECG data based on the combination of selected data was considered. A new visualization can be derived from this composition.

Phase 2: Presentation of a first prototype integrating the solutions and requiring user testing. Once the implementation of new visualizations performed, users can test and react by providing their feedback for possible extensions.

Feedback: The experts have identified their need to perform their own data selection in terms of ECG graph display and also to select peaks values between maximum and minimum values.

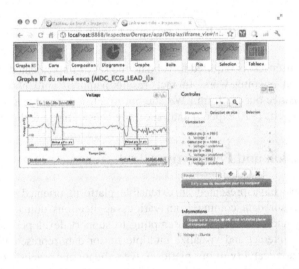

Fig. 2. Real-time visualization: dynamic visualization of a data record

Results: Our platform has been then enhanced with new functionalities and opened to new application domains such as medical by analyzing data coming from an ECG (Figure 2). With our platform, expert is leaded to upload files containing ECG data (i.e. *xml-hl7*) and to specifically select which data he/she wants to import (i.e. by date). Once the expert creates and selects a data record, he is able to display it with the different visualizations proposed on the dashboard. He can test several visualizations for the same record, for example in a table, in a static or in a dynamic graph (real-time simulation), etc. Indeed, all the proposed visualizations are adapted to visualize sensor data.

Thanks to our platform and by choosing a real-time representation, medical expert can simulate a dynamic sensor data stream and interact with data in different ways, for example: (i) manage graphs distribution over the dashboard (ii) zoom in a particular segment of the graph (iii) annotate the graph with markers (reference points) (iv) select some fragments of the graph (Figure 3) (v) compose a new graph based on selected data fragments.

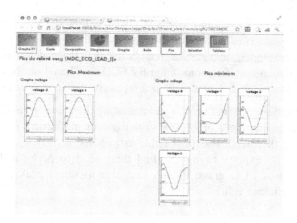

Fig. 3. Peaks detection and visualization

Phase 3: Other user test is required to validate the set of implemented functionalities. This aspect is an ongoing work. In fact, results acquired until now support us to increasingly enhance our platform. We attempt to introduce and test the platform by more medical experts (~10 experts) and especially considering a real scenario context.

5   Conclusion and Perspectives

In this paper, we have presented an extensible platform oriented to visualize and interact with sensor data coming from various applications domains. We propose several features and functionalities attempting to support developers and experts to simulate, create, interact and visualize multiple sensor data representations. In order to illustrate the applicability of our platform, we validate our proposal over a medical case study requiring a display of data coming from an ECG (Electrocardiogram). Results validate the extensibility of our platform and approach and motivate for further improvements.

The testing and enhancement of our platform is an ongoing work. At this time, we integrate new modules facilitating the implementation of features such as: preprocessing data to be displayed, managing composition of visualization tools and sensed data with an ergonomic point of view, relating patient health records, storing experts' visualization and interaction preferences, as well as migrating to mobile devices. In our future work, we aim to propose a more automatic visualization association and display, especially based on semantic rules and usage-based learning approaches.

This platform is currently used as part of a research project with specialists on cochlear and cardiac implants. Further experimentations with final experts will be performed on mobile devices should take place within a year. At present, experts and developers work closely to determine the visualization and interaction choices. Also, we plan to perform quantitative evaluations of platform's usability considering the measures proposed by ISO 9241-11 (Specifications and evaluation of usability).

Acknowledgments. This work is supported by the FUI project STM3[2] granted by the French SCS Cluster. We thank Sorin Group[3], members of the project and specialists in cardiac implants, for their support and collaboration. The authors would also like to thank the students Computer Science Department of Polytech'Nice Sophia Antipolis for their contribution to this project.

References

1. Stoicu-Tivadar, L., Stoicu-Tivadar, V.: Human-computer interaction reflected in the design of user interfaces for general practitioners. I. J. Medical Informatics 75(3-4), 335–342 (2006)
2. Stroetmann, K.A., Pieper, M., Stroetmann, V.N.: Understanding Patients: Participatory Approaches for the User Evaluation of Vital Data Presentation. In: ACM Conference on Universal Usability, pp. 93–97 (2003)
3. Campbell, B.D., Mete, H.O., Furness, T., Weghorst, S., Zabinsky, Z.: Emergency Response Planning and Training through Interactive Simulation and Visualization with Decision Support. Architecture, 176–180 (2008)
4. Niederauer, C., Houston, M., Agrawala, M., Humphreys, G.: Non-invasive interactive visualization of dynamic architectural environments. In: Proc. of 2003 Symposium on Interactive 3D Graphics (2003)
5. Grundy, E., Jones, M.W., Laramee, R.S., Wilson, R.P., Shepard, E.: Visualisation of Sensor Data from Animal Movement. Comput. Graph. Forum 28(3), 815–822 (2009)
6. Keim, D.: Information Visualization and Visual Data Mining. IEEE Transactions on Visualization and Computer Graphics 8(1) (2002)
7. Aigner, W., Miksch, S., Müller, W., Schumman, H., Tominski, C.: Visual Methods for Analyzing Time-Oriented Data. IEEE Transactions on Visualization and Computer Graphics 14(1), 47–60 (2008)
8. Luo, X., Teng, D., Liu, W., Tian, F., Guozhong, D., Wang, H.: A developing framework for interactive temporal data visualization. In: Proc. of the 3rd International Symposium on Visual Information Communication, September 28-29 (2010)
9. Shneiderman, B.: The Eyes Have It: A Task by Data Type Taxonomy for Information Visualizations. In: Proc. IEEE Symposium on Visual Languages (VL 1996), p. 336. IEEE Computer Society, Washington, DC (1996)
10. Stone, M.: Information visualization: Challenge for the humanities. Report of a Workshop Cosponsored by the Council on Library and Information Resources and the National Endowment for the Humanities. Council on Library and Information Resources, Washington, DC, pp. 43–56 (2009)
11. Richter, C.: Visualizing Sensor Data. In: Media Informatics Advanced Seminar on Information Visualization (2009)
12. Carmo, M.B., Afonso, A.P., de Matos, P.P., Vaz, A.: MoViSys – A Visualization System for Geo-Referenced Information on Mobile Devices. In: Sebillo, M., Vitiello, G., Schaefer, G. (eds.) VISUAL 2008. LNCS, vol. 5188, pp. 167–178. Springer, Heidelberg (2008)

---

[2] STM3 - Solution for the Treatment and Monitoring in Mobile Medicine
(http://www.pole-scs.org/projets?letter=S&page=5)
[3] http://www.sorin.com/

Graphical Controls Based Environment
for User Interface Evaluation

Selem Charfi[1], Abdelwaheb Trabelsi[2], Houcine Ezzedine[1], and Christophe Kolski[1]

[1] UVHC, LAMIH, CNRS, UMR 8201, F-59313 Valenciennes, France
{Selem.charfi,Houcine.Ezzedine,
Christophe.Kolski}@univ-valenciennes.fr
[2] University of Sfax, GIAD, 3018, Sfax, Tunisia
Abdelwaheb.Trablesi@fss.rnu.tn

Abstract. For more than two decades, the HCI community has elaborated numerous tools for user interface evaluation. Although the related tools are wide, the evaluation remains a difficult task. This paper presents a new approach for user interface evaluation. The proposed evaluation process focuses on utility and usability as software quality factors. It is based on the UI ergonomic quality inspection as well as the analysis and the study of the Human-Computer interaction. The proposed approach is mainly based on graphic controls dedicated to the user interface evaluation. These controls have, on the one hand, the role to compose graphically the interfaces. On the other hand, they contribute to the UI evaluation through integrated mechanisms. The evaluation is structured into two phases. The first consists of a local self-evaluation of the graphical controls according to a set of ergonomic guidelines. This set is specified by the evaluator. The second allows an electronic informer to estimate the interaction between the user interface (graphically composed by the evaluation based controls) and the user.

Keywords: User interface (UI), UI evaluation, utility and usability inspection.

1   Introduction and Background

The user interface (UI) evaluation is essential for interactive systems validation and test [10] [15] [16]. It is defined as the detection of UI aspects leading to use difficulties and errors. The HCI community has proposed many tools to evaluate UI for more than two decades. Although these tools are numerous, there are some difficulties related to this theme. As follows, an attempt is made to briefly summarize some of the main shortcomings in UI evaluation.

First, tools based on ergonomic guidelines (EG) raise difficulties for their exploitation for UI evaluation. Indeed EG are generally expressed in natural language [7]. Therefore, they are independent from any context of use [16]. Thus, their exploitation and interpretation are rather difficult [7]. Second, the evaluation results are hard to analyze [4]. Indeed, the evaluator is often confronted with a huge amount of data set. Their analysis turns out a costly task in time and resources [8]. Third, the

M. Winckler, P. Forbrig, and R. Bernhaupt (Eds.): HCSE 2012, LNCS 7623, pp. 360–367, 2012.

UI evaluation remains a neglected task by many designers. This negligence is essentially due to its high cost and its complexity. Another potential shortcoming is that the evaluation results can vary from a method to another one and from an evaluator to the other for the same UI [10]. Indeed, the evaluation often is based on the evaluator's quantitative judgments. Therefore, many works aim at automating the evaluation task to promote a subjective evaluation [1] [6] [15]. These shortcomings constitute motivations for the implementation of newer kind of UI evaluation tools. This paper falls within this line of work and aims at contributing by improvement of the existing tools. In this context, the proposed work consists in a framework for UI evaluation.

The remainder of this paper is organized as follows: the next section presents recent works related to UI evaluation tools. This section covers representative tools, their purposes and limits. Thus it provides the motivation for the presented work. Then, the proposed evaluation tool is presented: its general architecture, the proposed functionalities and the covered aspects of the evaluation process. The paper concludes with a summary, a brief overview of the proposed approach experimental validation and a discussion of the outcomes of the presented work.

2   Related Work

In order to contribute to UI evaluation, many tools were proposed [6]. These tools have essentially as an objective, automating the evaluation. In addition, they aim at detecting the problems engendering use difficulties. The proposed tools diverge on the aspects they cover, their efficiency, the degree of efficiency and the UI type that they evaluate.

2.1   User Interface Evaluation Tools

Many tools exist for UI evaluation [6]. These tools are mainly based on the utility, the usability and/or the accessibility as quality factors. The existing tools are so numerous that we consider it useful to classify them into categories. The first includes tools based on the usability inspection. The usability is defined as the ease of use and of learning UI system degree [8] [15]. The usability based tool focuses generally on the information display on the UI. The related tools are generally based on ergonomic guidelines and usability metrics, as in [14]. As example of usability inspection tool, we can mention MAGENTA [9]. The second set inspects the UI utility. The utility determines if the system allows the user realizing his/her task and if the system satisfies or not the needs for which it was elaborated. It corresponds to the functional capacities, the system performance and the provided technical support quality [10]. The related tools are generally based on the UI interaction study and analysis. Representative example of this class of tools is the electronic informer (EI) such as the case of EISEval [13]. The third category is based on the accessibility as a quality factor. The accessibility is defined as the UI capacity to be used and exploited by the largest possible users; as related tool we can cite EvalAccess [1].

2.2   Motivation of the Present Work

The present work is motivated essentially by the perspective that UI evaluation tools should be easier to establish and take into account the maximum of evaluation features. In addition, the provided evaluation process should be automated in order to provide better results. In [10], the authors recommend combining between several evaluation methods to get more reliable results. Then, we propose to adopt the ergonomic quality inspection and the EI for evaluation process. We intend to extend the range of functionality and the scope of existing tools. Through this environment, we intend to facilitate the evaluation process for the evaluators in order to make it more practical and easier. In fact, evaluation process is embedded into graphical controls[1]. Besides, the evaluation is established when conceiving the UI by composing it graphically.

In addition to that, our contribution major advantage is to support the evaluation process since the early stages (UI design) of the software development cycle. Indeed as expressed previously it is often neglected by software designers; more the evaluation process is too often located only at the end of software development cycle.

3   Graphical Control Based Environment for User Interface Evaluation

3.1   Global Overview of the Proposed Environment

The proposed environment is constituted mainly of two parts. The first one inspects the UI usability. It consists of the UI static display evaluation. The evaluation is elaborated while designing the UI. The graphical control inspects its conformity according to a set of ergonomic guidelines (EG). This self-evaluation process is established while adding a graphical control to the interface via drag and drop. The designer will be notified about detecting ergonomic inconstancies. The second inspects the UI utility. It analyses the interactions between the user and the interface. It is based mostly on an electronic informer (EI) for the capture and the analysis of the interaction sequences. Note that there is no mechanism implemented in the UI for the interaction capture. The UI is graphically composed by the evaluation based controls. These controls are similar to the graphical control proposed by the IDE. In fact, they ensure the same features and are exposed on the toolbar in the environments operating with the drag and drop principle, Figure 1. The prototype of the environment is developed using the "MS Visual Studio 2010", Framework 4.0. The applications were implemented in C# language.

The proposed approach allows only identifying UI use problems. It does not correct them or identify clearly the utility problems. Then, it assists the evaluator for UI utility inspection. The problems identified depend on the EG selected for the

---

[1] A control is an element used for graphical user interface composition. It displays information to the user and allows him/her to interact with the functional kernel. As examples, we can cite: combo box, button and text box.

evaluation process. This process is not totally automated. It only captures and analyses data automatically. The suggestion and the improvement phases are elaborated manually.

3.2   Usability Inspection Phase

This phase inspects the UI usability. The major advantage is to provide an early evaluation. It may be 100 times more costly to proceed for UI improvement at a late stage that early one [10]. This phase is based on graphical controls that evaluate themselves according to a set of EG. The guidelines are defined into XML files. Once added to the UI (and even modified in the UI), each evaluation based control loads the associated EG into the memory and then it inspects itself according to these guidelines. The inspection is done as mentioned in figure 2 by a comparison between the control value and the recommended value stored in the EG. For each EG is associated possible design errors and corresponding recommendations. At the end of the auto-evaluation process, the control notifies the designer by a message mentioning the design errors and recommendations, Fig 2.

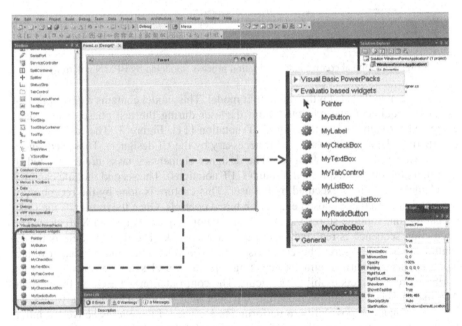

Fig. 1. Evaluation based graphical controls

3.3   Utility Inspection Phase

This phase is based on both an EI and evaluation based controls. The controls communicate the interaction data to the EI: elementary action execution time, action type (button click, check-list select, etc.), associated form (the interface containing the graphical control), graphical control text, control type (button, text-box, label, combo-box, etc.) and the machine IP address. The EI analyzes these data in order to detect UI utility problems. The proposed EI has a modular architecture; it is articulated around four modules: (1) Referential model generator, (2) Evaluated object model generator, (3) Confrontation and (4) Statistics generator.

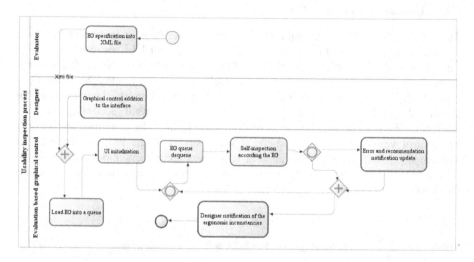

Fig. 2. Graphical control auto-evaluation process (modeled by BPMN notation)

The first module sets up the referential model. This model contains a description of the tasks required to be executed from the user during the test phase. The task is expressed through its sub-tasks in CTT notation [11], Figure 3. The task trees are specified by the evaluator (assisted if necessary by the UI designer). These sequences are determined by the UI designer. The designer elementary tasks are associated to the referential model (expressed through CTT notations). The second module captures the elementary actions executed by the user. This capture is done by the reception of information from the proposed evaluation based controls. Once the user ends the tasks execution, this module stores the elementary action sequences into an XML file. The interaction sequence is realized separately for each task. The third module is the EI central module. It insures the comparison between referential and evaluated object models. This comparison aims at detecting repetitive, useless and erroneous actions. Furthermore, it detects usability problems. The confrontation is based on Finite State Automaton [2]. They allow modeling the subtasks' various alternatives (often we have more than one possibility to perform a task). The CTT model is converted into a finished automaton. Then, the confrontation model inspects the elementary actions sequence (the evaluated object model) to detect inconsistencies and actions that are repetitive, useless, erroneous or missing. The fourth module generates statistics to simplify the evaluation process and to minimize the evaluator analysis and interpretation workload. These statistics concern the task execution rate, the tasks and sub-tasks execution average and the comparison between the evaluated object and the referential models through a graphic way with a colored legend, Figure 6. They cannot be described by lack of space.

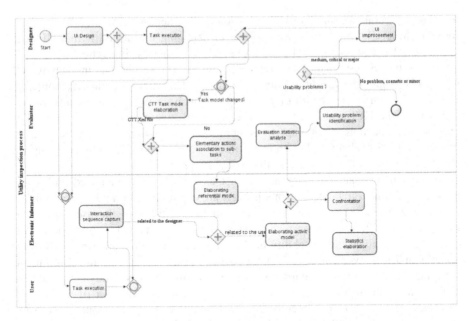

Fig. 3. The utility inspection process

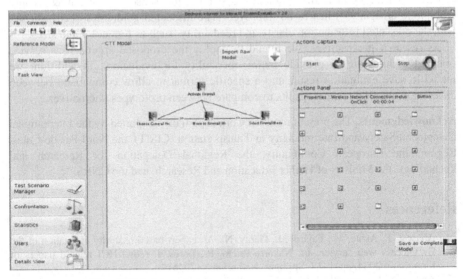

Fig. 4. The electronic informer for user interface evaluation

4   Conclusion

UI evaluation is the object of numerous researches for the last two decades. However, the evaluation remains a difficult task. Among the difficulties of the evaluation, we can underline the choice of the method and the tool to be used. In this paper we introduced several categories of UI evaluation tools. Then, we presented an approach for evaluating UI. Its goal is to contribute to obtaining useful and usable UI. It is constituted by two phases. The first one allows usability inspection by a self-evaluation process established by graphical controls. The second one inspects the UI usability through the evaluation controls and the EI. This approach aims at automating the UI evaluation during the information capture, analysis and criticism. Furthermore, it considers the HCI usability test since early interactive system design phase. The proposed approach is an attempt to combine two evaluation methods in order to contribute to UI evaluation. Different preliminary and deep evaluations may confirm the effectiveness and the easiness of the proposed approach.

In order to validate our approach, a first case study was conducted with eight novice users (undergraduate students in software engineering), one designer and one evaluator; their respective tasks are visible in Fig. 3. None of the users had deep knowledge at HCI. The study aimed at: identifying UI utility and usability problems, checking the evaluator acceptability of the proposed approach, gathering evaluators' remarks and improvement suggestions about the proposed evaluation environment, verifying that the proposed environment runs correctly. This case study concerned the evaluation of an interactive system evaluation in transport domain (the system is described in [5]). The result consists mainly on that 6 users among 8 executed successfully the required tasks. The evaluator signaled that the electronic informer is difficult to use: in fact, the guidance aspect (in the sense of Bastien & Scapin ergonomic criteria [3]) has to be improved. The inspected guidelines deal basically with the presented information clarity and readability (such as font color and size).

As research perspectives, we intend to deploy the proposed approach as service oriented architecture to provide better operability for evaluators. In addition, we intend to save evaluation result into a specific format to allow comparison between different evaluation process results to compare between prototypes alternatives.

Acknowledgments. The present research work is partially supported by the International Campus on Safety and Intermodality in Transportation (CISIT), the Nord-Pas-de-Calais Region, the European Community, the Regional Delegation for Research and Technology, the Ministry of Higher Education and Research, and the CNRS.

References

1. Abascal, J., Arrue, M., Fajardo, I., Garay, N.: An expert-based usability evaluation of the EvalAccess web service. In: Navarro-Prieto, R., Lorés, J. (eds.) HCI related papers of Interacción 2004, pp. 1–17. Springer, Netherlands (2006)
2. Anderson, J.A., Head, T.J.: Automata theory with modern applications, pp. 105–108. Cambridge University Press (2006) ISBN 9780521848879
3. Bastien, J.M.C., Scapin, D.L.: Evaluating a user interface with ergonomic criteria. International Journal of Human-Computer Interaction 7, 105–121 (1995)
4. Charfi, S., Ezzedine, H., Kolski, C., Moussa, F.: Towards an Automatic Analysis of Interaction Data for HCI Evaluation Application to a Transport Network Supervision System. In: Jacko, J.A. (ed.) HCII 2011, Part I. LNCS, vol. 6761, pp. 175–184. Springer, Heidelberg (2011)

5. Ezzedine, H., Bonte, T., Kolski, C., Tahon, C.: Integration of traffic management and traveller information systems: basic principles and case study in intermodal transport system management. International Journal of Computers, Communications & Control 3, 281–294 (2008)
6. Ivory, M., Hearst, M.: The State of the Art in Automated Usability Evaluation of User Interfaces. ACM Computing Surveys 33(4), 173–197 (2001)
7. Keith, V.: Using Guidelines to assist in the visualization design process. In: Hong, S.H. (ed.) Asia Pacific Symposium on Information Visualization, Sydney, Australia. Conferences in Research and Practice in Information Technology. Australian Computer Society, Inc. (2005)
8. Lazar, J.: Universal Usability: Designing Computer Interfaces for Diverse User Populations. John Wiley and Sons, Chichester (2009)
9. Leporini, B., Paterno, F., Scorcia, A.: Flexible tool support for accessibility evaluation. Interacting with Computers 18(5), 869–890 (2006)
10. Nielsen, J.: Usability Engineering. Academic Press, Boston (1994)
11. Paterno, F., Mancini, C., Meniconi, S.: ConcurTaskTrees: A Diagrammatic Notation for Specifying Task Models. In: Proceedings Interact 1997, pp. 362–369. Chapman&Hall, Sydney (1997)
12. Thatcher, J., Burks, M.R., Lauke, P.H., Heilmann, C., Kirkpatrick, A., Lawson, B., Henry, S., Regan, B., Rutter, R., Urban, M.: Web Accessibility: Web Standards and Regulatory Compliance. Friends of Ed (2006) ISBN-13: 978-1590596388
13. Tran, C.D., Ezzedine, H., Kolski, C.: Evaluation of Agent-based IS: Proposal of an Electronic Informer Using Petri Nets. Journal of Universal Computer Science 14(19), 3202–3216 (2008)
14. Rauterberg, M.: How to Measure the Ergonomic Quality of User Interfaces in a Task Independent Way. In: Mital, A., Krueger, H., Kumar, S., Menozzi, M., Fernandez, J.E. (eds.) Advances in Occupational Ergonomics and Safety I, vol. 1, pp. 154–157. International Society for Occupational Ergonomics and Safety, Cincinnati (1996)
15. Rubin, J., Chisnell, D., Spool, J.: Handbook of Usability Testing: How to Plan, Design, and Conduct Effective Tests, 2nd edn. Wiley (2008) ISBN: 978-0-470-18548-388
16. Vanderdonckt, J.: Development Milestones towards a Tool for Working with Guidelines. Interacting with Computers 12(2), 81–118 (1999)

Author Index